# *In Search of the Divine*

'Insightful and illuminating, Rana Safvi's extensive yet careful study contextualizes the traditions of Sufism within the larger historical framework of Islam. *In Search of the Divine* situates at its heart the enduring practice, impact and legacy of Sufism in India.'
—AANCHAL MALHOTRA, author of *Remnants of a Separation*

'With each page illuminated with selfless love and poetry, Rana Safvi's *In Search of the Divine* is a transformational book. The purity of faith that suffuses the book will find its way into the hearts of the readers. It sure reached mine.'
—GHAZALA WAHAB, author of *Born a Muslim: Some Truths About Islam in India*

'Rana Safvi is one of the finest chroniclers of our composite culture. This beautiful book is remarkable for its ability to bridge the gap between the past and the lived experience of today.'
—SUPRIYA GANDHI, historian and author of *The Emperor Who Never Was: Dara Shukoh in Mughal India*

'*In Search of the Divine* takes us deep into the Sufi tradition of India, which has been one of the major components of Islam in South Asia over the last century. Strongly recommended to all students of Islamic studies, as well as those wishing to learn about the long history of religious diversity in India.'
—OMID SAFI, professor of Islamic Studies, Duke University

'The many splendoured hues of Sufism that pervade the Indian landscape are brought to life by Rana Safvi in this fascinating book. A seamless blend of academic research, intriguing travel experiences and deep insights into what makes Sufism magnetic and timelessly relevant.'
—MOIN MIR, author of *The Lost Fragrance of Infinity*

Rana Safvi is a renowned writer, scholar and translator. She is a passionate believer in India's unique civilizational legacy and pluralistic culture which she documents through her writings, podcasts and videos. She has published nine books so far on the culture, history and monuments of India. These are *Tales from the Quran and Hadith* and the Delhi trilogy which includes *Where Stones Speak*, *The Forgotten Cities of Delhi* and *Shahjahanabad: The Living City of Old Delhi*. She has translated both the editions of Sir Syed Ahmad Khan's seminal work on Delhi, *Asar-us-Sanadid* and *Dastan-e-Ghadar*, and four accounts of nineteenth and twentieth-century Delhi from Urdu to English as *City of My Heart* and *A Saint, A Folk Tale and Other Stories: Lesser-Known Monuments of India*.

Also by Rana Safvi

*City of My Heart: Accounts of Love, Loss and Betrayal in Nineteenth-Century Delhi*

*Tears of the Begums: Stories of Survivors of the Uprising of 1857*

# In Search of the Divine

## LIVING HISTORIES OF SUFISM IN INDIA

Rana Safvi

First published in hardcover in India in 2022 by Hachette India
(Registered name: Hachette Book Publishing India Pvt. Ltd)
An Hachette UK company
www.hachetteindia.com

This paperback edition published in 2025

1



ISBN 978-93-5731-923-2

Hachette Book Publishing India Pvt. Ltd
4th/5th Floors, Corporate Centre,
Plot No. 94, Sector 44, Gurugram – 122003, India

Typeset in EB Garamond 10.5/14
by InoSoft Systems, Noida

Printed and bound in India
by Manipal Technologies Limited

*Dedicated to Hazrat Amir Khusrau,*
*whose poetry introduced me to the meaning of Divine Love*

*Khusrau darya prem ka –*
*Ulti wa ki dhaar;*
*Jo utra so doob gaya,*
*Jo dooba so paar.*

[O Khusrau, the river of love
Flows in strange directions.
The one who jumps in, drowns;
And the one who drowns, crosses it.]

– Hazrat Amir Khusrau

# Contents

## SHRINES AND DEVOTEES

# Preface

*Bismillah ar-Rahman i-Rahim*
(In the name of God, the most Gracious and the most Merciful)

This book is the result of a lifelong practice of Islam, and a decade-old journey into its Sufi traditions. It is the outcome of a personal and academic search of people's experiences of divinity in Sufi practices, focusing on its entire corpus of thought and discursive traditions, meditative and ritual practices, ethics of love and compassion, devotional poetry, music, art, and architecture.

Sufism is a vast ocean of mystical thought, doctrines, literature and poetry, and a legacy of its saints. The Arabic word *tasawwuf* means devoting oneself to the contemplation (of Allah)[1] but it is generally used today in the sense of 'a verbal noun meaning the act or process of becoming a Sufi'.[2] It is from this term that the word Sufism is derived.[3] The 'ism' in Sufism does not make it a system or philosophy. Instead, like *tasawwuf*, it is the act of following a mystical path, and a quest for ethical and moral perfection as one tries to realize Allah in one's self. It was always a part of Islam, though the term only gained currency around a century after the death of the Prophet (PBUH). It was at this time that an increasing number of Muslims came to feel that an entirely rational or intellectual relationship with what they considered God's revelation was inadequate; it needed to be supplemented by an experiential relationship, especially the sources of that revelation and the shifting body of hadiths. This emphasis on experience over intellect was the ethical and psychological beginning of Sufism.

There has been a recent resurgence in popular interest in Sufism in India. Indeed, many Sufi orders (*silsilah*s) are flourishing now. While not everyone can follow the intellectual and spiritual rigour that becoming a Sufi requires, thousands visit dargahs every day, seeking succour and peace, healing and care, love and compassion. I am one of them.

I have scratched just the surface of this great tradition, and my writing may reflect this, but the journey has enriched me as a person. Although I am not a Sufi, I am privileged for having got a small glimpse into the world of Sufism, and for being enriched by it.

While researching for this book, I conducted field visits to many dargahs across India, had conversations with devotees, descendants of the saints who run the shrines, and religious experts; and I have drawn from this experience. I focus on the changing character of the dargahs, and the crucial role saints play as *waseela* (intermediaries). The saints, who even after death continue to thrive in the shrine, are the link between the devotees and God.

Although traditionally India has been home to Sufism, of late a few detractors have appeared here too. And that's not all. The term 'Sufi' is bandied about casually as a kind of cool cult that showcases the secular spirit of Islam; or worse, it is seen as something that is outside Islam. There is even a longstanding trend in the early studies of Sufism where it has been differentiated from Islam. This book is an attempt to show that Sufism is, in fact, firmly rooted in Islam. I try to do this by describing it in its historical context and as a rigorous meditative discipline, highlighting every aspect of the tradition.

In addition to these attempts to delink Sufism from Islam and portray it as a different stream of thought, we see it being attacked both within and outside Islam. It is often critiqued as *shirk* (attributing a co-partner to God) or *bidat* (innovation), or even an internal threat to Islam. To discredit Sufism, such critiques often emphasize superstition, grave worship, music, and the fleecing of credulous believers by some shrine attendants.

These attempts began in the eighteenth and nineteenth centuries when Orientalists, with access to only limited literature regarding the subject, wrote of Sufism as outside Islam on account of the latter's 'essential characteristic of harsh legalism'. Sufism, on the other hand, was considered to be 'indifferent to matters of religious law'.[4]

The inherent secular nature of dargahs is a tradition inherited from the Sufi saints themselves, and visitors of all faiths flock to these dargahs. Of late, in India, there has been a campaign to discourage these visits by portraying saints as violent men who forcibly converted the Hindu masses. I have seen a few of such WhatsApp messages being circulated.

Today, despite having limited or no meaningful engagement with the religion and fuelled merely by news coverage of fanatical factions and Islamist militia, many see Islam purely as regressive and fundamentalist. Muslims are made out to be 'fanatical, violent, and those who lack tolerance'.[5] For people who defame the religion, the beauty of the Prophet's *ihsan* (doing all things beautiful) and *akhlaq* (exemplary character traits), his emphasis on beautiful deeds and conduct, and the *jawan-mardi* (chivalry) of Ali ibn Abi Talib are all alien to Islam. And according to them, the Sufi sheikhs' service to humanity, and the universality and spirituality of poets like Mevlana Rumi steeped in the Sufi tradition, can't be a part of Islam.

This book brings to light stories of how *ihsan* and *akhlaq* were practised by the Prophet and emulated by the Sufi saints, and of the belief and faith of the local populace in the saints, and later their shrines. It foregrounds the role of the Sufis in fostering a composite culture in India. If 'the presence of Sufis was the main factor in the conversion of large sections of the [Indian] population to Islam',[6] it is essential to know more about their practices.

Since my journey started in Delhi, which is called the *baees khwaja ki chaukhat* or 'the threshold of 22 saints,' I, of course, visited the shrines of these 22 saints. But I didn't stop with that. I have now made trips to every important shrine in Delhi. In a land where there are patron saints in every locality, where locals go and offer flowers and burn incense sticks and candles every Thursday, it is difficult to keep count, but I must have visited around fifty major shrines in Delhi while writing about the monuments of the city for my trilogy on the subject published by HarperCollins India. When I started researching for this book, I began travelling to other parts of India too. As I was describing the living histories of Sufism, it was important for me to visit the shrines and endeavour to get a personal sense of the place, locating its importance in the lives of the devotees and visitors. My attempt, for whatever it is worth, is to describe people's histories of

Sufism, instead of the 'formal' history on which there are already many books written.

My travels took me to Pandua and Kolkata in West Bengal, which is one of the important centres of medieval Sufism; the major shrines in Srinagar and Charar-e-Sharif in Kashmir; the shrines in Thanesar, Hansi, Bhatinda, Sirhind, and Malerkotla in Punjab and Haryana; the dargahs of Uttar Pradesh in Makanpur, Ayodhya, Dewa Sharif, Kakori, Lucknow, Bareilly, and Agra; Sarkhej Roza, Ahmedabad, and Pirana in Gujarat; the shrines in Bijapur, Gulbarga, and Hampi in Karnataka; the shrines in Burhanpur and Raisen in Madhya Pradesh; Khuldabad, Aurangabad, Pune, and Mumbai in Maharashtra; the shrine in Ajmer, Rajasthan; and the shrines of Hyderabad in present-day Telangana. These places and their shrines are described in this book. For the shrines in Odisha, Assam, Kerala, and Tamil Nadu, I rely on first-hand accounts of devotees and visitors because I could not visit due to the COVID-19 pandemic.

The scope of my book is ambitious as I have tried to present multiple facets that are important for the devotees and visitors – including an introduction to Sufism, its advent and spread in India, the major *silsilah*s, existing practices, music, poetry, and art. I present an interpretative study of the histories and contemporary cultures of Sufi practices in India, based on academic research, ethnographic observations, local and oral histories, and my personal experiences. In dargahs, a lot of the histories are oral and have been passed down through the generations. Those who retell it, and the devotees who gather to hear it, believe them to be true. The sceptics would stay away from these sacred spaces in any case.

The book is divided into three sections. The first, entitled 'Islam and Sufism', introduces readers to Islam, Sufism, and the Prophet and his family as the source of mystical practices. Every member of the Prophet's family was said to be endowed with esoteric wisdom. The *Ahl al-Bait,* or the Household of the Prophet, therefore, holds an important place in Sufi traditions. Any discussion revolving around the roots of Sufism would be incomplete without a discussion on the *Ahl al-Bait*. Key concepts and fundamentals of the Sufi path are introduced and explained for the lay reader.

The next section, 'Saints and *Silsilah*s', explores the advent of Sufism into India, how it spread, the need for and the concept of Sufi orders, and the major Sufi *silsilahs*, while also offering an overview of the important saints.

The third section of the book, 'Shrines and Devotees', presents shrines as places of devotional worship and healing, highlighting social relations, gender, and people's theological and historical experiences. It also offers a description of the popular dargahs of India.

Based on my visits, it became apparent to me that the major blessing said to be attached to a dargah today is the power of the saint's body to grant boons and remove the effects of the evil eye and possessions. I discuss this theme in the book, with a view to understanding who and what *jinn* are, how they are related to mental health, and why devotees think that coming to a dargah is more beneficial than visiting a doctor or a mental health professional. Chapter 16 in particular explores the visits of those said to be 'possessed' and dispossessed with historical and contemporary context.

The saint often becomes an integral part of the devotees' lives, and the saint's anniversaries as well as every festival are important events for the people. I describe this aspect of their faith practice in Chapter 17. In Chapters 18, I look at how mystical poetry and music can be transformative and uniquely universal. There is something for everyone, whether they are initiated into the path of Sufism or not.

The last chapter is on women devotees, who in most dargahs are separated from the shrine by a screen. This chapter is devoted to the important women Sufis. In it, I examine the contribution of women and consider why women are denied their due place in the scheme of things. It is not meant to hurt anyone's feelings or challenge the status quo, but to understand why it has happened and perhaps start a discussion on it.

A note on the spellings and terms: I have used the Quranic spellings for the names of prophets and angels, specifying their biblical equivalent in the instance of first use.

Sufi saints have been variously referred to as 'sheikh', 'khwaja' and 'hazrat'. The word 'sheikh' literally means a man of authority, prelate, prior, abbot, superior of the dervishes or Muhammadan monks,[7] while a 'khwaja' refers to a venerable old man, a man of distinction and a master. 'Hazrat' translates as 'Presence, dignity, majesty, dominion, and power; it is an epithet that is often joined with the names of the Deity', and is also a title by which kings and great men are addressed.[8] It is used only for those saints with an exalted status and a spiritual dominion. I have used 'khwaja' in the book as per the usage in Sufi texts and hagiography. According to Professor Raziuddin Aquil, 'Shaikh [spelt Sheikh in this book] is an Arabic term, meaning descendants of the companions of the Prophet, so perhaps lower in rank [than 'khwaja']. The title Khwaja was used for Syeds or direct descendants of the Prophet, while non-Syeds were Shaikhs, mashaikh, though sometimes such categorizations may not hold true.'[9] The word 'hazrat' is now often used while addressing any respected personage.

We have always referred to the Prophet as Rasool-e-Khuda, Allah's messenger or Huzur. The words affixed to his name are *Sallallahu alaihi wasallam,* meaning, 'May Allah's peace and blessings be upon him', often abbreviated as PBUH or 'peace be upon him'. For ease of reading, I have not added this in the book but have written his name with reverence and a prayer, and with these words in my heart. I request those reading it to also say it in their hearts.

Since childhood I have heard and used the word 'hazrat' for Ali ibn Abi Talib and I have used it in the book wherever I have addressed him simply as Ali. It is also used for Hazrat Nizamuddin Auliya, as he was the 'Mehboob-e-Ilahi' or 'beloved of God'. All translations of the Holy Quran are from Abdullah Yusuf Ali's magisterial work *The Holy Quran*, as that is a universally accepted translation, and word meanings are from Platts online dictionary.

Ultimately, I would like to apologize for any mistakes or failings in my understanding. As the popular saying goes: *durogh bar gardan-e raawi* (falsehood lies on the neck of the narrator).

# ISLAM AND SUFISM

# 1

## Sufism: An Introduction

*Moko kahan dhoondhe re bande?*
*Main to tere paas mein.*
(Where do you search for me?
I am within you.)

– Kabir

It is a Thursday evening and the dargah of Hazrat Nizamuddin Auliya in Delhi beckons. I am not the only one negotiating the narrow lanes full of vendors selling roses, incense, and *chaddars* – all the regular purchases of devotees. The faithful serve them as offerings to cover the shrine on this particular day of the week. In Islam, Thursday evenings are believed to be blessed with a bright night,[1] when Allah's *rahmat* or Mercy is said to flow.

Dargahs are a natural magnet for devotees and mystics seeking *barakat* (divine blessings) as the shrines inside are said to be sanctified by His *neamat* (divine grace). Devotees especially flock to the one I am visiting. After all, it houses the shrine of Mehboob-e-Ilahi (beloved of God).

As I walk barefoot on the cold stone, I think of those who walked here centuries before me. Devotees of yore were disciples, seekers of knowledge, and *saliks* (travellers) on the road to the truth. *Are those walking beside me also searching for the same things, or has the quest changed over the years?* I wonder.

I can hear strains of qawwalis being sung. The same tunes were sung, historically, in *sama mehfil*s (musical assemblies) that connected a lover to the beloved Divine through a mystical experience resulting in spiritual exaltation.

The heavy smell of incense mingled with rose petals beguiles the senses, and crowds of devotees are supplicating in various postures, praying, or simply listening to the qawwals. As I enter the shrine, I am greeted by the words being sung by these qawwals in the courtyard of the dargah:

*Aaj rang hai, Maa, rang hai ri*
*Moray mehboob kay ghar rang hai ri*

[There is a glow everywhere, O mother, a bright glow;
There is a glow in my beloved's house.]

This verse written by Amir Khusrau refers to the glow emanating from Allah that is reflected in his beloved Hazrat Nizamuddin Auliya's face, for he is Mehboob-e-Ilahi and Allah is pleased with him. The verses were composed by the poet at a very young age after his first meeting with the saint. Simply called *rang* (meaning colour or glow), they capture his rapturous emotions on finding a *pir* (spiritual mentor).

The singing overwhelms and encompasses me, and I sit down to hear the qawwals and savour the sense of continuity with the past. The timeless verses speak to everyone, each according to their sensibility and sensitivity. I am reminded of an ancient Indian parable where a group of blind men encounter an elephant for the first time. Through their touch, each of them perceives and describes the same animal differently. Sufism is like that elephant – it reveals its meanings to each seeker in a form that they can understand.

Sufism has developed over many centuries, starting with the Prophet himself in the seventh century, and has adapted to the local customs and traditions of each country in which it has flourished. It, therefore, has many faces, and those who come in contact with it experience different aspects of it, depending on their understanding. For some, especially the uninitiated, Sufism is defined by its music or the literature, while for others by visiting the shrines. But those who have taken the oath know that it is much more than all of these things.

With its mystical and esoteric connotations, Sufism has long fascinated people across borders and generations. But what exactly is it? And who is a Sufi?

Broadly, Sufism is a way of life and worship – a stream of interpretation emphasizing the interior path of mystical love and knowledge of God. But before we dive into its depths, it is important to understand that Sufism is neither a sect of Islam, nor is it different from the religion. While mystical impulses and a spiritual essence is present in all major religions, the concept of *tasawwuf*, the Arabic term from which the word Sufism is derived and is used interchangeably with, is rooted in Islam.

Thus, we must first understand Islam, for that is where the origins of Sufism lie.

'Allah is Great. I bear witness that there is no god but Allah. I bear witness that Muhammad is the Messenger of Allah; hurry to prayer, hurry to success.' The sound of the *azaan* calling the faithful to prayer with these words can be heard in most cities of the world.[2] Islam is the youngest Abrahamic religion, following in the tradition of the two earlier monotheistic religions – Judaism and Christianity – which claim Prophet Abraham as their common forefather. Today, it is the second largest religion in the world, but it started with a divine revelation and two followers.[3]

The first teachings of Islam were revealed to Prophet Muhammad (570–632), on a night in the holy month of Ramzan in 610, when he was in seclusion in the cave of Hira, the mountain of Al-Noor. Seyyid Hossein Nasr in his book on the Quran explains:

> According to the Prophet's wife 'Ā'ishah, 'The first thing that began happening with the Messenger of God from the revelation were dreams he would see in his sleep that would come true. He would not see any dream except that it would come to be, like the break of day in the morning. Then seclusion became beloved to him. So he used to go to the cave of Ḥirā' and devote himself to worship there for a number of nights, and would bring provisions. Then he would return to [his first wife] Khadījah and replenish his provisions for a similar number of nights. This continued until the revelation suddenly came to him while he was in the cave of Ḥirā'.'[4]

On this Night of Power, as it is called, the angel Jibraeel (known as Gabriel in the Bible) is said to have appeared before him in all his glory and, with a voice like thunder, commanded him:

> Proclaim (or Read)! In the name of thy Lord and Cherisher, Who created –
> Created man, out of a (mere) clot of congealed blood:
> Proclaim! And thy Lord is Most Bountiful –
> He Who taught (the use of) the pen –
> Taught man that which he knew not. (Quran 96:1–5)[5]

In this verse of the Quran, which is a part of the *Surah al-Alaq*, Jibraeel is seen instructing Muhammad to share Allah's message with humans, whom He had created from an *alaq*[6] which literally means something that is attached and hanging to something, and is translated as a 'congealed clot of blood' or a 'blood clot'. It refers to the 'early stage of the embryo'.[7] Muhammad was to proclaim that God was great and bountiful, for He had given humans the power to gain knowledge of new things every day.

The archangel also declared that there was only one god – Allah – and that Muhammad was His prophet. The revelations in the cave of Hira disturbed Muhammad, who had no idea whether he was hallucinating or had become insane. He ran to his wife Khadija, trembling with fear, and said, 'Cover me... Cover me.'[8]

Khadija supported him during this period. She assured him that Allah would never disgrace a man as pious as him, and that he was neither delusional nor hallucinating. This was endorsed by Khadija's christian cousin Waraqah ibn Nawfal who identified Jibraeel saying, 'This is "Namus" (i.e., the angel entrusted with Divine Secrets) that Allah sent to Moses.'[9]

The revelations were not repeated for a while – some say not for a few days, some say six months, and others claim it wasn't heard of again for years. Muhammad was in the throes of despair. *What had happened in the cave? Was it indeed a divine encounter or simply his hallucination? And what did it mean? What did God want of him?* he wondered. This was a period of disquiet, and it left him thinking that he was possessed.[10]

He returned again and again to the mountains, searching for answers, and was sometimes tempted to leap off the cliff. But each time he came close, he would hear a voice that said, 'O Muhammad! You are the apostle of Allah, and I am Jibraeel.'

Once, as he raised his head towards heaven to see who was speaking, he saw Jibraeel in the form of a man with his feet astride the horizon. According to his biographer Ibn Ishaq, Muhammad would say of this episode: 'I stood gazing at him, moving neither forward nor backward, then I began to turn my face away from him, but towards whatever region of the sky I looked, I saw him as before.'[11]

Every time he heard Jibraeel's words his heart would become calm, and he would return home, quietened.[12]

The complete Quran was revealed to the Prophet over a period of 23 years; sometimes, only a verse and at others, a whole chapter. Revelations came to him on different occasions – always when he could least predict it – while travelling, resting and even during a battle.

The first person to profess the faith, after Muhammad proclaimed his mission as a Prophet and messenger of Islam, was a woman – Khadija, Muhammad's wife. The second, a 10-year-old boy, was Muhammad's cousin and constant companion Hazrat Ali. Khadija and Ali were the first to read the *kalimah* or declaration of faith – '*La Ilaha illallah Muhammadur Rasulullah*',[13] which means, 'I bear witness that there is no god but Allah and that Muhammad is His Prophet.' The *kalimah* is now an integral part of the life of a Muslim. It is taught to every child born into the religion as soon as they learn to speak. I was so young that I don't remember when I was taught this. But ever since I can remember, I have recited it as soon as I wake up.

While the *kalimah* is something that is supposed to be on every Muslim's lips, and in their hearts, understanding what these words mean, beyond the obvious, can take time. It depends on how deep one plunges into its fathomless waters – some take years, and for some even a lifetime may not be enough.

With the recitation of the *kalimah,* Muslims assert the Oneness of Allah as explained in *Surah Ikhlas* (*Surah* 112). It professes the cluster of ideas that form the crux of Islam – that there is only one God, Allah, and that He is eternal and absolute, has no partners, neither did He beget anyone and nor was He begotten, and there is none like Him. Islam isn't just the acceptance of one God and all His manifold attributes and manifestations. It is accepting that all His followers are one people, united in their rise above divisions of tribe, clans, class, and race in order to submit to His will. In fact, the Arabic word 'Muslim' means submitting to God.

In order that we may begin to understand Allah, He describes Himself through the attributes listed in the Quran. There are 99 attributes of God mentioned in it; each one of them is a human characteristic, but Allah is much more than the sum of all, and His attributes are infinite. William Chittick explains:

> There is but a single Being, yet the names represent a multiplicity of faces that Being assumes in relation to the created things. The Essence Itself, or Being considered without the names, is what Ibn al-'Arabi sometimes calls the Unity of the One (aḥadiyyat al-ahad) in contrast to Being considered as possessor of the names, which is the Unity of Manyness (aḥdiyyatal-kathra).[14]

We only know as much as He chose to reveal, and what we know does not even begin to encompass His reality or the oneness of His manyness.

It was only three years after the first revelation of the Quran that Muhammad proclaimed its message to the people of Mecca. There had been many prophets before Muhammad, with Aadam (or Adam as he is known in the Bible) being the first. In fact, prior to the announcement of Muhammad's prophethood, no place on earth had been without a prophet at any point. Muhammad, however, is believed to be the last prophet of God as well as his messenger (*rasul*), because he brought the message of the divinely revealed book to the people.

In those early years, the word 'islam' was not used to refer to religion. As Carl Ernst writes:

> The Arabic term *islam* itself was of relatively minor importance in classical theologies based on the Qur'an; it literally means submission to God, and it denotes the minimal external forms of compliance with religious duty. If one looks at the works of

> theologians such as the famous Abu Hamid al-Ghazali (1058–1111 CE), the key term of religious identity is not *islam* but *iman*, or faith, and the one who possesses it is the *mu'min* or believer.'[15]

He further adds that historically the term was introduced into European languages by Orientalists like Edward Lane in the early nineteenth century 'as an explicit analogy with the modern Christian concept of religion'.[16]

> The 'religion' Muhammad proclaimed was simple and based on the idea of the oneness of God (that is, '*tauheed*' or 'monotheism') and universal brotherhood. The Quran revealed to him mentioned five important pillars of the religion: *tauheed* or monotheism; *salah,* called namaz in the Persianate world, or the ritual prayers performed five times a day; *sawm* called *roza* in the Persianate world or the fasting in the prescribed month of Ramzan; *zakat* or charity; and *hajj* or the pilgrimage to the house of God in Mecca, known as the Kaaba.

As he preached monotheism, the Prophet and his followers faced resistance and hostility in Mecca. Meccans then were essentially polytheists. His denouncement of their multiple idols and gods, and his criticism of the greed of local merchants – which he termed immoral – resulted in the hostility of the powerful Meccan clans. The Prophet was somewhat protected as long as his uncle Abi Talib, the head of the Hashim clan, was alive. But afterwards, when Abu Lahab took charge, the persecution increased. Waraqah ibn Nawfal had already predicted this when Khadija had gone to seek his advice after the first revelation, 'Thou wilt be called a liar, and they will use thee despitefully and cast thee out and fight against thee.'[17]

The persecution escalated to such an extent that, in 622, the Prophet and his followers had to migrate to Yathrib (now famous as Medina) to escape. The Islamic calendar, based on the lunar calculations, starts from the year of this migration.

The Prophet made his way out of Mecca secretly one night, while his cousin Hazrat Ali covered himself with his green mantle and slept in his bed in order to deceive the enemies. Hazrat Ali was also tasked with returning the valuables that the people of Mecca had left with the Prophet for safekeeping.

Accompanied by Abu Bakr, the Prophet reached Yathrib. Hazrat Ali would join him later with his mother Fatima bint Asad, the Prophet's daughter who was also called Fatima, and other ladies of the family.

Meanwhile, the journey to Yathrib took 10 days, including the time spent hiding in a cave while the men of the Quraysh hunted for them. There is a famous story from the time he spent hiding, which finds mention in the Quran (9:40).[18] It is said that a spider in the cave wove a web at the mouth of the cave, and two doves laid eggs in front of it, so that the hunters would be misled into thinking no one had entered it.

Yathrib welcomed the Prophet with open arms, and the city became Madinat-al-Rasul (the City of the Prophet). Since then, it has become famous as Medina. The foundation of the first mosque, known as Masjid-e-Quba, was laid here, as were the foundations of a just and egalitarian society governed by the rules of Islam.

Verse 72 of *Surah Anfal* in the Quran refers to a system of *mu'ākhāh* or brothering created by the Prophet shortly after the migration. It reads, 'In this "brotherhood" system, he assigned each Makkan migrant a role as a "brother" to one of the native Ansar [newly-converted Muslims of Yathrib].' In turn, it was Hazrat Ali whom the Prophet always saw as his own 'brother' and his most loyal and trustworthy companion. 'Ali is to me as Aaron was to Moses, except there will be no prophet after me,' he said.[19]

In addition, a constitution was drawn up to establish peace in Medina. Under it, all parties covered – the migrant Muslims (*muhajirs*), people of the book (Jews and Christians), important tribes of Yathrib and the Ansars – were given freedom of religious beliefs and practice.

> It [the Constitution] called for inclusiveness and transparency during negotiations with any outside forces as guiding principles of this alliance. It was all very empowering. All signatories to this arrangement were declared to be part of an *Ummah*, a term denoting community, or nation, and Medina itself was declared a

> sacred place where spilling the blood of any of the members of this alliance was forbidden.[20]

The final authority for mediation amongst the various members was the Prophet himself.

Prayers were established, and the community was flourishing in the peaceful surroundings. The Masjid-e-Nabawi was built in the vicinity of the Prophet's house. After Hazrat Ali's marriage to the Prophet's daughter, Fatima, the couple came to live next door to him.

In 624, the famous Battle of Badr was fought in which the Muslims defeated the Meccans led by Abu Jahl, one of the Prophet's main detractors in Mecca. This strengthened the Prophet's position. Later, the battles of Uhud and Khandaq were also fought in Medina. They exemplified the Prophet's keen military sense, bravery, courage, and above all his humaneness in dealing with the enemy.

In 628, the Prophet dreamt that he was circumambulating the Kaaba, taking that as a command from God to perform an *umrah* (minor pilgrimage);[21] he led a group of 1,400 unarmed Muslims dressed in *ihram* (the unstitched dress worn by male pilgrims) and camped outside Mecca at Hudabiyyah. The pilgrimage was opposed by the Quraysh. Eventually, the Treaty of Hudabiyyah was signed between the Prophet and the Quraysh, under which a 10-year 'no-war' pact gave the Muslims the right to go on a pilgrimage. It has been said of this that:

> No previous victory in Islam was greater than this. There was nothing but battle when men met; but when there was an armistice and war was abolished and men met in safety and consulted together none talked about Islam intelligently without entering it. In those two years double as many or more than double as many entered Islam as ever before.[22]

During this period, the Muslims consolidated their position in Medina too. The famous battle of Khaybar was fought a few months after this treaty between the Muslims and the Jews of Khaybar, who had allied with the Quraysh of Mecca. After a 40-day siege, Hazrat Ali smashed open the door of the fort in which the Jews had barricaded themselves.

The Jews were defeated and allowed to live peacefully in return for payment of a tax.

In 629, the Prophet thus led 2,600 men for the *umrah*. Despite the preceding conflict, their spiritual activities were appreciated by the Meccans.

As per the agreement that had been reached earlier, the Prophet had left in three days but in the following year led a second *umrah*, which was longer and even more impressive. This time around, 10,000 of his men accompanied him. The size of the pilgrimage party ensured that the Quraysh, who had planned to stop them, abided by the peace treaty. The Prophet's patience, kindness, and piety won the day.

The Kaaba had been a house of worship in pre-Islamic Arabia and had idols kept inside which were worshipped. Since Islam forbade idolatry, on this second visit, the Prophet and Hazrat Ali cleared the Kaaba of idols, breaking them. Mecca had been captured, and the Quraysh were disarmed. Many of them accepted Islam.

When the rest of the Arabs saw that the Quraysh who had declared war on the Prophet and opposed him were now subdued, and Mecca was now subject to his authority, 'they entered into God's religion "in batches", as God said, coming to Him from all directions'.[23]

Foreign delegations thus started coming to Medina to find out what was happening there and to meet the Prophet, and deputations to spread the message of Islam were sent to other countries. 'The year 630–31 is known in Islamic historiography as *sanat al-wufud*, the year of delegations or deputations. Two of the most important leaders contacted were Heraclius, the Byzantine emperor of the Eastern Roman Empire, and Khusrow Parviz, the King of Persia.'[24]

The monks of the monastery of St. Catherine in the valley of Sinai too came to meet the Prophet, leading to the signing of a covenant between them. That religious tolerance and peace-building with various communities were uppermost in the Prophet's mind can be seen in the words of the covenant:

> If a monk or pilgrim seeks protection, in mountain or valley, in a cave or in tilled fields, in the plain, in the desert, or in a church, I am behind them, defending them from every enemy... Moreover,

> no building from among their churches shall be destroyed, nor shall the money from their churches be used for the building of mosques or houses for the Muslims. Neither poll-tax nor fees shall be laid on monks, bishops or worshippers for I protect them... If a Christian woman enters a Muslim household [through marriage], she shall be given opportunity to pray in her church.[25]

The Prophet had performed three *umrahs* by 632 when, just before his passing away later that year, he performed his fourth along with his only Hajj (known as the Farewell Hajj). There, he once again laid down rules to be followed saying, 'Wrong not, and you shall not be wronged.' On his return to Mecca, he stopped at Ghadir and made the announcement about Hazrat Ali being the '*maula*' of all those who accepted him. (This is discussed at greater length later in this book.)

When the Prophet passed away, he was succeeded – as the temporal and religious authority – by four caliphs known as the *Rashidun* or the rightly guided ones: Abu Bakr (r. 632–634), Umar ibn al-Khattab (r. 634–644), Uthman ibn Affan (r. 644–656), and Ali ibn Abi Talib (r. 656–661). Hasan ibn Ali, the son of the fourth caliph, abdicated his claim to the caliphate after a series of letters with Muawiya I, the then governor of Syria.

> In them [the letters], he recognized Hasan's spiritual right to the caliphate but argued that he, Muawiya, was better suited to the task. He was the older man, he said, the more seasoned and the more worldly-wise in an uncertain world. He was the one capable of ensuring secure borders, of repressing Rejectionist terrorism and assuring the safety and integrity of the empire. Much as he admired Hasan's scholarship and piety, much as he honoured him as the grandson of the Prophet, the times called for a strong leader – a man of experience and action, not a man of intellect.[26]

Like his father before him who did not push his claim to be the first caliph, Hasan agreed for he did not want bloodshed as the unity of the *ummah* was more important. For him too, it was important that he strive in the way of 'the supremacy of the greater jihad – the lifelong struggle within oneself to become the ideal Muslim – over the lesser jihad, or armed struggle.' He believed, 'If the Kufans counted it shameful to turn away from war, [...] then "shame is better than hellfire."' And so he pledged to not seek not war with Muawiya 'but an honourable peace, and a general amnesty for all past bloodshed.'[27]

Muawiya in turn promised to name Hasan as his successor on his death. After this, Hasan retired to Medina, where he was allegedly poisoned later, in 669–70.

In the meantime, Muawiya I thus became the next caliph, leading to the rise of the Umayyad Caliphate (661–750).[28] On his deathbed, he went back on his word and named his son Yazid as his successor. That's when Ali ibn Talib's other son, Hussain, refused to take an oath of allegiance with Yazid, and the Battle of Karbala began.

The schism in Islam which had started during Ali's life now deepened with the establishment of two sects: the Shias (refers to partisans of the house of Ali ibn Abi Talib) and the Sunnis (whose name was derived from the phrase *'Ahl al-Sunnah wa al-Jamaaah'*, which means 'those who follow the [prophetic] traditions and the [official/orthodox] consensus.')[29]

It was after the death of Ali ibn Abi Talib that the egalitarian beliefs on which Islam was based were converted to a hereditary monarchy, with the establishment of the Umayyad and Abbasid Caliphates.

Sectarian controversies began to play an important role in Islam under the Umayyads, and the essence of spirituality and mysticism as taught by the Prophet was lost in this expansionist phase. The Umayyad Caliphate was eventually overthrown by the Abbasids (750–1258).

The Shias rejected the Umayyad and Abbasid caliphs and followed their own chain of leaders known as 'imams' (guides), who were the direct descendants of the Prophet. They are called the twelvers or *ashnaashriah* (believers in the divinely ordained twelve imams). Ali was the first imam. According to Shia belief, the twelfth imam is in occultation and will appear before the Day of Judgment. Along with the Prophet and his daughter Fatima, these imams are known as the fourteen Infallibles or *chahrdah masomeen* under the principle of *ismah*, which means protection and refers to the concept of incorruptible innocence, immunity from sin, or moral infallibility. Infallibility is defined as 'a spiritual grace *(lutf)* of Allah to a person which enables him to abstain from sins by his own free will.'[30]

According to Islamic belief, Muhammad was the last prophet, but he laid down laws for the guidance of his followers for all time. The areas of life that the Quran or hadiths are silent about are covered by Islamic jurisprudence. Learned and pious religious leaders of Islam interpreted these laws and advised lay Muslims on the principles of right and wrong.

The seventh century onwards, several attempts were made to codify the Islamic law or jurisprudence. Five major schools of jurisprudence called *madhab*s/*mazhab*s were established within *fiqh* (Islamic religious law), which collected and organized in one place the teachings of various great Islamic scholars according to their beliefs. Amongst the Sunnis, there were four schools: the Hanafi school founded by Abu Hanifa (699–767), the Maliki school of Malik bin Anas (711–795), the Al-Shafi school whose pioneer was Al-Shafi (767–820), and the Hanbali school founded by Ahmad bin Hanbal (720–855). Jafriya, the Shia school of jurisprudence, was founded by Imam Jafar al-Sadiq (700/2–765). Though these schools are based on the Quran and sunnah (traditions and practices of the Islamic prophet, Muhammad, that constitute a model for Muslims to follow), legal differences emerged between them according to their interpretation.

The esoteric teachings of the Quran and hadiths were lost, and with firming of laws and punishments, Allah's wrath took precedence over His *rahmat* in this phase. The simplicity and brotherhood that had been emphasized by Prophet Muhammad were forgotten in these power struggles and intrigues, leaving the newly converted Muslims in a flux.

Some Muslims, though, sought to go back to the basics of Islam, and it was in this void that a set of ascetic and renunciative practices rose and began to flourish. The emphasis was on a direct relationship with God, and tools such as *zikr* or remembrance of God were used to concentrate on His essence and purify the soul of materialism. It was from these that *tasawwuf,* from which the name Sufism was derived, emerged.

Sufi saints with their esoteric knowledge (*ilm-e-batin*) made the journey from the exoteric to the esoteric possible for the lay persons through their teachings, highlighting Allah as *rahim* (merciful) and *rahman* (benevolent).

Hassan Abbas, author of an acclaimed biography on Ali writes,

> Even in [the] modern era (the last 50 to 100 years), Sufism is seen as apolitical or perhaps [a] politically correct approach to Islam in the midst of sectarian hatred. Moderates among both Shiism and Sunnis have been gradually drifting towards Sufism for this reason also. In a way Sufism offers a middle ground in an increasingly polarized world and that's why both hardcore Sunni and Shia clergies are a bit wary of Sufi traditions.[31]

## What is Sufism?

> Light upon Light! Allah doth guide whom He wills to His Light
>
> – Quran 24:35

My first visit to a Sufi dargah was as a teenager. The dargah of Sheikh Salim Chishti in Agra is still clearly etched in my mind – the incense, the flowers, the joyous qawwalis, the threads tied on windows, and crowds of people supplicating. For the layperson today, the mention of a Sufi shrine is likely to evoke these very images and associations, along with those of dancing dervishes and fasting ascetics. However, Sufism is all this and much more.

At the core of Sufism is the direct personal experience of God – in whose likeness we are made – and union with Him is the ultimate goal. It is believed that God Himself guides the souls and actions of only those with the *junoon* (passion) to reach the divine. Sufism involves praying in such a way that one can experience the divine personally.

This is embodied in the hadith of Jibraeel, also known as Umm-e Hadith or 'the mother of all hadiths', narrated by Umar ibn al-Khattab, the second Caliph: One day the Prophet was sitting in the mosque with a few of his companions when a man appeared and questioned him on his *din* (faith).[32] The man was wearing pristine white clothes, without any signs of travel on them. He sat down so close to the Prophet that their knees pressed against each other. With his hands resting on his lap, he asked the Prophet five questions. They were about Islam (submission to God), *iman* (faith in God), *ihsan* (doing the beautiful), and the Day of

Judgment and its signs. The companions were surprised but kept silent as the questioning continued.

The Prophet, known for his eloquence and beauty of succinct speech, defined submission as bearing witness that there is no god but Allah and that Muhammad is His messenger, performing daily prayers, paying *zakat* (alms tax), fasting during Ramzan and performing the hajj, if one can find the means to do so.[33] (These are the five pillars of Islam.) Faith, he said, was to believe in Allah, His angels, His scriptures, His messengers and the Last Day, and to have faith that no good or evil comes without His providence.

On being asked what *ihsan* is, the Prophet Muhammad said, '*Ihsan* is to worship Allah as if you see Him, and if you do not achieve this state of devotion, then (take it for granted that) Allah sees you.'[34]

The stranger asked two more questions on the Day of Judgment and satisfied with the answers, he left. Then the Prophet identified him as Jibraeel to his companion Umar ibn al-Khattab and said that the angel had come 'to teach unto you your religion'.

This hadith also places Sufism – which follows these ideas of *iman* and *ihsan* – firmly within Islam. In fact, after submission to Allah, *ihsan* and *iman* are the two most important aspects of devotion. *Ihsan* is that level of perfect devotion wherein the devotee is so completely absorbed in God, they can feel the divine presence, seeing Allah with the eyes of the heart.[35] *Iman*, on the other hand, is the attainment of complete faith.

The two concepts are related. For some, this devotion may mean purifying the self of vices, the annihilation of ego and the attainment of complete faith (*iman*). For another, it may mean renouncing the world and performing *ihsan*.[36] And for still others, it may be nothing but absolute and complete love of the Divine, which leads the Sufi on to the path of eternal truth, beauty and goodness – towards the love of humanity and a life devoted to the service of people, irrespective of class, caste, or creed.

The beauty of Sufism is this personal experience of God, which can take myriad forms, and the many ways in which a Sufi may express their love for the Divine. It is the intense, unconditional love for God; Rabia al-Basri, the eighth-century saint from Basra wanted that God be loved for His sake alone – and not from fear of punishment or temptation of reward. But it is also the intoxication of Mansur al-Hallaj who annihilated himself in God, through intense Sufi practices, to the extent that only God was left in him so he kept repeating 'Ana'l Haq' (I am the Truth), and went to the gallows lost in that love. Sufism is the riverine generosity, the sun-like affection and the earth-like hospitality of Khwaja Muinuddin Chishti, and it is also the asceticism of Baba Farid, who performed the *Chilla-e-Maakoos*, a 40-day fast during which he hung upside down in a well as a test of his faith and courage. (More on all of these figures later in the book.)

Sufism is also the journey beyond the apparent or *zahir* (exoteric), into the hidden or *batin* (esoteric), for Allah Himself is both *al-Zahir* (manifest) and *al-Batin* (non-manifest), as He refers to Himself in the Quran. The Quran itself possesses many esoteric meanings, some which are known only to Allah.

Irrespective of how it is perceived or defined by its practitioners, Sufism has touched, and continues to touch, the hearts and souls of millions. There are thousands who take an oath of allegiance with Sufi masters even today. One master (he doesn't want to be named because he has reached a stage where his own identity is null now) told me that he has many *murids* (novices committed to gaining spiritual enlightenment under a guide), both men and women, who have taken an oath of allegiance with him. However, most of them are not the classical Sufis who immerse themselves in meditative discipline and pursue the goal of *marifah* (intuitive knowledge of spiritual truth reached through ecstatic Sufi experiences). They are content to just improve their life, live it according to the key principles laid down, and become better persons who serve humanity. The Sufi master told me he has four *khalifah*s (spiritual successors) and it is they who are following the path of *tariqah* (mystical path) and *haqiqah* (truth), explained later in the book. Whether they reach the stage of *marifah* is to be seen. Later, another Sufi master also told me the same thing. In any case, even apart from *murids*, there are many people who like me follow Sufism but are not ordained in its path; they visit dargahs (shrines of saints) for the powers of its *barakat* (blessings).

The long queues of devotees at various shrines all over the world, praying for intercession, and the popularity of anything to do with Sufism, bear testimony to its attraction for and influence on the masses.

'Sufism today is a name without a reality, whereas it was once a reality without a name.'

– Abu al-Hasan Fushanja[37]

The term Sufism was first introduced in a Latin work by a German – F.A.G. Tholuckin – in 1821, as an anglicized version of *tasawwuf*.[38] It was later popularized by British Orientalists describing those aspects of 'oriental' culture that Europeans found attractive. Thus, as mentioned earlier, there was an insistence on placing Sufism outside of Islam, which was believed to have the 'essential characteristic of harsh legalism'; Sufism, on the other hand, was considered to be 'indifferent to matters of religious law'.[39]

The first Orientalist to assert that Sufism was based on the Quran and the hadiths was Louis Massignon (1883–1962). A French Catholic scholar, Massignon greatly influenced the way Islam was perceived in the West through his work. Since then many Sufi texts have been translated and studied. Scholars such as Carl Ernst, Annemarie Schimmel, Seyyid Hossein Nasr, Sayyid Athar Abbas Rizvi, Bruce Lawrence and Raziuddin Aquil, to name a few, have written on Sufism, highlighting its historical and religious context.

Carl Ernst asks how it is possible to tell what Sufism is, questioning what it means to be a Sufi. The answer he arrives at is as follows: 'In Arabic and Persian, there are dozens of terms for Muslim mystics with distinct and sometimes conflicting meanings, all of which are subsumed by the English word *Sufism*' but concedes that '*Sufism* has now become a standard term, whether we like it or not.'[40]

Due to an increasing stress on sociology and ideology in the study of religion, in his view, Sufism was perceived as:

> [A] kind of mystical philosophy found in Muslim countries, which can include figures on the margins of society (dervishes and fakirs) along with politically important mass movements. This descriptive approach to Sufism contrasts sharply with the use of the term *Sufi* in Sufi texts. There we find a prescriptive use of the term which sets forth goals of ethical and spiritual perfection.[41]

There are many claims regarding the origin of the term 'Sufi'. Some say it comes from *Ahl al-Suffa/Ashab-e-Suffa* or 'people of the porch', a phrase describing the Prophet's companions who stayed on the porch of the Masjid-e-Nabvi, his mosque in Medina, and studied religious science there.[42] Some believe it comes from the Arabic word *safa,* meaning pure, for while ritual purity is essential for all Muslims, inner purity is a requirement for mystics. Yet others claim its origins lie in the Arabic word *suf* or wool, since the early Sufis, like ascetics of the far east, wore woollen cloaks. The coarse woollen cloak signified the humble, ascetic, and unmaterialistic spirit of the Sufis. It is now widely believed that this last theory is probably closer to the truth and it is indeed the word *suf* that led to the name, while the Arabic term that was translated as Sufism, *tasawwuf*, literally means 'the process of becoming a Sufi'.

Today the term Sufi encompasses many different types of mystics and saints. However, it was used infrequently in medieval texts; the popular words used then were *abid* (worshipper), *zahid* (ascetic), *salih* (righteous one), *salik* (traveller), *siddiq* (sincere one), *ahl-e-dil* (masters of the heart), and *mazjub* (the intoxicated).

The terms for a spiritual master were *sheikh*, *pir*, *or khwaja*, while the disciple was known as a *murid*. Just as temporal kings appoint their successors, so do the spiritual kings. The successor of a *sheikh/pir/khwaja* was called a *khalifa*. Highly acclaimed saints were given the title of *qutb* (polestar; a centre of sorts), *qutb al-aqtab* (chief of the *qutbs*, denoting their rank in the spiritual hierarchy), or *ghaus* (helper/redresser of complaints).

Terminology aside, the emphasis for Sufis is not on external rituals but on the experience of the inner self leading to the discovery of truth. This truth is achieved in three ways: one is obtained 'from' God, through the Quran and shariah (the Muslim code of religious law), which are obligatory for all Muslims; one is obtained 'with' God, on the mystical path; and the last truth is obtained 'of' God, and is called *ilm-e-marifat* (gnosis) – the knowledge possessed by prophets and saints, and is the final goal of all Sufis.

At the final stage on the spiritual path, the Sufi's heart becomes empty of everything except the remembrance of God; it is to be annihilated (*fana*) to become immortal (*baqa*) with Allah. Since God is always with us, and as close as our jugular vein, it is not a question of reaching Him, but recognizing His signs. The signs are always present everywhere and inside us. As one popular hadith puts it: 'My earth does not encompass Me, nor does My heaven, but the heart of My servant, the man of true faith, does encompass Me.'[43]

Thus, only He is worthy of worship and love, and to him will we return.

And the Sufi's (herein the lover's) love for God (the loved one), and closeness to Him has to be reflected in their conduct, which is a manifestation of Him. This sentiment comes across beautifully in Rabia al-Basri's immortal words:

> If I adore You out of fear of Hell,
> Burn me in Hell!
> If I adore you out of desire for Paradise,
> Lock me out of Paradise.
> But if I adore you for Yourself alone,
> Do not deny to me Your eternal beauty.[44]

# 2

# The *Ahl al-Bait*, or the Household of the Prophet

I [Gabriel] can go no farther, only human beings,
Once perfected through that Holy Light,
Can approach that unapproachable Light.
But you, Mustafa, have permission to
Go nearer, to intercede for humankind.[1]
– Paul Abdul Wadud Sutherland

The eve of the 27th Rajab – *Shab-e-Miraj* – is considered very auspicious. Throughout the world, Muslims commemorate this night with special prayers and *zikr* (remembrance of Allah, by chanting His names). Apart from praying on this night like millions of other Muslims, I cook *halwa* (a sweet) that I then consecrate in the Prophet's name.

On the night of the 27th Rajab (621), Prophet Muhammad undertook two journeys. The first – *Isra* – refers to him being taken by the Archangel Jibraeel from the Masjid al-Haram (Sacred Mosque) in Mecca, on a winged mule known as *buraq,* to the furthest mosque in Jerusalem, that is now identified as Masjid al-Aqsa. The Prophet found himself in the company of all the prophets and messengers from the time of Aadam, and he led the prayers. This was the physical journey.

The second was *Miraj,* or the spiritual journey undertaken by him to the heavens. As he crossed each of the eight heavens, he met the various other prophets. Jibraeel accompanied him on this trip till they reached the Lote Tree (*sidrat-ul-muntaha*), which marks the end of the seventh heaven. As soon as they got there, Jibraeel excused himself for being unable to accompany him any further, explaining to the Prophet that his wings would be singed if he did. The Prophet thus had to cross the last heaven alone.

At the end of the eighth, he found himself in divine presence. This symbolizes the state of pure consciousness of the Divine, which the Prophet was able to ascend to after overcoming physical barriers. Even Jibraeel had a veil between him and the Divine, but not so with the Prophet.

Prophet Muhammad is therefore called *ummi* or unlettered in the Quran. *Ummi* is the mystical symbol of a pure, uncluttered heart – one that can receive divine knowledge. It is believed that before starting on *Isra*, two angels who accompanied the Prophet took out his heart, cleaned and purified it, and put it back. That is exactly how a *salik* (traveller) starts on the journey of Sufism. The heart has to be open, washed of all impurities, and filled only with the remembrance of Allah. The night journey symbolizes the pursuit of the spiritual goal.

After the journey, Prophet Muhammad returned to his still warm bed in Mecca and resumed his life. He had returned from what was the zenith of spiritual experiences – a direct meeting with Allah – only so he could share it with his people, who could in turn experience a similar union. This is important. It signifies that after connecting with Allah we have to continue our service in His way, by serving humanity and proclaiming His message to all. Prophet did that and set us an example, earning himself another title: Habibullah (beloved of Allah).

It is thus from the Prophet's own behaviour that Sufis learn *ihsan,* or doing all things beautiful, a principle on which they lay great emphasis. In fact, Sufis believe that though the word 'Sufi' itself came up centuries later, in essence, Prophet Muhammad was the first Sufi. All Muslims look up to him as the *insan-e-kamil* (the complete man) and strive to emulate his qualities of mercy, knowledge, piety, and closeness to God.

The Prophet was also the first link of all *silsilah*s (Sufi orders).

> He [The Prophet] is said to have been the recipient of a two-fold revelation, the one embodied in the contents of the Quran, [and] the other within his heart. The former was meant for all and is binding on all; the latter was to be transmitted to the chosen few through these lines of succession. Hence it is that Muhammad's

> knowledge is described as being *'ilm-i-safina,* book knowledge, and *'ilm-i-sina*, heart knowledge.[2]

Moreover, every member of the Prophet's family was said to be endowed with esoteric wisdom, and the *Ahl al-Bait,* or the 'Household of the Prophet', therefore, holds an important place in Sufi traditions. Any discussion revolving around the roots of Sufism would thus be incomplete without a discussion about them.

According to Hassan Abbas, 'The central feature of Sufism is love of *Ahlul Bayt*[3] and the esoteric principles taught by Ali ibn Abi Talib and that connects Sufism and Shiism in an inextricable way as Shiism revolves around the love of Ali and *Ahlul Bayt*.'[4]

Therefore, what follows is a brief account of some key members of the Prophet's household with a view to understanding their significance in different sects of Islam more broadly and specifically for Sufism. But before that, here is a table to help follow the chronology:

## The Hashemite Family Tree

Hashim Abd al-Manaf
Abdul Muttalib
Abdullah ibn Abdul Muttalib m. Amina
Muhammad ibn Abdullah m. Khadija (daughter Fatima)
Fatima bint Muhammad m. Ali ibn Abi Talib

## The Twelve Shia Imams start with Imam Ali

Ali ibn Abi Talib (4th caliph, 656–661)
Hasan ibn Ali (imam, 661–679)
Hussain ibn Ali (imam, 669–680)
Ali ibn Hussain, popular as Zainul Abidin (imam, 680–712)
Muhammad ibn Ali, popular as Baqar (imam, 712–731)
Jafar al-Sadiq ibn Muhammad Baqar (imam, 731–765)
Musa al-Kazim ibn Jafar (imam, 765–799)
Ali al-Reza ibn Musa (imam, 799–818)
Muhammad al-Jawwad ibn Reza (imam, 818–835)

Ali al-Hadi ibn Muhammad al-Jawwad (imam, 835–868)
Hasan al-Askari ibn Ali al-Hadi (imam, 868–874)
Muhammad al-Mehdi (The 'Hidden Imam', 874 to date – as per belief he is in occultation)

What is meant by the Ka'ba is the heart
of the prophets
and the friends of God.
That
is where God is revealed.
– Mevlana Jalaluddin Rumi[5]

The account of the *Ahl al-Bait* begins with the Prophet himself. Muhammad was born in 570 into the Hashim clan of the powerful Quraysh tribe. The Quraysh was a mercantile tribe which historically controlled the city of Mecca and its pilgrimage centre, the Kaaba. The Hashim clan was named after Hashim ibn Abd Manaf (464–497), and they claimed descent from Ismail, the son of Prophet Ibrahim (known as Abraham in the Judeo-Christian world). The Hashimites had been the traditional providers of water to the pilgrims who came to worship the idols in the Kaaba, the house of God built by Ibrahim and Ismail. However, the holy Zamzam spring which had welled up because of the cries of Ismail and Hajira's prayer, when Ibrahim had left them in the desert of Mecca, had dried up so no one knew where it was.

Abdul Muttalib (470–578), Muhammad's grandfather, succeeded his father Hashim ibn Abd Manaf as the chief of the clan. He had a dream in which he was given detailed instructions about the location of Zamzam, which could now once again become a permanent source of water for the pilgrims. He found the spring by following the instructions, but the other Quraysh clans contested his claim to become its custodian. A diviner was called in to decide who would control the precious commodity. With the story of Ismail's (Biblical Ismael) sacrifice in mind, Abdul Muttalib made a vow that if God were to give him 10 sons, he would sacrifice one of them right there in front of the Kaaba. Soon, in accordance with the divine signs that were received, Abdul Muttalib and his descendants were made the custodians of Zamzam.

Eventually he was blessed with 10 sons, and the time to honour his vow came.

Traditionally, decisions were made by drawing arrows at the foot of the Quraysh's totemic icon, a stone called Hubal near the Kaaba. Various potential answers to any given question would be written on arrows, each of which was to be picked up by the priest who would say a prayer and let them fall. In accordance with this tradition, Abdul Muttalib took his sons there and wrote down the names of his sons on the arrows. The arrow that fell pointing at the Hubal would have the name of the son to be sacrificed. Every arrow that fell and pointed to the Hubal had Abdullah's name written on it.

Abdullah was the youngest and favourite son of Abdul Muttalib. Abdul Muttalib was shocked and inconsolable. But despite visions of Prophet Ibrahim (Abraham in the Bible) sacrificing Ismail haunting him, he started preparing to sacrifice his favourite son. That's when someone suggested they consult a famous *kahina* (female soothsayer) who lived in Yathrib.

Abdul Muttalib and his sons visited the priestess. She closed her eyes and invoked the spirits. 'What is the blood money for a man's life?' she asked. Blood money or *diyat* was paid to a murdered person's family by the family of the murderer, in exchange for the latter's life, if they agreed to settle the matter in this way.

'Ten camels,' was the reply.

'Go back to Mecca, take the young man and ten camels to the sacred stone and cast the arrows again,' she advised,[6] adding that if the arrows kept coming up with Abdullah's name, Abdul Muttalib would have to keep adding that number of camels to the sacrifice till the gods were satisfied. It ultimately took a hundred for the gods to be satisfied!

Muhammad would say, 'I am the son of the Two Sacrificed Ones.'

Soon after this incident, Abdullah married Amina bint Abd Manaf bin Zuhrah, daughter of the chief of another Quraysh tribe called Banu Zuhrah. Within a week of the marriage, Abdullah left with a trade caravan for work. According to Ibn Ishaq:

> It is alleged in popular stories (and only God knows the truth) that Amina bint Wahab used to say when she was pregnant with God's apostle that a voice said to her, 'You are pregnant with the lord of this people and when he is born say, "I put him in the care of the One from the evil of every envier; then call him Muhammad."' As she was pregnant with him she saw a light come forth from her by which she could see the castles of Busra in Syria.[7]

Abdullah may have been saved from the sacrifice just so Muhammad could be born from his union with Amina, for during his return journey he fell sick near Yathrib and died a few days later. Muhammad was thus born after the death of his father.

In the Arabia of those days, it was the custom of the townspeople to send their children to be suckled by Bedouin wet nurses. This was probably to ensure that they grew up in the free and healthy surroundings of the desert, where they could develop a robust frame and acquire the pure speech and manners of the Bedouins, who were noted both for the chastity of their language and being free from vices that usually develop in sedentary societies.[8]

Bedouin women would come to town looking for babies they could nurse for a fee. Halima was one such woman who set out looking for a child with her husband and baby, and other women of her tribe. There was a famine that year, and they were destitute. The female camel Halima rode was old and didn't yield a drop of milk. The woman herself was not lactating properly either, so her hungry child cried all night.

She was offered baby Muhammad to foster, but she refused because he was an orphan and she deduced that payment may therefore not be certain. Destiny, however, was at work, and when every other woman except her got a baby to foster, she told her husband that she would take the orphan rather than return empty-handed. In the words of Ibn Ishaq:

> He [The husband] replied, 'Do as you please; perhaps God will bless us on his account.' So I went and took him for the sole reason that I could not find anyone else. I took him back to my baggage, and as soon as I put him to my bosom, my breasts overflowed with

milk which he drank until he was satisfied, as also did his foster brother.[9]

In the morning, her husband said, 'Do you know, Halima, you have taken a blessed creature?' and Halima replied, 'By God, I hope so.'

Muhammad was weaned two years later. But before that, during those two years, Halima's family had an abundance of everything. When it was time to return the baby to the mother, Halima wanted to keep the blessed boy. So she brought him back after pleading to let her keep him. She said she believed he would be safer in the desert than in the city, where a certain infection affecting children was prevalent at the time. Amina agreed.

This is how it came to be that Muhammad lived in the desert for five years. Under the vast open skies and harsh climate, he grew up in the lap of nature. His mother died soon after and he returned to Mecca to his family. His grandfather Abdul Muttalib brought him and later entrusted him to the care of his son Abi Talib before dying.

In Mecca, Muhammad felt suffocated by the hypocrisy, injustice, and commercialism, and as he grew older, he turned inward, towards spiritualism and mysticism, slowly becoming a quiet, spiritual man. His behaviour and character earned him the reputation of being the Al-Ameen (The trustworthy one) in Meccan society. This was later demonstrated in an episode when he was 35.

The Quraysh decided to rebuild the Kaaba and add a roof to safeguard its treasures. The work of building the walls was divided equally among all the clans. The sacred black stone, which is revered as a relic, had also been removed and kept aside. When the time came to put it back none of the clans could decide which of them should have the honour of performing the task. Finally, they agreed that the first man to enter the premises of the Kaaba would arbitrate. The one chosen in this way was Muhammad. He proposed that they get a cloth and put the stone on it. Then the clans could hold onto its four corners and lift the stone together. All of the clans would thus be able to participate. Once they agreed, it was Muhammad himself who placed the stone in the centre of the cloth with his own hands. After this was done, the building work could resume.

This was the Prophet that the merciful God had sent for all humankind, a man whose *akhlaq* (exemplary character traits) was of the highest order and is described in the Quran (68:4) as follows: *Wa innaka la'alaa khuluqin 'azeem.* (And thou [standest] on an exalted standard of character.)

As the personification of virtue, Prophet Muhammad states in a hadith, 'I was sent to perfect good character,'[10] and to guide humans as they make decisions about right or wrong, so that they may reach their full potential.

In this aspect, *akhlaq* differs from the Western concept of ethics. While a strong moral outlook is needed in the former, it is not enough, unlike the latter. Piety, knowledge and awareness of God were all equally essential. The answer to finding the right balance is found in the Quran, hadiths, and the life stories of the *Ahl al-Bait*.

Every prophet has been given the power of performing some miracles called *mojeza*. Prophet Muhammad too is credited with many miracles, including his *akhlaq*. But the main *mojeza* (miracle) of the last prophet is the revelation of the Quran.

Despite The Holy Book being revealed in parts, over several years, it has one central theme –Allah is one, only He is worthy of worship, and obedience to Him and His prophets is a must. It contains the doctrine of reality, with God being the Absolute Reality, and the reality of creation. It lists Allah's names and attributes, by which we may know Him, for to Allah belong all the beautiful names. The Holy Book also lays down rules for the practical and ritual aspects of Islamic religious and spiritual life. It instructs readers in matters of ethics and morality, and good and evil, through various parables.

It is the single source of the shariah or Islamic law. The last Quranic revelation was made to the Prophet in 632. It reads: 'Today I perfected your religion for you and completed my favour to you and have chosen for you Al-Islam as your religion.'

The Holy Quran conveyed a deeper moral, spiritual, and theological truth by relying on historical memory. It is hortatory and calls upon Muslims to 'enjoin good and forbid evil'. (Quran 9:112)

To those who doubted that it was a divine book, Allah, via the Prophet, issued a challenge to create another book of the stature of the Quran or even reproduce 10 chapters: 'And if you all are in doubt about what I have revealed to My servant, bring a single chapter like it, and call your witnesses besides God if you are truthful.' (Quran 2:23)

Several orators and poets tried but they failed.

The Prophet's actions were a template for ethical behaviour and thus emulated by Sufi saints. He was the *insan-e-kamil* or 'the perfect man'. The perfect man is one who has 'perfectly realized the full spiritual potential of the human state, who has realized in himself and his experience the oneness of being that underlies all the apparent multiplicity of existence'. The term perfect man is, however, in itself 'more of a spiritual archetype than an actual human condition'.[11]

According to Annemarie Schimmel, the Prophet's *hijr* (migration) from Mecca to Medina became the prototype of the mystical path, the journey from home and back (and thus a microcosmic picture of the way of the soul from God and back to God).[12]

Muhammad lived an almost ascetic life, and his *faqr* (poverty) became the model for mystical poverty later – the mendicant 'who possesses nothing but is totally possessed by God, partaking of His everlasting riches'. His most popular title is Abdullah, which means servant/slave of Allah, and that is what he remained, setting an example for all Muslims to come. In fact, he is 'a mercy to mankind' who leads a divinely guided life with his *adab,* or 'conduct', being a continuous act of devotion. As Seyyid Nasr says in *The Study Quran*, 'Something of the reality of the Prophet's soul is present in the Quran, and that is why, when asked about his character, his wife 'Ā'ishah replied, "His character was the Quran."'[13]

The Prophet was sent to earth as *Rahmat al-Alameen* (mercy for all the worlds), and is the example for all men and women to follow. His life serves as a model for all those who seek to lead a life of piety, devotion, and humility; they emulate his ability to forgive, and, most importantly, his love for all.

As per one hadith, the Prophet loved perfumes, and today, some fourteen centuries after he left this world, his fragrance envelops millions around it and will continue to do so for as long as it remains.[14]

The Prophet left this world in 632. Most traditions describe an incident that is said to have occurred just before his death. One day, during his sickness, in a moment of lucidity, he said, 'Bring me writing materials that I may write something for you, after which you will not be led into error.'[15]

The people present in the room at that time were some of the prophet's wives, including his youngest wife Aisha, her father Abu Bakr, and Caliph Umar (another father-in-law of the Prophet). Since no one knew what he was about to write/dictate, and whether it would be a set of religious instructions, or a will naming his heir, there was confusion in the room. Some of those present felt he was too sick to undertake the pressure of such work and there were arguments to that effect. The noise disturbed him, and he finally said, 'Leave me. Let there be no quarrelling in my presence.'[16]

His voice was weak, but Umar who heard him said, 'The Messenger of God is overcome by pain. We have the Quran, the Book of God, and that is sufficient for us.'

After that the Prophet did not get a chance to voice any such wish, and whether he wanted to name Ali as his successor, reaffirm the words spoken at Ghadeer-e-Khumm, or something else, can now remain only a matter of conjecture.

However, Shia scholars believe that shortly before his departure from the earthly plane, the Prophet said:

> I leave among you something which is very important and should be followed; you will not go astray if you take hold of it after I am gone, one part of it being more important than the other: God's Book, which is a rope stretched from Heaven to earth, and my close relatives, who belong to my household. These two will not separate from one another till they come down to the pool [in the Hereafter]; so, consider how you act regarding them after my departure.[17]

These famous words constitute what is known as a hadith. Hadiths are the Prophet's sayings and they are a guide to the interpretation of the Holy

Quran. If the Quran is divinely guided rhythm, the hadiths are divinely guided prose. In fact, some of the hadiths known as Hadith-e-Qudsi are the words of God related by the Prophet as hadiths – and are thus not part of the Quran.

The hadith above is a particularly well-known one, and is called the Hadith-e Saqlain, or 'the hadith of two treasures'. It emphasizes the importance of the Quran and *Ahl al-Bait* as guides for the Muslim community, after him.

While the Prophet himself assigned the task of memorizing the revelations of the Holy Quran to various individuals he trusted as soon as they were revealed, the hadiths were all only documented *after* the Prophet's death. That would be as many as a hundred years later. Naturally the authenticity of the latter comes under question by some sections of Muslims. Besides, sometimes hadiths were written down after having travelled through many chains of transmission, so they were probably distorted.[18] In addition to the hadith compilations termed *sahih* or accurate, the Shias rely on the hadith compiled by the twelve imams as explained later on.

Learn how to act sincerely from Ali,
God's lion, free from all impurity.[19]
– Mevlana Jalaluddin Rumi

If Prophet Muhammad is universally accepted as the first Sufi and the first link of all *silsilah*s or Sufi orders, his cousin and son-in-law – Ali ibn Abi Talib – was the next link in that chain. As the Prophet's cousin, son-in-law, and father of the grandsons from whom the Prophet's line continued, Ali was a member of the *Ahl al-Bait* and is believed to be the one who inherited the Prophet's spiritual knowledge, *seena dar seena* (from my heart to yours). As per Islamic tradition the Prophet said, 'I am the city of knowledge and Ali is the gate of that city. (*Ana madina-tul-ilm wa Aliyun babuha.*)' So to enter the city, one has to go through its gate.

In fact, there are many hadiths in which the Prophet extolled Ali, and according to Schimmel, '[T]hese served the Sufis when they elaborated their own definitions of the various stages and states.'[20] Ali's chivalry and perfect behaviour or *adab* is seen as a continuous act of devotion in Sufism as it is a constant reminder of the existence of God and being on the right path.

In Ali, a man of medium build with piercing eyes, were combined not only mystical knowledge but also chivalry and bravery. The Arabic traditions of *futuwwah* (chivalry) were very different from its European connotations. After the advent of Islam, the word *futuwwah* meant a code of honourable conduct in the tradition of prophets, saints, and those who are Allah's beloved.

The noun was *fata* which meant an ideal, noble, and perfect person, generous to a fault, one ready to give up everything including their life for the sake of their friends, and of course follow the path of Allah. The Prophet was himself a supreme example of *futuwwah*. The Persian equivalent of this is *jawan-mardi* (chivalry), and Ali was the epitome of it. *Futuwwah* is also one of the essential requirements of a Sufi.

Ali – sometimes called Asadullah (Lion of Allah) – was not only brave but possessed exoteric and esoteric knowledge. His sword, known as Zulfiqar (two-edged), is one of the most famous in history; it is also linked to his mystical knowledge, and for Sufis, the two edges are said to metaphorically represent *zikr* (remembrance of Allah) and *fikr* (contemplation of Allah).[21]

Ali's *irfan* or mystical knowledge too is legendary, and three orders of Sufism – Qadriya, Chishti, and Suhrawardi – consider him their *khalifa* (spiritual leader), while the Naqshbandi *silsilah* is connected to him through his great, great-grandson, Jafar al-Sadiq. This connection and lineage was symbolically important for 'they provided a channel to divine authority through the horizontal medium of tradition. Regardless of their verifiability in external historical terms, the chains of masters and disciples were necessary for the transmission of spiritual power and blessings.'[22]

Traditionally, it is believed that the Prophet passed on the secrets of his esoteric knowledge to Ali and Abu Bakr. The two *silsilah*s of Sufis such as the Qadiriyya and Naqshbandiyya, believe that Ali was taught the *zikr* of '*lā ilāha illallāh*', while Abu Bakr was taught the *zikr* of '*Allāh Allāh*'.[23] *Zikr* (*dhikr* in Arabic) is a remembrance of Allah chanted repeatedly, and its count is kept either on a rosary, fingers, or said mentally. Both *zikrs* are meant to help the devotee concentrate on Allah's oneness and attributes.

The basis for this belief that Ali is his spiritual successor is related to the events that occurred after what is known as *Hajjat al-Vida* (Farewell Pilgrimage). On 18 Zill Hijj 10 AH (10 March 632 CE), just three months before his demise, Prophet Muhammad performed his first and only hajj. Realizing its significance, many people accompanied him. On his way back from Mecca, he stopped near a small pond in a place called Khumm (now the city of Juhfa in Saudi Arabia). Since *ghadeer* means 'pond' in Arabic, it came to be called Ghadeer-e-Khumm. It was a barren place with no potable water source, but it was the spot where caravans that had been travelling together from Mecca would split up and head on separate routes leading to destinations of their choice.

It was here that the Prophet said that he had received a revelation from Allah, and wanted to announce it to the people. (This is also supposed to be the last time he spoke to a large congregation of Muslim men and women.) The Quranic verse (5:67) said to have been revealed to him is: 'O Messenger, announce that which has been revealed to you from your Lord, and if you do not, then you have not conveyed His message. And Allah will protect you from the people. Indeed, Allah does not guide the disbelieving people.' After thus assuring the people of God's protection, he asked those who were getting ready to go their separate way to not leave.

A makeshift dais of palm leaves and sticks, topped with camel saddles, was set up. The Prophet climbed on to it and began his sermon: 'O people, Allah the Most Kind the Omniscient has told me that no apostle lives to more than half the age of him who had preceded him. I think I am about to be called (to die) and thus I must respond...'

He asked those assembled if he had acquitted his responsibilities equitably, to which they responded that he had informed and advised them well, assuring him that he had striven to do his best. After testifying that there is but one God, and reiterating his own prophethood, he talked of death and the Day of Judgment. The assembly bore witness to all of this.

Then the Prophet called his cousin and son-in-law – Ali ibn Abi Talib – and very dramatically lifting his forearm in line with his own went on to say:

*Man kunto maula*
*Fa hazaa Aliyun maula*

[Whoever accepts me as a *maula*
Ali is his *maula* too.]

The Prophet repeated this twice to the cheering crowd with Ali standing next to him, his forearm held up by the Prophet; in the moment of complete oneness, the spiritual knowledge – if not political mantle – was passed on.

Since the Prophet did not specifically use the word *khalifa* (successor), a dispute arose after his death as to whether Ali ibn Abi Talib was indeed his successor or friend. The root of the problem arises from the meaning of the Arabic word *maula*. Its root is the Arabic word *wali*, which means friend, guide, or to be close to. It can be interpreted in various ways and has over 20 meanings, such as master, protector, friend, owner of a slave, judge, and even servant.

Despite the controversy over the implication of the word *maula* that was used – a controversy that rages on to this very day between the Shia and Sunni sects – it is universally accepted that the word was used to declare Ali as his spiritual heir.

To celebrate the event and Ali, Eid-e-Ghadeer is marked every year with the Prophet'swords, '*man kunto maula*' resounding in millions of qawwalis in dargahs all over the world. Syed Salman Chishty, the *gaddi nasheen* (hereditary caretakers) of Ajmer Sharif Dargah, says, 'We celebrate Eid-e-Ghadeer with great reverence every year as we trace out the lineage to Hazrat Ali. It was the day the Prophet (peace be upon him) appointed Ali as his spiritual heir and guide for all believing men and women.'[24] It is celebrated by followers of Hazrat Ali as Eid-e-Ghadeer.

There is an interesting story around Hazrat Ali's birth which establishes the closeness between him and the Prophet. According to Shia beliefs, and as confirmed by some Sunni texts, Abi Talib's wife – Fatima bint Asad – was heavily pregnant with Ali, and had come to the Holy Kaaba to perform the ritual of circling it when she began to go into labour. While she was doing this, suddenly the wall of the Holy Kaaba cracked open. She entered it, and so it came to pass that she gave birth to a baby boy on the 13th Rajab (601) inside. To this day, Hazrat Ali's followers maintain that they can see the crack, even though it has been filled up since, and they try and touch the wall's surface during Hajj and Umrah. (I have also done it during the many Umrah pilgrimages I made to the Kaaba.)

It is said that once Fatima bint Asad had entered the Kaaba, the walls were sealed again; it was only on the third day when the baby's cousin Muhammad arrived that the locks on its doors could be opened. The baby's eyes had been closed all this while and opened only when Muhammad came; thus, his was the first face the new-born saw. Muhammad was the one who named him Ali (meaning 'exalted').

Ali followed his elder cousin everywhere, like a 'baby camel', and thus he learnt the lessons of the two worlds. At the age of 10, Ali was the first male to embrace Islam as his religion and Muhammad as the Prophet of God (although Khadija was the first person to accept Islam).

Hazrat Ali was with the Prophet throughout the years during which the Holy Quran was revealed, so he could rightfully claim, '[B]y God not one word has been revealed of which I know not where it was revealed what it concerns and its subject matter'.[25] There was no aspect of the Quran that Hazrat Ali did not understand. Hazrat Ali's knowledge of the Quran also extended to understanding, as Nasr puts it:

> [...the] remarkable mathematical structure that undergirds the Quranic text based on the mathematical symbolism of the letters of the Arabic alphabet. The traditional esoteric Islamic science known as *al-jafr*, whose origin is attributed traditionally to 'Alī ibn Abī Ṭālib (the cousin and son-in-law of the Prophet, who became the first Shiite imam and the fourth Sunni caliph), deals with the numerical values of the letters of the Arabic alphabet and their symbolic significance. [...] The science of *al-jafr* brings out remarkable aspects of the inner teachings of the Quran, including the meaning of the mysterious separated letters (*al-ḥurūf al- muqaṭṭa'ah*) that appear at the beginning of 29 sūrahs, and elucidates many basic doctrines.[26]

Fazle Haq's *masnavi*, which has been cited in Hassan Abbas's book *The Prophet's Heir,*[27] offers the following nugget from Islamic lore: The day after the *Miraj* (night of ascension to heaven), the Prophet had a conversation with four close companions. He told them:

> On the night of *Miraj* I have received the *kharqa-e-faqr* [roughly translated as 'cloak of transcendent spiritual knowledge'] from God and I wish to give it to one of you. However, first I must know – how will you do justice to this gift?' [...] The four men before him answered one by one, each convinced they were the right choice – the first one promising to spread justice, the second promising to proselytize Islam everywhere, the third promising to give a lot of charity. When the time came for Hazrat Ali's response to be heard, he said simply, 'I will conceal peoples' flaws.' And the Prophet replied, 'You, Ali, are the one who deserves to have this.[28]

This episode is mentioned by many writers including Nasr as it emphasizes Hazrat Ali's 'spiritual superiority and excellence in knowledge and wisdom.'[29] Nasr also mentions that 'Ali wore it and sewed patches on it until he said, "I have sewed so many patches on this cloak that I am embarrassed before the sewer." Ali made his son Hasan wear it after him, and then Hussain, and then the descendants of Hussain one after another, until the Mehdi [the 12th imam who is in occultation]. The cloak rests with him now.' According to Professor Ahab Bdaiwi, who teaches formative and post-classical Islamic thought at Leiden University, 'Alī's constant sewing of the cloak is both an act of modesty and continuity of the light of Muhammad.'[30] The passing on of the cloak to his sons and descendants symbolizes the passing on of that mystical knowledge.

On becoming the caliph, Hazrat Ali, dressed in the Prophet's turban, shirt, sandals and sword, revealed this knowledge to the crowd in the mosque of Kufa before him, saying from the pulpit:

> O people! Ask me anything you like, before I die. Verily, my heart is the storehouse of all knowledge. Ask me, because I have the knowledge of all that has passed and all that is to come.[31]

This call wasn't just about his esoteric knowledge but also accountability, as his justice was famed. Although there are no records of any interlocutions conducted with him, sayings, letters, and traditions attributed to him have been preserved in a compilation called *Nahj al-Balaghah* or the *Peak of*

*Eloquence*, which, in its present form, consists of 239 speeches, 79 letters and 480 wise and sagacious sayings. It was compiled by al-Sharif al-Raḍi (970–1016), a renowned Shia scholar of Abbasid Baghdad who scouted for material attributed to Hazrat Ali, often travelling great distances in his quest.

Once the *Nahj* was published it became the focus of many scholars and Sufis.

A saying attributed to famous Shia mystic and philosopher Haydar Amuli (1319–1385) goes, 'Shiʿism is the external teachings of the imams, while Sufism is the internal teachings of the imams.' Although I have not been able to find it in the books by him which I could access, it describes the point I am making perfectly.

Seyyed Mohammad-Mehdi Jafari, in an article, says that many great Persian poets, including Firdausi, Attar, Mevlana Jalaluddin Rumi, Sadi, and Hafez, were strongly influenced by the discourses of Hazrat Ali.[32]

Professor Prashant Keshavmurthy says that the *Nahj al-Balaghah* has been extensively 'quoted, alluded to and used for inter-linear imitation almost ever since Sharif al-Razi compiled it in mid to late 10th century Abbasid Baghdad.'[33]

In fact, Keshavmurthy quotes two verses by Rūdaki (c. 859–941), the 'father of Persian poets' who predated the compilation of *Nahj al-Balaghah*:

You must gaze upon the world with your heart's eyes
For your head's eyes do not see what's hidden.
With what's apparent to you, look upon the apparent.
What is hidden to you, leave to the hidden.

According to him, both these verses allude to Hazrat Ali's statement in sermon 49 on the possibility and nature of seeing God: 'Seeing Him with physical eyes is impossible, thus the eyes of someone who has not seen Him do not deny Him and the heart of someone who has known His existence is preeminent over, all.'

He adds many examples of poets who used Hazart Ali's sermons in their work. One example is Sanā'ī of Ghazna (1080–1131), the first major

Sufi poet in Persian who often alluded to Ali in his sayings. Here is one example from Sanā'ī, who reports that Hazrat Ali said: 'When there is no further recourse, the last resort is imperative."[34]

Hazrat Ali was not only the spiritual heir of the Prophet, but he was also his sword, instrumental in winning many battles. An Islamic proverb and very popular saying goes: 'Islam did not rise except through Ali's sword and Khadija's wealth'.

Hazrat Ali's legendary wisdom and bravery are often quoted by everyone. The chant of '*Ya Ali Madad*' (O Ali, help me) can be heard even today ever so often, and he is called upon as the *Mushkil Kusha* (remover of difficulties). *Naad-e Ali* is a popular prayer, used especially in times of difficulties, which translates as:

*Call Ali! Call Ali!*
*Call aloud to Ali*
*Who is the epiphanic source of wonders.*
*You shall surely find him helping in your troubles.*
*All grief and anxiety will disappear*
*By Your power and Authority!*
*O Ali! O Ali! O Ali*

The *Nahj al-Balaghah* too, bears testament to the fact that Hazrat Ali was rather unusual in that he was not only a man of wisdom and scholarship, but also one of the bravest warriors known to the world and a just administrator.When he became the fourth caliph (656–661), he appointed Malik Ashtar as the governor of Egypt. Hazrat Ali's instructions to Ashtar are a statement of good governance and quoted in the United Nations as an example. A line from it that can become a creed for all is: 'Remember that the citizens of the state are of two categories. They are either your brethren in religion or your brethren in kind.'

This statement is a legacy of the years Hazrat Ali spent with the Prophet Muhammad and captures the true spirit of the faith. It gives the lie to the rampant Islamophobia in today's world and the many misconceptions about Islam, not only amongst non-Muslims but within the minds of many Muslims as well. Hazrat Ali's words embody the Holy Quranic verse 2:256 that 'There is no coercion in religion.'

Today, Hazrat Ali is mostly remembered for his legendary bravery on the battlefield, and perhaps justifiably so. In the battle of the Trench, the famous Quraish warrior Amr bin Abd-e Wud challenged someone from the army of Muhammad to face a duel, which was the custom of war:

> 'So is there none among you who has the courage of a man? And what of your Islam? And your Prophet?' At this blasphemous taunt, Ali left his position in the front rank of the Muslims, approached the Holy Prophet and sought permission to engage the challenger and silence his insolent tongue once and for all. The Prophet replied, 'Sit down. This is Amr!' Ali returned to his position.
>
> There was another burst of scornful laughter, more taunts, another challenge. Again Ali went up to the Prophet. Again the Prophet declined permission. More laughter, more taunts. Again the challenge from Amr, and this time more insulting than before. 'Where is your paradise?' He shouted, 'Of which you say that those who lose in battle will enter it? Can you not send a man to fight me?'
>
> When for the third time Ali moved towards the Prophet, the latter saw in Ali's eyes a look which he knew well; and he knew that Ali could no longer be restrained. He looked at Ali fondly, for Ali was dearer to him than any other man. He took off his turban and wound it around Ali's head. He next took off his sword and girded it at Ali's waist. And he prayed: 'O Lord! Help him!'[35]

Hazrat Ali's agility and quickness with his feet helped him parry the giant's blows. Besides, he had his famous double-edged sword Zulfiqar in his hand. (The Zulfiqar was to become one of the deadliest legendary swords.) Soon, Ali had Amr flat on his back, on the ground. When Amr could not break Ali's hold and rise, he spat on his face. Ali, who had been lowering his dagger on Amr's throat, rose, took a step backwards and sheathed his weapons. When Amr then jumped up (to retaliate), Ali swung the Zulfiqar and killed him.

He then went back to the Prophet who asked him why he had sheathed his sword just as he was about to kill him?

This is a story that has been immortalized by Mevlana Jalaluddin Rumi in his epic poem named *Masnavi*:

He said, I use my sword the way God's planned
Not for my body but by God's command;
I am God's lion, not the one of passion
– My actions testify to my religion:
I am a mountain, God's my solid base,
Like straw I'm blown just by thought of His face;
My longing changes once His wind has blown,
My captain is the love of Him alone.[36]

Cries of triumph could be heard from the victorious army:

*La Fatah Ila Ali La Saif Ila Zulfiqar*

[Truly there is no victor like Ali,
And no sword like the Zulfiqar.]

If the Prophet is the first *insaan-e-kamil* or 'perfect man', Hazrat Ali is the second.

And Hazrat Ali was brave beyond the battlefield. Despite having lived his life by the Prophet's teachings, he was not afraid to adapt to changing circumstances. There is a hadith of the Holy Prophet that goes: 'With the help of hair dye, turn old age into youth so that you do not resemble the Jews.'[37] When Hazrat Ali was asked to comment upon this, he said that in that early stage of Islam, there were very few Muslims, so the Prophet had advised them to maintain their uniqueness by looking young and energetic – instead of adopting the fashion of the Jewish priests with their long, white flowing beards. However, Muslims were not a minority then; theirs was a strong and powerful state, and hence they could choose any style they liked.

Hazrat Ali was assassinated in the Great Mosque of Kufa in Iraq as he bent in prostration on the 19th Ramzan, 40 AH (661 CE) when a Kharijite (rejectionist)[38] struck with a poisoned sword. Hazrat Ali's last words were, 'By the Lord of the Kaaba, I have triumphed.' He knew that he had lived his life by the teachings of Islam and had protected and carried forward the Prophet's legacy.

'Today, they have killed a man on the holiest day, the day the Quran was first revealed,' Hazrat Ali's elder son, Hasan, said at the graveside. 'If the Prophet sent him on a raid, the angel Gabriel rode at his right hand, and the angel Michael at his left. By God, none who came before him are ahead of him, and none who come after him will overtake him.'[39]

After the death of Hazrat Ali on the 21st Ramzan 40 AH (660 CE), his eldest son Hasan ascended the pulpit in the Great Mosque of Kufa and addressed those gathered. As the grandson of the Prophet and *Ahl al-Bait,* the people pledged their allegiance to him as the next caliph. As discussed previously, a series of letters between him and Muawiya led to Hasan abdicating his claim, as he was content to become caliph on Muwaiya's death. This was not to be, though, as Hasan died before Muawiya. On his deathbed, the latter named his son Yazid as his successor. Hussain, Hazrat Ali's younger son, refused to accept him as caliph, which led to the Battle of Karbala.

Hasan may have given up his claims over the caliphate in the interests of the *ummah* (Muslim community), but I think he was undoubtedly the spiritual successor of his father. He had been brought up by his grandfather, who had showered him with immense love, thus imbibing the exoteric and esoteric knowledge of the Prophet and Hazrat Ali.

Like his father, Hasan was also very well-versed in all the aspects of Islam, a spiritual authority, and Hasan al-Basri, the Sufi, would seek his advice.

*Shah ast Hussain badshah ast Hussain*
*Deenast Hussain deen panah ast Hussain*
*Sar daad na daad dast dar dast-e Yazid*
*Haqq-e bina-e la ilaha ast Hussain*

– *Khwaja Muinuddin Chishti*

[Hussain is the ruler, Hussain is the emperor,
Hussain is faith, Hussain is guardian of the faith;
He offered his head but not his hand (in oath of allegiance) to Yazid;
Indeed Hussain is the foundation of La ilaha (No God but Allah – the Islamic creed).]

Imam Hussain, as he is popularly called, was the Prophet's grandson, and the son of Hazrat Ali and the Prophet's daughter Bibi Fatima. Both Hazrat Ali and Hussain play an important role in Sufi shrines. Most of the Sufi saints claim descent from the progeny of Hazrat Ali, and the aforementioned '*man kunto maula*' is the most commonly sung qawwali in dargahs.

Karbala (location of Hussain's shrine in Iraq) and the martyrdom of Imam Hussain is used as a powerful metaphor for the fight against evil and is very popular in Sufi literature, and hence it is important to understand it. On the fateful day of the 10th Muharram 61 AH (10 October 680 CE), a battle that was to change the history of Islam was fought. As mentioned before, this battle was between the small, determined band of followers of Imam Hussain and the mighty army of Yazid, the ruler of Syria.

Yazid wanted Hussain to accept him as spiritual leader and pledge allegiance to him. The latter replied to the envoy Yazid had sent as follows:

> Amir! We are the household of the Prophet, the substance of the Message, the ones visited by the angels; it is through us that Allah initiates and concludes. Yazid is a man of sin, a drunkard, a murderer of the soul the killing of which Allah has prohibited, a man who is openly promiscuous. A man like me shall never swear the oath of allegiance to a man like him.[40]

Yazid, according to him, had flouted almost every norm that had been preached and followed by his grandfather Prophet Muhammad and was unacceptable as a spiritual leader. Yazid kept sending emissaries, for he knew that to succeed in his ambitions it was vital to be accepted by the progeny of the Prophet as the spiritual and temporal ruler.

To avoid confrontation, Hussain left Medina and went on hajj to Mecca. There he received letters of support from Hazrat Ali's partisans in Kufa (Hazrat Ali had his capital in Kufa during his reign.) Hussain contented himself with *umrah*, the minor pilgrimage, when he began to feel stifled by the pressure Yazid had created; he left for Kufa to avoid bloodshed in the holy city. He was accompanied by his family, which included his wives and children, his sisters, nephews and nieces, and brothers and cousins. He had already sent his emissary, his cousin Muslim bin Aqil, ahead of him to the city to make arrangements for their arrival.

On their way, bad news arrived. Obaidullah Ibn Ziyad, Yazid's governor in Iraq, had managed to sway the fickle Kufians, and Muslim bin Aqil had been assassinated. Hussain's caravan was already in Iraq though, and so it continued on its journey. Obaidullah Ibn Ziyad did not allow them to reach Kufa, and they were forced to pitch their tents in the hot sands of Karbala.[41] Hussain called the tribal leaders of the Banu Asad tribe who owned the land there and pitched his tent after seeking their consent.

Initially, their camp was near the river Euphrates, but after a few days Yazid's commanders forced them to move further away from the river. Hussain did not want to start a war and be branded a rebel. So, on the sixth Muharram, they shifted their camp. Yazid's soldiers had blocked all the routes leading to the river. From the seventh Muharram, their water supply was exhausted, and there was none left even for the children. Hussain, and his family and friends, bore everything uncomplainingly. His was a righteous fight, and he was willing to lose all in his effort to preserve the religion his grandfather had preached.

On the ninth Muharram, Obaidullah Ibn Ziyad's military commander Omar ibn S'ad finally gave them an ultimatum: either agree to take an oath of allegiance with Yazid, or be ready to battle. Hussain asked for one night's reprieve, so that their last night on earth could be spent in prayers. Hussain dimmed the lights and announced that anyone who wished to leave him and his cause was welcome to do so. He assured them that there would be no rancour or anger on his part, since those on his side could be certain of death by the next day. He absolved everyone of all obligation towards himself. But no one left. In fact, everyone reaffirmed their faith in him and his war against evil.

On the morning of the tenth Muharram, the day commemorated as Ashura, Yazid's commander Umar ibn Sa'd ordered the opening of hostility, and their soldiers started shooting arrows at the tents of Hussain's caravan. Thus, the battle began.

One by one male members of Hussain's family went out to the battlefield and all of them were martyred, except Hussain's sick eldest son Zain-al Abidin. The commander of his army was the Lion of Arabia, Abbas ibn Ali.

Since in those days combat was one to one, Hussain could have single-handedly wiped out the other army. This was precisely why he wasn't given permission to go to war. He was martyred while bringing water from the river for the thirsty children who hadn't had a drop for three days.

In fact, Hussain was the last to be martyred. He had earlier helped his friends, followers, nephews, brothers, and sons to mount their steeds and go to battle. He had gone to collect their bodies and bring them back to the camp where the women could mourn their death. By late afternoon, Hussain was the only male member left to go to battle. As Hussain stood before his faithful steed Zuljana, his cloak, beard, and face splattered with the blood of his loved ones, he thought about how he had no one to help him mount the horse. But he was wrong. His loving and devoted sister Zainab came running outside and with her heart in her mouth helped him mount, despite knowing she was helping him mount to certain death.

Hussain had already bid farewell to his family and eldest son, appointing him the imam after his death. He now kissed his sister on her forehead and left the responsibility of his caravan on the shoulders of Zainab. His eldest surviving son Ali ibn Hussain, popularly known as Zain al-Abidin, was sick, and Zainab found herself in charge of this group of orphans and widows, and his ailing son.

A lesser mortal may have baulked at this task, but Zainab was Hazrat Ali's daughter. If Hazrat Ali was the Lion of Allah, Zainab was the Lion of Karbala. Earlier in the day, she had sacrificed both her sons, 12-year-old Aun and 11-year-old Muhammad, and rejoiced at their martyrdom for that meant her brother was safe that much longer. Now that she watched her brother ride to the battlefield, she did not have the time to stand there, watch and pray for him. The responsibility of the thirsty children and wailing widows was hers now. The thirsty, hungry children had not had water or milk for three days, and their cries were filling the air.

The camp was at a little distance from the battlefield. Zainab would run to the camp and then onto a mound now known as *Tila-e-Zainabiya* (Zainab's mound). This is the high point between the camp and the battlefield where, on the 10th of Muharram, Zainab stood to gain a vantage point. From here she could see what was happening on the battlefield. She ran several times, between the camp and the Tila in anguish, to see her beloved brother for one last time. Standing on the mound watching Yazid's soldiers cut Hussain's dry and thirsty throat with their daggers, she watched the jubilation of Yazid's army as they then celebrated the beheading. Today that mound has been made into a shrine. Many, like me, who visit Karbala mourn uncontrollably on seeing it, thinking of what she went through that day.

But was Hussain's beheading really a victory for Yazid's army? Not as long as Zainab bint Ali was alive. She single-handedly carried the message of Karbala forward, as will be discussed later in the chapter.

There are many lessons to be learnt from the Battle of Karbala. One of them is how to treat your enemy with mercy and justice – as exemplified in Imam Hussain's offering of water to Hurr's army. Hurr was Yazid's commander and had intercepted Hussain's caravan on its way to Kufa. When Hurr's army ran out of water, Hussain ordered that their water reserves be used to help Hurr, his soldiers, and horses. This is especially significant because later Hussain's camp would run out of water and suffer extreme thirst for three days.

Another lesson to take away is that of *sabr* and *tawakkul* (fortitude and faith in God), and the avoidance of confrontation, while trying for peace at every step. Both Zainab aided by her sister Kulsum, nephew Zain al-Abidin, and niece Fatima bint Husain kept rallying the spirits of the prisoners, bravely confronting Yazid's army and quoting from the Quran and hadiths.

When they were presented before ibn Ziyad, Yazid's governor in Kufa, Zainab was unbowed. He asked her:

> 'How have you seen what Allah has done to your Ahl al-Bayt ('a)?' She, peace be upon her, said, 'I have seen Him treating them most beautifully.'[42]

This speech is often quoted as 'I saw nothing but beauty.' It refers to submitting to Allah's will that her brother and family be martyred for the cause of Allah.

Both *sabr* and *tawakkul* stem from a deep trust in Allah and His power and justice. These are virtues captured well in the verses:

> '(He is) Lord of the East and the West; there is No god but He; Take Him therefore For (thy) Disposer of Affairs.' (Quran 73:9)

And *'hasbunallaahu wa ni'malwakeel'* (For us Allah sufficeth, and He is the best disposer of affairs) (3:173) and *'ni'mal mawlaa wa ni'man Naseer'* (The best to protect and the best to help). (8:40) These Quranic verses exemplify a believer's faith.

The biggest lesson from Karbala, however, is the power that doing the right thing bestows on the doer; one ought to stand steadfast in the battle of the right and not bow down to a tyrannical ruler, even if martyrdom is inevitable. As Mahatma Gandhi said, 'I learned from Hussain how to be wronged and be a winner, I learnt from Hussain how to attain victory while being oppressed.'

Its valuable lessons apart, the Battle of Karbala – like all battles – came with its share of negative consequences. It further cemented the divide between the two warring groups. The Shias (as they came to be known later) even now follow the imams who were the progeny of Hazrat Ali, rejecting the caliphate of Muawiya and those who followed him.

The word 'Shia', in fact, comes from *shiat-e Ali* (partisans of Ali), while 'imam' means 'to lead the way', and is the title used by the Shia community for their twelve leaders: Ali, Hasan, Hussain, Ali ibn Hussain (popularly known as Zain-ul Abidin), Mohammad Baqar, Jafaral-Sadiq, Musa-e Kazim, Ali Raza, Mohammad Taqi, Ali al-Naqi, Hasan Askari, and Mohammad Mehdi Sahib-uz Zaman.

O! My God, who is the one to have tasted the sweetness of Your love and then looked for a replacement in place of You?

Who can claim to have become familiar with
Your nearness, then wanted removal from You?
O My God, include us among the ones whom
You have chosen for Your nearness and friendship,
And (include us among the ones) whom
You have purified through Your love and affection.

– *The Whispered Prayers of the Lovers* by
Ali ibn Hussain Zain-ul Abidin.[43]

The lines above demonstrate the fourth imam Ali ibn Hussain's yearning for closeness with Allah. The imams were indeed granted such closeness and that made them great scholars and authorities on the Quran and the Prophet's teachings.

Ali ibn Hussain was the only one of Imam Hussain's five sons to survive the battle of Karbala. He was born in Medina in 38 AH/ 658–9 CE, and is said to be the closest in looks and temperament to his grandfather Hazrat Ali. According to Shia sources, his mother was Shahrbanu, the daughter of Yazdigird, the last Sasanian king of Persia, 'Thus he was said to be "Ibn al-Khiyaratayn", the "son of the best two", meaning the Quraysh among the Arabs and the Persians among the non-Arabs.'[44]

He was married to Imam Hasan's daughter and through their children the pure bloodline of the Prophet continued. After his release from Yazid's imprisonment he spent his life in devotion and was given the title of Sajjad or one who constantly prostrates [before Allah] and Zain-ul Abidin (adornment of the worshippers). He was an authority on the Quran and the hadiths. Some of the supplications that he wrote, preserved in the *Sahifa al-Sajjadiya*, bear testimony to his eloquence, humility, and total submission to the will of Allah. They are the oldest surviving seminal prayers. William Chittick, who translated it, writes in his translator's note, 'Al-Saheefat al-Sajjadiyya is the oldest prayer manual in Islamic sources and one of the most seminal works of Islamic spirituality of the early period.' He then goes on to add:

> No one with any sensitivity toward human weakness and Allah's love can fail to be moved at least by some of the supplications contained in the Saheefa. Here we have one of the greatest spiritual luminaries of Islam so overawed by the sense of Allah's goodness, mercy and majesty as to express his utter nothingness before the Creator in terms that may seem surprisingly explicit for one deemed by his followers to be the possessor of such holiness. In the Saheefa, we see Islamic spirituality – or that dimension of the religion of Islam which deals with the practical and lived reality of the personal relationship between man and Allah – expressed in the most universal of languages, that of the concrete and intimate yearning of the soul for completion and perfection.[45]

These are words that resonate with millions like me, offering us solace and comfort as we recite it regularly.

Ali ibn Hussain died in 713 and is buried in Medina near the Prophet. Data Ganj Baksh Ali Hujweri gives us an account of his teachings:

> He said that the most blessed man in this world and in the next is he who, when he is pleased, is not led by his pleasure into wrong, and when he is angry, is not carried by his anger beyond the bounds of right. This is the character of those who have attained perfect rectitude (*kamil-i-mustaqiman*).

Another imam who showed remarkable wisdom and learning was his son and successor, Imam Muhammad Baqar (676–732). The fifth imam was famous for his knowledge of the abstruse sciences and for his subtle understanding of the meaning of the Quran. Ayat 257 in *Surah Baqarah*, which talks of the evil ones who will 'from light they will lead them forth into the depths of darkness', has been interpreted by him as 'anything that diverts thee from contemplation of the Truth is thy *taghut* (false deity)'.[46]

'Whoever knows God turns his back on all else.'

This saying is believed to have been said by Jafar al-Sadiq (702–765), the sixth imam.[47] He lived in the latter half of the Umayyad dynasty and saw it replaced by the Abbasid caliphate. Like his father before him, he maintained a politically quiet stance during this turbulent period. He pursued his scholarship, studying and teaching in Medina. His discourses were very well attended, and he imparted knowledge on not only the Quran and hadiths but also on science. One of his students was Jabir ibn Hayyan, who is well-known as the father of chemistry. The founder of Hanafi *fiqh* – Qazi Abu Hanifa – was also his student.

Not only is Imam Jafar considered one of the famous Sufi masters, all Sufi *silsilah*s trace themselves back to the Prophet and Hazrat Ali via him. As the great, great grandson of Hazrat Ali and Abu Bakr who had inherited esoteric and exoteric knowledge from his forebears, Imam Jafar embodies in himself the connection of all *silsilah*s to the Prophet.

According to *Kashf al-Mahjub*, he 'is celebrated among the Sufi Sheikhs for the subtlety of his discourse and his acquaintance with spiritual truths, and he has written famous books in explanation of Sufism'. The influence of his ideas on the development of Sufism is all-pervasive.[48]

Knowledge was a central theme in his teachings, and in fact, in all imams' teachings; it is the duty of all Muslims to acquire knowledge through *aql* (intellect). For Imam Jafar, *aql* was the supreme faculty through which God is worshipped, and along with *ilm* (knowledge) and *amal* (action) would lead to self-actualization.

> The versatility and magnetism of Jafar in his own age was still more strongly felt by subsequent generations. His influence, or if one prefers it, the recurrence of his ideas, is particularly pervasive in the development of the Shia movement. The Sufis look up to those intimate spiritual issues of revelation and the search for *haqiqah*, of personal morality of individual communion with God, and of His continuing guidance, issues which will be seen to be the raison d'etre for the early Shi'i self-assertion. It was when sectarian considerations engrossed the Shiah that the responsibility

of such spiritual leadership passed to Sufis of both Sunni and Shi'i persuasion.[49]

Though spiritual communion with God is inward and an individual experience, for Jafar al-Sadiq and the Sufis who followed him, it was important to articulate their experiences for others to recognize and emulate. *Tasawwuf* was not to be understood as 'all ecstasy and escapism'.[50]

He introduced the terminology and concept of *marifah-e-qalbiya* (gnosis of the heart). This is illustrated in an incident described by Kulayni, the Shia hadith collector in the book *Al-Kafi:*

> A man of the Khawarij came into the presence of Abu Ja'far and said to him, 'Abu Ja'far, what thing do you worship?' 'God,' he replied. 'Do you see Him?' he said. 'No,' he replied, 'The eyes do not see Him with the vision of sight, but the hearts (*al-qulub*) see Him by the realities of faith (*bi-haqa'ia al-iman*). He is not known by analogy (*qiyas*), and He is not grasped by the senses (*bi al-hawass*) and cannot be likened to men. He is described by signs (*Mawsuf bi al-ayat*) and known by symbols (*Maruf bi-al-alamat*). He does not use force in His judgments. It is He Who is God, than Whom there is no other god.[51]

He wrote on *tibb* (herbal medicine), and included in his work, chapters on useful and harmful food, ethical food practices, and remedies for commonly known diseases. He is purported to be the founder of occult science in Islam.

He was seen as the transmitter of the Prophet's traditions, and it is his *mazhab* (laws of jurisprudence) – known as the Jafariya *mazhab* – that is followed by Shias.

Imam Jafar had designated his eldest son Ismail as the next imam, however Ismail predeceased his father. Later, a split occurred in relation to this, with some believing that he was not dead but in occultation, while others claimed that his son Muhammad should be the next imam. The former group went on to form the Ismaili sect. The Twelver Shias, on the other hand, consider the younger son Musa al-Kazim as the seventh imam.

The imams faced great persecution at the hands of the Umayyads and then the Abbasids. As a result, though the fourth, fifth, and sixth imams had long lives, their successors did not. Imam Hussain's successors were involved only in spiritual and ideological matters, but they were always seen as a threat and rallying point because of their direct descent from the Prophet. As per Shia belief, none of the imams had died a natural death.

This was also the time when Sufism was blossoming and many Shia intellectuals took the cover of Sufism to avoid persecution, thus linking Shiism and Sufism.

The 10th and 11th imams were kept under house arrest in Samarrah, a garrison city in present-day Iraq. It was here that the 11th imam married and had a son in secrecy. The son's given name was Muhammad, but he is called by many names by his followers. Since Shias believe that he is the *imam-e-zamana* (imam of the times), he has been given the title 'Sahib az-Zaman' (master of the age). In times of trouble believers call out to him and pray for his reappearance. Every year his birth is celebrated on 15th day of the Islamic month of Shabaan with great joy. Muhammad lived under his father's care and tutelage in Samarrah, away from public view and only meeting a few trusted Shias.

Muhammad Mehdi Sahib az-Zaman became the imam after his father was martyred in 872. According to Shia belief, he went into occultation due to divine command and appeared only to his deputies (*na'ib*) – that too only in exceptional circumstances. He will, it is said, reappear on the Day of Judgment and lead his supporters to victory, prevailing over evil and thus ushering in a period of justice and peace. Every year millions of his supporters send petitions called *arziyan* into running water, such as rivers, or still water with a certain specified depth, like wells, asking that he intercede on our behalf with Allah.

I too have been doing it since childhood and have great faith in it. Of course, over the years the petitions have changed from innocent pleas for good marks to prayers for humanity, the health, safety, and well-being of my family, and personal deliverance from evil.

Buehler co-relates the occultation of the imam to the emergence of Sufi saints. Since the last *hujja* (infallible proof of God, usually used to refer to the imams who were seen as living proof) had gone away from their midst, a lacuna was felt. Buehler writes: 'Soon after the Imâmî leader disappears in 260 AH/874 CE, the Sufi master becomes (newly?) imbued with many of the imam's traits.' He adds, 'Like the imams, Sufi *shaykhs* represent the indispensable repositories of divine knowledge as living inheritors of divine Prophetic knowledge.'[52]

In the same vein, Professor Hassan Abbas says, 'Some early mystics/Sufis were projected by Umayyads and Abbasids as alternatives to the spiritual attraction of Imams.'[53]

In his major work, *Jami' al-asrar* (*Compendium of Divine Mysteries*), the fourteenth-century Shia mystic Sayyid HaydarAmuli's 'main intention is to show that real Sufism and Shi'ism are the same'.[54]

Thus, while the imams as *wasi*s (legatees) of the Prophet were the *waseela* (intermediary) between humans and Allah, the Sufi saints inherited the same role as *auliya* (friends of Allah). The imams are believed to have been given supernatural qualities by Allah that enabled them to perform *mojeza* (miracles); the saints, on the other hand, were bestowed with the power for *karamat* (again, miracles).

*Auliya* (friends of Allah), the term used for Sufi saints, was initially used for the imams. As Hazrat Ali ibn Abi Talib said:

> The *awliyā' Allāh* are those who look at the inward side of the world while others look at its outward side. They busy themselves with its remoter benefits while others busy themselves in the immediate benefits. [...] Through them, the Book is learnt and they have learnt through the Book.[55]

In the Sunni tradition, the term *auliya* gradually came to be identified with the Sufis, or it can be said that the latter began to be identified with the former.

Many believers like me have visited the shrines of all the 11 imams in Saudi Arabia, Iran, and Iraq, as well as the underground chamber in Samarrah from where the 12th imam went into occultation. Visiting the shrines of Sufi saints is seen as part of the same tradition ultimately, whether one follows the Shia or Sunni tradition, because Sufism is the same the world over. It is finding the mystical and exoteric meaning in religion and serving humanity. It is above sectarianism.

*Ye sabirin-e-mohabbat ye kashifin-e-junun*
*Inhi ke sang inhin auliya ke sath hun main.*

[These patient lovers, these who are frenzied in love,
I am with them, I am with these *auliya.*]

– Ali Zaryoun

# 3

# Spread of Sufism

*Woh basti ujar jaaye jahan hoye na dervish,*
*Aabaad hai har shahr faqeeron ke qadam se.*

[The land where there is no dervish will be desolate.
Blessed are the lands where the footsteps of a fakir fall.]

– Shah Turab Ali Qalander

The famous hadith 'Whosoever knows his self, knows his Lord' is about the journey on which the Sufis embarked into the spiritual universe – a journey that leads to the Absolute Reality residing in our hearts. As Ibn al-Arabi propounded in his theory of *Wahdat al-Wujud*, all that is sought is indeed found in God. The path of this quest, leading through the dark corners of the soul, was lit up by the lamps of the Quran, hadiths and mysticism – the last developed and disseminated by Sufi masters and their teachings.

Abu Hisham of Kufa, Iraq was the first person to be called '*as-Sufi*' or 'the Sufi'. He preached that inner transformation should be the goal of all mystics and that pride and vanity were their greatest obstacles. He is believed to have remarked: 'It is far easier to dig a mountain with a needle than to cleanse the heart of arrogance and vanity.'[1]

His idea was reflected a few centuries later in a kafi (a kind of short poem) by Baba Bulleh Shah:

*Bulleh Shah gal taeeyon mukdee*
*Jadon mainu Dillon gawaayee.*

[Bulleh Shah, the ultimate [truth] is
when the I [ego] is removed from the heart.]

However, Imam Jafar al-Sadiq (702–765), Hasan al-Basri (642–728) of Basra in Iraq, Uwais al-Qarni (594–657) of Yemen, Rabia al-Basri (713–801), and Ibrahim ibn Adham (d.790)[2] were the first ones to gain prominence for their mystical knowledge and preaching. Among them, Hasan is mentioned in many mystical orders as part of the chain that goes up to the Prophet.

Sufism originated in Mecca and Medina with these individuals, but it goes all the way back to the Prophet himself. It spread to the cities of Kufa and Basra in Iraq after some time, and from there to Khorasan (comprising of modern-day north-eastern Iran, southern Turkmenistan, and northern Afghanistan), and Iran.

As Sufism was in itself a reaction to the growing materialism and worldliness, the first couple of centuries after the advent of Islam (that is, the seventh and eight centuries), the earliest period of Sufism was defined by ascetism, grief about the commitment of sins, and repentance. Most Sufis of this period were recluses living a very ascetic life. The emphasis was on salvation in the afterlife.

This early phase was characterized by the submission of human will to God. According to Professor Tara Chand, the early Sufis 'were seekers more of piety and other-worldliness than of divine knowledge, they had an exaggerated consciousness of sin and an overwhelming dread of divine retribution, yet they had developed emotional and ecstatic features and they negated the externalia of religion'.[3] Later, Rabia-al Basri introduced the element of ecstatic love for God and the idea that He was to be worshipped for His sake alone, not for gains in the next world.

The time of Abbasid Caliphate – the third of the Islamic caliphates, their rule lasted for five centuries from 750 in Baghdad – provided the stability that made the birth of the golden period of Islam possible. This was the age of enlightenment, and it led to many scientific discoveries, learning, and of course, mystical development. Muslims were now more involved in leading material lives; spiritual tasks were left to the saints and people accepted the Sufi saints as spiritual leaders. The ideas of Sufism were now put into words and actions, and simple asceticism gave way to mysticism.

In the ninth century, the Prophet's teachings were compiled in the form of hadiths.

The foundations of Sufism were strengthened in Baghdad. The most famous of the Baghdadi Sufis was Junayd (835–910), who is credited with helping establish the sober school of Sufism based on logic and scholarly works. Junayd tried to explain *tauheed* – 'the oneness of God' – to his fellow Sufis, from a point of mystical awareness, as the return of the soul to its primordial state where it has no individuality; it exists in God and is completely absorbed by Him.

> As long as he [the monotheist] preserves his individuality he cannot attain his full state of tawhid, as the continued persistence of his individuality means that something other than God is still present.[4]

Junayd's sober Sufism existed with Mansur al-Hallaj's intoxication with the Divine. Mansur al-Hallaj (858–922), one of the most celebrated martyrs of Sufism, was born in the Fars province of Iran. He famously chanted '*Ana'l-Haq*'. Since 'al-Haq' is one of the 99 names of Allah, *Ana'l-Haq* was understood as meaning 'I am God (the Truth)'. Mansur used the phrase to mean that he was in the state of ecstasy that prevented him from seeing anything except God and that for him, nothing existed except Him. He did not see himself and therefore could not affirm his own existence; it surely does not mean that he sees himself and considers himself God, as many believed it did. Rumi has been reported to say in Mansur al-Hallaj's defence:

> People imagine that it is a presumptuous claim, whereas it is really a presumptuous claim to say 'I am the slave of God'; and 'I am God' is an expression of great humility. The man who says 'I am God' has made himself non-existent and has given himself up and says 'I am nought, God is all: there is no being but God's.'This is the extreme of humility and self-effacement self-abasement.[5]

However, that is not how it was seen by the clerics, and Mansur al-Hallaj was imprisoned for sacrilege and hanged from the gallows. This marked an important turning point in the development of mysticism.

> His [al-Hallaj's] death epitomized the violent confrontation between the shariah (the orthodoxy that dominated Islam) and the *tariqah* (mysticism), but did not end the struggle, although this tragedy helped to bring orthodoxy and mysticism closer together. We can see in the teachings of Sulami, Qushayri, Imam Ghazali and Abdul Qadiral-Jilani, that it created a fusion of the inner and outer aspects of Islam, producing the union and interdependence of shari'ah and *tariqah*.[6]

This helped in the emergence of a new discipline of study – *ilm-e-tasawwuf*, the 'science of Sufism'. The new science 'gathered data on the mystical experience of various saints and the schools they represented. These experiences are substantiated by the support of the Quran and (practice) of the Prophet (s.a.w.s.).'[7] This helped in establishing three distinct levels of knowledge: *ilm al-yaqeen* (knowledge through information), *ayn al-yaqeen* (knowledge through experience) and *haqq al-yaqeen* (true knowledge through being) which was the highest level.

Three important books written on this subject are *Kitab al-luma* by Nasr al-Tusi al-Sarraj (d.988), *Tabaqat al-Suffiyah* by Sulami (d.1021) and the *Risalah* of Abdul Karim al-Qushayri (987–1074). These books began to be used in mosques, where only the Holy Quran and hadiths had been taught previously. 'The sheikhs taught this science of conscious being not as an abstract philosophy but as a way of life supported by the doctrine of Islamic orthodoxy.'[8]

## Sufism in India

| | |
|---|---|
| First half of 7th century | Arab trade with India began |
| 712 CE | Mohammad bin Qasim's conquest of Sindh |
| 1039 CE | Arrival in Lahore of Syed Hafiz Haji Abul Hasan Bin Usman Bin Ali al Jalabi al Hujwiri from Ghazni |
| 1192 CE | Muizuddin Muhammad bin Sam of Ghor defeated Prithviraj Chauhan and established the Delhi Sultanate |
| End of 13th century | Arrival of Khwaja Muinuddin Chishti in Ajmer |

From the dawn of history, India has been the meeting place of various cultures, making its landscape rich with complexity. India, being a 'civilization society',[9] has been the repository of various cultural, linguistic, and religious influences through the ages. All of these influences combined have resulted in its unique, rich, multi-layered culture referred to as a composite culture.

The various traders, conquerors, armies, migrants, crafts people, and professionals, who came to India in search of a better future, brought with them not just 'destruction but also valuable deposits that enriched the ancient soil, out of which grew fresher and more luxuriant cultures.'[10]

Navigational and commercial interests brought South Asia closer to Arabia; Muslim Arab traders travelled by sea to the shores of Gujarat and Malabar in the Indian subcontinent, and, as early as the seventh century, settled down in some of the cities in the Malabar region. They married local women and introduced Islam there. The Muslims, who were called 'mopillas' – a term meaning 'a great child' or 'bridegroom' – acquired great importance in the ensuing period and many privileges were showered on them. By the tenth century, Islam had spread to the east coast of India as well, and Muslims had acquired influence both in court and in society.[11]

Sufism was introduced in south India by such early Muslim traders and navigators from the eighth and ninth centuries onwards.

> Through the agency of incoming Sufis and the west Asian trading people who supported them, a chain of Muslim trading towns grew up along the Coromandel coast from Pulicat (30 miles north of the modern city of Madras) to the southern Tamil ports of Kilakkarai, Kayal and Kayalpatanam.[12]

The *maraikkayar*[13] built several shrines; several of such dargahs, from the 20 in Mahmud Bandar (Porto Novo), are said to contain the remains of *sahabi* (actual companions or contemporaries of the Prophet).[14] Even though, as Bayly says, 'It is impossible to say whether there really were *sahabi* who lived and died in south India,' the fact that they are believed to be *sahabi* shrines, it shows how early Muslims came to the southern coast of India.

Under Khalifa al-Walid bin Abdul Malik, who was the Umayyad caliph of Damascus, Muhammad bin Qasim was appointed by the governor of Iraq – Hajjaj – to lead an expedition into the Sindh. In 712, Muhammad bin Qasim's army defeated the army of Sindh ruler Raja Dahir, thus conquering Sindh and Multan. So by the eighth century, Muslim influence could be felt in both these regions where they now ruled, and in the coastal towns of Gujarat, Malabar, and Konkan where they had settled down as traders.

Saints soon followed the traders and the armies, and Sufism entered India through Multan and Punjab in the ninth century and spread to north India, in particular to Ajmer and Delhi. It then reached Bihar, Bengal, Kashmir, Gujarat, and the Deccan. In fact, the Deccan Sultans actively encouraged and invited Sufi saints of the Qadriya order to settle in their kingdoms.

The first Sufi to settle in Multan during the eleventh century was Sheikh Saifuddin Kaziruni, a native of Shiraz in Iran. He famously set off on a camel, after being appointed as his uncle's successor,. with orders to get off only after the animal came to a stop. The camel halted in the desert, and he founded the city of Uchh in Multan where it did. Uchh is now famous for its Sufi shrines. This story is probably mythical, but it is true that many turned to Sufism in this unpopulated area which was ideal for meditation and contemplation of God.

Though not much is known about Shaikh Saifuddin Kaziruni, he is mentioned in Nizamuddin Auliya's book *Fawaid al-Fuad* in connection with a yogi who challenged him to reveal his miraculous powers.

> The yogi flew to the celling and returned. Sheikh then prayed to God for power, imploring "O God, you have given this superiority to a stranger. Please grant me some miracle of like quality." After that the Sheikh soared from his place. He flew toward the qibla, that is, in the direction of Mecca. Then he headed north. Reversing himself, he flew south, finally landing in his original place.[15]

The awestruck yogi accepted his powers as miraculous and emanating from divine grace.

Soon, many other men of learning and religion too came to India. The most famous and the first known to arrive was Hazrat Syed Hafiz Haji Abul Hasan Bin Usman Bin Ali al-Jalabi al-Hujwiri, who is known in the subcontinent simply as Data Ganj Baksh. He went to Lahore in the eleventh century from Afghanistan, where his family had settled after the Battle of Karbala in seventh century. His Persian treatise *Kashf al-Mahjub*, the first work on mysticism, became a template for mystics.

Another famous Sufi to visit India in the twelfth century was Fariduddin Attar (1145–1221), celebrated author of the *Mantiq al-Tair* (*The Language of Birds*)[16].

In 1192, Muizuddin Muhammad bin Sam of Ghor defeated Prithviraj Chauhan, the ruler of Delhi, and established the Delhi Sultanate. When the Mongol hordes were conquering and destroying much of Central Asia, the Delhi Sultanate offered an oasis of peace, prosperity and learning. Many from Central Asia thus migrated to India during that period; among them were a vast number of Sufi scholars and mystics, including the parents of Hazrat Nizamuddin Auliya.

Khwaja Muinuddin Chishti came to India during the reign of Sultan Iltutmish (1211–36) and settled in Ajmer. He was the founder of the famous Chishti *silsilah* in India.

As numerous mystics came and settled in the subcontinent, they drew from local Hindu influences and developed a unique form of Sufism here. There was a great and constant cross-fertilization of ideas. With their understanding, acceptance and integration of local customs and influences, they carved their own unique space in the hearts of locals of every faith, class and caste. They could speak the local language and dialects, and as tales of their *karamat* (miracles) grew, so did their followers.

Regarding the matter of conversion, the majority of the saints believed in personal example, as is clear from conversations of Hazrat Nizamuddin Auliya in *Fawaid al-Fuad*, and not the use of force; many did accept Islam, impressed by the gentle and inclusive behaviour of these saints. Islam's democratic theories of social organisation also made an impression in a caste ridden society.

If it was the Chishtis and Qadriya saints who first came to the subcontinent and gained importance under the Delhi Sultanate, the Naqshbandi and Suhrawardi saints gained prominence under the Mughals.

Shaikh Bahauddin Zakariya of Multan established the Naqshbandi *silsilah* in India, a century after Khwaja Muinuddin Chishti settled in Ajmer. The establishment of the Delhi Sultanate saw many Sufi saints come to Delhi, especially during the reign of Sultan Iltutmish. Even today, Delhi is known as *baees khwaja ki chaukhat* (the threshold of 22 saints), after the famous saints who arrived in the sultanate era and were buried here.

Though dargahs are now an intrinsic part of our cultural landscape and are largely seen as oases of peace, but the oral and hagiographical histories attached to them are frequently beset with conflict. Specifically, there are tales of disputes with local jogis (Hindu ascetics) over territory – many constructed only in the postcolonial era. In them, the latter are invariably vanquished and either retire to some corner or convert with their flock.

Contesting the ones that reflect a colonial frame of mind, Muhammad Habib, in a series of essays from 1920–50, critiqued British administrator orientalists who consistently projected 'Muslim India' of 1000–1700 as a period of oppression and fanaticism from which colonial rule had finally liberated the grateful Hindus.

Historian Shahid Amin too writes in a similar vein:

> The tales of Muslim warrior saints detailed by balladeers, which bear a complicated relationship to the standard hagiographies, are evidence of the refashioning of sagas of 'religious' conflict in order to create communities in the past and in the present. To focus exclusively on the syncretism of such cults, without taking on board the narrative refashionings of conquest that these cults invariably entail, is to miss out on the creation of India's composite culture as a process. It is also to hitch popular remembrance to the temporal career of superstition, while remaining impervious to the literary, cultural and mnemonic devices through which popular assent is generated across religious divides.[17]

Thus, by simply associating dargahs with traditions of religious syncretism we ignore the dynamic role these places played in refashioning our understanding of Muslim conquest; it is therefore important to not see things in terms of fixed categories but to look at the creation of dargah cultures as processes of assent and conflict.

In recent years, we have seen attacks on Sufism by some Muslim clergy and scholars, especially those who adhere to Wahabi beliefs, who call it *shirk* (polytheism) or *bidat* (innovation), and perceive it as a threat that is internal to Islam. They consider it to be rooted in medieval superstition and idolatrous, derived from the practices of saint-worshipping Christians and from the heretical doctrines of pantheistic Greek philosophers. Two major dargah practices, in particular, have been declared un-Islamic: singing and grave worship, the veneration of the saint's body.

As discussed in the preface, this is not the only threat that Sufism faces. Attempts to delink it from Islam have been made in the past few centuries. In an interview that appeared in *The New Yorker* in 2017, Omid Safi, a professor of Middle Eastern and Islamic studies at Duke University, says that it was in the Victorian period that readers in the West began to uncouple mystical poetry from its Islamic roots. Translators and theologians of the time could not reconcile their ideas about a "desert religion," with its unusual moral and legal codes, and the work of poets like Rumi and Hafez. The explanation they settled on, Safi told me, was "that these people are mystical not because of Islam but in spite of it."'[18]

Known as Rumi to the West, the founder of the famous Mevlavi Sufi order was deeply religious. His title and full name is Mevlana Jalal al-Din Muhammad Balkhi with the Mevlana (our master) signifying his religious qualifications. His popular name Rumi, or the Roman, was given to him because he had spent many years of his life in the Seljuk Sultanate of Rum in Anatolia, which had previously conquered the area from the Byzantine Empire. His epic poem *Masnavi* is often referred to as the Persian Quran.[19]

Sufism and Sufi poetry, both extremely popular these days, are steeped in the mystical traditions of Islam and the beloved of the Sufi verses is Allah. Omid Safi has a point to make on why there are attempts being made to delink Rumi's poetry [or any other for the matter] from Islam. He writes,

> [T]he real crisis is not merely that the modern consumers of Rumi have taken the Islam out of Rumi in rendering him into a generic (and marketized) spirituality provider. There is a greater crisis that we have not done nearly enough to address: in far too many Muslim communities, it is Rumi and the entire path that produced Rumi which has been taken out of Islam. In far too many corners, we hear an Islam that is being preached without poetry, without humour, without spirituality, without compassion, and without reaching out to God as the Beloved. For every occasion that we

> critique the western commodification and perhaps appropriation of Rumi, we should be working to re-invigorate our own practice and understanding of Islam along the lines that produced the Mt. Everest of Rumi, and the whole Himalayan range of giants that led up to Rumi.[20]

The Prophet's *akhlaq* and *ihsan*, Hazrat Ali's *jawan-mardi*, the Sufi's earth-like generosity and inclusiveness, all bring the beauty and spirituality of Islam back into contemporary discourse.

## Stages of Sufism

> May God steal from you
> All that steals you from Him.[21]
>
> – Rabia al-Basri

The spread of Sufism also resulted in the formalization of its rules. *Kashf al-Mahjub* composed by Data Ganj Baksh – the most ancient and revered Persian treatise on Sufism – had already laid down doctrines and practices, which were further refined by the saints who came thereafter.

As per the classical belief of Sufis, there are four stages of Sufism, and any disciple desirous of travelling that path has to go through them after taking his/her *ba'it* or oath of allegiance under a *pir* (spiritual master). These stages are esoteric and exoteric, and not all are able to traverse the entire distance; only a very fortunate few reach the fourth.

The stages are integral to Sufism; 'Islam is like a walnut of which the shell is like the *Shar'iah,* the kernel like the *tar'iqah,* and the oil which is invisible yet everywhere present, the *Haq'iqah* [access to inner Reality of the divine message].'[22] The last stage of marifah (gnosis) is the most difficult to attain. It is a state of higer consciousness and reached not through 'intellectual exercises but ecstatic states'.[23]

Each of these stages is essential as a support for the next stage and needed for the totality of the tradition. On this path the Sufi will cross various *maqams* (stations) as they exercise spiritual discipline and experience various spiritual states (*haal*) and the divine favours them. 'Among the stations are "repentance," "renunciation," "destitution before God," "endurance," and "contentment." Among the states are "desire for God," "love," "contemplation," "proximity to God," and "intimacy."'[24]

During the *tariqah* stage some of the spiritual stations the Sufi has to cross are of repentance (*taubah*), renunciation (*zuhd*), and trust in Allah (*tawakkul*). While the state is temporarily induced by a changing condition, the stage is relatively permanent.

## Shariah: Knowledge of Religious Law

The root of the word 'shariah' means 'path'; shariah is thus the path which leads to God and refers to the revealed law. This stage emphasizes the reading of the Quran and hadiths, and the learning of Islamic laws – as sources and the basis of Sufi teachings. The early part of this stage is characterized by repentance, purification and reading, including memorizing and understanding the Holy book and scriptures. This stage deals with the outward practices of Islam.

## *Tariqah*: The Mystical Path

The journey towards God continues with *tariqah*. If shariah is a wide road that is easy to traverse, *tariqah* is a narrower one and not all can traverse it. This stage deals with inner practices. *Tariqah* (mysticism) teaches believers how to worship God with the awareness that He can see you, as explained in the Hadith-e-Jibraeel.

Sufism is essentially seen as the mystical dimension of Islam, where the seeker or traveller on the path of the divine is able to get in touch with their inner self and feel God within. To achieve this, the *murid* (seeker) must have a *pir-o-murshid* (a spiritual master) who guides them. The seeker takes an oath of allegiance with the master and follows the actions and path shown by him; slowly, their religious practice changes from *taqlid* (copying) to *tahqeeq* (realization). This cannot be achieved without a spiritual master. All prescribed practices must be carried out under the guidance of a master who has received that knowledge from his master.

Not everyone can stay the course; many sheikhs would put their disciples under probation to see if they could last before guiding them to the secrets of the true path.

How do you ever expect
for your heart to become polished like a mirror
without putting up
with the pain
of polish?[25]

– Rumi

The stage of *tariqah* is arduous and akin to the polishing of a mirror; only once this mirror is polished and all its impurities removed can it reflect the divine light. (A point to remember is that the mirrors being referred to were not made of glass but metal; they had to be perfectly polished and flat for a perfect reflection. If not, the image would be distorted.) For instance, Mevlana Jalaluddin Rumi writes:

Dost thou know why the mirror (of thy soul) reflects nothing?
Because the rust is not cleared from its face.[26]

According to al-Hujwiri, knowledge of the essence and unity of God, of the attributes of God, and of the actions and wisdom of God are essential at this stage.

Khwaja Muinuddin Chishti laid out nine principles of *tariqah* for a true dervish. These were:

1. Sufis should not earn money.
2. They should not borrow money from anyone.
3. They should not reveal to anyone or seek help even if they have not eaten for seven days.
4. If one gets plenty of food, money, grain or clothing, one should not keep it for the next day.
5. Sufis should not curse anyone – if very hurt, pray to God to guide the enemy to the right path.
6. All virtuous deeds should be attributed to the pir's kindness, to the intercession of the Prophet Muhammad, or to divine mercy (In

short, there should be no sense of pride or ego in having performed a virtuous act).

7. If a dervish has to commit an evil deed, then they should take full responsibility for the deed, and try and protect themself from committing any such acts in the future; one should always be fearful of God to prevent any recurrence of involvement in evil.
8. Having fulfilled these acts, they should fast during the day and spend the night in prayers.
9. A true sufi should keep quiet and speak only when necessary. The shariah makes it unlawful to speak unnecessarily. One should only utter those words that please God.[27]

## *Haqiqah*: Truth

When through proper guidance the *salik* (traveller) can feel the presence of God, they are said to have reached the stage of truth. In this stage, *nafs* or 'base desires' have been conquered, and one's heart and mind are filled with the Divine. One of the prerequisites for reaching the destination is to worship God as if you see Him, for He is seeing you all the time.

Masud-e-Bak explained these three stages beautifully in his book *Miratl al-Arifin*:

> The traveller on the path of sharia is the knower, the traveller on the path of *tariqa* is the perceiver and the traveller on the path of *haqiqa* is the taster. Thus, sharia is learning, *tariqa* is burning and *haqiqa* is illumination. The devotee should firstly acquire the knowledge of the sharia, then burn himself on the path of the *tariqa* and ultimately kindle the lamp of *haqiqa*.[28]

## *Marifah*: Gnosis

This is the final stage of knowledge of spiritual truth, and only the messengers, prophets, and saints reach it. It is the stage of gnostic knowledge of the divine and a state of constant spiritual experience.

Ibn al-Arabi (1165–1240), the famous Arabic Sufi master, poet, and philosopher, explained that shariah is the stage where there is the concept of 'yours and mine' as guaranteed by law, *tariqah* is the stage where 'mine is yours and yours is mine', and *haqiqah* is the stage where there is 'no mine and no yours', while the final stage of *marifah* is when there is 'no me and no you'.[29] It is at this stage that the Sufi achieves the state of *fana* (annihilation or the passing away of human attributes) in the Divine, and he no longer exists as a separate entity; he has achieved the stage of *baqa* (subsistence or existence in God).

Mansur al-Hallaj had achieved the perfect state of *fana* when he is said to have proclaimed 'I am truth', indicating that there was no 'you' and 'me'. He no longer existed as a separate entity; he had achieved the stage of *baqa*. He was not, as readers may remember, claiming to be God; what he meant was that the only reality is God, and so no one else can exist when God is present – there is no space for anyone else in the centre of human consciousness when God enters it. He was, however, misunderstood and imprisoned, tried, and executed in 922 for apostasy, as it was believed that he was claiming to be God.

> I am He whom I love and He whom I love is I;
> We are two spirits dwelling in one body,
> If thou seest me, thou seest Him,
> And if thou seest Him, thou seest us both.[30]
>
> – Mansur al-Hallaj

Similarly, when anyone called out to him, Bayazid Bastami (804–874), the famous Persian Sufi, would say that he was not there – as only God exists; he believed that his self had been annihilated in God. For both Bastami and al-Hallaj, God existed both outside and inside them, and nothing else did.

As Sufi activities gained popularity, there was a great deal of interest in the philosophical theory of *fana* and *baqa*. Bayazid Bastami and Junayd al-Baghdadi, were the great Sufi philosophers of this age. If Bastami talked of *fana*, the total destruction or annihilation of the self in God, Junayd al-Baghdadi, talked of 'unification'. Junayd believed that the one who preserves his individuality cannot attain the full state of *tauheed* (belief in One God); the persistence of individuality, to him, meant the presence of someone other than God, thus negating the principles of *tauheed* and *tasawwuf* meant that God would make you die for yourself, and live in Him.[31]

This 'dying-to-self' is called *fana* – a term reminiscent of the Quranic phrase 'Everything is perishing (*fani*) except His Face'; the 'life-in-Him' is *baqa* (continuance).[32]

Every Sufi strives to attain the last stage through various means as they travel on the path of truth. To belabour the point, it does not mean that the worshipper becomes identical with God. It means the loss or surrender of man's will, which characterizes his worldly individuality, for God's – being possessed by God and returning to the life of the eternal self in God.[33] Worshippers strive to achieve *akhlaq*, purify their hearts and souls, overcome ego and pride, be sincere in their devotions, tread the path of truth, and seek to annihilate themselves in the experience of union with God. This was Junayd's 'unification' and Bastami's '*fana*'.

Once *fana* has been achieved, the next state of being in *marifah* is *baqa*, where the Sufi finds everlasting life but not as themself. They find the 'self' that they had annihilated in divine essence, without any ego. In this stage, there is a perfect unity with the Divine. While *fana* is annihilation, *baqa* is abiding or continuing in God. Without *baqa*, *fana* is incomplete; this is exemplified in the saying of Hazrat Ali that goes: 'People are asleep; they awaken when they die'.[34]

Echoing this sentiment, Dhul-Nun, the famous Egyptian Sufi is said to have recited the following verses on his deathbed: 'Oh Ultimate Goal of all lovers, grant me a favoured place among Your visitors! For I care not for bygones, so long as You are my only Companion in the two abodes!'[35]

> Religion is a body; its head is knowledge of God, its spine obedience to him.
>
> – Ali ibn Abi Talib[36]

Knowledge is the cornerstone of all these stages. The importance of knowledge can be judged from the Quranic verse, 'O my Lord! Advance me in knowledge,' (20:114) and the Prophet's hadith 'Seeking knowledge is a duty upon every Muslim,' which goes on to say that one should seek knowledge even if it entails going to China (considered to be the end of the known world at the time). Knowledge should be linked to action and is required for righteous conduct, for it is *aql* (intellect) that separates man from other creatures, and *aql* is only honed by acquiring and using knowledge for the good of all. This knowledge should be used for service to humanity – because 'compassion is the pinnacle of knowledge; harshness is its scourge'[37].

Sufism, with its insistence on knowledge, self-introspection, and gnosis produced many great scholars. In fact, 'most of the outstanding religious scholars of Mecca, Medina, and the great cities of the Muslim world were intimately engaged with what we today call Sufism'.[38]

The Sufi writings on philosophy, metaphysics, logic, and cosmology are important treatises. Not only do they emphasize that knowledge was held dear by Sufis, but that Sufism wasn't quietist medieval obscurantism. The Sufi saints not only wrote books, they ran madrasahs to teach the populace, and maintained well-stocked libraries.

Not just knowledge but mystical knowledge is a central theme in Islam as can be seen from the Quranic story (*Surah Kahf*), which is symbolic of a Sufi's journey into the world of esoteric learning. Musa (known as Moses in the Judeo-Christian universe) is said to have asked God if there was anyone more learned than him. In response, he was sent on a quest to seek knowledge from 'one of Our servants, on whom We had bestowed Mercy from Ourselves and whom We had taught knowledge from Our own Presence,' (18:65). This servant, though not named, has been identified as Khwaja Khizr – often called The Green One. Khizr has been given knowledge called *ilm-e ladunni* by Allah himself, and Musa is the seeker of spiritual reality.

Musa set out on a quest to find the Absolute Reality. Accompanied by a servant who represented the reproachful self (*nafs-e-lawwama*) that resists evil, Musa was asked to take a fish that was a metaphor for *aql* (intellect) and meet Khwaja Khizr at the confluence of the two seas. The seas stood for the 'seas of Divine Knowledge and of human knowledge', and Ego was represented by Satan who tries to tempt at every step.

As soon as Musa crossed the sea of human knowledge and entered the sea of divine knowledge, intellect couldn't comprehend the reality of the

Divine Truth and parted ways. Moses did find his teacher Khwaja Khizr, but his ego prevented him from submitting fully to the teacher's will.

Khwaja Khizr had laid a condition that no questions be asked of him during the journey pertaining his actions, but Moses did not honour it and made a query. In response, Khwaja Khizr gave him an explanation of his actions but also said that it was time to part ways.

Musa is a prophet and the great law-giver, but even he was unaware of the mystical knowledge that the green saint has been blessed with.[39] Khizr is regarded as an eternal master in Sufi circles who still guides and even initiates certain people into the Sufi path through dreams and visions.[40]

## Important Concepts in Sufism

One of my favourite supplications is the *Dua-e-Kumail*, which Hazrat Ali taught his companion Kumayl Ibn Ziyad. The prayer seeking God's mercy and forgiveness is recited on Thursday evenings. It begins with: 'O my God! My master! My Lord! And my Nourisher! What! Wilt Thou see me punished with the fire kindled by Thee despite my belief in Thy unity?'

It then goes on to say:

> Nay, Thou art far too kind and generous to destroy one whom thyself nourished and supported, or to drive away from Thyself one whom Thou has kept under Thy protection, or to scare away one whom Thy self hast given shelter, or to abandon in affliction one Thou hast maintained and to whom Thou hast been merciful [41]

A dua is an invocation to God and this dua not only reaffirms the believer's *iman* but is also inextricably linked to the belief in the mercy of God and His acceptance of repentance which is described below. This dua emphasizes the importance of remembering God (zikr) and His bounties and blessings even if sent to Hell.

## *Taubah* or Repentance

While every Muslim should practice *taubah* daily, it is especially so for the Sufi, who is supposed to introspect, retrospect, self-examine, repent, and continually strive for self-purification. And the Hadith-e-Qudsi 34 promises that repentance will be met with forgiveness:

> Allah the Almighty said: O son of Aadam, so long as you call upon Me and ask of Me, I shall forgive you for what you have done, and I shall not mind. O son of Aadam, were your sins to reach the clouds of the sky and were you then to ask forgiveness of Me, I would forgive you. O son of Aadam, were you to come to Me with sins nearly as great as the earth and were you then to face Me, ascribing no partner to Me, I would bring you forgiveness nearly as great as it.[42]

While outer repentance involves shunning wrong deeds and turning to righteous ones, the Sufi's *taubah* (literally means 'return') includes the shunning of the material world and turning towards Allah. It goes without saying that outer *taubah* means not only repentance, but also abstention from further sins and a resolution to never to return to them.

## *Ikhlas* or Sincerity

Sincerity is worshipping Allah for His sake, and not with the expectation of rewards or out of fear of punishment. This is best exemplified in Rabia al-Basri's aforementioned verse.

> Sincere worship is to embrace the divine command with utmost humility – in heart and spirit. Sincerity in oneself is to avoid being critical of others; sincerity of the heart is to be oblivious to others' opinions about you, and sincerity of the spirit is cleansing oneself of the desire to be distinguished.[43]

## *Zikr* or Remembrance

*Zikr* is the remembrance of Allah, and it is something that all Sufis strive towards. In the Quran (2:152) Allah says, 'So remember Me; I will remember you.'

The Sufi concept of *zikr* is exemplified in a saying of the tenth-century Arab scholar Al-Qushayrī that goes: 'Be consumed in our existence through your remembrance after your annihilation from yourselves.'[44]

In any mosque, dargah, or religious space, the most common sight is of people with rosaries in their hands, reciting Allah's names or some Quranic *aayat* (verse), *taubah,* or *shukr* (thanksgiving). Most of these people are not Sufis, but just ordinary Muslims in whom *zikr* is ingrained since childhood as an integral and essential part of life. Most Muslims don't go to sleep until they have say a few rosaries glorifying some of Allah's beautiful name (*zikr*), one asking for forgiveness and repentance, and one thanking Him for his daily mercies.

## *Ishq-e-Haqeeqi* or the Love for the Divine

> I was a [hidden] treasure that was not known, so I loved to be known. Hence, I created the creatures and I made Myself known to them, and thus they came to know Me.[45]
>
> – Hadith-e-Qudsi

As is apparent from this hadith, God became manifest because of love. Since love was the reason behind the creation of the universe, love between the creator and the creation remains the only reality, and it is this love that the Sufi seeks – to receive and to give it. As God's love is the source of all love, everything revolves around this love. *Mahabbah* or *mohabbat* (love) is the ultimate station for the Sufi and is achieved at the stage of *marifah*. Total love demands annihilation (*fana*), total self-effacement, and for the lover to be consumed in the beloved.

Another famous Hadith-e-Qudsi (25) that speaks of such love reads as follows:

> Those who seek nearness to Me seek nearness through nothing I love more than the performance of what I have made incumbent upon them. My servant never ceases to seek nearness to Me through supererogatory works until I love him. Then, when I love him, I am his hearing through which he hears, his sight through which he sees, his hand through which he grasps, and his foot through which he walks.

Human beings are constantly seeking love, affirmation, and admiration from their fellow beings, but those who are spiritually inclined seek it from God. When that love consumes the body and soul, it becomes *mazhab-e-ishq* (religion of love).

For the mind, heart, and sight, the first *sheikh* (spiritual leader) is *ishq* (love). In the absence of love, Islamic law (shariah) and religion (*deen*) become but idols of whimsical ideas.[46]

But those of Faith are overflowing in their love for Allah. (*Surah* 2:165)

Though the Arabic word for love, *hub*, is used in many verses of the Quran to describe love between God and humans, or as a human emotion, the word most commonly used today in relation to Allah is *ishq*. It is derived from the word 'ashiqah', a vine: the common belief is that when love takes its root in the heart of a lover, everything other than God is effaced.

*Haqeeqi ishq ki ishq-e-majazi pahli manzil hai*
*Chalo su-e-Khuda ai zahidon ku-e-butan hokar*

[The way to love divine is human love;
O devotees, let us go towards God, via the street of the beloved.]

– Unknown

*Ishq* or love has been classified as *ishq-e-haqeeqi* (love for the divine) and *ishq-e-majazi* (which literally means metaphorical love but refers to love for God's creation or carnal love). The way to *ishq-e-haqeeqi* is often through *ishq-e-majazi*. The latter is often seen as a way of learning how to love someone selflessly, and the natural progression of this is *ishq-e-haqeeqi* – that is, identifying and drowning oneself in the love of God. It conditions the heart and mind to be immersed in love to the exclusion of all else, as Baba Bulleh Shah says:

*Ranjha ranjha kardi ni main aape ranjha hoyi*
*Saddo ni main no deedo Ranjha, mainu heer na aakho koyi*

[Having chanted his name for so long, I have become Ranjha myself,
Call me Ranjha, but there is nobody with the name Heer here.]

If one can be so immersed in the love of the created, then how much more love can one pour out for the Creator? Perhaps the answer is: so much that one ceases to be and finds only the divine everywhere. Kabir expresses this closeness between God and His creation, which the Sufi attempts to experience, as follows:

*Jab main tha Hari nahi jab Hari hain main nahi*
*Prem gali ati sankri taame do na samaahi*

[When I was there, God was absent; now God is there and I am missing;
The lane of love is very narrow – two cannot fit in it at the same time.]

– Kabir

This sentiment is reflected in a Quranic verse (2:186): 'When My servants ask thee concerning Me, I am indeed close (to them).' Yet, it is not always possible to see what is in you and around you.

The Sufi lover (*aashiq*) wants to make this possible and believes that the way to do this is through *ishq-e-haqeeqi,* or pure love, which is only concerned with loving the Divine (beloved/*mehboob*/*mashuq*) and not the outcome; the Sufi is willing to forgo all worldly desires to achieve this. In *ishq-e haqeeqi*, the presumption is that only God is worth loving, and He is the only one who can return His creature's love – all other forms of love have a selfish motive embedded in them.

There are many difficulties in the path of true love, which only *ishq-e-haqeeqi* can surmount. Hazrat Amir Khusrau speaks of these difficulties when he says:

*Bahut kathin hai dagar panghat ki*
*Kaise bhar laaun main Jamuna se matki?*

[The way to the riverbank is very difficult.
How can I fill my vessel with Jamuna water?]

On the journey to finding real love, strewn as it is with obstacles, the first step is to forgo *nafs* or 'ego', and give up worldly desires. The lover must be conscious only of the beloved, spend their time in *zikr* (remembrance of the beloved) till they can see Him (the beloved) with their heart's eyes, feel Him to be closer than their own jugular vein, and long and prepare for the final union (death) when the eternal soul meets and is united forever with the beloved.

This path is not easy and the Sufi needs a spiritual master to help in this quest, a person under whom they take a formal oath of allegiance. Sufism is knowledge passed on from master to disciple and is called '*seena dar seena*' (from my heart to yours). The heart in Sufism is seen as a spiritual organ.

## *Wahdat al-Wujud*

Oh God! Thou pervadeth the soul of every human being.
The blackness of Kufr doth emanate from thee:
And Thou art the light of every faith.
Idol worship, prayer, Kaaba, fire worship in temple,
To me art identical for the essence of each faith art Thou,
How long should I say 'I am Thou',
For only Thou existed and not Masud.
In reality it is not I who reciteth these verses,
Thou reciteth them.[47]

– Masud al Bak

*Wahdat al-Wujud* is made up of two words*: wahdat* and *wujud. Wahdat* or 'unity', beyond its apparent meaning is an important metaphysical concept in Sufism. It is a complex subject and may be hard to understand for a layperson. It needs a spiritually evolved mind to grasp. I can only try and explain the concept to the best of my limited ability, as I have understood it, and may not be able to capture its reality.

The word *wahdat* means to be alone, single, and when used as an attribute of Allah, it means oneness, unity, or singularity. *Wahdat* is derived from the same root as *tauheed* and is used as a belief in the unity of Allah. *Tauheed* has acquired a specific equivalence with Oneness of Allah, on which the *shahada* (bearing witness to the Oneness of God), or *kalima* (Islamic creed) is based, and is the basis of Islam. It states: There is no God, but Allah.

*Wujud* means to be, or to exist. When used to refer to God, it means the necessity of being *wajib-ul-wujud* – that which cannot not be. Thus, God becomes *al-wujudal-haq* or the Necessary Being. God is the ultimate source of existence.

The concept of *Wahdat al-Wujud* existed well before its most famous exponent Ibn al-Arabi was born. Much before, Maruf al-Kharki (c. 750–815) had said, 'There is nothing in *wujud* but God', or Abul Abbas Qassas said in the tenth century, 'There is nothing in the two worlds as my Lord: the existent things (*mawjudat*) – all things except His *wujud* – are non-existent (*ma'adum*)'.[48]

And Khwaja Abdullah Ansari (1089) goes so far as to say that no one exists other than He:

> What is *tawhid*?
> God and nothing else.
> The rest is folly (*hawas*).[49]

Al-Ghazali (1111) too said that there is nothing in existence save God, and that the world is sheer non-existence.[50] However, the theory of *Wahdat al-Wujud* (unity of existence/being) was most clearly formulated and promulgated by Ibn al-Arabi, a.k.a. Shaikh al-Akbar, the Greatest Master (1165–1240). With him, it became an important milestone in the development of Sufism.

Ibn al-Arabi was born in Spain and an early vision changed his life. He studied Islamic sciences under various teachers and was a prolific writer himself. He regarded both man and nature as mirrors displaying God Himself – that God manifested Himself through every atom of creation. His major contribution is the reconciliation of the work of various Sufi scholars into the theory that became famous as *Wahdat al-Wujud* or 'unity of existence'.

According to him, there is only one reality, which is God, and everything is His manifestation. This implies not only that Allah is the only God in existence, but that He is the only Being in existence, and there is nothing in this world but Allah.[51]

He is all of being
and He is the one in whose
Being my being resides[52]

– Ibn al-Arabi (in *Fusus al-Hakim*)

If anything else exists, it does so only because God has allowed it, or willed it to exist, or bestowed existence upon it. The easiest way to describe this is in these words: 'If things other than God appear to exist this is because God has lent them *wujud*, much in the same way that the sun lends light to the inhabitants of the earth.'[53] So when whatever exists does so because of God, He is the only reality. Everything else is his shadow which can't exist without Him.The cosmos is God's self-manifestation and every particle reveals His attributes.

*Whichever way you turn there is the face of God.*

– Quran 2:115

Though *Wahdat al-Wujud* is actually the inward experience of a Sufi, the philosophy has been explained by scholars as follows: the only reality is God, there is no ultimate truth except Him and all things exist within Him. This does not mean, however, that because we see God in everything, God has been reduced to everything – for He resembles no one and is only Himself. Or more simply, as Holm puts it, Ibn al-Arabi used metaphors 'to describe this relationship between God and the world; almost like a light – a pure white light which is called Being that travels through the prism creates multitude of colours which would be the world. The colours themselves are never the same as the white light, just as the creatures of creation are never the same as God but at the same time they consist of nothing but the white light.'[54]

Interestingly, Ibn al-Arabi himself never used the term, even though it is most frequently associated with his teachings. Somehow it became the designation for an expression of *tauheed,* typified by the writings of Ibn al-Arabi and his followers.[55]

When we think of God, we think of Him in terms of one of the beautiful names or attributes that He has. Every seeker calls Him by one of the 99 names we know based on how they relate to God in that moment. When asking for His mercy, for instance, we call him Ar-Rahim; when asking for forgiveness the term used is often Ghafur ar-Rahim. Each attribute is specific and relatable.

If God created the world as a mirror of His manifestations because He wanted to be known, 'God becomes the mirror in which the spiritual man contemplates his own reality, and man in turn becomes the mirror in which God contemplates His Names and Qualities.'[56]

Does this mean that the term *wujud* means 'to be found'?[57] Because if it does, then that is what the Sufi spends his life doing. Thus the goal is the realization that there is nothing but God and our being is His being.

In the *Fusus-ul-Hiqam,* Ibn al Arabi says:

> If the believer understood the saying of Junayd 'The colour of water is the colour of the vessel containing it', he would not interfere with the beliefs of others, but would perceive God in every form and every belief. He has opinion, not knowledge. Therefore, God said, 'I am in thy servants' opinion of Me', i.e., I do not manifest myself to him, save in the form of his belief.[58]

*Wahdat al-Wujud* was also important for it implied that since the entirety of mankind is one and is reflected in God, there is harmony between followers of all faiths. As Mevlana Jalaluddin Rumi said, 'The lovers of God have no religion but God alone.' Many scholars have found similarities between this idea and the Advaitva Hindu philosophy.

During the reign of Akbar (1556–1605), when he was preaching *Sulh-e-Kul* or universal peace, there was a revivalist movement spearheaded by the Naqshbandi Sufi saint Ahmed Sirhindi. He felt that the *Wahdat al-Wujud* philosophy was tantamount to pantheism and that what existed was *wahdat-ash-shuhud* (unity of vision or appearance), which holds that God and his creation are totally separate.

> Sirhindi exemplifies this distinction by describing two views which a person can take of a natural phenomenon. The wujüdi would deny the existence of the stars whilc looking at the sun because he

> is overwhelmed by the spectacle and cannot see anything except the sun itself. His view is patently wrong. The shuhüdi, on the other hand, knows that the stars do exist, though he also sees only the sun. His consciousness is in the stage of ayn al-yaqin [the vision of certainty], while that of the wujüdi remains at the lower stage of ilm al-yaqin [the knowledge of certainty]. The highest stage of consciousness, that of haqq al-yaqin [the final level of certainty gained through experience], can be reached when the sight of the onlooker is sharpened to an extent that enables him to see the stars and the sun simultaneously.[59]

Shah Waliullah Dehlvi (1703–62) tried to reconcile the two by calling them verbal controversies, saying that it rose out of ambiguous language and insisting that both were actually in agreement.

To put it simply, according to *wahdat-ash-shuhud,* one does not merge into Allah but reaches the stage where you can feel Him in every moment of your life. There is a complete and essential unity with the divine being. The ultimate aim of the lover is not attaining Allah but loving Him with every breath in his self.

In fact the perfect human or *insan-e-kamil* is one who has reached a stage of complete self-annihilation and recognizes that he is nothing but God's reflection and acts accordingly.

According to a hadith that resonates this idea, when you stand to offer your prayers, Allah is in front of you. Though the hadith was meant to ensure that worshippers don't spit in front of themselves while praying, the fact that Allah is watching was established through it.

Therefore, God is reality, and one of His creations (the Sufi) becomes so overwhelmed by His existence and conscious of it that they become oblivious to all else and spend their entire life trying to be one with Him. For the Sufi saint, the path to union with God was through complete devotion to God and service to his creation. One important point to note regarding *Wahdat al-Wujud*, however, is that according to the theory, though mystically united, God's creation is not identical or interchangeable with Him. Love is the essence of God and though the lover yearns to be united with God, that is an impossibility since the created can't unite with the essence.[60] That love resonates through a poem cited in Aishah Al-Bauniyyah's book on Sufism:

I erased my name and my body's trace,
so I disappeared from me while you stayed.
In my passing, my passing passed,
and in my passing, you were found![61]

# SAINTS AND *SILSILAHS*

# 4

## *Silsilahs*: The Mystic Orders

The paths
are many
The destination
is one
Do you not see?
There are many paths
to the Ka'ba.[1]

– Mevlana Jalaluddin Rumi

I am standing in the courtyard of Dewa Sharif, in Uttar Pradesh, surrounded by a sea of yellow as I wait for the *urs* ceremony to start. A first-time visitor may not know that the Warsis of Dewa Sharif wear this distinctive shade of yellow or about its significance.

Haji Syed Waris Ali Shah (1817–1905), the founder of this *silsilah*, not only wore yellow in his daily life, he also performed his hajj in an *ahram* (unstitched robe worn by pilgrims) of the same colour. Was it because yellow symbolizes paleness? The lover is pale and anguished, longing for his Beloved Divine, and he suffers till he becomes 'golden', like metal, in the crucible of love.[2]

Is yellow associated with Sufism? Or do followers of a certain saint wear it? To understand this one must understand what a *silsilah* or Sufi order is.

When the uninitiated think of Sufism in India, it is the very popular dargahs of Khwaja Garib Nawaz and Hazrat Nizamuddin Auliya that come to mind. Most people probably don't know that they belong to the Chishti *silsilah*, or indeed what *silsilah*s are, and how they helped in the spread of Sufism.

The Arabic word '*silsilah*' literally means chain, and in Sufism it refers to the formal chain of spiritual descent. The chain runs across centuries but starts with the master who passes on their mystic wisdom to disciples, who in turn pass it on to theirs and so on.

In the previous chapter, we have seen how the first Sufis came to the Indian subcontinent in the eighth and ninth centuries. But it was only with the establishment of the Sufi *silsilah*s (orders) in the twelfth century that Sufism became popular. Many graves of *pir babas* (saints) from the early period are revered even today. They are scattered across various parts of the subcontinent. Although they often have a strong localized following, not much is known about them.

For instance, Haji Rozbih, the first Sufi saint to reach Delhi, lies buried just outside the walls of the Chauhan Fort, Lal Kot, Mehrauli in Delhi. Next to his simple open air grave in the forest is the grave of another devotee, said to be his female disciple from the Chauhan clan and a daughter of Prithviraj Chauhan.[3] This claim maybe far-fetched, especially because Prithviraj Chauhan never came to Delhi. Besides, we don't know enough about the saint, so we can't be certain he had disciples at all. Chishti saint Qutub Sahib, too, is in Mehrauli; he holds sway over the hearts of not just the locals but people the world over. In his case, because the Chishti *silsilah* is well documented, we know of his history and *karamat* and disciples.

With the consolidation of the Delhi Sultanate came the establishment of *khanqah*s (Sufi hospices), and state patronage of saints; with the new conducive atmosphere, the Sufi orders were able to establish themselves firmly in the Indian subcontinent. The *urs* (death anniversary) celebrations of Sufis slowly began to attract thousands from across the globe, and it continues to do so even now. The most popular *urs* ceremony in India is that of the Chishti saint of Ajmer, Khwaja Muinuddin Chishti, known popularly as Khwaja Garib Nawaz.

In this and the subsequent chapters, I delve into the formation of *silsilah*s, as their emergence is a very important to understand Sufism.

From the tenth century onwards we see the popularity of Sufism spread across Central Asia. The establishment of the Delhi Sultanate (1192) coincided with unrest in Central Asia due to the Mongol invasions,[4] leading to the large scale exodus of immigrants into India. Many Sufi saints, too, thus arrived in India during this period and set up their *khanqah*s.

This led to the emergence of many new traditions and according to Raziuddin Aquil, an academic, the 'interactions between various strands of Islam and diverse Indic religious traditions led to the emergence of new forms of religiosity, cults and sects, the most prominent being Sufism, Bhakti and Sikhism.' Aquil then proceeds to elaborate on this succinctly:

> Sufis were able to evolve an acceptable language and common grounds, which the self-styled guardians of Islam, the ulama, could not. Low-caste Bhakti saints could speak against social inequities, the Brahmin pandits could not. Some of the exalted gurus did speak of social harmony, but their ill-trained *chelas* [disciples] did not. For some, bigotry was the guiding principle of life; for others, justice and humanity were the ideals to adhere to.[5]

As the number of Sufis began to increase, they began to feel the need to formalize and legitimize their spiritual training. This led to the rise of mystical orders or *silsilah*s from the twelfth century. *Silsilah*s gave the followers a spiritual hierarchy and a place within it, along with 'greater respectability and a stronger base of defence against the onslaught of the orthodox'.[6]

The earliest stage of the formation of such orders was marked by the presence of ascetic Sufis who renounced worldly pleasures, and lived in constant remembrance of Allah, and in solitude. They were mainly based in the cities of Basra and Kufa in Iraq. This was in adherence to Prophet Muhammad's example.

A very popular hadith given in Sahih Muslim (no. 1479) describes the time when the second caliph of Islam, Umar ibn al-Khattab, found the Prophet lying on a straw mat with only a handful of barley in the corner of the cell. The imprint of the Prophet's bare upper body was still on the mat. On seeing the extremely austere life the Holy Prophet was leading, Umar ibn al-Khattab started weeping. When the Prophet asked him why he was crying, he replied that he was saddened by the realization that the Caesars and Khusraus of the world (kings) lived a life of luxury, while the Messenger of God was living in such poverty. The Prophet said that he was satisfied with the prosperity of the hereafter – meaning he didn't hanker after worldly pleasures, which were temporary.

Aquil summarizes the spread of Sufism, 'Beginning with the influential mystic circles of Baghdad, Sufi networks were established in lower Iraq, Iberia, Egypt, north-eastern Iran and Central Asia between the ninth and twelfth centuries.'[7] The rise of *silsilah*s was a natural progression when Sufi saints became more organized.

To understand Sufism and its impact in India, it is essential to understand the various *silsilah*s that flourished here and their important saints, for it was these saints who attracted people to their *khanqah*s in the early stages. The major saints of each order sent their disciples to various parts of the subcontinent to establish their mission. These were called *vilayat*s (spiritual territories). Today the teachings, legacy, and the *karamat* (miracles) attributed to these disciples draw people seeking their intercession to the shrines.

Though there were many female Sufi saints, they did not establish *silsilah*s which remained a male privilege.

The *silsilah*s began to develop in the *tariqah* stage, discussed in the previous chapter. They were built around a particular saint and his teachings, and the rules of *khilafat* (succession) were formed. The relationship between the *pir* and *murid* became very clear.

The initial *silsilah*s were formed and named after their masters. Take the example of the first group to organize itself as an order, the Qadriya *silsilah*; it was named after Sheikh Abdul Qadir Jilani. There was also the Muhasibi *silsilah* named after Abu Abdullah al Harith Ibn Asad al Anazi al Muḥasibi (781–857), and the Junaydi Order named after Junayd Baghdadi (830–910).

As the Sufi *silsilah*s developed, they split into a number of branches (as will be discussed in detail later). Today, there are innumerable *silsilah*s in the world, but I will limit myself to the major Indian *silsilah*s.

As these *silsilah*s formalized their teachings, they also imbibed many other regional influences, which they adapted within the Islamic framework. So while Sufism didn't grow out of these, as its main source is the Quran, and the life of the Prophet, the monastic traditions of Buddhism and Christianity, and the philosophies of the Vedas, the Upanishads, and Neo-Platonism were all absorbed into its discourse.

Every *silsilah* had its own particular methods, rituals, and techniques. There is, for instance, a difference in the method of *zikr* (remembrance of Allah) in each order. While the Naqshbandi order lays emphasis on silent *zikr,* with breath control and meditation, the Chishti order does it aloud – almost always through the medium of *sama mehfil*s (musical assemblies) to create momentum to lead to a state of trance. The Chishti *silsilah* today is the main promoter of the tradition of qawwali; you will always find qawwalis being sung in their dargahs. Scholar and author Omar Khalidi writes about this:

> Of the four Sufi orders popular in India the Chishtis alone sought ecstatic inspiration in music. The Suhrawardis were generally indifferent to it and recommended instead the chanting of the Quran; the Qadiris were opposed to music generally, and to instrumental music in particular. The Naqshbandi attitude to music was even more hostile.[8]

The *silsilah*s are of two types: those that adhere strictly to shariah and are called *ba-shara,* and the non-conformist ones referred to as *be-shara*.

According Aquil, the terms and the 'distinction smacks of *fatwa-baazi* [Islamic rulings] in Islam. If at all one needs to identify and judge some people such as the madaris or qalandars, they may be referred to for being non-conformist, and even somewhat deviant.'[9]

Therefore, the term used in this book is non-conformist.

The non-conformists called *qalandari* or *mazjub* (intoxicated) do not belong to any one *silsilah* and spend their time wandering from one place to another. They believed in rejecting the material world, according to scholar Ute Falasch, 'opting for celibacy, itinerancy, poverty, and mendicancy instead'.

> The deviance from social and moral norms in the attitude towards piety is often presented to the community by peculiar dress and paraphernalia, or the lack of appropriate clothing, as well as a provocative behaviour that is regarded as offensive. Not only the neglect of social standards may characterize this piety, but also that of religious normativity, which is why they are labelled antinomian. It may be expressed in different ways, such as ecstatic states that revolve around music and dance or the experimentation with

> drugs, mostly hashish, as well as a disregard for religious duties, such as fasting and praying. Because of these aspects, these groups always have been an object of criticism. Movements such as the Qalandariyyah, which spread in the thirteenth and fourteenth centuries across the Muslim world up to India, have been looked down upon by the intellectual elite of the society, regarding them as false Sufis who lack religious sentiments or imposters that misuse the sensitivities of the people.[10]

This is not to say that these fakirs or qalandars were rejected by Muslim society. They found a space for themselves in society and dargahs. Though they did not follow the widespread social norms, there is nothing to suggest that they rejected normative Islamic practices.

Many Sufi *silsilah*s have flourished in India over time. Abul Fazl lists fourteen orders that were functioning in sixteenth-century India. Of these, the four most prominent *ba-shara silsilah*s are the Chishti, Suhrawardi, Qadriya, and Naqshbandi. Among the non-conformist *silsilah*s, the *dewangan* section of the Madari *silsilah* and the Rasul-Shahis are two prominent ones in India.

While mystic centres had been established in many areas by Muslim saints long before the establishment of Turkish rule, the establishment of the Delhi Sultanate saw the emergence of Sufi saints and systematic organization of *silsilah*s in India. Two of the most important mystic orders – the Chishti and the Suhrawardi – were also introduced in north India during the Delhi Sultanate years. These *silsilah*s often played an important role in society of the times, as will be discussed later.

The Suhrawardi and the Chishti *silsilah*s were and are on friendly terms with each other, and the latter even rely on the works of the saints from the former *silsilah*, like Sheikh Shihabuddin Suhrawardi and Sheikh Hamiduddin Nagauri. The goal of both the orders is to surrender their souls to God's will and achieve union with the Divine.

Yet, despite all these similarities, there are also differences. The rituals and ceremonies of the two orders reflect their contrasting attitudes towards society and politics. While the Suhrawardis emphasize *salat* (prayers) and *zikr*, fasting only in the month of Ramzan, the devotion of the Chishtis leads them not just to offer prayers but indulge in difficult ascetic practices and fast almost continuously. The former believe in eating all that is pure, and in acting righteously, while the latter focus on self-mortification, penance, and meditation.

Their contact with yogis has led the Chishtis to practice *zikr* with strenuous coordination of limb movements and postures associated with exhalation and inhalation.[11]

The *sama mehfils* of the Chishtis are attended by the Suhrawardi saints of Delhi but not encouraged by the Multani Suhrawardis.

The Naqshbandis felt it essential to connect and interact with the powers that be, as the life of the rulers had a deep impact on the life of the people.[12] The Suhrawardis mixed with the kings, and 'gave moral support to them but did not attempt any reorientation of their thought'.[13]

The Chishtis, on the other hand, didn't seek active involvement but they didn't shun the rulers totally either, accepting grants and land from them. The well-known Chishti Hazrat Nizamuddin Auliya did seek to stay away from rulers, though, and there is a famous incident pertaining to the time when Sultan Jalaluddin Khilji wanted to visit him. Hearing of the ruler's desire, he is said to have famously quipped that a Sufi *khanqah* has two doors and if the sultan entered by one, he'd use the other to leave.[14] However, his relations with Alauddin Khilji were cordial – with the sultan seeking 'Nizam-ud-Din's spiritual assistance for knowing the fate of his campaign in southern India – the Sufi master had predicted its victory'.[15]

A very famous story described in *Fawaid al-Fuad* is of a Sufi saint named Shaikh Ali. The saint was sitting with outstretched legs repairing his tattered cloak when the ruler and his *wazir* (prime minister) visited him. The *wazir* asked him to fold his legs, but he remained still and unperturbed. When the ruler drew closer, he showed his fists and said that he has closed his hands instead!

This should not be taken to mean that these saints did not influence the rulers – only that they did it indirectly by narrating stories and parables, or quoting from the hadiths and the life of the Prophet, to show rulers that their tyranny was wrong.

The Naqshbandi order was the last of the major *silsilah*s to find its way into India via Khwaja Nasiruddin Ubaidullah Ahrar's descendants, Khwaja

Abdul Shahid, and Khwaja Kalan. The two men came to the Mughal court on Babur's invitation but didn't stay long. This *silsilah* attained popularity later via Khwaja Muhammad Baqi, also known as Baqi Billah Berang.

Apart from the four main *silsilahs*, there were many offshoots and independent *silsilahs*, such as the Sabri, Firdausi, Shattari, Kubravi, Warsi, and Kazmiya Qalandari.

Throughout the lands where the *khanqahs* and dargahs established were governed by the local rulers, the Sufi saints were considered the spiritual rulers. According to historian Sunil Kumar, the political ruler with his army 'were the intrusive and sometimes violent and usually coercive element that appeared in South Asian history with the establishment of the Sultanate (c. 1200+).' Further, he says:

> 'Conversely, as proponents of a mystical Islam, Sufis have been regarded as the ecumenical face of Islam, preaching to the commoners, often using the vernacular, and communicating complex aspects of Islam and Sufi philosophy through pithy maxims derived from the quotidian experiences of the common people and not just the elites. As an extension of this idea, since Sufis were not involved in the mundane temporal world but with abstract, spiritual praxis, historiographical narratives often placed them outside the realm of history and the vicissitudes of change.'[16]

The role of the Sufi was multi-layered and thus they played a very important role in shaping the religious outlook of the rulers, thereby shaping history. Sheikh Abdul Quddus Gangohi, the Chishti Sabri saint, in a letter to Babur sets forth his views in regard to the functions and duties of a Muslim king. He expressed his faith in Babur's firm conviction in Islam and Hanafi law, and his devotion to the ulema and the Mashaikh, whom he entreated for the theologians, mystics, weak, and the depressed to be maintained and subsidized by the state. In M. Zameer Uddin Siddiqi's words:

> It was specially stressed that the obligation of deep gratitude to God demanded that [the] all-pervading Justice of the King cast its

> shadow on the people and that no one should subject another to torture and tyranny and that all the people and soldiers hold fast to all that has been ordained by *shara* and abstain from all that is forbidden.[17]

Since each *silsilah* had its own dynamics with the rulers and the people of the subcontinent, I will examine each one separately in the subsequent chapters.

# 5

# The Chishtis

Agreed that you perform a lot of namaz
And also fast for many days,
Yet, if your heart isn't cleansed of anger and hatred
It's like dumping a hundred mounds of flowers on top of a thorn.[1]
– Hazrat Nizamuddin Auliya

At any given moment of time, outside the dargah of Khwaja Muinuddin Chishti, one will find a huge crowd milling around trying to get a glimpse of the shrine. My first visit to this shrine, known as Ajmer Sharif Dargah, had been part of a college trip, and I was unprepared for the crowds, and the palpable sense of piety and devotion that greeted me there. Even today, as I walk into the courtyard and sit on the porch built by Princess Jahanara, I am transformed into a whole other world of goodness and reverence.

Almost nine centuries have passed since Khwaja Garib Nawaz started living and preaching in Ajmer. His illuminating and instructive discourses, full of spiritual insights, drew the local populace to him then, and even now attracts devotees from far and wide. His is by far the most popular *silsilah* in India, with shrines of Chishti saints in almost every town and city.

> Kings have come and gone, emperors have risen and fallen
> but the graves of the great saint and his illustrious disciple are still
> visited by the pilgrims year in and year out, and the people
> irrespective of castes and creeds pay their homages to them;
> Mankind still draws inspiration from their messages of universal
> love and tolerance, unity and catholicity, humanity and
> brotherhood.[2]

The Chishtis are the most popular and enduring Sufi order. The root of the order's name lies in a small town named Chisht near Herat in Afghanistan. Abu Ishaq Shami (d. 940), the founder of the Chishti order, as his name 'Shami' (Syrian) implies belonged to Syria. He went to this remote town on the behest of his Sufi master Ulu Dinawari. The reason for this directive is not known, but Abu Ishaq went on to become one of the most famous Sufis of his age. He returned to Syria before his death as he wished to be buried in Damascus. His successor Khwaja Abu Ahmad Abdal Chishti (d. 966), the son of the Amir of Chisht, dropped the Shami (Syrian) in his name, and added Chishti. And so was born the Chishti *silsilah*.

The Chishti saints lived very austere lives, eating very frugally, and spending their time in *zikr*, devotion, and the service of people. At the heart of their teachings lay the values of humility, modesty, patience, and fortitude, and a call to seek purification of the heart. They believed that leading pious lives prepared people not just for this world but also the next. Each of the saints preached this philosophy in their own unique way.

Once Khwaja Muinuddin Chishti was asked to explain the highest form of religious devotion which endeared man to God. He replied: 'Develop a river-like generosity, sun-like bounty, and an earth-like hospitality.'

Hazrat Nizamuddin Auliya shared this belief. According to him,

> Devotion to God is of two kinds: *lazmi* (intransitive) and *muta'addi* (transitive). In the *lazmi* devotion, the benefit, which accrues, is confined to the devotee alone. This type of devotion includes prayer, fasting, pilgrimage to Mecca, recitation of religious formulae, turning over the beads of rosary etc. The *muta'addi* devotion, on the contrary, brings advantage and comfort on others; it is performed by spending money on others, showing affection to people and by other means through which a man strives to help his fellow human beings. The reward of *muta'addi* devotion is endless and limitless.[3]

It was this identifying of religion with the service of humanity that led to its far-reaching impact, for it could now be used for both spiritual and physical benefits of humankind.

The simplicity of the teachings and their emphasis on love and service to humanity were the reasons for the success of the Sufi saints in medieval India, with the aforementioned Ajmer Sharif Dargah housing the most popular one.

Khwaja Muinuddin Chishti was born in Sijistan (modern-day Sistan) in Iran around 1141. His parents named him Muinuddin Hasan and affectionately called him Hasan. Today, he is known by many names, the most popular of them being Khwaja Garib Nawaz (patron saint of the poor). His life is described in the famous book *Siyar al-Arifin* (*Biographies of Mystics*) written in the sixteenth century by the renowned Sufi saint Maulana Jamali, who collected stories from Iran and India.

Muinuddin was a special child: he showed his famous 'earth-like' generosity right from infancy. It is said that whenever any woman with a child came to his house and the child cried for milk, he would signal to his mother to give his share to that baby.

The turning point in his life, though, came when he was in his teens. His father Saiyed Ghiyasuddin Hasan had died, and Muinuddin Hasan was living on his earnings from a garden and water mill left to him by his father. One day, a *mazjub* (saint), Ibrahim Qandoozi, intoxicated by the thought of nearness of God came into this garden just as Hasan was watering it. The young boy welcomed him and offered him some grapes. The saint was greatly pleased; taking out a piece of cake from his bag, he chewed on it, and then put it in the mouth of the young boy. As soon as Hasan ate it, he experienced a change within himself – a strange repulsion towards worldly goods. He thus sold his garden and water mill and distributed the proceeds among local mendicants.[4]

The search for knowledge led Muinuddin Hasan to many cities, and he spent time with the famous Sufi masters of his time there, including the famed Baghdad Sufi saint Ghaus-ul-Azam Abdul Qadir Jilani.

Khwaja Muinuddin was 52 years old when his master Sheikh Usman Harawani appointed him as his *khalifa* or spiritual successor. This appointment did not mean the end of his quest and once again, the Khwaja set out on his travels and went to Ush, Isfahan, and then Mecca for Hajj, and finally Medina.

While he was praying in the Prophet's mosque in Medina, the Khwaja is said to have heard the Prophet's voice telling him to go to Hindustan (present-day India), and to the city of Ajmer. At the time, he had no idea where Ajmer was. However, he found his way and proceeded via Baghdad and Herat to Lahore, and thence to Delhi and Ajmer.

The Delhi Sultanate has been established, and it was in Sultan Iltutmish's reign (1211–36) that Khwaja Muinuddin Chishti came to Ajmer. His illuminating and instructive discourses, full of spiritual insights, soon drew the local populace to him, and devotees from far and wide began to throng towards him.

Khwaja Muinuddin Chishti earned the sobriquet of Garib Nawaz around this time; even today, thousands are fed in his dargah daily. The two huge *degh*s (pots), donated by Mughal emperors Akbar and Jahangir, in which rice is cooked and distributed daily are world famous. The pot presented by Akbar holds 4,800 kg of food and the one by Jahangir holds 2,400 kg. Many grateful devotees whose prayers have been fulfilled contribute to it.

Khwaja Garib Nawaz passed away in 1236, but even today devotees visit from all over the world, across boundaries of region and religion, caste, and sect. There are always hordes of people doing what is known as *haziri*: sitting, meditating, praying, and supplicating. It is a dargah that has been visited and endowed by rulers, nobles, and common folk alike. They are all united in their love for a saint who loved them.

Khwaja Muinuddin Chishti appointed Sheikh Hamiduddin Nagauri as his *khalifa* (successor) in Rajasthan and Qutub Sahib as his successor in Delhi, the capital of the Delhi Sultanate.

Sheikh Hamiduddin Nagauri was born in 1192; he was the first native of Delhi to become a Sufi saint. A profligate and ne'er-do-well as a youngster, Nagauri transformed after meeting Khwaja Muinuddin Chishti, and he decided to become the Khwaja's disciple in Ajmer.[5]

Of an ascetic nature ever since his discipleship, the saint shunned the society of people, and preferred remaining immersed in remembrance of Allah, desiring nothing more than surrendering himself to the divine will. Khwaja Muinuddin Chishti gave him the title of Sultan-ul-Tarikin (King of Hermits). He lived a very simple life as a farmer on a small plot of land in the village of Suwali near Nagaur, selling the milk of the one cow he possessed. He refused all offers of gifts from his followers.

The area he lived in had a large Jain population, and he was very influenced by them. He was against the killing of animals; a strict vegetarian, he advocated the same for his followers.

For him, ignorance was the greatest curse on man, and a man without knowledge was no 'better than a fossil'.[6]

He shunned fame and believed that a saint's spiritual powers should be hidden from the gaze of ordinary men: just as women would hide their menstrual flow, so too should Sufis hide their *karamat* (miracles).[7]

He was well versed in Persian, Arabic, and the Hindavi[8] languages spoken in the land of his birth.

He died in November 1274 and was buried in Nagaur.

His dargah in Nagaur is popular among locals. During the *urs*, his followers come in procession, with their chief on a camel and offerings in their hands. They carry *chaddar*s (shrine covers) in ceremonial processions. Huge pots of *langar* (communal meals) are cooked to feed the attendees and for distributing. In the medieval ages when the *khanqah*s and dargahs received state and aristocratic patronage, *langar*s were a daily affair in dargahs, but now, with a few exceptions, it is limited to *urs,* or other special occasions such as Ramzan.

In the by-lanes of Delhi's bustling Mehrauli locality is a small mosque with a very fascinating and endearing legend concerning Khwaja Garib Nawaz's other successor. Its entrance as well as main mosque are recent constructions, but there is a small three-doorway pavilion, which according to the imam of the mosque, is a thirteenth century *mehfil khana* (place of assembly).

During my first visit to the mosque, in 2014, I met Maulana Mohammad Idrees, who had been the Imam of Masjid Auliya there for the previous 55 years. He was extremely welcoming and learned, and (unlike many others) had no hang-ups about engaging with a woman intellectually or answering my innumerable questions. He explained the significance of this small mosque in the history of Sufism and in particular the Chishti *silsilah*. He narrated tome the story of a miracle that had taken place in the mosque, earning Qutub Sahib the titles of Bakhtiyar and Kaki – as a result, he is now popularly known as Khwaja Qutbuddin Bakhtiyar Kaki.

According to the story, three important Chishti saints, Khwaja Muinuddin Chishti (a.k.a. Khwaja Garib Nawaz), Qutub Sahib, and Baba Farid, had lived in the mosque intermittently for 12 years. Qutub Sahib was the *khalifa* of Khwaja Muinuddin Chishti, and the *pir* of Baba Farid. The three saints used to have discussions on religion and spirituality in the *mehfil khana*.

One day, Allah sent food for them in the shape of *kaak,* a kind of flatbread. When the basket of food appeared in the air, the saints Khwaja Muinuddin Chisti and Baba Farid asked for it by turn, but it eluded their hands and kept floating away. Qutub Sahib was sitting outside with the slippers of Khwaja Muinuddin Chisti, who now asked if the food was meant for someone in particular and if that person was absent. In response, Baba Farid, the disciple of Qutub Sahib, said that perhaps it was meant for his master who was waiting outside. The Khwaja promptly asked that Qutub Sahib be brought inside. As soon as the latter came in, the Khwaja said, 'Qutbuddin, we have all asked for this thing that Allah has sent but somehow, it's not coming in our grasp. Perhaps you should ask for it... Maybe it's in your destiny.' Qutub Sahib put the Khwaja's shoes under his armpits, spread out his *daaman* (the edge of his dress/scarf) and said, 'Oh Allah, only you can save my reputation, today.' The basket came into his grasp as soon as he said this.

Khwaja Garib Nawaz, who was watching, said, 'Oh Qutbuddin, I didn't know that your station was so elevated. If I had known, I would have been your disciple and not the other way round.' He was then given the title of 'Bakhtiyar' – one who is very fortunate and has *ikhtiyar* (control) over things.

Irrespective of whether this story is authentic or not, it is widely accepted and has endured for many centuries, bearing testimony to the popularity of the Chishti *silsilah,* and the grasp that it has had over the minds of people.

The protagonist of the story, Khwaja Qutbuddin Bakhtiyar Kaki, is popularly known as Qutub Sahib, after his title Qutb al-Aqtab or the central axis around which everything revolves. This denoted his rank in the Sufi hierarchy. He was born in Ush in the Fergana Valley of Kyrgyzstan in 1173, and met Khwaja Muinuddin Chishti in Baghdad, becoming his disciple soon after.

He had come to Delhi in 1221 after spending some time in Multan, and was Sultan Iltutmish's spiritual master and had great influence in the Delhi Sultanate. At the request of the Sultan, he shifted from Kilokari (modern-day Maharani Bagh in Delhi) to Mehrauli, which was the seat of governance. Though he wanted to shift to Ajmer to be with his master, he was ordered by the latter to stay in Delhi, as the capital of the Delhi Sultanate had become an important centre for Sufis of various orders to gather.

Among other things, Khwaja Muinuddin Chishti advised his *khalifa* to always feed the hungry, hear the complaints of the distressed and stand by them. And the disciple obeyed.

Qutub Sahib died on the on 27 November 1235. Just before, he was in a *mehfil-e-sama* in the house of the dervish Ali Sanjari when he went into a state of *wajd* (ecstasy) induced by the recitation of the couplet below by Sheikh Ahmad Jam, a poet of Chisht:

*Kushtagan-i khanjar-i taslimra*
*Har zaman az ghayb jan-i digar ast*

[For the victims of the dagger of divine love,
There is new life every moment from the unseen.]

On being taken back to his house, he asked for the verse to be repeated every time he gained consciousness (at times of obligatory prayers). He would then again lapse into an ecstatic state each time. This went on for five consecutive nights. On the fifth night, he passed away.

He is also called *Shaheed-e-Mohabbat*, a martyr of Allah's love, because of his extraordinary death. Sultan Iltutmish himself is said to have led his funeral prayers.

His death has been recorded by Amir Hasan Sijzi with the following lines added before the original couplet of Sheikh Ahmed jam:

The saint who gave up his soul on this verse
Take note: what a rare gem he was.[9]

Qutub Sahib appointed Sheikh Fariduddin Masud Ganj-e-Shakkar as his *khalifa*. Popularly known as Baba Farid, he was born in 1173/74 in

Kathwal, a small town in Multan where his father was the *qazi* (judge). His mother was an extremely pious lady, and her influence on her son was immense, leading to the development of his exceptionally ascetic nature. He met Qutub Sahib in Multan, where at the age of 18 he had gone for further studies. He became his disciple there but was advised to finish his studies. Later he came to Delhi to be with his spiritual master in Mehrauli. He performed many austerities and ascetic practices there.

At the entrance of the dargah of Ashiq Allah in Mehrauli is a well where Baba Farid is said to have performed the difficult *chilla-e-makus* (inverted penance), which entails being suspended upside down for 40 days in a state of fasting. The dargah itself is built around a cave where Baba Farid did another *chillah*. The cave is a low vaulted cell – 5ft 8 inches in height, with a floor that is 16ft by 7ft 6 inches. It has a simple qibla niche on the western wall.

While researching the monuments of Mehrauli for another book,[10] I was a constant visitor to this area. During that time, I had many conversations with ascetics and devotees gathered there. Asif Khan Dehlvi, a resident of Mehrauli with Sufi sensibilities and the founder of the Delhi Karavan group which specializes in immersive heritage experiences, would often accompany me. He would tell me stories he had heard from the fakirs gathered in Qutub Sahib's dargah. According to the fakirs, he said, Khwaja Moinuddin Chisti once visited his disciple Qutub Sahib and asked all his disciples to assemble. When everyone gathered, the Khwaja noticed that someone was still missing. Qutub Sahib realized that it was his disciple Farid (Baba Farid) who was away at his spiritual retreat. They then decided to locate him. He was found in a semi-comatose emaciated state in this cell, where he had been praying for the past 40 days, oblivious to his physical needs. The Khwaja lifted up Baba Farid in his arms and prayed to Allah to accept his prayers.

Baba Farid 'became exalted with the auspiciousness of kissing the hand' of Hazrat Khwaja Muinuddin Chishti.[11] The Khwaja turned to Qutub Sahib and said a number of times: 'Hey Bakhtiyar! You have captivated a great falcon that it will not nestle at any other place than *sidrat-ul-muntaha* [the heavenly tree, beyond which Jibraeel Aleh can't go]. This Farid is a candle, with which he will enlighten the *Khanwadah* [family] of the mendicants.'[12]

Nowadays, many devotees flock there daily, supplicating for the fulfilment of their desires. They offer mustard oil for the burning of the diyas there. One can indeed experience a strong force of spiritual power in the cell which brings a sense of peace.

Baba Farid's epithet Ganj-e-Shakkar (store house of sweetness) comes from his extreme fasting of which this story is only one example. Another time, in a state of hunger, it is said that he put a few pebbles in his mouth, and they turned to sugar. He spat them out believing it to be the work of the devil, but it happened every time he put the pebbles in thereafter. Eventually overcome by extreme hunger one day, he ate the pebbles-turned-sugar just so that he could continue praying.

At the time of Qutub Sahib's passing, Baba Farid was in Hansi where he had gone to pray and meditate as solitude was difficult for him to have in Delhi. He thus reached five days late and was inconsolable. As Qutub Sahib's *khalifa*, Baba Farid was given the master's robe, turban, staff, and wooden sandals by Qazi Hamiduddin Nagauri, who had been entrusted the task of passing on the belongings.

Baba Farid then settled down in Ajodhan (Pakpattan in present-day Pakistan), where he built a small mud house with a thatched roof and a mosque, married and started a family. He spent most of his time there in meditation and devotion.

Like his *pir*, he was also *mazjub* (intoxicated by Allah's love), and experienced the most intense moments of spiritual communion with God in the semi-privacy of his cell. According to Bruce B. Lawrence, Hazrat Nizamuddin said that he would often see the saint, with a grave demeanour and bare head, reciting the following verse:

> I wish that I may live always in loyalty to You,
> May I become dust and live under Your feet;
> My goal beyond both worlds is You –
> It is for You I die and it is for You I live.[13]

After reciting this verse he would prostrate, and only then would the disciple enter and ask his master for some spiritual gift, which would invariably be granted.

All these stories are useful to foreground the Chishti practice of *sama*.

Baba Farid had few possessions – just a rug which he covered himself with at night and sat on during the day. Khwaja Qutbuddin's stick rested behind his head as a pillow.[14] Like his disciples, he slept on the floor.

As his spiritual powers became more well known, many started flocking to him. He spent a great deal of time meeting people and his popularity, in his lifetime itself, was immense.

Food was usually a broth of wild berries collected from the forest or offerings made by locals, and was shared by everyone. No borrowing was allowed and if any donations were received, they had to be used for necessities or distributed amongst the poor. Faith in God and His ability to provide was the principle on which life was spent.

Baba Farid's *Jamatkhana* (assembly room) at Ajodhan was one of the most famous centres of spiritual activities in the medieval era. His doors were open for all and he preached the lesson of love. As his assembly room was located along a major arterial road, people visited it from all over: some to seek blessings, others to have spiritual discussions. The discussions were free and could be on any topic. Many of them are known to have involved Muslims and non-Muslims. In fact, there are some interesting ones recorded with *nath* yogis. One of them relates to a disciple asking one of the yogis for a recipe to grow hair!

For Baba Farid, the most important thing was to reduce the distance between human beings, and the highest form of religious devotion was to give happiness to all irrespective of caste, creed or colour.

He wrote poetry in Arabic, Persian, and in the local dialect that is popular even today. He is said to be the first classical poet of the Punjabi language. His sayings are included in the Guru Granth Sahib, the sacred book of the Sikhs, and Farid *bani* – as his sayings were called – are said to have influenced Guru Nanak's poetry, too.

In an article written for *Scroll*, Haroon Khalid, the author of *Walking with Nanak,* writes:

> The Sufi saint's poetry had a huge influence over Guru Nanak, who used several symbols similar to those espoused by Baba Farid. In the Punjabi literary tradition, Guru Nanak is believed to be the

> second classical poet. It is through Guru Nanak that the poetry of Baba Farid found its way into the Guru Granth Sahib, considered the eternal, living Sikh Guru. Today the Sikh holy book is the only written source of Baba Farid's poetry.[15]

A famous anecdote describes his philosophy best: when he was offered a pair of scissors by a disciple, he refused it saying that he'd rather be the needle that darns, than the scissors which cuts. Some of his teachings were:

1. Pray to God alone, for everyone else takes away but He gives.
2. Do not utter a truth which resembles a lie.
3. Do not regard the ignorant as amongst the living.
4. Avoid the ignorant who pose as though they were wise.
5. Do not satisfy the demands of the carnal self for its demands know no limits.[16]

Baba Farid passed away on 6 October 1266. He died while prostrating. As he lived, so he died – in the path of Allah.

He left behind seven *khalifa*s, but it was to the most famous of them, Hazrat Nizamuddin Auliya, that he passed on the cloak he had received from his *pir*, Qutub Sahib. It was Hazrat Nizamuddin Auliya who would firmly establish the Chishti *silsilah* not only in Delhi but in various parts of the Indian subcontinent, ensuring that to date the *silsilah* remains the most popular in this part of the world, even if it remained comparatively unknown outside.

Hazrat Nizamuddin Auliya, popularly known as Mehboob-e-Ilahi (beloved of God) and Sultan ji, short for Sultan-ul-Mashaikh (king of saints), was born in 1238 in Badayun, a town in present-day Uttar Pradesh. He was named Muhammad at his birth. His grandparents had migrated from Bukhara to Badayun sometime between 1202–09 in the wake of the Mongol attacks. His father, Ahmed, died when he was five years old. He was brought up by his mother Bibi Zulaikha, an extremely pious lady.

Despite severe financial hardships, Bibi Zulaikha ensured the best for her children, and that made sure her son was educated by the best scholars of Badayun. She then shifted to Delhi so he could continue his education once she felt her son had outgrown what Badayun had to offer. Nizamuddin was 16 at that time.

During this time, due to their strained circumstances, there would often be no food at home. On such days, she would tell her son, 'Nizam! Today we are the guests of Allah'. Bibi Zulakiha had complete faith in God's will and taught her children that He would send spiritual nourishment. Before she passed away, she entrusted them to God's care.

In Delhi, they lived in a rented house next to that of Sheikh Najibuddin Mutawakkil, the brother of Baba Farid. The young Nizamuddin expressed a desire to become a *qazi* and asked Sheikh Najibuddin Mutawakkil to pray for him. The latter dissuaded him from being a *qazi* and asked him to be something else.

One night, while he was praying the *tahajjud* (supererogatory prayers) in the Jama Masjid of Delhi (today famous as the Quwwat-ul Islam Mosque in Mehrauli), he heard the call for the dawn prayers. The muezzin recited a verse from the Quran:

Has not the time arrived
For the believers that
Their hearts in all humility
Should engage in the remembrance of Allah?

– Quran 57:16

When he was 12 years old, Nizamuddin had already heard of Baba Farid's *jamatkhana* and the discussions held there, from Abu Bakr Kharrat, a musician in Badayun. He felt a spiritual and emotional bonding with the saint since and had a longing to go there. Feeling emotionally overwrought, he immediately left for Ajodhan to meet Baba Farid. The year was 1257/58, and Nizamuddin was 20 years old.

When he reached Ajodhan, the 90-year-old saint welcomed him with this verse:

The fire of your separation has burnt many hearts,
The storm of [the] desire to meet you has ravaged many lives.[17]

Baba Farid saw his nervousness and welcomed him, asking his disciples to give the youth a bed in the *jamatkhana*. Nizamuddin was hesitant as other devotees and people who knew the Quran by heart were sleeping on the floor. However, he relented when he was asked if he would disobey the master.

Nizamuddin was immediately initiated, and contrary to a rule that was meant to help disciples rid themselves of worldly conceit, Baba Farid didn't ask this young disciple who had long, curly hair to shave it off. Nizamuuddin had not wanted to shave his head in his heart of hearts, but later when he saw the others, he requested permission for the same and it was granted. He thus became like everyone else.[18]

Baba Farid encouraged him to continue his studies along with his prayers and to immerse himself in ascetic exercises in Delhi. In Ajodhan, Nizamuddin learnt patience, tolerance and how to deal with people. No one ever left the *jamatkhana* of Baba Farid dissatisfied or hurt.

Nizamuddin visited Ajodhan twice after that. He was given permission to initiate people into the order. On his third and final visit in June 1265, Baba Farid gave him his *khilafat nama* (letter of succession) and blessed him saying, 'You will be a tree under whose soothing shadow the people will find comfort.'[19]

Nizamuddin had been given the 'spiritual empire of Hindustan' by Baba Farid and told to go and take it, but he remained undecided whether to stay on in Delhi or move to some provincial town. Ultimately, he decided to stay in the capital of the Delhi Sultanate, living in appalling poverty for many years and shifting many residences. Eventually he settled down in Ghiyaspur on the banks of the river Yamuna, now famous as Hazrat Nizamuddin Basti. A quiet village at that time, it became much busier after Sultan Balban's death when his grandson shifted his capital to Kilokari (1288–1289) near modern-day Maharani Bagh.

Hazrat Nizamuddin Auliya wanted to leave Ghiyaspur when a handsome stranger appeared and said:

> That day that you became the moon you did not know
> That to behold you throngs and throngs would forward press.

Today, when the hearts of all are trapped by your cress,
To remain in seclusion is worse than useless.[20]

He went on to advise the saint to stay amongst the people, for true benefit comes from serving them and not turning a deaf ear to them. 'What power, what gain is there in retreating from people and immersing yourself in God?'[21]

Ghiyaspur continued to flourish under Alauddin Khilji. By that time Hazrat Nizamuddin's own reputation had grown, and he attracted many disciples from amongst royalty, nobility, and the common people. He refused to entertain or meet royalty but kept an open door for the needy. It was under him that the Chishti *silsilah* grew immensely. He sent 700 disciples to open *khanqah*s in various parts of the country, and from the Deccan to Bengal, Gujarat to Bihar, and Awadh to Rajasthan, his disciples established *khanqah*s and taught the lesson of love.

As Hazrat Amir Khusrau said:

You have put the beads of Shaykh Farid in a rosary.
It is on this count that your title has become Nizam (stringer of pearls).[22]

Unlike his spiritual master, Hazrat Nizamuddin did not practice ascetism, or do *chillah*s for penance. He drove the devil out 'by the quiet joy that inspired his heart',[23] and his greatest miracle was the greatness of his sympathetic and inclusive heart. His doors were wide open for all and people from every class and creed came to his *khanqah*; he talked to each of them according to their own knowledge and understanding. He initiated many into the Chishti *silsilah* himself. He accepted all who came without enquiring about their antecedents, for he believed that everyone should be able to benefit from him.

It was this policy of universal admission that turned 'a mystic movement which earlier aimed at mere[ly] individual[s] into a mass movement for the spiritual culture of man. It marks the beginning of a new phase in the history of Islamic mysticism in South Asia.'[24]

Like his master, he darned the social fabric in India and spread spiritual enlightenment. His belief, in his own words, was:

*Har Qaum raast raahe*
*Din wa qibla gaahe.*

[Every people has a path, a religion and a focus of devotion.]

Thus, like the Sufi saints before him, he attracted people of every faith and religion.

*Fawaid al-Fuad* describes a very interesting conversation between Hazrat Nizamuddin Auliya and a yogi who had come to his *jamatkhana*. Asked for the secret behind and real essence of his mystic path, the yogi responded:

> [A]ccording to our doctrines the self of man is composed of two regions, one is spiritual and the other is profane. From the crown to the head to the navel is the spiritual region and from the navel to the foot is profane. The essence of the doctrine is that the spiritual region is all truth, purity and ethics. The profane region demands strenuous efforts for self-control and morality.

This impressed the saint greatly.[25]

The saint steadfastly refused to meet the Delhi Sultans, who were influenced by him or his teachings, and kept away from the corridors of power. However, he was caught in the political upheavals that followed the death of Alauddin Khilji.

A protégé of Alauddin Khilji's son Mubarak Shah, Khusrau Khan assassinated his master and ascended the throne. He gave the Sufi saints of Delhi large sums of money to ensure his success as a ruler. Hazrat Nizamuddin Auliya accepted the gift of 5,00,000 tankas and distributed it amongst his followers.

When Khusrau Khan was overthrown by Malik, who took over the throne of Delhi as Ghiyasuddin Tughlaq Shah, the latter recalled the money from these saints. Hazrat Nizamuddin refused to refund the money saying that it was *bait al-maal* (from the public treasury), and he had anyway already distributed it to the deserving, without keeping a single coin for himself. Though the Sultan stayed silent at that time, this incident attracted royal displeasure in the long term, and led to a conflict that continued till the Sultan's death.

There is a legend that the Sultan in fact ordered the saint to leave Delhi, threatening to have him killed on his return from Bengal. The saint continued living there in contentment and full faith in God, using the now famous phrase '*Hanuz Dilli dur ast*' (Delhi is yet far away). Ghiyasuddin Tughlaq Shah never returned to Delhi; he died when the tent built by his son Muhammad (who reigned as Muhammad bin Tughlaq) to felicitate him, collapsed.

Professor Muhammad Habib writes that this story appears to be a later-day fabrication as neither Ziauddin Barani nor Amir Khurd, the two main historians from this period, mention anything concerning the 'unpleasantness between the two old men, who were so eminently virtuous in their different spheres of life.'[26]

Hazrat Nizamuddin Auliya passed away on 3 April 1325. Sheikh al-Islam Sheikh Ruknuddin Multani led his funeral prayers. Muhammad bin Tughlaq is said to have been one of the pallbearers.

Though the Hazrat had wanted a simple open grave, a dome was built over it by the Tughlaq sultan. Today, his grave is one of the most popular dargahs visited by people from all classes and walks of life.

Peerzada Altamash Nizami, one of his direct descendants who has been giving *haziri* (attendance) at the dargah all his life, says that he has seen heads of states, film stars, Sufi saints, priests from other religions, and writers, intellectuals, students, and ordinary folk visiting. Most stop by to ask for the saint's intercession as they pray for their problems to be solved; a few come because it's a popular tourist spot, and some just to hear the qawwalis – but none go away unmoved by the atmosphere.

Still, Hazrat Nizamuddin Auliya's life is yet to be fully appreciated. In author Mohammad Habib's words:

> The Shaikh's [Hazrat Nizamuddin's] life was, in fact, the embodiment of what psychological research shall one day prove to be the deepest principle of our human nature: that salvation, or happiness in its highest form, lies not in a war with attractions of worldly life or in indifference to them, but in a healthy

> development of 'cosmic emotion' in a sympathetic identification of the individual with his environment, so that the distinction of the *I* and *not-I* disappears in a mystic absorption of the human soul in the Absolute.[27]

Before his death, Hazrat Nizamuddin Auliya had ensured that not a morsel of food was left in the *langarkhana* (community kitchen), and everything had been distributed to the poor. He called for his meagre bundles of clothing and from it gave away small portions to those followers whom he wanted to appoint as his *khalifa*s. He gave Maulana Burhanuddin one of his *dastar*s (turban), a robe and the sheet he used for prayer and sent him to Deccan. (The city of Burhanpur in the Deccan was named after him.) Another *dastar* (turban), a robe and a sheet he used for prayer were given to Sheikh Yaqub, whom he sent to Gujarat. Similarly, Maulana Shihabuddin Imam, Maulana Shamsuddin Yahya, and Maulana Jamaluddin Khwarizmi were also given a *dastar* and other personal belongings.

To everyone's surprise, the day he distributed all his meagre possessions, he gave nothing to Sheikh Nasiruddin Mahmud. But after prayers on Wednesday, he called him and gave him the beads, wooden bowl and all that he had got from his master Baba Farid, asking him to stay in Delhi, look after the people there and ease their oppression.[28]

The beloved of Allah was thus succeeded in Delhi by the lamp of the city, Sheikh Nasiruddin Mahmud who was popularly known as Roshan Chiragh-e-Dilli (lamp of Delhi). Nasiruddin was the last great Chishti saint of Delhi and the *khalifa* (successor) of Hazrat Nizamuddin Auliya. He was born in Awadh (present-day Uttar Pradesh), and the *Siyar al-Arifin* in fact says that his name was Hazrat Sheikh-ul-al-Mashaikh Naseer-ul-Millat wa din Mahmood Awadhi.

His father Sheikh Yahya, an affluent wool merchant, died when he was nine years old. His mother, a very pious and devout lady, was very particular about his education. He acquired knowledge under excellent teachers but his mind was more attracted to the life of an ascetic, and at the age of 25 he chose a life of solitude, with which he began to concentrate on devotion and self-improvement.

At the age of 43, Sheikh Nasiruddin came to Delhi and was admitted as a disciple of Hazrat Nizamuddin Auliya; he remained in attendance there, going to Awadh only to visit his mother and sister. He was very popular with the mendicants who took to calling him *ganj* (storehouse/treasure), as he was indeed a spiritual treasure to them.[29]

He wanted to leave Delhi and go away to a quieter and less populated place, but Hazrat Nizamuddin Auliya dissuaded him, saying he had to stay, to serve the people, and bear the oppression and injustice that came his way as a result.[30]

Sheikh Nasiruddin Roshan Chiragh-e-Dilli was very different from his master and was indifferent to poetry and *sama*. Even today, unlike other Chishti shrines, there are no qawwals sitting in the courtyard of his dargah. The qawwals perform there only during his *urs*. The Sheikh preferred a reclusive life and though he himself prostrated before his *pir*, he discouraged the custom for himself.

He escaped the forced migration to Daulatabad under the reign of Sultan Muhammad bin Tughlaq; hundreds of Sufis had to shift to his new capital at the time. But he was compelled to travel and serve as a *jamdar* (one who helps with dressing up) to the Sultan. He bore it with fortitude nevertheless, following his master's advice, and never sought royal patronage. Nor did he give the royals importance over others. Sultan Firoz Shah Tughlaq who was his devotee had to wait his turn to meet the saint like the rest.[31]

Like the other Chishti saints, he too lived an ascetic life, spending his time in prayers and self-mortification. He believed that if a Sufi went to bed hungry and woke up in the early hours to practice meditation, they would experience a divine light in their soul.[32]

During meditation he would practice breath control; he believed that a Sufi was a master of articulated breath (*sahib-e-anfas*) and each breath should be measured. This is a practice very similar to that of yogis. Many Sufi practices do, in fact, resonate with Yogic philosophy. Dara Shukoh has quoted a disciple of Miyan Mir in *Sakinatal-Auliya*, saying that the saint didn't sleep at night and would often pass the entire night in one breath. Dara Shukoh himself also practiced breath control, as did many saints.

Once, while he was praying in the solitude of his room, a *qalandar* named Turabi stabbed him, but the Sheikh did not deviate from his namaz. Later he forgave the would-have-been assassin and helped him escape from Delhi and the wrath of his followers.

Sheikh Nasiruddin Mahmud left this world on 14 September 1356.

He did not consider any of his vast number of disciples to be worthy of the honour of bestowing the relics he had received from his spiritual master, so he instructed that they be buried with him. Thus, as per his instructions, the patched garment he got from Hazrat Nizamuddin Auliya was placed on his chest and the Hazrat's stick was placed by his side, the beads [rosary] of the Hazrat, the spiritual guide, tied on his index finger and in place of the brick, the wooden sprouted jar [used for ablutions] placed under his head, and even the wooden sandals were placed in his embrace.[33]

Some of these relics would have been the ones passed down from Khwaja Muinuddin Chishti to Qutub Sahib, then Baba Farid, Hazrat Nizamuddin Auliya, and finally, to Sheikh Nasiruddin. It shows the importance they were accorded. This unorthodox mode of burial was to prevent any misuse or misappropriation of these relics after his passing away, and so nobody could claim that they were given to them in order to become the *khalifa*.

Sheikh Nasiruddin Roshan Chiragh-e-Dilli's most famous disciple is Khwaja Gesu Daraz Banda Nawaz who settled in the Deccani city of Gulbarga. He was present, according to Maulana Jamali, at the time of his death and funeral. He took out a rope from the cot on which the *ghusl* (funeral bath) was given and tied it around his neck saying that this was his patched garment.

Popularly known as Khwaja Banda Nawaz Gesu Daraz (1321–1422), Saiyed Muhammad ibn Yusuf al-Husayni moved to Gulbarga during his master's lifetime. His father Syed Yusuf, also known as Raja Qattal, was a Sufi saint. Khwaja Banda Nawaz Gesu Daraz was ordered by Sultan Muhammad bin Tughlaq to shift to Daulatabad in the Deccan. When he returned some years later to Delhi, he became the disciple of Sheikh Nasiruddin to whom he was greatly devoted.

A popular story describes how once while walking alongside his master's palanquin his long hair got tangled in its wooden legs. As he did not want to disturb his master, he continued walking, hiding his pain and discomfort. This was how it came to pass that the master gave him the title of Gesu Daraz (one with long locks).

Khwaja Gesu Daraz moved to Gulbarga on the eve of Timur's invasion of Delhi and was responsible for spreading the Chishti Sufi message there. He was very similar in his devotional practices to his spiritual master's master Hazrat Nizamuddin Auliya. He avoided the company of the wealthy, preferring to maintain a veil of secrecy around his mystical accomplishments.[34] The compositions of this saint who was so fond of verse survive even now. He was also devoted to *sama mehfil*s as a means of spiritual growth. Adapting quickly to the ways of the Deccan, Khwaja Gesu Daraz established the Chishti *silsilah* in the region.

Ahmad, the brother of the Bahmani Sultan Tajuddin Firoz (1397–1422), became his disciple and built a *khanqah* for him. When the saint refused to endorse the Sultan's good-for-nothing son as the next ruler, throwing his weight behind Ahmad instead, he was banished from the city. This was how he came to the spot where his dargah was later built. In time, Ahmad went on to become the Sultan.

Though Ahmad shifted to Bidar, he continued to be devoted to the saint, and after he passed away built a massive dome on his dargah. It is said to be the largest ever dome to shelter a shrine. The dargah complex itself is massive, dominated as it is by the white-domed structure, yet it is also beautiful and serene. One of the most popular dargahs in the Deccan, it is always full of visitors from far and wide. As per the Chishti tradition, women are not allowed inside.

No discussion on the Chishti saints can be complete without talking of Amir Khusrau referred to fondly as Hazrat Amir Khusrau. I often go to his shrine to ask the man called the Tuti-e-Hind (parrot of India) to supplicate Allah on my behalf for increase in my knowledge and power to my pen as a *sadqa* for his master.

Amir Khusrau was not an Auliya, but he was Mehboob-e-Ilahi's favourite disciple and the man responsible for some of the most enduring verses that colour our Sufi experiences.

*Khabaram raseed imshab ki nigaar khwahi aamad*
*Sar-e man fidaa-e raah-e ki sawaar khwahi aamad*

[Tonight I received word that you, O beloved, would come;
May my head be sacrificed to the road along which you come riding.]

– Amir Khusrau

Amir Khusrau was born as Abul Hasan Yameenuddin in Patiyali village of modern-day Kasganj, in 1253, to Amir Saifuddin Turk Lachin Mahmood, a Turkish soldier from Balkh, and an Indian woman. His maternal grandfather Imad-ul-Mulk Rawat Arz was Sultan Balban's minister of war. It is said that when he was born, his father swaddled him in a piece of cloth and took him to a mystic neighbour. The mystic cast a glance at the baby and said, 'Amir Lachin, you have brought to me one who will go two steps beyond Khaqani.'

There is a popular story that describes the first meeting of a young Khusrau with Hazrat Nizamuddin. The former had composed a quatrain sitting on the steps of Hazrat Nizamuddin's *khanqah*. He remarked: 'I shall choose my "*pir*/spiritual guide" myself, and if bestowed with Divine Power, he will converse with me even from a distance.' The saint replied and the boy became his disciple.

This is however, not born out by biographical account of Amir Khusrau from Amir Khurd's *Siyar al-Awliya* or *Biography of Saints*. The saint was a tenant of Amir Khusrau's maternal grandfather in Delhi and that is where they met. Hazrat Nizamuddin Auliya had a great affection for him and 'singled [him] out for all kinds of favours and kindnesses and held [him] in special regard. In those days, Sultan al-Mashayikh used to live in the house of Ravat-i'Arz, the maternal grandfather of Amir Khusraw, near the Manda bridge gate.'[35]

According to one legend, Mehboob-e-Ilahi – as Hazrat Nizamuddin was called – rubbed his *luab-e-dahan* (saliva) on his disciple's lips, and that led to his voice and words becoming sweeter. He then recited the verse:

> While your tresses shed lovers' blood from both sides,
> Your face, in the middle, robs them of any power to complain.[36]

Thus he received the title of Tuti-eHindustan (the parrot of Hindustan).

That was an era of cultural attainment and there were many incomparable poets in the Khilji Sultanate, but according to the famous historian Zaiuddin Barni:

> The incomparable Amir Khusrau stands unequalled for the volume of his writings and the originality of his ideals; for, while other great

> masters of prose and verse have excelled in one or two branches, Amir Khusrau was conspicuous in every department of letters. A man with such mastery over all forms of poetry has never existed in the past and may perhaps not come into existence before the Day of Judgment. He (Amir Khusrau) was one of the chief disciples of Sheikh Nizamuddin Auliya; and a disciple with a firmer faith in his master I have never seen. Of love and affection, too, he had his full share, and he was a man of ecstasy and rapture. He excelled in the playing and composition of music.[37]

After the congregation's night prayers, Hazrat Nizamuddin Auliya would retire to his room. Amir Khurd informs us that during that time none except Amir Khusrau could remain in the presence of the saint. The poet, who was always full of reports, news, and reviews, would talk about different matters as the Hazrat approvingly nodded his head. Sometimes the Hazrat would ask: 'What more, O Turk?' and Khusrau would offer an exposition on a whole different topic.[38]

Khusrau, a fervent devotee of Hazrat Nizamuddin Auliya, was devastated when the saint left this world. At the time, he was in Lakhnauti on official work and upon hearing the tragic news, he gave up all his worldly possessions, left the imperial service and immediately left for Delhi. He then composed and recited this *doha*:[39]

> *gori sove sej par mukh par daare kes*
> *chal Khusrau ghar apne saanjh bhain sau des*
>
> [The fair maiden rests [on the wreath of roses],
> Her tresses covering her face,
> Let us, Oh Khusrau, go back now,
> The dark dusk settles in four corners.]

Amir Khusrau refers not only to his own grief here but also that of the world. '[T]he gloom, which has enveloped the world after the saint's death, is also the darkness of ignorance, yet another veil, separating the Sufi from the Truth.'[40]

Though those around him tried to alleviate his agony, especially Sheikh Nasiruddin Chiragh-e-Dilli, but Khusrau was utterly inconsolable. He spent all of his last few months alive weeping at the foot of his master's shrine. Six months after this, he died at the age of 74 on a Friday, 20 Zil Qayda 725 AH (1324 CE).

Their love for each other had been so great that the Mehboob-e-Ilahi had said that Amir should be buried near him, as they could not share a grave as per Islam. And so he was buried at the Yaarani Chabutra – next to his spiritual master, Hazrat Nizamuddin Auliya.

For a long time, Amir Khusrau's grave had no dome or enclosure; one was built much later in 1014 AH/1605 CE. During the last years of Akbar and the initial years of Jahangir's reign, Imaduddin Hasan – known as Tahir – had an enclosure and a beautiful marble dome constructed on his grave, with the following verse inscribed on it:

> Oh matchless Khusrau,
> I have faith in your shrine.[41]

Hazrat Nizamuddin Auliya used to compare the poetic talent of Khusrau and Hasan using the following analogy: 'Our Khusrau is like a saltish river, while Hasan is like a sweetish rivulet.'[42]

Thus my visit to the Deccan took me to the shrine of Amir Hasan Sijzi, the writer of *Fawaid al-Fuad,* in Khuldabad.

Saiyid Zaheer Hussain Jafri, professor at the department of History at Delhi University, says that *Fu'ad* was the first book of its kind in India. It was for the first time that anyone had written about the day-to-day interactions, reactions and teachings of a Sufi sheikh in his *khanqah*. He says:

> In this book, you find the principles of Sufism being talked about in the simplest of terms by the great Sheikh, and we also see that every section of society is represented. The Sheikh is not only talking to the elites but to the common man as well. It's not that Sheikhs didn't speak earlier, but a mature scholar, recognizing the value of these discourses, recorded it for posterity. The entire book is in the

> form of conversations supported by examples. It is a lively speech that captures the reader's imagination.[43]

The saint himself checked the account for veracity. Very simply written, this book is an important historical, social, and literary document as it recorded life and society at the time.

Professor K.A. Nizami has written in his preface to the *Fu'ad*'s English translation by Bruce Lawrence: 'It soon found a distinctive place in Muslim mystic literature.' In fact, Amir Khusrau offered to exchange all his works for it.

> In the lanes of taverns and the inns of vagabonds
> There is no restriction – come, sit and be at home.[44]
>
> – Amir Hasan Sijzi

When I reached Khuldabad, I had to ask many people about the shrine. I was told to look out for a big gate with an old man sitting in front of it. This was to the west of Khuldabad and it seemed as though not many people visit it. I found the old man, the caretaker, sitting in front of the big gate, which he opened when my car stopped before it. He took me inside and I offered my prayers.

It is believed that the original copy of the *Fawaid al-Fu'ad* is buried with Amir Hasan Sijzi, as per his will. The caretaker told me that children who can't talk are brought to this shrine and given sugar, which is believed to give them the power of speech. On hearing that I was a writer, the caretaker offered me some sugar to sweeten my pen. I pray that it works.

# 6

# The Suhrawardis

If a heart has no burning love for God, it is merely a dead piece of flesh, but if it possesses the love of God, it is a mirror of divine presence and blessings.

– Sheikh Bahauddin Zakariya

Bengal was called the chief centre of the Islamic world; one of the reasons for this was the Suhrawardi saint, Sheikh Jalaluddin Tabrizi. When I visit his Badi Dargah in West Bengal's Pandua district, I can sense divine blessings. Standing in one of the earliest parts of the dargah, the sun setting on the pond, I experience the sense of serenity and calm that has always enveloped me when I visit places with spiritual energy. Most visitors have not yet evolved enough to feel love for the divine, but a mortal's love for their children, relatives, and partners, and the saint's famed powers to intercede with Allah draw them to it.

A couple of girls sitting near the pond with their feet dangling in the air tell me about a henna tree here, which they have come to visit to pray for a good match. The tree has many petitions tied to its branches. Praying for a wide range of things, from marriages and the welfare of children to health and prosperity, devotees flock here from near and far. The *khadim*s (hereditary caretakers) were very welcoming and showed me all the relics so I could seek the blessings attached to them.

The Suhrawardi *silsilah* originated in Iraq in the twelfth century and spread throughout the Muslim world. One of the earliest Sufi *silsilah*s, it is known for its strict spiritual observances and discipline, including the ritual prayers that repeatedly invoke the seven names of God. It lays emphasis on the observance of external forms of religious belief and advocates a fusion of *ilm* (scholarship) with mysticism.

The Suhrawadi order was founded by Sheikh Shihabuddin Abu Hafs Suhrawardi (1145–1234) who was initiated into Sufism by his uncle, Sheikh Abun Najib Suhrawardi, a disciple of Ahmad al-Ghazali. Sheikh Shihabuddin Abu Hafs Suhrawardi was a great scholar who wrote the *Awarif al-Ma'arif* (The Gifts of Spiritual Perceptions), which became one of the most popular Sufi books for seekers to read, memorize, and study regularly. 'This book marks a watershed in the reconciliation of Sufism with orthodoxy.'[1]

He used the Quranic verses to support his theory that knowledge, not in the legalistic exoteric sense but in the spiritual esoteric sense, are the basis of Sufism. According to him, the Quranic term 'those firmly rooted in knowledge' applies to those whose hearts have a total perception of truth, and this knowledge cannot be learnt in schools. It is a legacy from the prophets and can be learnt only from them.[2]

In *Fawaid al-Fu'ad*, there is a reference to Baba Farid using a copy of the *Awarif al-Ma'arif* to provide *fawaid* (morals) for his disciples. As the script on the copy was not very clear, Hazrat Nizamuddin Auliya suggested that he take his brother Sheikh Najibuddin Mutawakkil's copy instead. This lead to Baba Farid getting angry with his disciple. The script was faint and contained numerous errors. In the *Fawaid*, Nizamuddin Auliya records, '[T]his remark greatly offended my master. For an hour he kept asking: "Has the dervish *no* power to correct a defective manuscript?"'

Sheikh Shihabuddin was sent by the Abbasid Caliph Al-Nasir li-Din Allah (r. 1180–1225) as his ambassador to various Islamic countries.

He believed that there are two types of Sufis: those whose spiritualism was based on their own perceptions and those whose path to spiritual enlightenment was caused by self-deprivation. According to him, reason and intellectual discussions did not lead to the path of Sufism; rather it was hunger, abstention, and the renunciation of all things, including those that were permitted in Islam.[3] However, he reminded Sufis that mysticism was not the same as poverty or asceticism, though they nevertheless could lead to *fana* (annihilation). He felt that a fakir who had made *faqr* (poverty) as his goal was inferior to the real Sufi as this was just one of the stations of the Path.

According to Sheikh Shihabuddin, opposing wealth obsessively was in itself a weakness, and a true Sufi would not differentiate between wealth and poverty, fear, or recompense. These things created a dependence on the idea of causation and the expectation of a reward.

The Suhrawardi saints were thus not against accepting grants and gifts from the kings, and believed that a Sufi should own property, knowledge, and mystical enlightenment in order to serve the poor better.

The sheikh agreed with other orthodox Sufis in that people with spiritual knowledge were not exempt from the shariah. He believed that reality and the law were interdependent.

He had many disciples. From among them, he appointed *khalifa*s to spread the Suhrawardi *silsilah* in other parts of the world. Many of these disciples travelled around the Islamic world. Several also came to the Indian subcontinent, but the three that really brought the Suhrawardiya *silsilah* to India were: Sheikh Bahauddin Zakariya, Sheikh Jalaluddin Tabrizi, and Sheikh Hamiduddin Nagore. The first two belonged to India and travelled to Baghdad where they became disciples of Sheikh Shihabuddin. Upon their return, they spread the knowledge of the *silsilah* and their teachings in India.

Like the Chisti *silsilah*, the Suhrawardi order and its saints were very popular in the Indian subcontinent in the early medieval period and continue to remain so to date. The spread of the Suhrawardi *silsilah* in India has been linked to the efforts and popularity of Sheikh Bahauddin and Sheikh Jalaluddin, both disciples of Sheikh Shihabuddin Abu Hafs Suhrawardi.

Among the most famous Suhrawardi saints was Sheikh Bahauddin Zakariya, born in 1182 in the Multani village called Kat Karor. He was a contemporary of Baba Farid and Qutub Sahib, and had amiable relations with them. A pious child, he had learned the entire Quran by heart. His father, Khwaja Wajihuddin, died when he was 12 years old and he went to Khurasan for further studies of the esoteric and exoteric branches of knowledge. Later he went to Bukhara.

He acquired great fame in both Khurasan and Bukhara, earning the title of *ferishta* (angel) in the latter on account of his extreme chastity and piety. He went to Mecca to perform the hajj pilgrimage and stayed in the two holy cities of Mecca and Medina for five years, engrossed in devotion and acquiring knowledge of hadiths from Sheikh Kamaluddin Muhammad Yemeni, one of the most famous religious scholars of his age. Sheikh Kamaluddin certified him as a scholar of hadiths and gave him written permission to teach them to others.[4]

His next destination was Baghdad; there he met Sheikh Shihabuddin Suhrawardi and became his disciple. His training lasted for only 17 days, after which Sheikh Shihabuddin made him his *khalifa*. The pre-existing disciples who had been there for many years were naturally upset at his elevation in the order in such a short time. Sheikh Shihabuddin, on hearing of it, said that when these disciples had come to him, they were like green wood that would not catch fire, whereas Sheikh Bahauddin 'was like dry wood, which had begun to burn with a single breath'.[5]

After this, Sheikh Bahauddin returned to Multan.[6] There the holy men and religious dignitaries requested him to settle somewhere else through the symbolic gesture of sending him a cup full of milk. The sheikh, understanding the meaning, returned the cup by placing a rose on the milk. The cup symbolized that the city was already brimming with the presence of innumerable scholars and holy men, and the rose placed by the sheikh indicated that he would be like that rose in the milk and would meld in and add value.

Following the Suhrawardi philosophy that Sufis should maintain a relationship with rulers and officials, he had a very good relationship with Sultan Iltutmish who conferred the title Sheikh al-Islam on him. This was an honorary title signifying his elevated status amongst religious dignitaries, but it carried with it monetary stipends and lands.

During the struggle between Sultan Iltutmish and Nasiruddin Qubacha, the ruler of Multan, the saint openly favoured the Delhi Sultan who wanted to add Multan and Sind to the Delhi Sultanate. In 1228, Multan and Sind were annexed by Sultan Iltutmish.

The Sheikh was extremely popular in and around Multan and used his fame and influence, to successfully negotiate peace with the Mongols, who besieged the Multan fort in 1247.[7]

Sheikh Bahauddin preached that Sufis should not seek multiple *pir*s; rather they should stay with one. Emphasizing the significance of namaz, he is known to have said that all his accomplishments were due to his daily prayers.

He died on 21 December 1262. His dargah in Multan (present-day Pakistan), with its warm bricks and blue ceramics, is an architectural beauty and perhaps the earliest example of tilework in the subcontinent. It was built during his lifetime, in 1236.

Fakhruddin Iraqi (1213–1289) was a well-known Persian poet and disciple of Sheikh Bahauddin Zakariya. His songs continue to be sung at his master's tomb in Multan even today.

In *Siyar al-Arifin*, Maulana Jamali narrates a story about him that goes as follows. Once Sheikh Bahauddin Zakariya was sitting on a cot and had taken off his *dastar* (turban), unwound it and put the cloth on one of the sides of the cot. His son, Sheikh Sadruddin Arif, was sitting respectfully on his knees on the floor, and Sheikh Arif's four-year-old son, Ruknuddin, was tottering around the cot, clutching at each of its sides for support as he went along. When he reached the side where the turban cloth was kept, he picked it up and put it on his head. The father immediately scolded him for being disrespectful and asked him to put it down. Sheikh Bahauddin asked his son not to scold the boy saying that the boy had placed it on his head as he was worthy of it, and that he granted the dastar to him. Sheikh Ruknuddin wore the same turban when he succeeded his father Sheikh Sadruddin Arif (d.1286).

As per the custom, the *khirqa* (patched garment) which had in turn been given by Sheikh Shihabuddin to Sheikh Bahauddin was passed on to Sheikh Sadruddin Arif, and then to Sheikh Ruknuddin at the time of their initiation.

Sheikh Ruknuddin, also known as Shah Rukn-e-Alam (the pillar or the world), was extremely popular. He visited Delhi twice under Sultan Alauddin Khilji's rule; both times, the Sultan rode out to meet him and then later to see him off. He visited Delhi thrice in the reign of Sultan Alauddin's son, Sultan Qutbuddin Mubarak Shah.

Just as his grandfather had been on very amicable terms with Qutub Sahib and Baba Farid, Sheikh Ruknuddin had great respect and affection for Hazrat Nizamuddin Auliya and said that he travelled to Delhi primarily to meet the great Sufi. A simple mosque which exists even today in Delhi was the Jama Masjid of Kilokari; it bears witness to their many meetings. Sheikh Ruknuddin and Hazrat Nizamuddin said their Friday prayers there.

Some parts of the medieval mosque still exists, but most of it has had a makeover to serve the needs of modern worshippers.

It is said that since Hazrat Nizamuddin did not visit the royal court; he passed on all the petitions of the people of Delhi to Sheikh Ruknuddin, who would then take them to the reigning Sultan for consideration.[8]

Sheikh Ruknuddin died in 1334. He was initially buried in his grandfather's tomb, but later shifted to the present tomb built by Sultan Ghiyasuddin Tughlaq in Multan. It is a popular pilgrimage spot and is now a UNESCO heritage site. His *urs* is celebrated for three days every year at his tomb from the 6th to the 9th of Jumada.

After Sheikh Ruknuddin's death, the Suhrawardi *silsilah* became popular in Bengal and Bihar. In Bihar, it later led to the establishment of an offshoot – the Firdausi *silsilah*, another popular medieval *silsilah* in the subcontinent.

The other saint who along with Sheikh Bahauddin has been credited with increasing the reach of the Suhrawardi *silsilah*, as mentioned before, is Sheikh Jalaluddin Tabrizi. He was responsible for spreading the message of the *silsilah* to Bengal and other parts of eastern India. The sheikh had studied in many places, including Bukhara, before becoming a disciple of Sheikh Shihabuddin. The sheikh and his father had been disciples of Sheikh Abu Said Tabrizi, but after the death of his father he decided to go to Baghdad.

When Sheikh Jalaluddin became a disciple of Sheikh Shihabuddin, the great Sufi was getting on in years. In spite of this, Sheikh Shihabuddin performed a pilgrimage to Mecca every year. But doing so was becoming increasingly difficult, because he could no longer consume cold food. Sheikh Jalaluddin devised a method whereby he could keep food warm by storing it in special pots. He carried these pots on his head. Sheikh Jalaluddin served his teacher with absolute dedication for seven years.

Upon completion of his training, Sheikh Jalaluddin travelled back to India. He made his way to Delhi where Sultan Shamsuddin Iltutmish received him warmly. The saint's coming to Delhi was resented by the Sheikh al-Islam, Najmuddin Sughra. An interesting anecdote regarding this pertains to the time when Sultan Iltutmish asked Najmuddin Sughra to assign a house to him. Najmuddin Sughra assigned a house named Bait al-Jinn (house of jinn), which was believed to be haunted by evil spirits. His explanation for this was that the spirits could not harm a man as spiritually perfect as the sheikh, and if they did he wasn't perfect after all! To Najmuddin Sughra's amazement, the spirits departed before the sheikh could enter the house.[9] However, the animosity continued, and finally the court intrigues and jealousies compelled Sheikh Jalaluddin to leave Delhi as they contributed to his unhappiness in the city.

Sheikh Jalaluddin ultimately settled in Lakhnauti (present-day Gaur in West Bengal). There he built a *khanqah* that had many gardens and he gathered several disciples. He remained in Lakhnauti for some years, but then moved to Devatalla or Dev Mahal near Pandua in West Bengal. The sheikh was popular among Hindus and Buddhists as well as Muslims in the area. His reputation attracted many visitors, which eventually led to the place being known as Tabrizabad.

His popularity was such that he inspired the writing of a Sanskrit biography, *Shek Subhodaya* (*The Blessed Advent of the Sheikh*).

However, nothing is known about his disciples, and by the fifteenth century, the Jalali Suhrawardi saints of Bengal were forgotten. In the pre-Mughal times of the fourteenth and fifteenth centuries, it was in the north-west part of the subcontinent that the Suhrawardi saints flourished. We know of the later Suhrawardis of Multan mainly from the Chishti records and *tazkiras* (Sufi hagiographies), as the records of the Suhrawardis themselves have not survived.

That is thankfully not the case with the shrine associated with Sheikh Jalaluddin Tabrezi in Pandua in West Bengal; his Badi Dargah (*badi* means 'big') is extremely popular. It has several buildings, some of which were built by Sheikh Jalaluddin, while other saints added to it over time. There is in addition to the dargah, a *chillahkhana* (a place to retreat), a *tanurkhana* (kitchen where the langar might have been prepared), a store house and a *salami darwaza* (entrance gate). Devatalla, also called Tabrizabad, close to Pandua has relics that prove that the sheikh lived many years of his life there. There is a theory that he was buried there,[10] but his place of burial is not known for certain. He passed away sometime in the mid-thirteenth century; the exact date is uncertain.

Badi Dargah, situated on the edge of a pond, remains popular even today. The place where he sat for his prayers has been covered with *chaddar*s and flowers and acts like a shrine in a normal dargah. Though most of the building is medieval, the mosque has been renovated and made quite modern. A marble imprint of the Prophet's foot is kept in the dargah, which is described in chapter 13.

Sheikh Hamiduddin Nagauri was born in Bukhara, and his birth name was Muhammad. He travelled to the Indian subcontinent from Uzbekistan with his father Ataullah Mahmud sometime before 1200. He was appointed the *qazi* (judge) of Nagaur by Sultan Iltutmish after the death of his father, who had held the post until then. He served in this role for three years before leaving for Baghdad to pursue his interest in Sufism. There he met Sheikh Shihabuddin Suhrawardi and became his disciple first, and later, *khalifa*. He should not be confused with Sheikh Hamiduddin Nagauri of the Chishti *silsilah*.

During his travels, he met Khwaja Qutbuddin Bakhtiyar Kaki (Qutub Sahib), and the two became close friends. Both of them were very fond of *sama mehfil*s and attended many together. An interesting anecdote regarding this is described in the *Fawaid al-Fu'ad*. Once, both Qutub Saheb and the *qazi* were attending a *sama* party in someone's house. Maulana Ruknuddin Samarqandi, who opposed *sama* parties, accompanied by some people, arrived to stop the party. The *qazi* told the owner of the house to hide so that the Maulana couldn't seek permission to enter the house. Entering anyone's house without permission is against the shariah, so the Maulana had to leave without creating any disturbance. And the *sama* continued!

The *qazi*'s knowledge of Islam and Islamic jurisprudence was enormous, and he had the honour of teaching Qutub Sahib the *Ulum-e-Zahiri* or 'external sciences'. Dara Shukoh too has praised his knowledge of the external sciences and internal sciences (*Ulum-e-Batini*) in his book, *Safinat al-Auliya*. His book *Lawa'ih* (*Flashes of light*) no longer exists, but was a very important text of its time and was used by Baba Farid while teaching his disciples. The three books of his that have survived are *Ishqiyya* (where he explains the relationship between the Sufi lover and Beloved God), *Tawali al-Shumus* (an exposition of God's names) and *Risala Min Kalam*. In *Ishqiyya*, he said that although the lover and beloved appear as two separate identities, they are in fact identical. According to him seeing the two separately is absurd, and anyone who can't see them at all is insane. Further:

> One who is lost in Being is a part of God's Attributes. This state makes Sufis present everywhere. The extinction of 'I' leads to the predominance of 'He'. Both Lover and Beloved mirror each other. Love is the source of everything that exists. Fear is the burning quality of love, air is the aspect of restlessness in love, water is the movement of lobe and earth its immutable aspect. The essence of all existent beings is Allah, everything else are His branches, which are dependent on the main trunk.[11]

In *Tawali al-Shumus* he gives a detailed exposition of Allah's name, referring to '*Huwa*' (pronounced hu and is literally the Arabic word for 'He') as the greatest name. This should bring to mind the great qawwalis which have the catch phrase *Allah Hu*!

The mystical insights of the *qazi* are amazing. For instance:

> When God is the first He is Rahman and when He is the last He is Rahim, hence every creature stands between the two attributes, that is everyone dwells between Rahman and Rahim. Rather the world is the dot of the [letter] 'nun' of Rahman. God is always looking with a merciful glance at that dot and everything is maintained because of that glance.[12]

A witty man, he refused to give payments to visiting dervishes saying that he too was running a spiritual shop so it was most improper of them to ask for anything.

It was in Qazi Hamiduddin Nagauri's lap that Qutub Sahib breathed his last. Later it was Qazi Hamiduddin Nagauri who passed on the late saint's relics to his successor, Baba Farid, who was not present at the time of the demise.

Qazi Hamiddudin died in 1245, and his grave is also in the same complex – close to his friend's shrine in Delhi's Mehrauli. It is on a high platform just outside the enclosure with Qutub Sahib's shrine, and it is easy to fancy that he is still there sitting with the saint's head on his lap.

At the entrance of his shrine this quatrain by him is inscribed on the wall:

*An aql kuja ki dar kamal-e to rasad*
*Van ruh kuja ki dar jalal-e to rasad*
*Giram ki to parda bar girifti zi jamal*
*An dida kuja ki dar jamal-e to rasad*

[Where's the mind to grasp Your sovereignty?
Where's the soul to mirror Your majesty?
Beauty's face, I know, You could unveil
But where are eyes to behold Your beauty?][13]

Mehrauli is also home to the shrine of another great Suhrawardi saint, and the two shrines are within walking distance.

Sheikh Makhdoom Samauddin Suharwardi (d.1496) was a very important saint of the Suharwardi order and was, along with his *khalifa* Sheikh Jamali, responsible for its popularity in Delhi. He was the disciplc of Hazrat Kabiruddin Ismail and a descendant of Sheikh Jalaluddin Makhdum-e-Jahaniyan Jahangasht (d. 1383), the world traveller instrumental in popularizing the *silsilah* in Uchh.

Sheikh Makhdoom Samauddin came from Bayana, where he had originally settled, to Delhi during the reign of Sultan Sikandar Lodi (1489–1517). Lodi had great respect for the saint and valued his opinion on matters of religion and state. Sheikh Makhdoom Samauddin had told the sultan in one of their discussions that 'there are three types of people who could never hope to receive blessings; one, is old men who sinned, second, young men who did likewise but hoped to repent at a later date, and the third, the king who lied'.[14]

He was as active in the field of letters as he was politically. He wrote *Miftah-ul Asrar* (*Key to the Divine Secrets*), and a commentary on the Suhrawardi poet Iraqi's book *Lamat*.

The saint died in 1496 and was buried at Mehrauli. According to legend, he had informed his disciples about the exact spot on the banks of Hauz-e-Shamsi where he wished to be buried, which was shown to him by Qutub Sahib in a dream.

While Sheikh Samuddin Suhrawardi's shrine is tucked away in the by lanes of Mehrauli, and only those who know of him go there, the shrine of his son-in-law Sheikh Jamali is extremely popular with tourists and has become a part of folklore. No longer open to tourists, the tomb is like a jewel box with glorious colours. It is one of the most exquisite tombs in India, with incised paintwork on the circular ceiling and the Sheikh's Persian verses inscribed along its circumference.

> On the day of separation from you in helplessness and loneliness,
> nothing consoles us but the sorrow we feel for you.
> O Jamali! Resort to the door of the friend,
> for our refuge is the door of the beloved.[15]

Better known as Sheikh Jamali or Dervesh Jamali Kambo Dehlvi, Sheikh Hamid bin Fazlullah was a renowned Sufi saint and a celebrated poet. In addition to being Sheikh Makhdoom Samauddin Suharwardi, he was also his disciple, and it was on his suggestion that he changed his pen name from Jalali (anger) to Jamali (beauty).

Sheikh Jamali was very devoted to his spiritual master and served him sincerely as long as he lived. His fame as a mystic was widespread, and Sultan Sikander Lodi was his devotee. The Mughal emperors Babur and Humayun also respected him and visited his house in Mehrauli in Delhi to pay him their respects.

Sheikh Jamali's famous work *Siyar-ul Arifin* (*Biographies of Mystics*) is a comprehensive and extensively quoted treatise on Sufi saints, which I too have used for this book.

He was a prolific poet and also wrote a masnavi (a poem written in rhyming couplets) called *Miihr o Mah* on the love story of a childless king of Badakshan who finally had a son thanks to the prayers of a mountain dervish. The young Prince grows up and falls in love with princess Mihr. The two meet after many adventures but are unable to get married, as the king dies before they can wed. The two die, distraught, one after another. The tomb of the prince, who died first, breaks in half and the princess is buried along with him.

Jamali was a favourite of Sultan Sikander Lodi, who was devoted to the poet saint's company. The former was the court poet and corrected the verses of the sultan, who wrote under the pen name Gul-rukhi.

He wrote a *qasida* (panegyric) on the Mughal victory in the battle of Panipat in 1526.

Jamali died on 1 May 1536 while on a trip to Gujarat with Emperor Humayun. His body was brought back and buried in the house where he had lived. His Persian couplets are incised on the borders of the house. One of them reads:

Cast your eyes upon Jamali with kindness
And do not look at his idleness and shortcomings.

# 7

## The Qadriyas

Listen to your heart and not your ego. Your ego prompts you to boast of vain assertions to obtain the glory of this world. Turn away from vanity and seek Him in the recesses of your heart and soul.

– Sheikh Abdul Qadir Jilani

Standing in the Akhund Shah mosque in Srinagar, I am transported back to the seventeenth century – to the time of a princess and a prince who had taken an oath of allegiance with a Qadriya saint and left a legacy of their faith in him. Jahanara Begum built a mosque and *khanqah* for her spiritual preceptor Mullah Shah Badakshi, a Qadriya saint. It came to be known as the Akhund Shah mosque, while Dara Shukoh built the Pari Mahal. The city still echoes of their devotion.

The Qadriya or Qadiri *silsilah* was named after Sheikh Abdul Qadir Jilani, who was born in 1077/78 in the town of Jilan in Iran. It is the oldest and a very important *silsilah* in the spiritual journey of Sufism. Sheikh Abdul Qadir Jilani preached that spiritual values far outweigh material ones, and that the latter only erodes social structures. His teachings impressed many, and the Qadriya *silsilah* formally came into being in Baghdad, 50 years after his death in 1166.

From Baghdad, the *silsilah* travelled to Morocco, Egypt, Central Asia, and finally India. Sheikh Abdul Qadir Jilani laid the spiritual foundation on which all the later *silsilah*s were built. He had said, 'My foot is on the neck of every saint of God.' The famous Sufi Ibn al-Arabi was also a Qadriya.

Sheikh Abdul Qadir Jilani preached a balance between the material and the spiritual. According to him, a good Sufi saint should not be a recluse;

instead he should live among people, so they might be led by his example. A saying attributed to him is: 'God said, through the Prophet, "Man is my secret and I am his secret. The inner knowledge of the spiritual essence is a secret of My secrets. Only I put this into the heart of My good servant, and none may know his state other than Me."'[1]

Since the Qadriya *silsilah* was established after Sheikh Jilani's death, many of the practices associated with the order took shape later. For instance, Sheikh Jilani emphasized *zikr*, but how to do it was formalized later.

*Zikr* is one of the most important spiritual practices of the Qadriyas, and it is done with different degrees of intensity and emphasis. Qadriyas also places emphasis on *pas-e-anfas* (controlled breathing), so that the name of Allah reverberates and circulates inside the whole body while it is being chanted. This is very similar to the chanting of '*Om*' during certain Yoga exercises. The next step after *pas-e-anfas* is a *muraqabah* (contemplation) of some verse from the Quran.

Sheikh Abdul Qadir Jilani is extremely popular in the Indian subcontinent. His *urs* on the eleventh Rabi us-sani is simply called *gyarvi sharif* (the blessed 11th) and is celebrated all over the country. It was traditionally celebrated under the later Mughals, where it is reported:

> [A]ll kinds of fireworks, some in the shape of animals, are set off in the courtyard of the Diwan-e-Khas in Red Fort, Delhi. A bamboo frame covered with shimmering red paper, called a *mehndi*, is placed in the Diwan-e-Khas. It is made for illuminating candles and lamps. The *dastarkhwan* [tablecloth] is spread out, and every type of food is laid on it. The Badshah [emperor] lights the *mehndi* and consecrates the food in the name of Ghaus-ul-Azam.[2]

Sheikh Abdul Qadir Jilani's relics and the places associated with it are scattered over the countryside. In Bareilly, for example, there is the Jhanda Sharif, where his *urs* is celebrated. A *jhanda* means a flag in Hindi. The shrine is so named because of the flag around which it has come up. The flag in question was brought from his shrine in Baghdad by a devotee Mir Wattan and installed here; such is the saint's draw that even this flag-shrine attracts many devotees.

The very popular shrine called Dastgeer in Srinagar houses the saint's relics (a strand of hair from his beard and a skull cap). Made of wood and papier mâché, it is one of the prettiest shrines. It was destroyed by a fire in 2012 but has been since rebuilt. The relics were miraculously saved.

The Qadriya *silsilah* was quite popular in West Asia, but it spread to India only in the fourteenth century. It became very popular in the Deccan where the Bahmani Sultans were looking towards West Asia, particularly Iran, for inspiration and guidance – rather than north India.

In 1422, the Chishti saint Khwaja Banda Nawaz Gesu Daraz passed away, and in the same year the Bahmani capital shifted from Gulbarga to Bidar. The Bahmani Sultan, Shihabuddin Ahmad I, requested Shah Nuruddin Muhammad Nimatullah Wali bin Abdullah (1330–1431), a Sufi saint and prolific writer of mystic poetry and prose, to send one of his sons to Bidar. The latter sent his grandson Mir Nurullah bin Shah Khalilullah, as he didn't want to send his only son Shah Khalilullah. Mir Nurullah was welcomed with pomp, and a new town was built close to Bidar called Nimatabad; he was given the title of Malik al-Mashaikh and preference over all other Sufis in the Deccan area. The Sultan continued to honour the Shah's family; he also married his daughter to Mir Nurullah. Their impact continued to affect the culture of the Deccan, introducing Persian influence into the local culture. One of the main effects of the royal patronage of Shah Nimatullah's family was the reduced influence of the descendants and followers of Khwaja Gesu Daraz, the Chisti saint who had settled in Gulbarga.

Sufis of the Qadriya *silsilah* started arriving from Najaf, Baghdad, Mahan, and Multan. Other Sufis were also invited by the sultans. After the Bahmani kingdom was split into five territories, it was Bijapur that became the centre of the Qadriya saints.

One of the most popular Sufis of Bidar, whose shrine is still a popular place of pilgrimage, was Sheikh Makhdum Muhammad Multani (d. 1529). Known popularly as Multani Pasha, he was however, born in Bidar; his father was Sheikh Ibrahim Multani (d. 1463), and his mother a descendant of Makhdum Jahaniyan Jahan Gasht. He was one of the outstanding personalities from his age, and his piety, knowledge, and spiritual powers were legendary. The Barid Shahi rulers of Bidar were his devotees, and

Sultan Qasim Barid (1489–1504), the founder of the Barid Shahi dynasty and the reigning king of the time, is said to have compared him to Khwaja Gesu Daraz saying that the Deccan only produced these two great saints.

The spread of the Qadriya *silsilah* in other parts of India took place between the fifteenth and the eighteenth centuries.

Meanwhile, saints of the Qadriya *silsilah* had already settled in Uch, Multan (in present-day Pakistan), where a direct descendant of the founder of the Qadriya order, Sheikh Muhammad al-Hussaini al-Jilani, had founded a *silsilah* in the mid-1400s. The ruler of Multan welcomed Muhammad al-Hussaini as there were few spiritual leaders in their midst.

The Qadriya saints gained a lot of popularity and won over many disciples in Multan and Uch. One of the earliest was Sheikh Abdul Qadir Sani (d.1533), the eldest son of Muhammad al-Hussaini, who became the leader of the Qadriya order in Uch. He was loved by the people in Multan and Uch. Many miracles are attributed to him, which led to the spread of the Qadriya order in the Punjab and Sindh regions of the Indian subcontinent.

Sheikh Abdul Qadir Sani was succeeded briefly by his son, Sheikh Abdur Razzaq (d. 1535). The latter was succeeded by his son Sheikh Hamid who had trained under his grandfather. He succeeded his father during the early days of Akbar.

Sheikh Hamid was very popular with the Muslims of Uch, who feted him with gifts which he then invariably disposed. The *sadr al-sadur* (chief judge) of Akbar got him summoned to the emperor's court at Agra. This greatly annoyed him, and he is said to have cursed both the *sadr* and his patron, Bairam Khan. Both were disgraced by 1560, and their fall from grace was said to be the direct result of this curse.[3]

Upon his death in 1571, there was a controversy regarding which of his sons should succeed him, and the matter was taken to Akbar's court.

However, it was Sheikh Dawud (1513–1575), another of Sheikh Hamid's disciples, who was the most famous. In his youth, he was constantly in a state of ecstasy and wandered around in Ajodhan in that state for twenty years before having a dream where Ghaus al-Azam told him to become a disciple of Sheikh Hamid and live in a *khanqah*.

Once, one of Akbar's famous courtiers and biographers Abdul Qadir Badayuni travelled to Shergarh to visit the sheikh. Though the sheikh refused to go to Akbar's court in 1573, saying that he read secret prayers for Emperor Akbar and that was enough for his spiritual welfare, members of the Qadriya order reached Delhi and Agra under his leadership. The sheikh was tremendously popular, and the spread of the Qadriya *silsilah* across northern India can be attributed to him. He is said to have converted many people into believers with his teachings and life.

Sheikh Dawud died in 1574, and his dargah is in Shergarh, on the banks of the river Beas in Pakistan, where he spent his life. He was succeeded by his son-in-law and nephew Sheikh Abul Maali.

Amongst the other famous Qadriya saints of this period is Sheikh Hussain Lahori (1538–1599) and his disciple Sheikh Madho (1575–1647). They are known by the composite name of Madho Lal Hussain.

Madho was a handsome youth with whom Sheikh Hussain fell in love. After seeing him Sheikh Hussain had become intoxicated and went into a mystic trance. He spent many years circumambulating his house at night and following him in the day. Initially Madho ignored him, but after some years embraced his love and Islam. Sheikh Hussain made him his disciple and successor. Because of his association with Madho, Sheikh Hussain had a fondness for Hindu festivals such as Holi and Basant; he would dance and sing on the festival days, throwing colour. Both of them are buried in the same tomb in Baghbanpura, adjacent to the Shalimar Gardens, Lahore, with the simple inscription *Sakhi Sarkar Madhu Laal Hussain* (friend and master Madho Laal Hussain) uniting the two forever.

Sheikh Hussain's *urs* known as *Mela Chiraghan* (Festival of Lights) has a celebration involving the throwing of colours. The *dhamaal* (a form of ecstatic dancing) performed there by dervishes is world famous. Their tomb stands as a symbol of religious harmony, love, and their defiance of social norms.

Sheikh Hussain was one of the pioneers of kafi (a kind of short poem) and his poems are sung by many famous qawwals. One of his poems goes:

*Ranjhan Ranjhan phiraan dhouda indi,*
*Ranjhan mairay nal.*

[I wandered looking for Ranjhan Ranjhan,
But Ranjhan is within me.]

His disciple Madho also wrote emotive kafis, which expressed *Wahdat al-Wujud*.

Another very famous and popular Qadriya Sufi and one of the foremost proponents of *Wahdat al-Wujud* was Sheikh Aman Panipati (d. 1550). He lived in a simple house and did not establish a *khanqah*, although he had many famous disciples. While praying he would go into ecstasy when reciting the fifth line of *Surah Fatiha*: 'Thee do we worship and Thine aid we seek.'

One of his well-known disciples was Sheikh Saifuddin, born in 1514 in a family of literary scholars and those in military service. However, he preferred the life of a Sufi. Originally a follower of the Suhrawardi *silsilah*, he decided to become a disciple of Sheikh Aman Panipati after hearing him.

Like many other mystics, Sheikh Saifuddin believed in *Wahdat al-Wujud* (unity of being). In fact, his writings on *Wahdat al-Wujud* and *tasawwuf* were very famous in mystical circles. He was greatly moved by divine love; even within his home, passages from the Quran that talked about hope and promises were chanted loudly, while those that carried threats from God were read quietly. His lectures were often very emotional and his listeners would request the Sufi to talk about the longing for God, divine love, and the pain of separation.

Sheikh Saifuddin died in 1582 at the age of 68. He is buried in the compound that houses the shrine of his son Sheikh Abdul Haqq Muhadith Dehlvi near Hauz-e-Shamsi in Mehrauli, New Delhi.

Sheikh Saifuddin did not take many disciples, but he did instruct his son on spirituality and mysticism. Sheikh Saifuddin's son was born in 1551, when the Sheikh was around 37 years old. He named him Abdul Haqq. Abdul, like his father, was a somber child. He was ahead of his peers in many aspects, and with his father's teaching he became wise beyond his years. With encouragement from Sheikh Saifuddin, the young Abdul Haqq explored a range of subjects and read many classical texts. He was so devoted to his studies that he would often be in the classroom before daybreak and continue to study well through the night. When his parents insisted that he sleep, Abdul Haqq would pretend to fall asleep only to get up again and resume studying.

Sheikh Abdul Haqq was initiated into the Qadriya *silsilah* when his father sent him to become a disciple of Sheikh Musa, son of Sheikh Hamid, and great grandson of Sheikh Abdul Qadir Sani. Sheikh Musa initiated Sheikh Abdul Haqq in 1577. Sheikh Abdul Haqq lived with Sheikh Musa in Emperor Akbar's court in Fatehpur Sikri. There were religious debates between the two main Islamic scholars of the day – Sheikh Makhdum al-Mulk and Sheikh Abdun Nabi – as well as religious discourses in Akbar's *ibadatkhana* (house of devotion) in Fatehpur Sikri. Akbar invited Jain, Jesuit, Hindu priests, ulemas, and Islamic scholars to debate religion in these discourses.

Sheikh Abdul Haqq was unhappy with the religious developments of the court and, like his father, was upset with the egocentric discussions of the theologians and scholars. He never participated in the debates there and remained neutral to imperial policies.

Sheikh Saifuddin's death in 1582 prompted Sheikh Abdul Haqq to return to his mother's side in Delhi. During this time, although he was taking care of his widowed mother, he felt a strong urge to visit Medina and Mecca, and he managed to go there in 1588. Once in the holy city, Sheikh Abdul Haqq studied the hadiths and the Hanafi school of law. He was also taught and initiated into other Sufi *silsilah*s like the Chishti, Madayniya, and Shaziliya *silsilah*s. In 1590, Sheikh Abdul Haqq saw a dream in which Prophet Muhammad was delivering a sermon on a hadith. This dream made him feel that he had reached the pinnacle of his religious and spiritual aspirations, and so he decided to settle in Mecca.

Though Sheikh Abdul Haqq wanted to continue living in Mecca, in pursuit of an intellectual and spiritual life, his teacher reminded him of his responsibilities back in India. Sheikh Abdul Wahhab advised him to go back to India and carry forward on the Sufi path, teaching him that the duty of every Muslim was to reinforce their beliefs based on the shariah law. Sheikh Abdul Haqq returned to India in 1592.

Even after his return, he stayed away from the emperor's court and chose instead to focus on writing about the hadiths and go on teaching. After Akbar's death, it is said that the sheikh wrote to members of the court to reverse the emperor's policy of *Sulh-e-Kul* (universal peace), and replace it with the strict rules prescribed by Ghazali. He wrote that their first duty was towards the shariah and he should not forget that while conducting his worldly affairs.

In his lifetime Sheikh Abdul Haqq wrote almost a hundred books, which included long and short manuscripts. All of this work propagated orthodox Islam with the Sunni shariah way of life. Sheikh Abdul Haqq died a celebrated Sufi saint in 1642 at the age of 94. After his death, his writings ensured that his name was held in high esteem by learned men across the Islamic world.

His simple but well-maintained shrine near Hauz-e-Shamsi is visited by followers of the Qadriya order from all over the world. The mosque attached to his shrine is a busy hub, as children come there to study the Quran.

The *Qadriya silsilah* gained popularity in the Punjab region of undivided India. It retains its popularity in India till date. The most famous Sufi saints of the Qadriya order in the Indian subcontinent are Miyan Mir (1531/32–1653), Sultan Bahu (1630–1691) and Bulleh Shah (1680–1757).

Miyan Mir preached that there were two paths to finding God. The first was when a devotee was drawn to God himself; the other was through meditation and contemplation under a Sufi saint's guidance. Dara Shukoh records that one of his disciples claimed that Miyan Mir never slept at night and for several years used only one breath lasting the entire night till sunrise. Even at 80 he was inhaling and exhaling only four times nightly.[4]

Miyan Mir attracted the attention of the Mughal emperor, Akbar. His fame spread and even Shah Abbas Safavi of Iran asked Akbar to request Miyan Mir to pray for him.

Both Emperors Jahangir and Shah Jahan were greatly influenced by the saint. Emperor Shah Jahan visited the saint in his *khanqah,* as did his son Dara Shukoh. Miyan Mir refused to accept human help throughout his lifetime. Even as he was ageing, he would not accept assistance – financial or otherwise – from his many disciples and believers. Such was his faith that Allah would provide for him, he would not allow the physician of the Governor of Lahore to treat him when he was very ill with dysentery.

He would throw away water to ensure that none remained for the next day!

He died in Lahore of an unknown cause and his disciples performed his last rites. There were many that were a part of his funeral procession, including the Governor of Lahore. He is buried in Alam Ganj, an area close to Lahore.

Miyan Mir was a close friend of the fifth Sikh Guru, Arjun Dev. It is said that the guru approached his Sufi friend to grace the occasion of the laying of the foundation stone of the Harminder Sahib – famous as the Golden Temple in Amritsar. This fact shows how greatly the people appreciated the catholicity of his views.[5]

Miyan Mir had many successors, of which the most famous is Mullah Shah Badakshi (1584–1661), also known as Mohammad Shah and Hazrat Akhund (revered teacher). As is obvious from his name, he was born in Badakshan. His disciples believed him to have received the title *Lisanullah* (tongue of Allah).

His initial religious training was in Balkh, where he migrated at the age of 24. From there he moved to Kashmir and became deeply interested in mysticism and ascetism. After a residence of three years in Kashmir, he wanted to go to Lahore to meet Miyan Mir but was dissuaded by a friend who advised him that there was a more eminent Sufi in Agra. However, he was quickly disappointed by this other Sufi, so he came back to Lahore and became a pupil of Miyan Mir.

The teacher put his disciple through many tests and after he passed, introduced him to mystical exercises. Miyan Mir was very proud of his disciple and he prophesied that the Qadriya order and his own brand of spiritual discipline would gain fame through Mullah Shah.[6]

Mullah Shah perfected the control of self and felt that all stages of divine mystery were reflected in him. In 1628–29, he moved to Srinagar, Kashmir.

Mullah Shah would practice breath control while doing *zikr*. He was a firm believer of *Wahdat al-Wujud*. In 1660, he moved back to Lahore, where he died a year later. He is buried near Miyan Mir; Jahanara Begum had a red sandstone tomb erected over his grave, adding a garden to it.

As mentioned before, Dara Shukoh and his sister Jahanara Begum (the eldest son and eldest daughter of Shah Jahan and Mumtaz Mahal) were the disciples of Mullah Shah Badakshi and it is now time to turn to the former.

Born in Ajmer, Dara Shukoh (1615–1659) was named by his grandfather, Jahangir. He received the traditional education given to Mughal princes, including literary, and religious education as well as training in administration and warfare. He was fascinated by mysticism and wrote the *Safinat al-Auliya* (*Ship of Saints*), a biographical dictionary of Sufism. In it, he included the biography of Miyan Mir and his sister Bibi Jamal Khatun. While writing the book, his dreams were full of visions of him circumambulating the shrine of Imam Musa Kazim in Kazmain a suburb of Baghdad and that of Ghaus al-Azam in Baghdad; he took it as their approval of his work.[7]

In 1640, he became the disciple of Mullah Shah and learnt many spiritual exercises from him.

In a mystical *ghazal*, Dara praised his spiritual master:

> As my Lord and master is the *pir*,
> My Kaaba is the blessed Kashmir.
> Whoever has seen the Shah has not sought the Kaaba,
> This is the effect of gazing at his countenance.
> O Kaaba-goer, grasp the Shah's hem!
> Since you are the Kaaba's hem-grasper.[8]

Dara Shukoh's quest for knowledge and spiritual attainment led him to explore the ancient Indic knowledge:

> Now, thus sayeth this unafflicted, un-sorrowing fakir Dara Shukoh that after knowing the Truth of Truths and ascertaining the secrets and subtleties of the true religion of the Sufis and having being endowed with this great gift, he thirsted to know the tenets of the religion of the Indian monotheists. And having had repeated and continuous discussion with the doctors and perfect divines of this Indian religion... He did not find any difference, except verbal, in the way they sought and comprehended Truth.[9]

Dara realized that there was only one truth and went on to translate the Upanishads as the *Sirr-e-Akbar* (*The Great Secret*) in 1657.

In a dream during or before 1655/6, inspired by reading a translation of *Jog Bashisht*, he had seen the sage Vashishta tell Rama to embrace Dara with the following words: 'O Ramchandra! This is a disciple who is absolutely sincere, please embrace him.'

'With the utmost affection, Ram took me into his arms,' Dara relates. 'Thereafter, Basisht gave Ramchandra sweets to feed me with. I ate the sweets.'[10]

He was thus anointed the *maryada purushottam* (a man who is supreme in honour) of his times, carrying forward ancient traditions. In him was clear proof that an ascetic could be a model ruler.

He also got the *Jog Bashisht* retranslated in Persian.

However, fate had other things in mind and the battle of succession did not go in his favour. He was defeated by his brother Aurangzeb, who ascended the Mughal throne after imprisoning his father and sister in the Agra Fort.

Dara was executed on charges of apostacy in 1659.

If some Qadriya saints came from royalty, others didn't have much to do with worldly affairs. Some of them made the teachings of renowned and widely revered saints popular through songs. Two such Sufis were Sultan Bahu (1630–91) and Bulleh Shah (1680–1757).

Sultan Muhammad adopted the name Bahu, which he used to sign off at the end of his poems, as he grew up. The pen name has a deep spiritual significance; it means Ba (with) Hu (literally means 'he', and is a name by which Allah is referred). Sultan Bahu's father died soon after his birth, and so he was brought up by his mother, Bibi Rasti. She was the greatest influence on his life.

One night, Sultan Bahu saw a dream. In it, he was being presented to Prophet Muhammad by Hazrat Ali himself, and then the Prophet entrusted him to Sheikh Abdul Qadir Jilani. After this, he became aloof and started spending time in spiritual pursuits. Seeing this, his mother advised him to seek the path of Sufism. The young boy argued that he had already been initiated into Sufism in his dreams, but his more practical mother insisted that he find a spiritual master and take an oath of allegiance. Sultan Bahu then went to Hazrat Shah Habibullah Jilani and lived with him for some time. Shah Habibullah later told him that he was incapable of conferring on him the kind of knowledge that he deserved, thus advising him to go to Delhi and take an oath of allegiance with Sheikh Syed Abdur Rahman Qadiri, a noted Qadriya Sufi of his times who was responsible for setting up the order in Delhi. Later Sultan Bahu returned to Punjab and founded the branch of Sarwari Qadriya Sufis.

Sultan Bahu wrote 20 Persian treatises, but he is best remembered for his Punjabi poetry. His verses were set to music and have inspired several generations. His poems talked of *Wahdat al-Wujud*. Even today his 'Jugni' continues to enthral listeners.

> *Alif allah chambay di booti, tey meray murshid mann vich lai hu*
> *Nafi asbaat ka paani de ke, har raage harjaai hu.*
>
> [Alif [with which the name of Allah starts] is a fragrant jasmine flower planted in my heart by my master.]

He watered it with negation and affirmation[11], so that it reached each vein and pore.

Sultan Bahu was buried in Kaharjanan on the banks of the river Chenab near Sherkot. His mortal remains were, however, shifted to the present shrine in Garh Maharaja of Jhang district (in Pakistan) due to floods in the river.

The other musical Sufi was Abdullah Shah, born in 1680 in Uch, Bhawalpur. He adopted Bulleh or Bulleya as his name for writing his verses. He belonged to the Qadriya-Shattari *silsilah*.

Bulleh Shah was initiated him into Sufism by Shah Inayatullah Qadiri. He initially preached on the banks of the Chenab, and after a few years, on the instruction of his spiritual master, he settled in Qasur. He passed away in 1757 and was buried in Qasur. His kafis are extremely popular and explain the universal truth of overcoming ego and greed. His most popular poem is: *ilmon bas kareen O yaar* (Enough of learning O friend) from which I quote the the last eight lines:

*parh nafal namaaz guzaareyn*
*uchiyaan baangaan chaangaan maarey*
*mimbar te charh waaz pukaarey*
*keeta teyniin hirs khawaar*
*jad mein sabaq ishaq da parhyaa*
*daryaa weykh wahadat da waryaa*
*ghuman gheyraan dey wich aryaa*
*Shah Inayaet laayaa paar*

[You meditate and you say your prayers
You go and shout at the top of the stairs
You cry reaching the high skies
It's your avarice which ever belies
The day I learnt love's lesson
I plunged into the river of divine passion
An overwhelming gale. I was confused and lost
When Shah Inayat cruised me across
Enough of learning, my friend!][12]

– Bulleh Shah

# 8

# The Naqshbandis

For the mind, heart and sight, the first shaykh is *ishq* (love). If there is no *ishq* then shariah (Islamic law) and din (religion) become but idols of whimsical ideas.[1]

– Faqir Zulfiqar Ahmed Naqshbandi

In 2014, I set off on a quest to find the graves of the Mughal princes executed by Major Hodson in the aftermath of the Great Uprising of 1857, and it introduced me to a great saint of the Naqshbandi *silsilah*. The *Waqeat-e Darul Hukumat-e Dehli*[2] recorded that they had been buried in the dargah of Khwaja Baqi Billah. Entering through the Buland Darwaza, the first thing that struck me were the innumerous graves; this emphasizes the *barakah* (blessing) of the shrine, as devotees believe that burial near a saint makes the journey in the afterlife easier.

The children of a family living there are playing, fighting, and having fun amongst the graves, as I stand and watch them, absorbing a life lesson. The sight of children playing amidst the graves seems to reiterate the philosophical message that life and death should hold no fear for the devout.

The Naqshbandi *silsilah* was the last major order to came in India. Sufis from this order arrived during the reign of Akbar. Timur, from whom the Mughals claimed descent, was a follower of this *silsilah,* and so it was only natural that the emergence of the Mughals as a reigning dynasty in India coincided with the order's rise and establishment in India.

Khwaja Ubaidullah Ahrar, the fifteenth-century Central Asian Naqshbandi saint, envisaged himself as not only the spiritual but also the political patron of his disciples. Babur's father, Umar Shaikh Mirza, was

Khwaja Ahrar's disciple, and Babur attributed his success to the Khwaja's blessings even though the Sufi saint had passed away by then.[3]

When the battle of Panipat took place in 1526, between Sultan Ibrahim Lodi and Babur, the most popular saint of northern India, followed even by the sultan, was the Sabri-Chisti saint Sheikh Abdul Quddus Gangohi (d.1537). Though the sheikh did not approve of Sultan Ibrahim Lodi, his disapproval of the Mughals was greater; he saw them as a divine scourge – God's retribution in the world of the sinful Afghans.[4] He was humiliated by the Mughals after the defeat of the Lodi sultan and remained opposed to them, spending his life in Gangoh.

Sheikh Abdul Quddus Gangohi was a mendicant whose belief in *fana* and *baqa*, is reflected in his words: 'The self was freed by the Self, then the Self itself became captive'[5]

Babur and Humayun continued with their allegiance to the Naqshbandi saints of Transoxiana, and this was strengthened by Timurid princesses being given in marriage to the Naqshbandi saints. During Akbar's reign, the *silsilah* was established in India – by Khwaja Baqi Billah (d.1603) in Delhi, and Khwaja Khawand Mahmud Alavi Hussaini (d. 1652) in Kashmir. One of his four successors, Sheikh Ahmed Sirhindi, founded the Mujaddadi branch of the *silsilah* and went onto play a very important role in it.

Humayun had been greatly impressed and influenced by a Shattari saint named Sheikh Phul, who shared his interests in astronomical sciences and occult. His brother was Sheikh Ghaus Gwaliori.

Akbar 'favoured a kind of universal kingship, emphasizing an undisputed and all – encompassing power for the ruler'.[6] Although he was initially inclined to supporting the Chishti saints, and even built his capital Fatehpur Sikri to pay homage to the Chishti saint Sheikh Salim Chishti, it was ultimately he who was the centre of authority – not the saint.

The language of pluralism used by Chishti saints appealed to Akbar. Chishti treatises of his era even make a plea for the illegitimacy of considering Islam as superior to any other religion. They say:

> The whole world is a manifestation of love (*ishq*) to one such treatise and we see everything as perfect. [...] As you begin *iradat* [become a murid and join the order] you stop quarrelling over *kufr* [disbelief] and iman [faith]. There is no precedence of one religion

> over the other; after you experience the limitlessness of unbounded beauty you can see His Grace present both in a kafir and a Muslim.[7]

While the Chishtis shunned contact with royalty, the Suhrawardis met them, mixed with them, and gave them moral support but did not seek to influence their decision-making. The Suhrawardis remained aloof despite maintaining contact; the Naqshbandis on the other hand actively sought to establish contact with and influence the decisions of royalty, as they felt that it created a deep impact on public life.[8]

Much has been written on the influence of Sheikh Ahmed Sirhindi on contemporary politics and some of this will be examined later in the chapter. According to famous Sufi scholar Nizami,

> The history of the Naqshbandi order is closely related to the period of the rise and fall of Mughal power in India, so much so that the change from Akbar to Aurangzeb is inexplicable without a clear and unbiased appraisal of the part played in it by the Naqshbandi saints.[9]

The Naqshbandi order was built on the principles of an order called the *Silsilah-e-Khwajgan* (the path of teachers) started in the twelfth century. This older order was initiated by Khwaja Abu Yaqub Yusuf al-Hamadani and his disciple, Khwaja Abdul Khaliq bin Abdul Jamil Ghujduwani. Khwaja Bahauddin Naqshband (1318–1389) revitalized this *silsilah* in the fourteenth century, and eventually the followers of Khwaja Bahauddin Naqshband became known as Naqshbandis.

The Naqshbandi saints pass knowledge from one master to the other through what is called the 'Golden Chain of Spiritual Transmission'. According to them, Prophet Muhammad, is 'not only the recipient of revelation and the expositor of the divine message, but also – for the Sufi – the first link in the initiatic chain and the supreme guide on the path. It is, in the ultimate sense, incorrect to regard anyone other than the Prophet as the founder of a legitimate Sufi order.'.[10]

The teachings of the Naqshabandi *silsilah* were formulated by Khwaja Abu Yaqub Yusuf al-Hamadani and his disciple Khwaja Abdul Khaliq bin Abdul Jamil Ghujduwani. Though the writings of the latter were based on the shariah, the principles he based a Sufi's life on were based on yogic teachings present in the Bukhara region. According to Nizami, the teachings bore a deep impact of Buddhist ideas.[11]

Eight principles are described in detail in Khwaja Ahrar's treatise *Rashhat Ain-ul Hayat*. They are:

1. *Hosh dardam* (awareness of every breath), so that the Sufi is aware of each inhale and exhale and associates it with the Divine. Khwaja Ghujduwani writes that Sufis should not take any breath distractedly.
2. *Nazar bar qadam* is walking mindfully towards the goal without distraction and with continuous awareness of the presence of divinity.
3. *Safar darwatan* (journey to land of origin) is the spiritual journey leading to a transformation from human vices to angelic ideals. This necessitates purification of heart, dedicated to the early phases of spiritual training.
4. *Khalwat daranjuman* (seclusion in crowds) is recommended so that the Sufis are engaged in *zikr* even in the midst of a crowds. This meant that the Sufi should be so absorbed in meditating on the divine that he is unable to register anything else even among people.
5. *Yaadkard* (remembrance) is the oral and mental state of *zikr*.
6. *Baz gasht* (control), especially of thoughts, so that a Sufi's *zikr* is always pure.
7. *Nigahdasht* (alertness), so that a Sufi is always alert against evil thoughts entering his mind during meditation.
8. *Yaaddasht* or recollection, a state that all trainees should be in permanently. This is a state of innate insight wherein the Sufi is always aware of the presence of divinity.[12]

Khwaja Ghujduwani (d. 1179) had four successors, just as his master Khwaja al-Hamadani did before him. Of these four, Khwaja Ghujduwani passed the secrets of the Golden Chain to Sheikh Arif Riwgari.[13] Sheikh Arif Riwgari became the first of the mystic teachers to be known as Khwajgan (the masters).

One of the main saints of the Naqshbandi *silsilah* was Khwaja Bahauddin Naqshbandi, the fifth generation of Khwaja Ghujduwani's disciples. He was born in a village near Bukhara, and his family name Naqshband means embroiderer/painter, either referring to his family profession or to his spiritual abilities.

It is from his name that the *silsilah* gets its name. The term Naqshband thus incorporates two basic ideas: the naqsh or 'engraving the name of Allah in the heart', and the bond 'describing the link between the individual and creator'.[14] They are also called the silent Sufis because of their practice of silent *zikr*.

Khwaja Bahauddin was also called Sultan al-Arifeen (the King of Gnostics). He acquired a wealth of knowledge and was one of the few students of *Ilm ash-Sharia* (the Science of Divine Law) and *Ilm al-Haqiqat* (the Science of Reality in his time).

Like most Sufis, Khwaja Bahauddin too lived a life of austerity. He spent most of his days fasting and usually only ate bread made of barley that he harvested from the fields, grinding the grain, and baking the bread himself. He would often invite the poor to his home and feed them with his own hands, while also encouraging his followers to take his example.

Khwaja Bahauddin added three principles to the eight existing ones prescribed by Khwaja Ghujduwani. They were:

1. *Wuquf-e-Zamani* (being aware of time);
2. *Wuquf-e-Adadi* (being aware of numbers), to prevent evil thoughts; and
3. *Wuquf-e-Qalbi* (being aware of the heart): This message is an addition to Khwaja Ghujduwani's principle of *Yaaddasht* or 'recollection'.

Khwaja Bahauddin was immensely popular during his life. His generosity and wisdom attracted people; they would come from far and wide to seek his blessings and aid. He died on 1 March 1389 and was buried in his garden in the village of his birth, Qasr al-Arifan, as per his request.

His successors, as stated by him, were Sheikh Alauddin Attar, his son-in-law and Sheikh Muhammad ibn Muhammad ibn Mahmud al-Hafizi (also called Muhammad Parsa). The secrets of the Golden Chain were passed on to Sheikh Alauddin Attar.[15]

The Naqshbandi lineage, however, was carried forward by Maulana Yaqub Charkhi, a disciple of Sheikh Bahauddin Naqshbandi. After the death of his *pir*, he received guidance from Sheikh Alauddin Attar, his *pir's khalifa*.

Khwaja Ahrar (1404–1490) was his *khalifa* and the saint responsible for the spread of the Naqshbandi *silsilah* and its teachings across Central Asia, establishing centres in Herat, Badakshan, and Balkh and further across the Muslim world.

Babur even translated in verse Khwaja Ahrar's treatise *Risaliya-e-Walidiya* when the latter fell sick in 1528, in the hope of curing him.

Babur invited Khwaja Ahrar's grandsons from Samarqand to India. They were Khwaja Khawand Mahmud (known as Khwaja Nura) and Khwaja Abdul Shahid, and his great grandson was Khwaja Kalan. The latter two came to Agra and were feted by Babur. However, they did not stay for long.

Khwaja Khawand Mahmud came to India in 1530, but by that time Babur had died. He was received with a lot of respect and honoured by Humayun. Nonetheless, he left for Kabul after some time, as he was annoyed by the Shattari influence on the emperor.

Khwaja Abdul Shahid returned to Akbar's court and was given a pargana in Punjab. However, the Naqshbandi saints could not fully establish their presence till later.

It was Khwaja Khawand Mahmud Alwi Hussaini (1557/58–1642) and Khwaja Baqi Billah (1564–1603) who finally prevailed in getting a firm footing in India.

Khwaja Khawand Mahmud Alwi Hussaini was educated in Samarqand. He was a descendant of one of Khwaja Naqshband's disciples, Sheikh Alauddin Attar. He was given the responsibility of the Naqshbandi *silsilah* at the age of 23 and left for the Indian subcontinent.

When he was travelling through Kabul to assume his responsibilities, the Khwaja met a caravan bound for Lahore and decided to join them. In Gujarat, there was a point where the group was meant to turn and take the road to Lahore, but the Khwaja fell into a trance. Unguided, his horse left the group and went on a different path towards Kashmir. Deciding that this diversion was divine interference, he decided to continue on it.

True enough, the Khwaja became very popular among the people of Srinagar; even the ulema of the region approached him to become disciples.

The Mughal government converted the house of the sultan of Kashmir, Hussain Shah, to a *khanqah* and gave it to the Khwaja.

Before Emperor Akbar died, Khwaja Khawand visited Agra. Many prominent officials and ladies of the harem became followers of the Naqshbandi philosophy. He started his journey back after Emperor Jahangir had assumed the throne. Along the way, Prince Khusrau, who had rebelled against his father Jahangir, asked the Khwaja to bless his uprising but was disappointed. Khwaja Khawand said he only prayed for people with pious motives.

The Khwaja died on 4 November 1642. He had several disciples and 16 *khalifa*s at the time. He was succeeded by the eldest of his six sons, Khwaja Khawand Ahmad. However, his most well-known son and disciple was his fourth-born, Khwaja Khawand Muinuddin.

Khwaja Muinuddin travelled to Srinagar to lead the disciples of his late father. He remained away from politics. He was quite a significant presence during Emperor Aurangzeb's reign, and is buried in the beautiful Khanqah-e-Naqshband built to honour Khwaja Babhuddin Naqshband in Srinagar. When I visited it in 2018 and 2021, despite the turmoil in downtown Srinagar, it was an oasis of tranquility and drew many locals to prayer.

Though the Naqshbandi *silsilah* was introduced in India by Khwaja Ahrar's disciples, the spread of the philosophy is attributed to Khwaja Muhammad Baqi, also known as Baqi Billah Berang. He was born in 1564 in Kabul. The Khwaja's father, Abdus Salam, was a judge who was greatly influenced by spirituality and began to seek spiritual knowledge after a visit to India. Khwaja Baqi was a descendant of Khwaja Ahrar from his mother's side.

Khwaja Baqi was introspective even as a child. After finishing his scholastic education, he was taken under the tutelage of Maulana Sadiq Halwai, a poet and scholar from Samarqand. While there, he studied and performed *zikr* and *tauba* (repentance) under the guidance of many Naqshbandi saints in the area; yet he was not spiritually fulfilled. While on his travels, he met Maulana Khwajagi Amkinagi, a Naqshbandi saint part of the Golden Chain, and was initiated into the order. The *pir* was so impressed by Khwaja Baqi, he told his other disciples that the Khwaja had already become a perfect Sufi in the short time. Khwaja Baqi was soon sent back to India to spread the teachings of the *silsilah*.[16]

On his way to Delhi, the Khwaja visited a famine-stricken Lahore. While he was there, he refused all food, sending his rations to the starving locals instead. He took those who were too weak with him when he left for Delhi a few weeks later, mounting them on his horse. He would climb on to his horse whenever he came close to a town, so no one would know the extent of his charity. In Delhi, he lived in Firozabad Fort (present-day Firoz Shah Kotla) near the river Yamuna.

Khwaja Baqi was a strong believer in *Wahdat al-Wujud*. He placed much emphasis on humility, ensuring that his charity was inconspicuous. According to him, vanity was the biggest hurdle in living a pious life. The Khwaja was always polite; he would often take responsibility and apologize for any errors committed by his disciples. Though he was a learned and pious man, Khwaja Baqi was humble, too, and did not consider himself better than any of his disciples. Despite his efforts to remain inconspicuous, he was very popular and had many high-ranking people as his disciples.

People around the subcontinent knew that Khwaja Baqi had miraculous spiritual powers. Followers reported that if they looked into his eyes while performing *zikr*, they would reach a state of *fana* in just one meeting.[17] This power prompted many to become his disciples and he came to be well-known around the Indian subcontinent and the entire Islamic world. He achieved immense popularity although he only lived in Delhi for a short period of about four years. Khwaja Baqi died in 1603 at the age of 40. He had many disciples, including his two sons.

Khwaja Baqi's dargah in Delhi's Paharganj area is very popular. It became very popular as a cemetery during the Mughal era because its proximity to the saint's shrine was considered blessed by devotees. The sons and grandson of Bahadur Shah Zafar, the last Mughal emperor, all of whom were killed by Major Hodson after the fall of Delhi in 1857, are also buried here. The saint's shrine enclosed by a wall is a very simple one. The mosque attached to it is maintained by his descendants, who are the *sajjada nasheen;* it is beautiful. There are no crowds of supplicants or beggars, and it is a place of solitude and meditation.

Sheikh Ahmad Sirhindi, Khwaja Baqi's most popular disciple, was born on 26 May 1564 and named Khwaja Ahmad. His father Sheikh Abdul Ahad had travelled all through India and received the spiritual blessings and wisdom of many Sufis and scholars. By the time his son was born, he has settled in Sirhind in a *khanqah* and was a scholar of *Wahdat al-Wujud*.

Sheikh Ahmad received his early education from his father, who also initiated him into the Chishti order. He was later associated with the *Qadriya silsilah* and had performed *tauba* (repentance) under the Naqshbandi saint Khwaja Ubaid Kabuli.

Even as a child, he showed a lot of interest and promise in theological studies and learned from eminent teachers like Sheikh Yaqub Kashmiri, with whom he visited Emperor Akbar's capital at Fatehpur Sikri. Khwaja Ahmad was disappointed by the impunity with which the scholars and theologians present discussed controversial subjects like miracles and prophethood.

Sheikh Ahmad returned to Sirhind and remained with his father until the latter's death in 1599.

Despite his early Chishti initiation, he was disinclined to practice *sama* and lived a rigidly austere orthodox life. In 1599, he departed for Mecca but on the way a friend suggested he meet Khwaja Baqi Billah. Although Khwaja Billah did not readily accept disciples, he invited Khwaja Ahmad to postpone his journey to Mecca and spend time in his *khanqah*. He was greatly inspired by his new *pir*'s mystical powers and made swift progress in his spiritual learning after his initiation into the Naqshbandi order.

In just two days, Sheikh Ahmad had reached the point of *fana* and at the suggestion of Khwaja Baqi, he continued his meditation achieving *fana al-fana* (a state in which his personality disappeared absolutely into the Essence). He then went on the next stage, where he perceived both God and each realized the existence of the other. This was the last stage of the beginning of the Sufi journey in the Naqshbandi *silsilah*. Sheikh Ahmad completed his entire training in three months; it took most Sufis years to reach the same level. Khwaja Baqi was pleased with his student's progress and granted him permission to return to Sirhind with some of his other disciples.

Even though he had been a follower of *Wahdat al-Wujud* like his father, he gradually came to accept the superiority of *Wahdat ash-Shuhud* (unity of vision or appearance) explained above, propagated by Sheikh Alaudaula Simnani (1261–1336), a Persian Sufi of the Kubravi/Firdausi *silsilah*. In a series of letters to Khwaja Baqi, he wrote about his realization.

After the death of Khwaja Baqi, Sheikh Ahmad visited Delhi. Through there were other contenders to the succession of Khwaja Baqi, Sheikh Ahmad claimed spiritual supremacy in India. At the age of 40, according to his followers, he received, in Sirhind, the grace to be the *mujjaddid* (renewer) and became known as Mujaddid-e-Alf-e-Sani (the renewer of the Second Millennium).

As per a hadith found in several collections, the Prophet is reported to have said: 'Islam began as a stranger and it will return to what it was. How blessed are the strangers.' This is a belief that was held by Sheikh Sirhindi, too. In his time, he thought, Islam had become weak and its followers were few, and though he did not believe that it was the end of the world, he did believe what the hadith foretold that Islam had become a rarity and the Muslims were strangers in an alien environment, in which no godly person will soon remain. Since Prophet Muhammad is the last of the prophets and another prophet cannot be expected to come, a *Mujaddid* (renewer of faith) is chosen from among the Muslim *ulema* on the eve of every century, not to bring a new sharia, but to revive the existing one. That's why Sheikh Ahmed Sirhindi is considered the renewer of the second millennium.

He is seen as a reformer who came at a time when the teachings of Islam were felt to have been diluted in India due to the addition of indigenous practices. He wanted to maintain the social order of the time, which he felt was being affected by Akbar's decisions. He believed that certain mystic practices had become closer to yogic practices, rather than being based on the Quran and hadiths, and set about rectifying this. He wanted to purge Islam of the heresies that he felt had crept in. Music and *sama mehfils* found no place in his tradition, and his followers were forbidden to participate in them.

Sheikh Ahmad Sirhindi believed that the Naqshbandi *silsilah* was superior to the others, as it had inherited the Sufi traditions of both Hazrat Ali and Caliph Abu Bakr through the sixth Shia Imam Jafar al-Sadiq, whose mother was a descendant of the caliph. So the Naqshbandi methods were based on the methods of Hazrat Ali, which were rooted in an abundance of knowledge, and the Sufi methods of Abu Bakr, who founded them on his love of the Prophet.[18]

The Sheikh is believed to be 'the person who defended Islamic orthodoxy against the heterodoxy of Akbar and his imitators, the leader whose descendants supported Aurangzeb against his mystically inclined brother Dara Shukoh.'[19]

Scholars like Nizami and S.A.A. Rizvi have argued that Sheikh Ahmed Sirhindi had great influence on Mughal policy and governance, and that Aurangzeb's 'more severe treatment of the Hindus' in the eighteenth century was the culmination of the religious programme inaugurated by Sirhindī. This programme in turn was a reaction to Akbar's policies, deemed not only to be too tolerant to non-Muslims, but also too aggressive to the Muslim clergy.'[20]

There is no doubt that Sheikh Ahmad Sirhindi played an important role in the history of his era and sought to influence the actions of the Mughal emperors. He vociferously opposed Akbar's attempts at what he saw as *bidat* (innovation), with his policies of Din-e-Ilahi and attempts to interfere in religion; he wanted a return to Sunni orthodoxy.

Sheikh Ahmad Sirhindi is seen as a highly orthodox figure who is said to have reversed the heretical traits of the period of Akbar and restored the pristine purity of Islam and inspired the orthodox reforms of Aurangzeb.[21]

Once Sheikh Ahmed Sirhindi and his movement were introduced into the Mughal court, according to Nizami, there was a gradual change in the religious life and attitude of the Mughal rulers. Akbar's religious cosmopolitanism was abandoned by Jahangir; Jahangir's indifference to religion was given up by Shahjahan; and Shahjahan's attempt to keep personal religious ideas out of politics was ignored by Aurangzeb, who applied his religious views to administration. Akbar had brought religion into politics inspired by his zeal for religious cosmopolitanism; Aurangzeb introduced religion into politics impelled by an orthodox, religious attitude, created by the Naqshbandi saints.[22]

However, Professor Irfan Habib has argued against the view that the sheikh had such an influence over Aurangzeb. He builds his argument as follows. First, he says, 'What is supposed to distinguish Sheikh Ahmed from all this is that he was a kind of a leader of the whole movement and that he attained, after great labours, decisive success. There is however little truth in either of these two notions.'

According to Habib, Sheikh Ahmed wasn't a leader of the masses but had his sights 'fixed upon the king and his nobles and he held the view that the Shariat could only be restored and protected by the king, for "the king is to the universe what the heart is to the body"'. He was keen on establishing the perfect rule of the shariah and *accordingly* wrote a large number of letters to the nobles, especially Jahangir's Mir Bakshi Nawab Murtaza Khan Shaikh Farid, exhorting them to convince the king of his views. His appeal was never to Muslims in general but only to superiors and to the main authority.

Since there are well-preserved historical records of Jahangir's reign, including his own memoirs, Habib says, 'we are fortunately in a good position to judge how far the claims of his success advanced in the hagiology of the Sheikh's later disciples and by his modern admirers are correct.' The two points where the Sheikh's role is emphasized is, first, in 1605 when Akbar died and second, when Jahangir ascended the throne a month later. The Sheikh was said to have enjoyed great influence on one of Jahangir's nobles, Sheikh Farid, who in turn had an equally great influence in Jahangir. 'Jahangir under his pressure is said to have abandoned Akbar's anti-Islamic policies. Secondly when in 1619 Jahangir released Sheikh Ahmed from the short imprisonment he is said to have come under his direct influence.'[23]

Examining the influence that Sheikh Ahmad had on Sheikh Farid and the latter's influence on Jahangir, and asking whether Jahangir abandoned Akbar's policies, Habib opines:

> There is no real proof apart from the large number of Sheikh Ahmed's letters addressed to him that Sheikh Farid ever took Sheikh Ahmed's advice. The letters were gathered in a volume and published only in 1617 when Sheikh Farid was dead. There is no proof that he received them at all or at least in the form we have them now. It seems very difficult to believe that such a high official of the Empire would have dared to entertain letters which spoke in abusive terms of the reigning king's father. Sheikh Farid seems on the contrary to have had a great sense of loyalty for Akbar, for he commissioned Illahdad Faizi to write history of his reign in which a lot of praise was showered on Akbar.[24]

Habib goes on to say that in 1619, after the letters were published, Jahangir imprisoned Sheikh Ahmad for a year in Gwalior Fort. In his words:

> Before these letters were circulated or published Sheikh Ahmed was not important enough to merit any attention. But now that his views were put down on paper for all to see he could hardly be ignored. It was not enough that Akbar had been denounced and the Hindus abused in letters addressed to the greatest nobles of the court. Shias had been second subjected to vituperation at a time when his favourite queen was Nur Jahan, and her father is Itmadud-daula and brother Asaf Khan occupied the highest ranks in the Empire. But with his innate shrewdness Jahangir picked an issue where he could have the full weight of the Sunni orthodoxy behind him.

Jahangir levied charges that his book was the 'carrier of meaningless things' with 'many absurdities which lead to infidelity and heresy'. He also said that he felt that the Mujaddid was presumptuous and opiniated.

There is therefore no contemporary evidence of the sheikh's influence of Prince Khurram (later given the title of Shah Jahan). The sheikh predeceased Jahangir. There is no evidence of his influence even later, says Habib, especially on Aurangzeb. A reference by Nimat Khan-e-Ali, the merciless satirist of the time, to the sheikh being the emperor's spiritual preceptor must thus be understood as satire in the wake of Aurangzeb's conquest of Golconda.

Yohanan Friedmann, in his book on *Shaykh Aḥmad Sirhindī* has argued that Sheikh Ahmed Sirhindi wanted to place Sufi doctrines within Sunni orthodox beliefs but did not break away from the mainstream Sufi thought of his time.[25]

As Professor Prashant Keshavmurthy puts it, 'The scholarship of Yohanan Friedmann and Shankar Nair on Sheikh Ahmad Sirhindi's intellectual genealogies and legacies has shown that his modern salience as a so-called anti-ibn 'Arabi reformer stems from twentieth-century South Asian Muslim nationalism and not from his importance in his own milieu where he was taken up far more significantly in Ottoman lands than in

Mughal ones; and there for mainly ontological reasons rather than reformist or nationalist ones.'[26]

Sheikh Ahmed Sirhindi died on 10 December 1624. His very grand dargah in Sirhind is extremely popular even today and is frequented by devotees from India, Pakistan, Bangladesh, and Afghanistan. After his death, the order was taken forward by other Sufi sheikhs, namely Mirza Mazhar Jan-e-Janan and Shah Waliullah.

Jan-e-Janan was born to Mirza Jan, an officer in Aurangzeb's court, in Malwa on 13 March 1699. He was named Jan-e-Janan by Aurangzeb, as per a custom of the emperor naming his officer's sons. Aurangzeb said that 'a son is the soul of his father. Since the name of the father is Mirza Jan, the son's name will be Jan-e-Janan.'[27] He took the *takhallus* (pen name) Mazhar and was given the title Shamsuddin Habibullah. His father died when he was around 19, but the young boy continued his religious education. He was initiated into the Naqshbandi order by Sheikh Saiyid Nur Muhammad Badauni, a *khalifa* of one of Khwaja Ahmad Sirhindi's grandsons and part of the Golden Chain.

According to lore within the Naqshbandi order, Jan-e-Janan saw Prophet Ibrahim and spiritually received miraculous powers from him. It is said that anytime the name of Caliph Abu Baqr Siddiq was mentioned, the Mirza would see him, Prophet Muhammad and all his companions, and all the Khwajas of the Naqshbandi *silsilah*. When Sheikh Nur Muhammad began teaching Jan-e-Janan, he took him to new heights of spiritual awareness and showed him the secrets of the world. After Sheikh Nur Muhammad passed away, he learned under many prominent spiritual teachers of the time, including Sheikh Muhammad Afzal and Sheikh Muhammad Abid. He studied under these sheikhs for 20 years and became an ocean of knowledge.[28]

Mirza Mazhar Jan-e-Janan began initiating disciples into the Naqshbandi *silsilah* after Sheikh Muhammad Abid's death. He wrote letters to his disciples sharing his philosophy that there was no real difference between *Wahdat al-Wujud* and *Wahdat ash-Shuhud*, and that people should not question saints of God. He was a staunch believer and defender of the Mujaddid (Khwaja Ahmad Sirhind). His teachings focused on *zikr* and reaching a state where the heart was tranquil and journeying towards the divine.[29]

As a poet, Mazhar wrote in Persian. Some of his Urdu verses survive too. He wrote about the excitement of love he had experienced when he was young. He said that he was considered a poet only because his rhythmic cries were considered poetry.[30]

One of his significant contributions is that he vociferously rebutted the views of the orthodoxy regarding Hindu scriptures and gave them an important place in the evolution of the religious thought of mankind. K.A. Nizami writes about him in his account of state and culture in medieval India:

> Sheikh Ahmad Sirhindi and his school of thought is labelled as representing orthodoxy but it is completely forgotten that one of his spiritual descendants Mirza Mazhar Jan-e-Janan gave evidence of great spiritual virility and dynamism when he included the Hindus among *ahl-eKitab* [people of the book] and declared the Vedas to be a revealed Book.[31]

Jan-e-Janan believed that since no place on earth was left without prophetic guidance, and the prophets that were sent spoke in the language of the people they were sent to guide, Shri Krishna and Shri Rama – called avatars in Hindustan – were actually prophets or messengers.

> On the basis of this view he interprets a dream in which Krishna is seen in a desert full of fire, saying that the fire is not to be understood as the fire of hell, tormenting Krishna the infidel, but as the fire of Sufi love (*ishq*), in which Krishna was immersed. Krishna and Rama were not mentioned in the Qura'n and it is not permissible to declare any ancient (*azguzashtagan*) pre-Islamic person as infidel without scriptural evidence.[32]

Thus Jan-e-Janan concludes that the religion of the Indians (by which he seems to have meant Hindus) was one that pleased God in the past. Till the mission of the Prophet, it was incumbent upon them to follow the other prophets sent to their country. After Prophet Muhammad, a fundamental change was brought about and all former religions were abrogated. So while those before the Prophet's mission were not truly infidels, those who don't follow his mission are now seen as such.[33]

Jan-e-Janan died in 1781 and was buried in Shahjahanabad (Old Delhi). His dargah is known Khanqah-e-Mazhariya or Shah Ghulam Ali ki Khanqah, and it houses the shrines of four very important saints of the Naqshbandi *silsilah*. It is right in the heart of the old city of Delhi, and the mosque is very popular with the locals who use it to say their daily prayers. It is very well-maintained, too.

Qutubuddin Ahmad, known popularly as Shah Waliullah, was born on 21 February 1703. His father Sheikh Abdur Rahim was a learned man, from the Naqshbandi *silsilah*. He had remarried when he was 60, and it was through this marriage that Shah Waliullah was born. Sheikh Abdur Rahim believed that his decision to remarry was inspired by God.

Like his father, Shah Waliullah was devoted to studying theology. The home in which he was raised provided the perfect environment to fuel this passion for knowledge. He completed his religious education by the age of 15, at which point his father gave him charge of Sheikh Abdur Rahim's seminary and initiated into his *silsilah*.

Studying at the grave of his father, Shah Waliullah developed an extraordinary understanding of Sufism. He studied for 12 years after the death of his father and learned all four schools of Sunni jurisprudence. In 1731, the Shah travelled to Mecca and Medina, meeting many interesting scholars and kindling an interest in Ibn al-Arabi. He had many visions of Prophet Muhammad and his family and many inspirations from God. These visions were recorded in a book called *Fuyuz al-Haramain*.

Returning to India in 1732, full of ideas to transform its social, religious and political life, he began lecturing and writing. By the time of his demise, Shah Waliullah had written several books, letters, and treatises. Although most of this was on Sufism, he also wrote on theology, mysticism, sociology, and politics.

Shah Waliullah died on 20 August 1762. He had many disciples but they were trained in their own specialized fields of knowledge. Shah

Waliullah's interest and knowledge in multiple fields was inherited by his son Shah Abdul Aziz. After the death of his father, the young man joined the seminary and completed his studies under his father's eminent students including Sheikh Muhammad Ashiq and Shah Muhammad Amin.[34]

Shah Waliullah is buried in a simple grave in the area of Delhi known as Mehdiyan near Maulana Abul Kalam Medical College. It is a very popular cemetery and is also the resting place of the famous poet Momin Khan Momin and BJP leader Sikander Bakht.

The dargah is a popular place not just for the devotees of Shah Waliullah, but also for the relatives of others who are buried there. And though the place is being seriously encroached upon, the dargah and cemetery are rather well looked after.

Near Mehdiyan is an area now known as the Khwaja Mir Dard Basti (adjacent to Zakir Hussain College). There, in a simple tin-shed dargah, a famous mystic poetrests eternally. Khwaja Mir Dard (1721–1785) – along with Mir Taqi Mir and Mirza Sauda – is considered one of the three major poets of the Delhi School. What is often missed is that Khwaja Mir Dard was a very famous Sufi saint of the Naqshbandi Majdudi *silsilah*. His greatness lay in translating his mysticism into verse. An instance of his craft is seen in the following verse:

*Shamaa ki maa nind ham is bazm men*
*Chashm-nam aaye the daaman-tar chale*

[Like a candle to this gathering
I came with wet eyes, and left with a damp hem.]

His father Mohammad Nasir 'Andalib' (d. 1758) was also a mystic poet. Mir Dard had descended from Sheikh Bahauddin and was a disciple of his father and of Pir Mohammad Qayyum, a disciple of Sheikh Ahmed Sirhindi. From his father he learnt *Tariqa-e-Mohammadiya* (the path of Prophet Mohammad).

Mir Dard lived through the terrible period when Delhi was devastated by the raids of Nadir Shah and Ahmed Shah Abdali. He captured it in his poetry:

*Tar-damani pe Sheikh hamari na jaiyo,*
*daman nichod den to farishte wazu karen..*

[Don't be deceived by my tear-soaked hem, O Sheikh;
If I were to wring it, angels could perform ablutions.]

The Naqshbandi *silsilah* is one of the most popular *silsilahs* in the world with disciples and masters of the golden chain in almost all countries.

# 9

# Qalandars and Other *Silsilahs* in India

*O laal meri pat rakhio bala, Jhoole Laalan,*
*Sindri da Sehvan da,*
*Sakhi Shabaaz Qalandar,*
*Dam-a-dam mast Qalandar,*
*Ali dam dam de andar.*

[Please preserve my name and protect me O the red robed, Jhulelal;
O friend of Sindh and Sehwan,
The generous red-robed one,
The red-robed God-intoxicated *Qalandar*,
Ali in every breath of mine.]

– Unknown/Traditional song

This qawwali dedicated to the popular Sufi saint Lal Shahbaz Qalandar is one of the most easily recognizable songs in the Sufi milieu. Like the song, the qalandars with their colourful attire and dramatic aesthetic stand out at any dargah. They are not connected with any of the *silsilah*s and roam around from dargah to dargah.

The qalandars, with their flowing robes, tangled locks and sometimes a wild look in their eyes, are free spirits who have renounced the world for the love of God. In fact, the word qalandar is used to refer to someone who has renounced all worldly belongings and is engrossed in selfless devotion to God. They perform only the bare minimum religious duties and are unfettered mystics, roaming the countryside from dargah to dargah.

Razzaq Ali, an elderly qalandar I met, reflected a simple joy on his face and a sense of freedom from all norms as he described the life of a wandering fakir who went from one *urs* to another.

> I am mystic gypsy called qalandar;
> I have neither fire, home, nor monastery.
> By day I wander about the world, and at night
> I sleep with a brick under my head.[1]

A qalandar is unlike the Sufis in that they are not affiliated to any *silsilah* and are normally always on the move. In contemporary times, they go from one dargah to another, wherever an *urs* is taking place and perform services there. A common sight in most dargahs is the qalandar fanning devotees with huge cloth fans, as providing comfort to the devotees is considered *sawab* or an act worthy of divine reward.

In his study, Digby says that those recruited to the qalandar bands are usually people who find the lifestyle associated with them more attractive than what society currently has to offer, or who are seeking escape from punishment (presumably from minor crimes), or oppression.[2]

The first references to qalandars are found in the eleventh-century treatise of Khwaja Abdullah Ansari titled *Qalandarnam*. The treatise describes the author's conversations with a qalandar. According to the book, qalandars should be humble, lowly, selfless, and ascetic.[3]

By the end of the twelfth century, a distinct Qalandariya *silsilah* that could be differentiated from Sufis and *malamati*s (those mystics who blamed themselves) emerged. Much of their differences centred on their dress choices and lifestyle. Being wandering fakirs, they came into contact with other ascetics. Their association with *nath yogi*s, for instance, led to their practice of wearing earrings and they shared with them the habit of consuming Indian hemp and other drugs.[4]

According to Trimingham, a well-known author on the subject:

> [T]he term qalandariyya is applied to people so possessed by the intoxication of 'tranquillity of [the] heart' that they respect no custom or usage, and reject the regular observances of society and mutual relationship. Traversing the arenas of 'tranquillity of [the]

> heart', they concern themselves little with ritual prayer and fasting except such as are obligatory (*faraid*).[5]

Trimingham differentiates between a Sufi and a dervish, with the former being those who follow the mystical doctrines, and the latter, those who follow the mystical way.

In India, the Qalandar *silsilah* was introduced by Shah Khizr Rumi, a native of Anatolia, during the reign of Iltutmish (1210–1236). Bu Ali Qalandar is said to have been his disciple. The two most famous Indian qalandars are Bu Ali Qalandar of Panipat and Sheikh Hazrat Abu Bakr Tusi Haideri Qalandari.

There are many legends concerning Bu Ali Qalandar Bu (1209–1324). One such legend describes him as a disciple of Hazrat Ali, with whom he had taken an oath of allegiance in a dream.

Bu Ali lived in Delhi for some years before returning to Panipat, where he practiced extreme ascetism and mortification of flesh. True to the nature of a wandering dervish, he travelled extensively – even going to Konya where he met the son of Mevlana Rumi.

He was also a gifted poet and his Persian masnavi is very famous. He was supposed to be in a perpetual state of spiritual ecstasy. He wrote:

> Recognition of Beauty is a step leading to the understanding of the Beloved. This made the lover and the Beloved identical. Beloveds were created in the form of human beings in order that they might lead people to the righteous path. Both heaven and hell were born of the beauty of the Lover and none of these were meant for anyone but lovers. Heaven was the stage of union; hell was the station of separation and was intended for enemies.[6]

The only other qalandar as popular as Bu Ali was Sheikh Hazrat Abu Bakr Tusi Haideri Qalandari. The latter is popularly known as the *Matka Peer* of Delhi to his numerous devotees. According to a local legend, he who lived during the reign of Sultan Ghiyasuddin Balban cured an incurable disease by giving the suffering man a sip from his *matka* (pot). On hearing of this incident, Sultan Balban sent clay pots filled with mud and iron balls to the saint as an offering. The saint covered the pots and started praying;

at the end of his prayers, the covers on the pots were lifted and the iron balls and mud were gone. The people around saw that the pots now had roasted gram and jaggery in them. Even today devotees whose *mannat*s (wishes) have been fulfilled offer *matka*s and jaggery and gram at his dargah.

All around the dargah one can see *matka*s, either hanging from trees or stacked around the shrine. The shrine is now on a 10-metre high hillock, which can be approached by steps. It is a very beautiful shrine of modern construction. Sixteen delicate pillars form engrailed arches and support a flat roof that houses the shrine. Mirror work decorates the insides. The courtyard that surrounds it is always full of visitors and qawwals. An inscription on the outside wall mentions many details about the saint, including the fact that he left this world in 1257. Though next to a very busy road, the place is very calm and peaceful. No one asks devotees for money or subscriptions, as is often the case in religious places in India, so one can sit and pray in peace.

One of the most renowned ones is the Pakistani qalandar from the mid-thirteenth century; the real name of Lal Shahbaz Qalandar (the Red Falcon), the patron saint of Sehwan, was Mir Saiyed Usman. It was he who inspired the popular and evocative qawwali *dum-a-dum mast qalandar* mentioned at the beginning of this chapter. He was a wandering poet, dancer, and musician who always wore a red dress and thus earned the sobriquet *lal* (red).

He was a *mazjub* (intoxicated) Sufi who considered himself to be a spiritual descendant of Mansur al-Hallaj. His annual *urs,* from 8th to the 11th in the Islamic month of Shawaal, attracts a huge crowd of devotees from Pakistan and abroad. According to one newspaper report, his 765th *urs* celebration in May 2017[7] saw over two million people at the three-day event.[8] The festival of dance, music, and love took place with the *dhamaal* celebrations after evening prayers that year. The word *dhamaal* means enjoyment, and the *urs* indeed saw a full-throated abandonment of worldly cares as the dervishes, qalandars, and other mystics gathered celebrated with their dance which is also called *dhamaal,* despite the blazing heat and threats of bombs being planted at the venue.

Jamaluddin Hansawi, the famous Sufi and contemporary of Hazrat Nizamuddin Auliya, would also visit *Matka Peer*. He gave him the nickname *Baaz-e-Safid* (White Falcon), as if in contrast with the Red Falcon, Lal Shahbaz Qalandar.[9]

Along with *silsilah*s, subsidiary *silsilah*s also took root. Those with slightly different ideas branched off, and a number of offshoot *silsilah*s came into being. These orders were named after the Sufi masters who exemplified the distinguishing teachings and practices of the new branch.

The Chishti *silsilah* developed the most offshoots with many of the popular saints having *silsilah*s named after them. The followers of Hazrat Nizamuddin Auliya are called Nizami Chishti but they stay within the Chishti fold.

The Sabri-Chishti *silsilah,* named after Sheikh Alauddin Ali Ahmad Sabir (1196–1291), is another of its bifurcations. The Sabris developed a distinct identity, which according to Ernst, intensified during British colonial rule.[10]

Sheikh Alauddin Ali Ahmad Sabir was a *khalifa* and nephew of Baba Farid. He settled in Kaliyar near Roorkee (present-day Uttarakhand).

There is a very interesting story about Sheikh Sabir from the time when he was appointed in-charge of the *langarkhana* by Baba Farid. His mother – Baba Farid's sister – came to visit him and found him severely emaciated. Upon enquiry, he told her that while he had been given the charge of the *langarkhana*, he had not received permission to eat! This earned him the sobriquet of *sabir* (the patient one), the name by which he is famous today. He is also called Sabir Ali Piya (beloved) by his followers.

According to *Siyar al-Auliya,* he was a gifted mystic who showed a high level of spiritualism and self-control.[11] Baba Farid held him in great respect and once remarked that while Hazrat Nizamuddin has received the knowledge of the chest, Sabir has inherited the knowledge of his heart.[12]

The Sabri-Chishti *silsilah* became famous because of Sheikh Alauddin Ali Ahmad Sabir's disciples, the most famous among them being Sheikh Abdul Haq of Rudauli (near Barabanki, Uttar Pradesh) and Sheikh Abdul Quddus, who was born in Radauli but settled later in Gangoh near Saharanpur (also in Uttar Pradesh).

Sheikh Alauddin Ali Ahmad Sabir's disciple Sheikh Jalauddin Panipati inducted Sheikh Abdul Haq into the folds of Sufism. This is how the Sabri-Chishti *silsilah* went from Panipat to Radauli and later to Gangoh.

His other renowned disciple Sheikh Abdul Quddus Gangoh (1456–1537) was one of the most prominent Sufi saints during the reign of Sikander Lodi and Mughal Emperors Babur and Humayun.

He began his formal studies in external sciences (*ulum-e-zahir*) but got diverted and consumed by the love of God (*ishq-e-maula*). In letters to his disciple Sheikh Jalauddin Thaneswari (also known as Maktubat-e-Quddusiya), he writes that love *(Ishq)* is the principal cause for the creation of the world. From a superficial point of view love appears easy, but in reality it reduces the lover to ashes. The sheikh was a staunch exponent of *Wahdat al-Wujud.*

He was very fond of *samameh fil*s with *raqs* (rhythmic movement) and deliberately adopted elements of Yoga in his mystical thought. He often remained in a state of *sukr* (mystical intoxication) but all this was within the precepts of the shariah. Apart from prescribed prayers, he spent considerable time performing supererogatory prayers and rituals, and did strenuous spiritual exercises.

He performed the *salat-e-makus* (inverted prayer) and during it experienced a mystical state called *sultan-e-zikr* (a spiritual and physical state resulting from constant *zikr*). Though Baba Farid also performed *chillah-e-makus, sultan-ul-zikr* was a new term in Chishti writings.

The Radauli area of Uttar Pradesh has been described as:

> [A] stronghold of Nath-Panthi and other yogic traditions, and Abd al-Quddūs drew upon Vedantic philosophy and yogic practices in his teachings and rituals. His work on Sufi themes entitled *Rushd-nāma* (*The book of rectitude*) reveals such yogic influences. For instance, it draws links with yogic practices in the description of *pas-eanfas* (breath control), and it identifies *Wahdat al-Wujud* with the teaching of the Naths, as well as *salat-emakus* with *ultisadhna (trans*gressive (lit. "upside down") way to salvation).[13]

He interspersed his work with Hindavi dohas and composed poetry in Hindavi under the pen name Alakhdas.

He wrote extensively in Persian, Arabic, and Hindi and his *Rushd-nama* is very famous. He made a comparison between the Nath terminology *dvaid advaita-vilakshanavada* (the monism-dualism distinction debate) and the terminology of Sufism and *Wahdat al-Wujud.* (Though Dara Shukoh was not aware of *Rushd-nama*, it is the same philosophy that he has written about in *Majma-ul-Bahrain.*)

His followers visit his simple domed dargah in Gangoh with great devotion. His disciple and *khalifa* Sheikh Jalaluddin Faruqi Thaneswari (d. 1581) has a small but extremely popular dargah behind Sheikh Chehli Ki Mazar in Thaneswar.

The saints of the Sabri-Chishti *silsilah* played an active part in the Uprising of 1857 against the British East India Company.

The most important dissident was Haji Imadullah (d. 1899). 'A Sābrī Chishtī master, Imādullāh looms as a giant amid all the reform movements of the late nineteenth century that adapted and transformed their Islamic renewal into a pan-Indian force.'[14] He was exiled by the British to Mecca after the uprising.

The Firdausi *silsilah*, a branch of the Suhrawardi *silsilah*, was one of the earliest offshoot *silsilahs* to be established in the Indian subcontinent. It traces its origin to Saifuddin Said Bakharzi (1190–1260) who was a disciple of Sheikh Najmuddin Kubra (1145–1221). Sheikh Bakharzi had been given the title of Sheikh al-Firdaus (sheikh of paradise) and so his followers came to be known as Firdausis. This *silsilah* spread across the subcontinent courtesy of his disciple, Sheikh Saiyed Badruddin Samarqandi (d. 1315), who was sent by Bakharzi to India in order to spread its spiritual message.

Sheikh Saiyed Badruddin Samarqandi came from Bukhara to Delhi as Khwaja Qutbuddin Bakhtiyar Kaki and settled on the banks of the River Yamuna. His great and well-known contribution to the growing reach of the *silsilah* apart, Sheikh Saiyed Badruddin Samarqandi was on very friendly terms with the Chishti saints of his time and often enjoyed the company of Hazrat Nizamuddin. He was one of his followers and would often go to Hazrat Nizamuddin's *khanqah* to enjoy the *sama mehfils* held there.

His dargah is just off one of the key main roads in Delhi – M.G. Marg. It is also one of the few dargahs where women are allowed to go in. When Sultan Firoz Shah Tughlaq was building his citadel (Firoz Shah Kotla), he ensured that the walls of his citadel circumvented the saint's dargah. This respectful diversion of the walls can be seen from inside the dargah itself.

The dargah is very popular, especially among the locals, and receives regular visitors. One such regular is Amarnath ji, who pays his respects to the saint daily. His father was a devotee, and so it has been a practice to visit daily since he was a baby. He told me to ask for whatever I wished, reassuring me that it would be granted.

Khwaja Ruknuddin Firdausi and Khwaja Najibuddin Firdausi were disciples of Sheikh Saiyed Badruddin Samarqand. They succeeded him as *khalifa*s in Delhi. The former was the first to add the word Firdausi after his name. Khwaja Ruknuddin Firdausi's dargah is in Kilokari while Khwaja Najibuddin Firdausi's shrine is in Mehrauli; both are well regarded among followers of the Firdausi *silsilah*.

The Firdausi *silsilah,* however, could not flourish in Delhi and made a more significant mark for itself in Bihar. Sheikh Sharfuddin was one of the leading lights in that region.

Born as Ahmad Yahya (1263–1381), this saint began to be known as Sharfuddin which means the 'glory of the faith'. His ancestors had settled in Maner (now in the state of Bihar) at the end of the thirteenth century. He had a traditional education as a young boy and became a disciple of Sheikh Abu Tawwama when he was about 15 or 16, moving to Sunargaon in Bengal and living with his *pir*'s family. He was so devoted to his spiritual education that he would often not even stop to read letters from his family. However, when Sheikh Sharfuddin's father died in 1291, he had to leave Sunargaon to be with his grieving mother in Manyar. A little later, he came to Delhi and after a lengthy search for a spiritual preceptor, eventually becoming the disciple of Khwaja Najibuddin Firdausi.

Popularly known as Makhdoom-ul Mulk Bihari, Sheikh Sharfuddin performed very difficult ascetic exercises in the forests near Rajgir in Bihar. While it is commonly believed that he spent 12 years in the forests performing these exercises, the real number is unknown. As the Sheikh's fame spread, many visitors would come to the forest to meet him.

Eventually, the Sheikh started coming to Manyar near Rajgir every Friday for congregational prayers, so he could meet people, after which he would return to the forest.

Maulana Nizam Madani, a disciple of Hazrat Nizamuddin Auliya, was quite attached to the Sheikh and built a small *khanqah* for his use in Manyar. Moreover, on Sultan Mohammad bin Tughlaq's orders, the governor of Bihar Zainuddin Majd al-Mulk built him a *khanqah* and assigned the revenue district of Rajgir to it in order to meet the sheikh's expenses. The sheikh reluctantly accepted this kindness.

Like other Suhrawardi saints, although of an ascetic temperament, Sheikh Sharfuddin reluctantly accepted gifts and presents of land and money from rulers and nobles. He was not averse to giving the sultan suggestions on occasion, and he wrote two letters to Sultan Firoz Shah Tughlaq advising him to be impartial in dispensing justice.[15]

Sheikh Yahya al Maneri believed in mercy, compassion, humility, and generosity. Once, while he was observing a supererogatory fast, someone offered him food. He accepted it; he explained that he could recompense for breaking the fast by keeping more later, but that there was no atonement for the sin of breaking someone's heart!

According to him, the *nafs* or ego was the biggest evil and every Muslim was duty-bound to wage a war against it. The true jihad 'was to be waged not against non-Muslims but against the heretical *nafs* (ego).'[16]

His dargah is often confused with that of his father, which is in Maner near Patna. Sheikh Sharfuddin's dargah is a simple one in Bihar Sharif. The old shrine and mosque have been completely renovated. His mother is buried next to him, and it is another one of the few dargahs where there is no restriction on the entry of women. In fact, even at his master's shrine in Delhi, and also where his father is buried in Maner, women are allowed to enter and pray. As one of the *khadims* at his dargah told me: 'With his mother buried beside him, how could anyone stop women from entering?'

The Kubravi *silsilah* was founded by Sheikh Najmuddin Kubra (1145–1221). Born in Khwarezm in Central Asia, Sheikh Najmuddin was an outstanding personality and prolific writer. His teachings spread to many parts of Central Asia and Iran, and eventually found their way to India via Kashmir, where they remain popular till date.

Sheikh Najmuddin Kubra lived during the period of turmoil in Central Asia and Persia when Chengiz Khan and his army were sweeping through the area, sacking city after city and adopting the scorched earth philosophy. When Khwarzem was attacked by the Mongols, Chengiz Khan offered protection to Sheikh Najmuddin Kubra. The great sheikh, who had predicted that calamity would come from the east and ruin the flourishing city of Khwarzem, refused to accept and instead rode out against the Mongols in defence of his city, dying during the battle in 1221.

His disciples spread the teachings of the Kubravi order in various parts of the Muslim world.

One of his many famous disciples is Saiyed Ali Hamdani (1314–1385), popularly known as Shah-e-Hamadan. He introduced the Kubravi *silsilah* in Kashmir, one of the most popular Sufi orders there now. His uncle, a very pious saint, tutored him, and at the age of 12, introduced him to Sheikh Muzdaqani. Sheikh Muzdaqani initiated the Sheikh into the Kubravi order and taught him the principles of Sufism. After his initiation, he became the student of Sheikh Taqiuddin Ali Dusti, a disciple of Sheikh Alaud-daula Simnani. After studying under his new teacher for two years, Saiyed Ali Hamdani returned to Sheikh Muzdaqani to complete his education.

Saiyed Ali Hamdani came to Kashmir in 1381; the new kingdom offered him the stability and opportunities he needed to propagate Islam. But his stay was to be cut short.

The sultan of Kashmir in those days was Sultan Qutbuddin, who following the policies of his predecessor Shah Mir maintained friendly relations with his Hindu subjects and let Brahmin elite dominate the administration. 'Although, the Sultan did not wish to alienate the migrants from Iran, their activities shocked him and a conflict between them became inevitable. After a stay in Kashmir of about three years, Saiyyed Ali [Hamdani] left Srinagar a frustrated man,'[17] with the stated objective of performing hajj.

While Sufi scholars like Sadia Dehlvi praise him for his 'greatest achievement', 'creating an ambience for the evolution of an Islamic consciousness', Saiyed Ali Hamdani is not without his detractors on another count as well. His classification of state subjects as Muslims and non-Muslims has sometimes been criticized.[18] In response, Dehlvi tries to set the record right, saying: '[H]e wrote that a Muslim ruler being the shadow of God should render equitable justice and beneficence to both believers and non-believers. He was concerned with maintaining the visibility of the Sharia through reforming the behaviour of the Sultans and the ruling elite.' In fact, during his stay in Kashmir, one of the points of friction between Shah Qutbuddin, the ruler of Kashmir who reigned from 1373 to1389, and Saiyed Ali Hamdani was regarding the implementation of shariah.

Dehlvi quotes M. Ishaq Khan, who says, 'Although Sayyid Ali was deep-rooted in the Sharia, his chief mission was not to enforce religious laws through the state machinery. His primary objective was to sensitize the ruler and the small minority of his Muslim subjects in respect to following the Sharia in personal matters.'[19]

However, Saiyed Ali Hamdani's followers were not like him. They were overtaken by a missionary zeal, which resulted in temple destruction and many forced conversions. And their saint's proselytizing zeal is praised, although they offer no description of his methods are available.[20]

Though Sufi saints did not emphasize miracles and instead laid emphasis on good conduct and service, one anecdote is often used to suggest that Saiyed Ali Hamdani gained converts because of his miracles. It describes his visit to a renowned ascetic in Srinagar. The ascetic tried to impress him by saying he could fly through the air and immediately demonstrated it. Saiyed Ali Hamdani asked one of his followers, Saiyed Kabir, to teach the man a lesson. Saiyed Kabir instructed his slippers to bring the man down by beating him on his head. The slippers followed the orders and brought the man down, who now became convinced of Sheikh Hamdani's superiority. He and his followers accepted Islam.[21] Similar anecdotes are attributed to many other Sufi saints including Khwaja Muinuddin Chishti, and this continuing tradition could be a way of gaining legitimacy in the eyes of local populace and disciples.

Despite this turbulent history with Kashmir, the *khanqah* of Shah-e-Hamadan, built in 1395, on the banks of River Jhelum remains. It is a beautiful wooden building with intricate papier mâché designs, and a focal point for Kashmiris today. There is a sense of peace and harmony in the *khanqah,* and devotees from far and wide flock to it, either seeking the saint's blessings or simply to meditate.[22]

Besides, he came to Kashmir with many other Sufis and travelled extensively through the valley. He is said to have come with 700 or so followers, out of which many settled down in Kashmir and carry on his work.

Saiyed Ali Hamdani was also an *alim* (scholar) and wrote many books.

Finally, the Sheikh died on his return journey in 1385. His followers took his body to Khatalan in Tajikistan.

Saiyed Ali Hamdani appointed Sheikh Ahmed his *khalifa*. Sheikh Ahmed was a local Kashmiri whose father was Sheikh Sulaiman. He had converted to Islam before Sheikh Hamdani's arrival. Both father and son are buried in the Jami Masjid of Srinagar.

Sheikh Ahmed was succeeded by his son Sheikh Fathullah Hafiz, who in turn was succeeded by his son Sheikh Ismail. Sultan Hassan Shah conferred on Sheikh Ismail the honorary title of Sheikh al-Islam. When he died in 1510, he was buried near his *khanqah* in Koh-e-Maran in Srinagar. His *khalifa* was Baba Ali Najar, who came under the influence of Sheikh Shamsuddin Iraqi and joined the Shia sect.

The *khanqah* and its responsibility then fell on Sheikh Ismail's son Sheikh Fathullah. However, the Shia–Sunni strife that gripped Kashmir in that period forced him to migrate to Sialkot in Punjab, where he spent the rest of his life.

The Kubravi *silsilah* continued through another route, though. Mir Muhammad (1372–1405), the son of Sheikh Hamdani, was born in Khwarezm and was 12 years old when his father died. He became the disciple of Khwaja Ishaq and Jafar Badakshi, and came to Kashmir in 1393 where he lived and preached. Sultan Sikander (r. 1389–1418) became his disciple during his time there. The sultan built the *khanqah* of Shah-e-Hamadan for him.

Mir Muhammad's most famous disciple was Suha Bhatta, a Hindu minister of the Sultan. Suha Bhatta took on the name of Saifuddin after converting to Islam. His daughter was married to Mir Muhammad.

After staying in Srinagar for 12 years, Mir Muhammad left for Khattalan via Mecca. He died in Khattalan and was buried in the same tomb as his father.

The Shattari *silsilah* has its roots in Iran where Bayazid Bastami founded it as the Ishqiya *silsilah*. It is one of the oldest Sufi orders. Shah Abdullah, a descendant of Sheikh Shihabuddin Umar Suhrawardi, brought it to India in the fifteenth century and named it *Shattari* (meaning lightening quick), because of the speed with which the Sufis of this order trained in order to achieve *fana*. Their techniques to achieve mystical perfection were such that they could achieve it at the beginning of their Sufi ascension.[23]

Shah Abdullah travelled to many parts of India. He would travel in royal robes, accompanied by Sufis dressed in black, holding banners and beating kettle drums, and would cry out, 'Is there any seeker, whom I can show the way of God?' His explanation for this was that he was searching for the secrets of *tauheed* (unity of God) from those more perfect than him, while inviting others to learn from him. He finally settled in Mandu, Malwa, where he died and is buried.

The Shattari *silsilah* spread to Gujarat, Madhya Pradesh and Bengal. The most famous saint of the order is Muhammad Ghaus Gwaliori, a musician and author of *Jawahir-e-Khams* (*The Five Jewels*). He also translated the Yogic text *Amrit Kund* from Sanskrit into Urdu; it is named *Bahr-ul Hayat*.

During Akbar's reign, Muhammad Ghaus Gwaliori settled in Gwalior and visited the Mughal emperor. Akbar visited his *khanqah* too during a hunting trip in 1559. The saint, who raised livestock on his considerable tracts of land, gifted a pair of fine bullocks to the emperor. He also initiated him into the Shattari *silsilah*, but it is said that the emperor was more interested in the bullocks than the initiation ceremony!

Another spiritually uplifting dargah is in Dewa. Popularly known as Haji Sahib, Haji Syed Waris Ali Shah (1817–1905) founded a comparatively recent *silsilah* – the Warsi *silsilah* – in Dewa near Barabanki (in the heart of Uttar Pradesh today).

There is a beautiful legend regarding how this dargah came to be constructed. Thakur Pancham Singh, a landlord in Etah district of Uttar Pradesh and an ardent devotee of Lord Krishna, once desired to see a *rasleela* (dance form dedicated to Lord Krishna). The deity appeared in a dream and told Singh that the only person who could help him achieve this desire was Haji Syed Waris Ali Shah, thus urging him to go to his *khanqah*. Through his divine knowledge, Haji Sahib knew of the arrival of Thakur Sahib and so he sent his men to meet and greet him. Before Thakur Sahib could explain the purpose of his visit, Haji Sahib told him to close his eyes and Lord Krishna's *rasleela* began to unfold before him. Thakur Sahib immediately became a devotee of the saint and stayed on in Dewa. He spent his wealth to make the beautiful dargah complex for him.[24]

Haji Sahib was initiated into Sufism through the Chishti and Qadriya saints. Perhaps it is fitting that his teachings and practices should also be steeped in the Ganga-Jamuni *tehzeeb* (syncretism) of the Awadh region. He emphasized love as the primary condition to gain knowledge – both worldly and spiritual.

Since Haji Sahib lived not so long ago, his life is well documented. He is said to have great healing powers and one is likely to meet many sick people in his dargah praying to God for a cure and seeking the saint's intercession.

His devotees are from all faiths and regions. Haji Sahib donned unstitched yellow robes and one can find many of his devotees to be similarly clad. (It is said that he performed hajj in a yellow *ahram*– that is, mandatory robes for a pilgrim.) His followers included not only Indians of all sects and faiths but also British and Europeans residing in Awadh, as by then the province was under British rule.

Haji Sahib's dargah is one of the most popular ones in Uttar Pradesh and its annual *urs* is celebrated on a grand scale. Lakhs of people come to attend and camp in the huge complex for days, to pay homage to their beloved saint. It is fitting that women are allowed here, too. A huge fair is held and it is a local highlight, especially as a well-attended cattle and horse auction is held. His followers also wear yellow robes and his shrine is a sea of yellow during his *urs* ceremony.

Apart from his *urs*, the festival of Holi is celebrated with great enthusiasm in the dargah's courtyard.

Perhaps the most fascinating of the existing orders is the Madariya *silsilah*. Saiyed Badiuddin Ahmed (856–1434), famous as Zinda Shah Madar (living saint) and Qutb-ul-Madar (axis of saints) – the highest title given to a Sufi saint, established the Madariya *silsilah*. Born in Aleppo in Syria, he came to India in accordance with a revelation he received on a pilgrimage to Medina, whereby he was ordered to go to Hindustan and dedicate himself to the welfare of mankind.[25] The exact date of his advent into India isn't known, but he arrived during the reign of Firoz Shah Tughlaq (1356–88), and travelled to many parts of the country before settling and building his *khanqah* in Makanpur near Kanpur. The old name of the area was Khairabad and the name Makanpur was derived from Macknadeo, a Hindu disciple of his.[26]

Many legends surround Shah Madar and his life. He is linked with those associated with roads and journeys and is said to be an epitome of Hazrat Khizr, the patron saint of travellers and wayfarers. The breathing or *dum* practiced by Shah Madar and the Madaris led to the belief among a section of his followers that he was alive within his *mazar* (shrine), and just in a state of deep meditation – thus the epithet *Zinda* (alive) is associated with him. As per another legend, he lived for 12 years on one breath and that is why he is also known as Dum Madar. According to a book, *Makanpur Sharif Itihas ke Aaine Mein* (*Makanpur Sharif in the Mirror of History*), written by Saiyed Zahir Hussain Jafri al-Madari who is associated with the dargah, the saint lived to the unbelievably long age of 596 years.

Shah Madar gained much fame in his lifetime for the healing of snake and scorpion bites, and the curing of male impotency. According to legend, so much heat was generated from the face of Zinda Shah Madar that people gazing directly at his face, especially unbelievers, would get burnt; so he wore a veil on his face.

A certain author who goes by the name of Mrs Meer Hassan Ali, an English lady married to a nobleman in Awadh, made a record of the denial of entry for women after her visit to the annual *urs* or *mela* (fair), as it is called here, in her diary. Her words are available to us through the fascinating book *Observations on the Mussalmauns of India*. She notes:

> I have conversed with a remarkably devout person, on the numerous extraordinary stories related of Maadhaar's life, and the subsequent influence of his tomb. He told me that women can never, with safety to themselves, enter the mausoleum containing his ashes; they are immediately seized with violent pains as if their whole body was immersed in flames of fire. I spoke rather doubtingly on this subject, upon which he assured me that he had known instances of one or two women who had imprudently defied the danger, and intruded within the mausoleum, when their agony was extreme, and their sufferings for a long time protracted, although they eventually recovered.[27]

Apparently women were not allowed because it was believed that they would be 'overcome with agony' since the saint is directly connected to male potency.

However, at some point after the description by Mrs Meer Hassan Ali, entry was forbidden for men and women. At present, no one is allowed inside the tomb. It is only on special days, such as *urs* or when the chadors have to be changed, that the designated hereditary Saiyeds and dargah custodian enter to do all rituals such as ghusl, etc.

There are two celebrations in the dargah – one being the annual *urs* ceremony and the other is for Basant Panchami.

Shah Madar's nephews who are said to have accompanied him to India, became his spiritual descendants. Known as *khademan*, their sub-order maintains his dargah in Makanpur, organizes the *urs* festivals and looks after the devotees who come to pray or pay respect to the saint. The piri-muridi (master-disciple) tradition that exists in the dargah has been passed on by them. The takht-nashin (head of the order) is from this lineage.

The *dewangans* are a sub-order of the Madariya *silsilah*. Their sub-order began with Syed Mohammad Jamaluddin Janeman Jannati, the disciple of Shah Madar whose dargah is in Nalanda, Bihar. The *dewangan* are wandering ascetics who can be found at the *urs* ceremonies of saints of every order across dargahs in India. They are also known as Madariya Fakir. Two other sub-orders of the *silsilah* are *aashiqan* (seekers of love) and *Taliban* (seekers of knowledge). The *Taliban* trace their lineage to Qazi Mahmud (d. 1485–6) who is buried in Kantur, UP and the *ashiqan* to Qazi Muntahar (d. 1507–8) whose tomb is in Kalpi, UP.[28]

Additionally, Kalleswari and Mahmud Kanturi are both successors of Shah Madar.[29]

These four groups are known collectively as Madaris, each distinguished by the way they observe customs and rituals. According to one account:

> The customs and rituals observed by the *deewangan*s are distinctive. They do not observe the Shariati (Islamic scripture) rituals, their unorthodox outlook identified them with the *be-shara* group of *faqir*s [mendicants]. It is learnt from an oral discussion with the members of the *deewangan*s of water living in Makwanpur that though they model themselves on the immediate predecessors in general they follow the custom and manners of Syed Mohammad Jamaluddin the founder of the order.[30]

While the *dewangan* are non-conformists, the *khademan* are strict adherents to shariah.

The *dewangan* concentrate on the feeling of spiritual ecstasy, and the relationship between the master and the disciple – rather than on Islamic rituals, including prayers and fasting. In the seventeenth century, they were heavily influenced by Hindu yogis and would move about with heavy iron chains on their bodies – at times even naked, according to one historical account.[31]

They were closer in practice to nath yogis and sanyasis than to the Sufis. They covered their bodies with ash and consumed hemp. In a state of intoxication, they often got into scuffles. They wore black turbans and carried black flags in their hands. Akin to yogis, they often wear just a loincloth and practice the control of breath. Like the nath yogis, the *dewangan madaris* practice strict celibacy.

During the *urs* of Shah Madar, his followers walk on burning coal calling out 'Dum Madar' (breath of Madar) to prevent their feet from being burnt! It is the *dewangan* sub-order that has become more famous as they were and are more visible. They perform acrobatic tricks and even today street jugglers are called Madari, with Shah Madar being their patron saint. In fact, some Madari Fakirs actually dance or perform juggling and other acts on streets or in trains, for money. Madaris consider begging in this way for alms acceptable way to sustain themselves.

In the eighteenth century, the Madaris participated in a revolt against the British in Bengal, in what became famous as the fakir–sannyasi revolt.[32] This uprising against the British was in the wake of restrictions put on fakirs and sannyasis after the Battle of Plassey in 1757. The Madari Fakirs were joined by Hindu sannyasis and fought a guerrilla war against the British for 15 years between 1771 and 1786, till their leader Majnu Shah Malang of Makanpur was wounded and returned to live in hiding in his home town, where he died in 1787.

Majnu Shah, also known as Malang – another name for a dervish, fakir, or *deewangan* as in this case, caught the public imagination. He was born in the Mewat region of Haryana and became a Sufi with deep attachment to Hazrat Ali. No one knows his real name; he was probably given the sobriquet Majnu (someone madly in love) and was also called Majnu Shah Burhana (come without clothes).

Unfortunately, the grave of this early freedom fighter of India is in a neglected state.

His dargah bears testimony to his influence and the syncretic nature of his teachings and followers. Its history is available in *Makanpur Sharif: Itihas ke Aaine mein.*[33] The fascinating shrine was built by a Sharqi ruler of Jaunpur, over a period of four years from 1420; additions were subsequently made by various emperors and local rulers. On my visit, the dargah committee members showed me around and identified its era for me. No inscriptions providing the dates of the construction exist.

Being a woman, of course I couldn't go into the shrine but based on what I could see, the description given and images available, it is a plain building – 315 square feet in area, with a low-domed white roof, with the walls covered by a black cloth.

There is a gallery – made on the orders of Emperor Shah Jahan – called the Shah Jahani Dalan, and an ornamental gateway and mosque made by Emperor Aurangzeb Alamgir. Both rulers are said to have visited the dargah during their respective reigns.

When Emperor Aurangzeb visited the tomb somewhere around 1664, he is said to have crawled up to the shrine on his elbows and knees, both of which were well covered with cotton. On reaching the tomb he repeated the following verse, which is believed to have been composed by himself:

Approach! For here is the summit of perfection!
Approach! For here is a refuge for the guilt of kings!
The pure lord, the king of kings, the centre of the universe,
With reverence approach, for here is the light divine.[34]

The emperor was accompanied by two Hindu nobles, one of whom composed the following verse:

Who goes to Salon, or to Karra, or Hilsa?
Who goes to Bihar or Bukhara?
Who cares for Ajmer, or Muner,
When a much greater saint is here?
A brilliant light, and a holy delight.
So says Shiva Pandit the poet –
For he whom the maker chooses to favour,
Comes to the shrine of Madar.[35]

The verse refers to popular Sufi shrines, with Salon being the nearest and having the same syncretic traditions.

According to the *khademan* of the dargah a mirrored hall was built by the Rani of Datia and a hall for recitation of the Holy Quran by Puttulal Khatri, a devotee.

The Maratha chiefs and Nawabs of Bengal also patronized the Madariya *silsilah*. Their influence spread all the way up to Bengal and even Nepal and Bhutan where they had properties.

The history of the dargah is indicative of Majnu Shah's and the Madari *silsilah*'s vast following in the past. The *silsilah*'s most visible presence is now found in dargahs in Delhi, where many Madari fakirs or *malang*s offer their services. You are likely to be struck by their free spiritedness. They are easy to spot in their long green gowns and matted hair. The Madariya *silsilah* is also very popular in present-day Uttar Pradesh, the Mewat region, Bihar, Gujarat, and Bengal.

In Kolkata's busy Khidirpur, which once upon a time used to be a hub of trading activities because of its proximity to the sea, is the dargah of Syed Ali Shah Baba – a saint of the Madariya *silsilah*. Earlier, sailors would come here for blessings before sailing. Even today, the dargah is visited by numerous devotees. In fact, a flyover had to be designed and built such that it would go around it. Regular traffic and passers-by have to take an extra turn, so as to not disturb the saint. With the flyover next door and cars and buses whizzing about, this dargah with pigeons flying around signals a message of peace and calm. Many bus drivers, be they Hindu or Muslim, slow their vehicles down in deference as they pass by. They also throw coins towards it and supplicate in its direction from the flyover, keeping Shah Madar and his Khwaja Khizr connection alive even after all these centuries.

In the dargah, a very low wall between the shrine and an area next to it separates the male and female sections.

Love and devotion towards Hazrat Ali and Lord Krishna is part of the Awadhi Ganga Jamuni (syncretic) culture manifested at a famous set of Sufi shrines in Kakori, a town nearly 15 km from Lucknow. The Takia, as the shrine complex is called, with its four whitewashed domed dargahs in the middle of mango groves, is an oasis of peace and beckons to those with a thirst for spirituality.

The Kazmiya Qalandariya *silsilah,* to which these shrines belong, was established by Shah Muhammad Kazim Qalandar (1745–1806). He belonged to a family of scholars and soldiers who served in the Mughal courts and army. At the age of 15, he joined the Awadh army.

However, Shah Kazim enjoyed the company of ascetics and mendicants much more and would follow their practices.[36] Eventually, he met a qalandar in Allahabad named Shah Basit Ali Qalandar. On his advice, he settled in Kakori, teaching and guiding the people of Awadh. Later on, Shah Basit declared Shah Kazim as his successor in meditation and mystical practices.[37]

Since Shah Kazim's condition was straitened, Shah Basit ordered his follower Maharaja Takait Rai, the very rich and influential diwan of Awadh, to help him out. The Maharaja built him a *khanqah* that became a centre that captured India's syncretic culture. Shah Kazim was followed by rulers and commoners alike, and this holds true even today, with millions from all faiths and walks of life thronging to the Takia (as the complex is known) to celebrate his *urs* ceremony.

Shah Kazim was very fond of music and composed a book of poetry titled *Naghmat ul-Asrar*, also known as *Sant Ras*, in Braj *bhasha* based on classical ragas, which contained a *thumri* of 5,000 verses.[38] An excerpt from it that reflects the syncretic nature of his ideas reads:

> I fall at your feet, Uddhav,
> take me to the flute-playing friend.
> The day God made him a raja,
> he cast me out of his memory.
> In Gokul, we played together;
> now those games are all forgotten.
> Those days when he used to herd the cows
> still linger in my eyes, bringing tears.
> When a memory comes of those days
> a fire lights up deep in my heart.
> Shyam has been with Kazim from the First Dawn;
> may he remain with him till the End of the Days.[39]

One of the conversations that deepened my understanding of this syncretism involved Shams Ur-Rehman Alavi, a descendant of the saint. After talking to Shah Ain-ul-Haider Qalander 'Zia Miyan', the current *sajjada nasheen* (hereditary caretaker) popularly known as Ainul Bhai, he gave me an account of their conversation. It went as follows:

> [Krishna bhakti] begins from none other than Shah Kazim Qalandar and the tradition is well-known. Once he (Shah Kazim Qalandar) was in a state of deep anxiety when he saw Krishna ji in his dream. He said, 'I want death.' Krishnaji soothed him and said: *Tum amar ho* (You are immortal), suggesting that someone whose

heart is lit up with love is freed of the bondage of time and space, life and death.[40]

This idea was apparently mentioned by the saint's son and successor, Shah Turab Ali Qalandar (1768–1858), in the introduction to Shah Kazim Qalandar's collection of poetry, *Naghmat ul-Asrar*. It is a well-known and well-documented story; along with innumerable anecdotes and stories, it has been recounted for generations, and it has been part of folklore in Kakori, Shams ur-Rehman Alavi tells me. The Sufis of Khanqah-e-Kazmia say that Krishnaji was a beloved in the metaphorical world, but for the Sufis who believe in *Wahdat ul-Wajud*, the reality is crystal clear: Krishna is an *aarif haqeeqat-shinaas* (Enlightened Truth-follower).

Shah Kazim Qalandar was succeeded by his son Shah Turab Ali Qalandar, who took his father's teachings and syncretic traditions to the next level. Shah Turab Ali Qalandar was also devoted to Lord Krishna. Shah Turab Ali wrote the *Amrit Ras*, which is steeped in spirituality and devotion with many verses for Krishna.

Even if we set aside these amazing ideas behind them, the shrine complex still remains culturally important – as it is also a wonderful specimen of architecture. The Takia Sharif shrine complex has multiple structures on its premises, but it is the three beautifully constructed and maintained dargahs of Shah Kazim Qalandar, Shah Turab Ali Qalandar, and Shah Ali Anwar Qalandar that catch the visitors' attention. There is a *baradari* (pavilion) with exposed lakhauri brick and vaulted arches resting on a high platform; this would have been the place where the saints met their devotees. There is a *langarkhana* and kitchen to the southeast of the complex and various houses built for the saints' families and for devotees.

There is a fascinating story behind a colonial style bungalow in the complex called Iona Bai Ki Kothi, built by a Parsi lady for the use of devotees. The story behind the *kothi* (bungalow) too was narrated to me by Shams Ur-Rehman Alavi, who had heard it from his ancestors. Sona Bai once dreamt that she was being asked to light a lamp for Hazrat Ali and was told to go to a place named Kakori. She somehow located it and came down. After that she visited often, becoming a disciple. She never married and instead adopted a girl, Temi Bai, who also became a disciple.

This girl and her descendants too kept coming and helped in the restoration work of the dargah.

The sleepy town of Kakori is more famous for its kababs than its spirituality, but this wasn't always so. Shams tells me of a time when people came not just to experience healing and for lessons in spirituality, but also for secular learning. There would be scholars coming here from far and wide who would stay at the *khanqah* to avail the library, have scholarly discussions and write books. A very far cry indeed from many other hospices today where the emphasis is more on buying flowers and *chaddar*s, with shopkeepers pushing their wares at us.

In the dargah complex in Kakori, though, this tradition continues. There are no flower shops or sellers. It is complete peace, serenity, and silence. No one disturbs us as we enter (women were allowed), and inside, we sit in peace, praying, and meditating. An annual *urs* is held and people from all parts of the country, including faraway regions, arrive for the occasion.

# SHRINES AND DEVOTEES

# 10

# At the Saint's Threshold

*Bulhawas paanw na rakhiyo kabhi is raah ke beech,*
*Koocha-e-ishq hai ye rahguzar-e-aam nahin.*

[O lustful one, never tread on this road;
Not everyone qualifies for the lover's abode.]

– Shah Niaz Beniaz

It's a Thursday night – 'a very bright night'.[1] The deeds of a believer are being presented before Allah, the gates of paradise are open, and every believing servant is forgiven save the ones who have 'severed ties of kinship'.[2] On this night we offer special prayers at home, in mosques and shrines, and ask for that mercy which is integral to Islam, for Allah's mercy encompasses all things,[3] and fills our life with the reality of a God that is ever merciful and compassionate.

Heads covered, floral offerings, and *chaddar*s in hand, tonight I head towards the dargah to seek the blessings of the saint and participate in the prayers there along with other devotees. The mind is hopeful and the heart emotional, for we are going to give *haziri* (attendance) at the saint's shrine. I have lost count of the number of such scenes I have seen or participated in, for almost every city in India is dotted with dargahs – some are big; others, simple small roadside graves with a green *chaddar* (sheet/shroud) spread over them. Every Thursday evening one can see huge crowds thronging the dargahs as *shab-e-juma* (Friday eve) is considered very auspicious and special prayers are prescribed for the night.

It is considered a time when the chances of prayers being heard are at a high and praying for the souls of the departed is recommended. While most pray at home and mosques, many devotees do go to the dargah of their choice, to not just to pay their respects to the saint but also ask for intercession so their desires are fulfilled and the souls of their departed loved ones are forgiven.

Dargahs are usually brightly lit with electric lights and candles; the heady fragrances of incense and rose petals intoxicate the senses, while the sound of qawwalis lifts the spirit into another world. It is a spiritual experience for devotees and an unforgettable one for those visiting more casually. There are also those who have been wronged, betrayed, or hurt by the world and its people, the wounded in spirits, who have come to find compassion and mercy in the dargah; along with fellow seekers, they too find an oasis of peace.

This is the threshold of the house of saints who emphasised repentance and forgiveness, not punishments. Repentance (*taubah*) as described in the previous chapter is an important fundamental tenet of Sufism for as Hazrat Ali said, 'There is no intercessor more effective than repentance,' and 'Do not despair if you have sinned, for the door of repentance is open.'[4]

Just as integral to a believer is the belief in the Day of Resurrection, when the angel Israfeel will blow the trumpet, and on that day, all living creatures will die and the earth will split into two. Seas will submerge mountains, and the mountains will come crashing down. The universe will be destroyed. And then nothing else will remain except Allah. He will recreate the Heavens, earth, and the angels, but there will be no trees, seas, or mountains on it. Israfeel will once again blow the trumpet and the earth and all creatures in it will return from their graves to their original form, in which they were before their death. The souls will re-enter the body and proceed towards the plains where the final Day of Judgment will be held. The sun will be only a mile above the heads and under its fiery rays, people will be sweating in their sins waiting for their deeds to be read out. The day of reckoning will be long with a single day being as long as 50,000 years as they wait for God's decision. Do they get the promised reward for their virtues or are they condemned to burn in hellfire for ever after?

The graphic descriptions of that day and punishments and the torments of hellfire are dinned into a believer's heart and mind. Fire and brimstone are common themes in every religion, and the bread and butter of orthodox preachers. Sinners will suffer and suffer grievously in the afterlife. Surrounded as we are with temptations and the human propensity to err, it is important for us to remind ourselves of God's mercy and have faith that He will surely forgive those who repent sincerely as that's our only hope.

Law givers and orthodox preachers emphasize wrath over mercy, but we forget the well-known hadith-e Qudsi which says, 'When Allah decreed the Creation, He pledged Himself by writing in His book, which is laid down with Him: My mercy prevails over My wrath.'[5]

The word of God the Quran are in itself an act of mercy. Being a revelation of Allah, its teachings were central to Sufi thought as well, but in the early commentaries we find mystical interpretations of it. Thus, going with a more mystical interpretation, the Sufi saints spoke of a loving God who forgave, encouraged the followers to embrace His teachings, taught them that the path to Him was also through love, and offered a 'theory and practice of holistic, experiential knowing of Divine Truth'.[6] The popularity of this theory and practice can be seen from the number of Sufi dargahs and the *silsilah*s that sprang up all over the world, where inclusiveness was practised and religious pluralism and multiculturalism embraced.

Faraz Arif Ansari, a filmmaker immersed in Sufism told me about his introduction to it. His words reflect what many devotees experience in a dargah:

> When I was forced to learn Arabic as a child, in the first few lessons that followed after learning [the] Arabic alphabet was a talk on Heaven and Hell. The Maulana barely spoke of Heaven but went on for a good 20–30 minutes talking about Hell and God's wrath. Something that was deeply problematic and scarring for a child. My introduction to Sufism happened because of my *Khalajaan* [maternal aunt]. She had taken me to Hazrat Baba Bahauddin Shah Asfahani Dargah on a Thursday. I remember her telling me, *'Yeh bhi Khuda ka ghar hai: Mohabbat ka ghar.'* [This is also God's house: a house of love] I'll never forget that. It made me feel accepted, loved and welcome immediately. Since then, my relationship with Sufi shrines is about that – love, acceptance and immense peace.[7]

Like Faraz, I too am drawn to dargahs for their inclusiveness of rich and poor, pious and sinners, low and high born, powerful and powerless, and above all, the feeling that Allah will forgive me as long as I repent and don't repeat the mistake. Though it may seem that Allah's mercy and wrath have a yin and yang relationship, they are not equal in measure; His mercy easily outweighs His wrath. The shariah may be stern and strict but underneath the threat of hell is the promise of mercy. The image of Allah in my mind: the One, the Supreme, the Master, the Nourisher and at least for me He is a father figure, a *parwardigar* (nurturer) as it were – someone who will always cherish me, as *parwardigar* implies 'to care again and again'.

These are lessons also taught by Sufi saints through their insistence on the daily remembrance of Allah (zikr) and *tawakkul* (faith in Allah). Scholar William Chittick explains:

> Once we see the parallel between the Sharia and the divine majesty and wrath, it is easy to discern a relationship between the spiritual perfection that is sought by the Sufis and the divine mercy, gentleness, and beauty.[8]

Every dargah has its own caretaker who may be hereditarily appointed from the family of the saint, or selected by the state or a local committee. They are called *sajjada nasheen* (literally, the 'one who kneels' on the prayer carpet of the late sheikh and is his spiritual heir), *gaddi nasheen* (one who sits on the seat of the previous sheikh and is a hereditary administrator who tends to the saint's shrine*), pirzada* (descendant of the saint) *mujavir* (caretakers of the shrine), *khadim* (a caretaker of the shrine), or trustees (one who looks after the administration or running of the shrine).

Every evening, the Chishti dargahs have a *dua-e-Roshni* (prayer of light) just before dusk and the *maghrib* (evening) prayers. The senior *sajjada nasheen* or *gaddi nasheen* will recite the prayer. It has a magical feeling to it – the candles lighting up through the slowly darkening evening, the bowed heads and the always beautiful rendition of the prayer, requesting the saint to intercede on behalf of the devotees and asking Allah to grant their wishes. The prayer ends with the following lines:

Oh, Almighty as the Sun and the Moon endure;
May the Chishti lamp resplendently sparkle.

According to Saiyed Salman Chishti, *gaddi nasheen* of the dargah of Khwaja Muinuddin Chishti, this ritual is inspired by the traditional ceremony that took place in the blessed mosque of the Prophet, Masjid-e-Nabwi in Medina.[9]

All dargahs have their own set of daily rituals which are performed by the caretakers, but in effect they all transport the attendees to a higher spiritual level. Those who visit them take all these celebrations and daily rituals for granted, but how did these rituals evolve? It is a long and complex historical process and not easy to understand.

The initial period of Sufism was centred around the *khanqah*s and the *takia*s (convents) of the saints. Their disciples gathered at these places to hear the saint, be with him, follow his teachings, and serve him.

The first scholar to study it in detail, J.S. Trimingham identified three distinct phases that Sufism passed through, organizationally: the *khanqah*, the *tariqah,* and the *ta'ifa*.

The *khanqah* phase is considered the true golden age of Islamic mysticism in terms of creativity of thought, the quantity of original mystical literature produced and the simplicity of the Sufis' social organization.[10] This was the period in which the saints were alive, their disciples took their oaths of allegiance with them, and they appointed *khalifa*s from among them.

In the *tariqah* phase, the *silsilah*s were formalized, and their teachings and practices were fixed. The differences between the various orders now became prominent.

The *ta'ifa* stage started in the fifteenth century. In this phase:

> To be a Sufi [...] came to mean more the belonging to a cult-association called a *ta'ifa* than the submitting to a method of discipline. Moreover, Sufism's mystical element, which in its unrestrained abundance had characterized the *khanaqah* phase and which in the *tariqa* phase was subjected to a good deal of systemization, now played a minor role in the movement.

> In this stage a Sufi's direct communion with God was replaced by the veneration and even worship of a *pir* who now occupied the position of spiritual intermediary between the disciple and God.[11]

In this third stage, the *pir*s (spiritual masters) became *wali*s (friends of God), and saint-cults were established. The descendants of the saint became their successors, as family replaced merit, and the emphasis was on veneration of the saint buried in the shrine known as the dargah. The system of *khanqah*s was replaced by dargahs. The emphasis was on devotion to the saint rather than mysticism, and it was no longer restricted to an elite group of Sufis. This resulted in the broadening of the movement and association of the masses. The *barakat* or blessings that the saints possessed were transferred to their shrines and in some cases even came to be associated with their successors and the hereditary caretakers of the shrines.

These three stages outlined by Trimingham also presume that there was a decline in Sufism.

Ernst criticizes this theory. He says, 'Trimingham's observations contain a modern and strongly Protestant attitude that champions personal religion over institutionalized religion, and his theory of decline logically derives from his assumption that mysticism must be a personal and individual phenomenon.'[12] He adds, 'The notion of historical decline is basically a rhetorical strategy for evaluating and classifying history, according to what one considers to be of real value and what constitutes a departure from that.' That this notion helped colonizing nations in their so-called mission of 'civilizing nations', and in carrying the 'white man's burden', added to this image of a decline in Muslim nations.

Ernst quotes Isma'il R. al Faruqi to sum up this position:

> The decline of Islam as a result of colonization was seen as a result of the growth of Sufism. Under the Sufi spell, the Muslim had become apolitical, asocial, amilitary, unethical, and hence non-productive, unconcerned for the umma (the world brotherhood under the moral law), an individualist, and, in the last resort, an egotist whose prime objective was to be saved himself, to be absorbed into the consuming majesty of the divine being. He was

> shaken neither by the misery, poverty, disease, and subjection of his own society nor by the lot of mankind in history.[13]

Ernst rejects that theory and questions 'the basis for assuming that Islam in general and Sufism in particular rose, then fell – both marked by a period of classicism and greatness, followed by another period of stagnation and decline'.[14]

In Turkey, many prominent Sufi orders were banned in 1925. But since it was a matter of the heart, *tasawwuf* (mysticism) itself flourished and Sufi orders continue to operate.[15]

However, in South Asia itself, Sufism has held its own and we see a worldwide resurgence, especially in the West where many Sufi orders are flourishing.

In this chapter, we will study the stages that led to the popularity of dargahs and how they became an organic part of social life. But before that, a brief word on the terms *khanqah*s and dargahs.

In the cases of saints, most of whom wanted to be buried in open mud graves after death, their disciples built elaborate structures as a mark of respect and for the convenience of the devotees. In most cases, they were buried in what were called *khanqah*s, and a mosque, *jamatkhana* and *langarkhana* would already exist there.

The word dargah literally means 'threshold' or 'door'. It has now come to signify a shrine where people come to pay their respects and plead for the intercession of the saint buried there. The general belief is that the spirits of the saint live in these graves, and they have power granted by God to intercede; they are Auliya Allah (literally, friends of God).

This idea is based on a verse from the Quran (3:169):

> Think not of those who are slain in Allah's way as dead;
> Nay, they live, finding their sustenance in the presence of their Lord;
> They rejoice in the bounty provided by Allah.

Orthodox Muslims think of the idea as an innovation, for according to them one should ask God directly rather than relying on divine intermediaries. I receive many such comments on Instagram and Twitter when I post details and photographs of the dargahs I visit every Thursday as part of a series I created with the label #SufiThursdays.

However, most people who visit dargahs don't ask think of the saints as divine. Instead, many believers see the saints merely as someone who holds a blessed position in the eyes of God, on account of which their prayers are more likely to be heard. *Waseela* (intercessions) are thus a means of reaching Allah.

As mentioned before, the hospices or convents where the saints lived and had spiritual discussions are called *khanqah*s. The disciples lived here and served their master as they sought the path of spiritual enlightenment.

Though there were *khanqahs* in the subcontinent before the advent of the Delhi Sultans, their stable rule afforded a peaceful atmosphere for many Sufi saints who had migrated to India to build *khanqah*s. The systematic organization of *silsilah*s happened during this period, with the Chishti and Suhrawardi saints setting up their centres and establishing themselves. While the Chishti *khanqah*s were simple with everyone living in a large community hall, the Suhrawardis had more commodious arrangements for each inmate.

Some *khanqah*s insisted on the new followers going out to beg to teach them humility and to reiterate that they were the lowest of creatures.

Soon, areas from Multan to Lakhnauti (present-day Gaur in West Bengal) and Panipat to Daulatabad had flourishing *khanqah*s and *jamatkhana*s where people gathered to meet and hear the saints. These *khanqah*s became a centre for cultural synthesis where different ideas were heard, discussed, and often assimilated.

These *khanqah*s offered board and lodging to Sufis who were often in pecuniary conditions, and they were a great space for the exchange of ideas. It was a space where travellers in search of truth – such as dervish and *qalandar*s – could get some respite too. While the younger ones generally helped in the upkeep and maintenance of the place and lived in *jamatkhana*s, older Sufis would be housed in cells so that they could devote their time often to rigorous prayer and devotion.

The *khanqahs* were run on *futuh* (unsolicited gifts) and grants, and elaborate rules regarding them were laid down by each *silsilah*. With the Chishtis, for instance, the gifts received should not have been asked for, for solicited contributions were deemed illegal. Besides, the gift could not be immoveable property, or a regular payment, and they had to be used/distributed as soon as they were received.

The Sufi saints led a tough life indeed. Bibi Zulaikha, Hazrat Nizamuddin Auliya's mother, would often say, 'Nizam, today we are guests of Allah', which meant there was no food in the house. Baba Farid's family and the residents of his *jamatkhana* would live on berries or starve.

Even as they lived in such austerity and braved all manners of difficulties, the saints also dealt with all the problems brought to their *khanqah*, whether big or small. They never let any devotee go away feeling unsatisfied.

Others started flocking there for the saints, who while 'concerned more with emotional harmony than ideological synthesis, which was a very slow process and touched only a limited section of intellectuals, created an atmosphere of mutual trust, good will and understanding by emphasizing respect for basic human values'.[16] Such was their popularity that a traveller in the early fourteenth century is said to have informed Shihabuddin-al Umari at Damascus: 'In Delhi and its neighbourhood are *khanqahs*, and hospices numbering two thousand.'[17]

To a significant extent, the popularity was due to the fact that dargahs are very accepting spaces. At a time when caste and class restrictions, autocratic regimes, zealous priests, and the orthodoxy were all placing restrictions on the movement and behaviour of the common man, this was the place where all of itcounted for nothing; it was the love for saints' humanity that attracted the devotees. The saints, and later their dargahs, welcomed everyone, and they were almost never judgmental.

The 'Dispute Between Love and Law' (*'ishḳ shara' dā jhagaṛā*), a *kāfī* attributed to (but probably not actually authored by) the most widely sung Sufi poet of the Punjab, Bulleh Shah (1680–1758), showcases this best:

> Law says, 'Go to the Mullā and learn the rules and regulations!'
> Love says, 'A single word is enough: shut and put away all other books!'...
> Law says, 'Have some shame and decency: put out this light!'

Love says, 'What is this veil for? Let the visions be open!'
Law says, 'Come into the mosque and perform the obligatory prayer!'
Love says, 'Go to the wine-tavern, and having drunk, perform the superogatory prayer!'...
Law says, 'O, Believer! Go for Ḥajj – for you will have to cross the Ṣirāt Bridge!'
Love says, 'The door of the Beloved is the Ka'bah, don't move from there!'
Law says, 'We strung Shāh Manṣūr up on the cross!'
Love says, 'Then, you did well; for you sacrificed him at the Beloved's door![18]

From the first ever *khanqah* on Indian soil, established by Khwaja Muinuddin Chishti in Ajmer, to the present-day dargahs, they are not only sacred but also welcoming spaces without restrictions based on religion, caste, or class. This is the reason why people started flocking to the saints during their lifetime and continued to visit their shrines after they left this world. These places became community centres for the dispossessed, desperate and diseased of heart, mind, and body.

In the medieval era, the lower castes lived outside the cities and were deprived of basic amenities of daily life. If a careful survey is made of the sites where the earliest Muslim saints built their hospices in India, it will surely be found that they existed outside the caste cities. They were often built on the outskirts in separate cities, where workers and artisans – Hadis, Domas, Chandals, and Badhatus – and the mass of humanity then known as Antyaja (the newer and better term is Dalits) were forced to live deprived of all amenities of civic life.[19]

The *khanqah*s provided a beacon of hope for these people who had been deemed untouchable by society. The Sufi saints and many of their followers who had come with them from Central Asia came from a custom of brotherhood as preached by Islam and believed in community living, praying, and eating together. The custom of eating in one plate irrespective of class or caste was a novelty in the caste-ridden society of the day. This was responsible in many areas for the success of the Sufi saints who warmly welcomed all.

This emphasis in dargahs on service to mankind is not disjointed from the Islamic belief that bringing solace to one human heart is more important than a hundred pilgrimages to Mecca. As Sheikh Sharfuddin Maneri said, 'In this dark world, one should help people with pen, tongue and money. Though namaz and *roza* are the fundamentals of Islam, [they are] not better than providing comfort to the heart.'[20]

Apart from being tolerant of all other faiths, the saints also believed that there are many ways of reaching the 'one' God, and laid much emphasis on harmony. Since the doctrine of *Wahdat al-Wujud* implies that it is His existence which pervades the whole universe and 'entire mankind is one and it reflects the glory of God', it 'was instrumental in promoting communal harmony by eliminating formal differences of faiths'.[21]

Reflecting this belief, Sheikh Abdul Quddus Gangohi, a distinguished Chishti saint of the sixteenth century, declared in his book *Maktubdt-i'Quddusi*: 'Why this meaningless talk and clamour about the believer, the Kafir, the obedient, the sinner, the rightly guided, the misdirected, the Muslim, the pious, the infidel, the fire-worshipper. All are like beads in the same rosary.'[22]

The *khanqah*s also contributed to the growth of cosmopolitan centres and thought. With travellers and locals coming to these centres, the areas around developed and as they were open to people of all classes, genders, religions and persuasions, healthy discussions helped develop a more cosmopolitan approach. Free men and women would mingle with slaves (that is, in separate assemblies/spaces for each gender), as did Hindus and Muslims, the rich and poor, the urban and village dweller. These *khanqah*s thus 'became veritable centres of cultural synthesis where ideas were freely exchanged and a common medium for this exchange was evolved.'[23]

The success of the Sufi saints thus lay in their approach to the society of medieval India. They had to deal with (1) the caste structure of Indian society, (2) the narrow and racially conditioned ideology of the Muslim governing class, and (3) the rigid and orthodox thinking pattern of the ulema.[24]

Saints like Hazrat Nizamuddin Auliya exemplified this by using kindness and charity as a way to reform the populace. Under the reign of Kaikubad (Balban's grandson), drinking, debauchery, and licentious ways were the norm and to counter this, Hazrat Nizamuddin Auliya got many platforms with thatched roofs constructed from the king's court in Mehrauli to Ghiyaspur (modern-day Hazrat Nizamuddin Basti) where he lived. The idea behind the move was that the construction would keep people cool, and that might serve as an additional incentive for those who wanted to turn away from bad ways. On the roofs little pits were built and vessels full of water were kept in them. Prayer rugs were spread out, carpets kept ready, and a servant and a Hafiz (those who know the Quran by heart) were stationed along the route to help disciples reach the *khanqah*. This helped counter the prevailing atmosphere and his followers refrained from improper acts, conscious as they were of their responsibility as his disciples.[25]

According to Hazrat Nizamuddin Auliya, retribution and revenge are laws of the animal world: 'If a man puts a thorn in my way and I also put a thorn in his way, it will be thorns everywhere.'[26] He argued that if wrong is returned by good, it saves conflict and tension, and creates a healthy atmosphere in society.

The saint thus promoted large-hearted forgiveness. In patience and tolerance, he saw the secret of social well-being. He used to say: '[If] one man vents his wrath on another and the second man is patient, the virtuous attitude belongs to him who is patient and not to him who gives vent to his wrath.'

He would also recite the following verses of Sheikh Saifuddin Said Bakharzi, which reiterates the same sentiment:

> He who is not my friend – may God be his friend,
> And he who bears ill-will against me, may his joys (in life) increase.
> He who puts thorns in my way on account of enmity,
> May every flower that blossoms in the garden of his life, be without thorns.[27]

*Jamatkhana* are assembly rooms, where discussions were held and the saints met their disciples, followers, and visitors. They also doubled up as a place for them to live. The *jamatkhana* would become welfare centres for the neighbourhood over time, as the saints ensured that any offering that came to the *khanqah* was not kept for more than a day. Stipends were given to the needy, and food was distributed through *langar*s.

Baba Farid's disciples lived in the *jamatkhana* and slept on the floor. Hazrat Nizamuddin's senior disciples had small cubicles in his *khanqah,* while the rest lived in the hall.

Here, the senior disciples would undertake the spiritual training of novice initiates and as each group learnt the principles, they in turn became in charge of the newcomers. This system ensured that everyone was trained adequately. The senior disciples were under the saint's direct care for only he could lead them to the final path.

A *chillahgah,* the cell or sometimes cave where the saints performed spiritual penance was another feature of dargahs.

There is a hadith about a man who once asked the Messenger of Allah: 'Which act in Islam is the best?' He replied, 'To give food, and to greet everyone, whether you know [them] or you do not.'[28]

This was the model followed by the Sufi saints who kept their house and kitchens always open. Thus the *langarkhana* was a very important part of the *khanqah* complex and today, it is of the dargahs. Everyone who came was served the same food, and the dignity of those who ate there was maintained uniformly. No indigent person was left feeling in any way less worthy than the richest person there.

In fact, the first *langarkhana*s to be established were the ones in the dargahs, before they were adopted by Guru Nanak and Sikh gurdwaras. Today, the Sikh community is famous for its *langar*s (free meals), and they are the first to provide aid in any humanitarian crisis. According to Professor Harbans Mukhia:

> If Guru Nanak Dev's new religion of Sikhism brought forth the message of social harmony in the midst of social tensions, it acquired immense power as it incorporated other similar messages of his time, those emanating from great Sufis like Baba Farid and Sants like Kabir. From Baba Farid he also inherited the marvellous

institution of *langar*, signifying both selfless service and social equality.[29]

There are numerous legends associated with dargahs, and a well-known one has to do with *langar*s. One evening in 2016, when I was at the dargah of Hazrat Nizamuddin Auliya, I met Pirzada Altamash Nizami, who has always graciously welcomed me there. Altamash invited me to a *langar* he was organizing, and when I demurred explaining that I had to leave early as it was getting dark, he regaled me with a famous anecdote about Zafar Khan (who was later crowned Alauddin Hasan Bahman and founded the Bahmani Kingdom in the Deccan in 1347) and Mahboob-e-Ilahi. And of course, after hearing the story, I stayed back.

According to the legend, Alauddin Hasan Bahman (who founded the Bahmani Kingdom in the Deccan in 1347 and was not yet known by that name then, as he had not yet been crowned) was once standing at the door of the Hazrat Nizamuddin's *khanqah* and a *langar* was customarily being held in the dargah. Sultan Muhammad bin Tughlaq, a devout disciple of the saint, was leaving after having tasted the *langar*. Mahboob-e-Ilahi, who was watching all this said:

*Yak shah raft wa deegrey bur astana niojood.*
[One king has left and another is again at the door.]

When asked about what he meant, he told one of his followers to go out and escort Alauddin Hasan Bahman, then known as Zafar Khan, in. The saint shared a piece of bread kept for his iftar with the young man and prophesied that he would become a sultan one day.

It is not uncommon for such stories to come to be attached to dargahs. Here, it's not the brain that works but the heart. Asghar Gondvi expresses this poetically in a ghazal:

*Ye ishq ne dekha hai, ye aql se pinhan hai,*
*Qatre mein samundar hai, zarre mein bayaban hai*

[It is revealed to love, reason can't see it,
A drop can contain the ocean, a grain can hold the desert.][30]

– Asghar Gondvi

The common visitor associates Sufi saints not so much with their teachings as with their dargahs. Although according to Islam no concrete structure should be built over the mortal remains of a Muslim, very few adhere to it. In the cases of kings and the rich, a grave with an exposed mud top is built at the ground level and a cenotaph on top, with the size and design reflecting the power and position of the person buried.

According to historian Nile Green, not only were these dargahs valuable, albeit neglected, resource for historians, the 'shrines of the immortalized Sufi saints were crucial in the making of Muslim space on Indian soil.' Green adds that Sufi shrines offer continuity as they are 'arguably the only spaces to survive with their rituals, book collections and even family lineages intact: they are "places in which memory is crystallized".'[31]

Dargahs are not only a rich source of history but repositories of knowledge, mystical discussions, and that custom must continue, for as Green writes, Sufism is 'a powerful tradition of Muslim knowledge and practice bringing proximity to or mediation with God and believed to have been handed down from the Prophet Muhammad through the saintly successors who followed him,'[32]

Every dargah attracts crowds – whether locally, or from far and wide. Visiting numerous dargahs, called *haziri dena* or *salam karna* (both terms mean paying respects to the saint), is rather enriching experience. *Haziri* is a derivative of Islamicate court culture where one paid obeisance at a royal court. It reflects continuity with a pluralistic past – dargahs being spaces where many before have come and still to do so irrespective of faith, class, and gender.

The most well-known and famous dargahs in India are those of Hazrat Nizamuddin Auliya in Delhi, Khwaja Muinuddin Chishti in Ajmer, Charar-e-Sharif and Makhdoom Sahib in Srinagar. And the ones of Data Ganj Baksh in Lahore and Baba Farid in Pakpattan in Pakistan. During the *urs* celebrations, lakhs throng the dargahs to offer their respects and pray for their needs.

Delhi, Hyderabad, Srinagar, Khuldabad, and Bijapur have a concentration of dargahs, and every dargah is full, especially in the evenings.

However, it must be pointed out that the hereditary caretakers of some dargahs need to reflect on their past. For many, the shrines are oases of peace; for some, it is a place where one goes for spiritual enrichment. Unfortunately, not catering to either of these kinds of visitors, they sometimes get caught in the melee of caretakers and alms seekers out to enrich themselves.

I once had a bad experience in the dargah of a lady saint. I was rudely interrupted while praying and nudged to put money in the donation box. I am afraid I lost my cool and requested the person who did this to leave me alone and go away, while urging him to think whether asking for money in the name of a lady who was famous for not seeking anyone's help was respectful to her memory.

Author Annie Zaidi too describes an unpleasant experience in the dargah of Beema Beevi in 2019:

> Shangumugam beach reminded me a bit of Juhu in the Bombay of the early 1990s.Relatively clear water, a few food stalls, soft sand. I had gone to Shangumugam with a friend and we spotted a 'tota' astrologer sitting nearby. This was a man with a caged parrot and a box with a set of cards in it. You pay 50 rupees for the parrot to pick a card, and for the astrologer to read your palm and tell your fortune. Although I don't really believe in fortune-telling, on a whim, I decided to go along with it. After the astrologer had told me a few promising things about my future, he asked whether I was Hindu or Muslim. I was somewhat reluctant to answer. He looked at me keenly then and said: If you follow Allah, you must go to Beemapally, offer flowers and incense and pray.
>
> I had never heard of Beemapally until then and I initially assumed it was a mosque. Having gone along with my whim thus far, I decided to take his advice and go further. My friend drove me down and it turned out to be a dargah, painted bright pink. Women could go right in, but there was a barricade preventing me from touching the covered grave of the saint within. It was cordoned off by metal barriers and the *khadim*s took your offerings

from your hands. There had not been any crush of flower or incense stalls outside the dargah, as I have seen at Nizamuddin in Delhi. However, this also meant that I could not choose what I wanted to offer, or how much. The *khadims* I was talking to told me that I could take a 'package' which included a glittering *chaddar*, and which cost 501 rupees.

I have always resented having other people control what I offer, and how, but having come here, I decided to follow instructions and made a *mannat* as directed. The *khadims* gave me their blessings while reciting an *ayat* (verse from the Quran). Then, one of them probably decided that since I have travelled a great distance (since I did not speak Malayalam) and could afford the 501 package, I could be persuaded to part with more. He called me aside, asked me if there were problems in my life, any pain or grief. I said, yes. Then he asked for 10,000 rupees in exchange for a *tabeez* and a prayer that he guaranteed would 'work' in three months.

I did not have 10,000 rupees. The man began to bargain with me. Seven thousand, he said. I said, I do not have even that. Then he said, go home and return with the money. I told him that I am not a rich woman. He sized me up again and realized that I was not feeling desperate in the way he had assumed. So he said, just pay us a thousand rupees to feed the poor. I scrabbled about in my purse. By now, my initial sweet mood was starting to turn sour. I did not want to leave in anger though, so I gave him a few hundreds and left.[33]

Archaeologist and epigraphist Desai, who has studied many dargahs describes the problem well:

Today, it is difficult to say that these establishments have much spiritual guidance to offer. The main activities seem to be confined to the maintenance of the tomb building, the management of whatever land and property endowed by the Muslim rulers in the past has escaped the vicissitudes of time and the greed of those in charge, and to looking after the flow of believers who come with offerings of flowers, coconuts, scented sticks or cash.'[34]

To continue the glorious traditions of spiritual enrichment, it is important that the attendants and caretakers embody the spirit of their blessed ancestor or master and make dargahs once again the centres of spiritual training and learning that they were historically, staying away from the evils attached to materialism. Ultimately, devotees come to receive spiritual, physical, material and economic succour, and enlightenment depending on their purpose for coming to the dargah. They should go away fulfilled and feeling closer to the Divine.

*Kabhi yahan tumhein dhoonda kabhi wahan pahuncha*
*Tumhari deed ki khaatir kahan kahaan pahuncha*
*Gareeb mit gaye pamaal ho gaye lekin*
*Kisi talak na tera aaj tak nishaan pahuncha*
*Ho bhi naheen aur har jaa ho*
*Tum ik gorakh dhanda ho*

[At times I searched for you here, at times I went there;
I have come very far for the sake of seeing You.
Fellow seekers have been ruined in this journey, but
Your signs are not visible to all;
You are a deceptive puzzle.][35]

– Naz Khialvi

# 11

# Dargahs Containing Relics of the Prophet and the *Ahl al-Bait*

*Shah-e-Medina suno, iltija Khuda ke liye,*
*Karam ho mujh pe Habib-e-Khuda, Khuda ke liye*
*Huzur guncha-e-umeeed ab to khil jaaye.*
*Tumhare dar ka gada hun, to bhik mil jaaye.*
*Bhar do jholi, bhar do jholi meri, Ya Muhammad,*
*Laut kar main na jaaunga khaali.*[1]

[Emperor of Medina listen to my plea; for the sake of God,
Shower your kindness on me, O beloved of God. For God's sake
Your honour, let the buds of hope, blossom.
I am a beggar of your threshold, may I be given alms.
Fill the beggar's pouch; fill my pouch, O Muhammad,
I will not return empty handed.]

As a child of three, I had gone on a pilgrimage with my grandmother and mother to Iran and Iraq. Somewhere along the journey, I fell sick as it was very cold and I wasn't used to the snow. My grandmother immediately vowed that once I got well, she would take me to the shrine of Imam Hussain (in Karbala, Iraq) in a *chaddar* and make me do my namaz there.

In Karbala and other shrines in Iraq, people whose vows have been fulfilled distribute sweets. Since it's difficult to give these to the thousands of visitors individually, they raise their hands high and throw them into the crowd. I was too small to run and grab one. When we were there, I have a very clear memory of me pestering my mother for sweets: '*Amma, mithai. Amma, mithai.*' (Mother, sweets. Mother, sweets.) My mother, busy praying, told me to ask Maula (Imam Hussain) for what I wanted. I have always had a one-track mind and pay full attention to whatever I am doing. I started off with my tiny hands lifted in the air, 'Maula, *mithai*, Maula, *mithai*.' To this day I get goosebumps when I remember the very beautiful young woman who came over and pressed into my palm a handful of sweets just for me. Hazrat Ali and Bibi Fatima have since remained my personal saints and I pray to them all the time.

Since it is not possible to visit their and other shrines dedicated to The Infallibles (*Ahl al-Bait*) in Iran, Iraq and Syria, dargahs were constructed in India. Thousands flock to these local shrines to take a *ziarat* (pilgrimage) and seek the fulfilment of prayers.

In this chapter, we will talk about the famous dargahs in this part of the world which, while they don't have bodies of saints buried there, have relics of the Prophet, his progeny, or of Hazrat Ali. Though they receive visitors from across regions and faiths, these dargahs are especially revered by Shias.

There are no restrictions on women entering these sacred spaces. Indeed, even in Iraq, Iran and Syria, women are allowed in these shrines. There are separate rows and queues – sometimes even areas – for women, but everyone has access to at least some part of them.

Among them are many *Qadam Rasul* dargahs here which have an imprint of the Prophet – including Gaur in West Bengal, Paharganj in Delhi, Asar Sharif in Delhi's Jama Masjid, Lucknow in Uttar Pradesh – or a relic like a strand of hair from his beard (as is the case in Hazratbal in Srinagar and Hazrat Nizamuddin in Delhi). These dargahs are extremely popular with the devotees. The *Qadam Rasul* in Gaur, housed in a beautiful mosque, was an important medieval shrine. Unfortunately, with the passing of the dynasty of the Sultans of Bengal, it fell into a state of disrepair. Today it is just another monument, and the room with the footprint is kept locked.

The Hazratbal Dargah in Srinagar contains a relic – the *Moi-e-Muqqadas* – which is said to be a hair from the Prophet's beard. 'Bal' means place, and Hazratbal means revered place. Indeed, it is extremely revered and the holiest shrine in Kashmir.

According to a story on the board outside, the dargah's main relics once belonged to Syed Abdullah, a descendant of Prophet Muhammad who came from Medina (Saudi Arabia) and settled in Bijapur (Karnataka, India) in 1636. This individual had many relics of the Prophet, which were inherited by his son Syed Hamid after his death. A rich Kashmiri trader Khwaja Nooruddin Ashawari, who had accompanied Syed Hamid, asked for one of the relics when he was leaving Bijapur. Initially Syed Hamid refused, but then Prophet appeared in a dream and asked him to hand one of them to the trader.

The next day when Syed Hamid asked the Khwaja what he would like him to carry along, he chose the blessed hair. On his way to Kashmir, Khwaja Nooruddin was imprisoned by Aurangzeb in Lahore and the relic was confiscated and kept in the Ajmer Sharif Dargah.

After the Khwaja's death, Aurangzeb had a dream asking him to fulfil the Khwaja's dream of taking the relic to Kashmir. Aurangzeb then had it enshrined in the Khanqah-e-Naqshbandiya in Srinagar in 1700.

From there it was shifted to Bagh-e-Saif Khan and housed in the mansion of Sadiq Khan, a Mughal descendant. The mansion came to be known as Asar-e-Sharif Hazrat Bal. According to a verse by poet Mirza Qalander Baig:

> *Kashmir, Medina bishud az moi e Nabi (SAW).*
>
> [Kashmir has become [like] Medina because of the sacred hair of the Prophet (SAW)]

Over the years, the building of Hazratbal has been rebuilt and considerably enlarged, but it remains central to the lives of the Kashmiris. The present building with its beautiful white dome gives a sense of peace; its location on the bank of the Dal Lake only adds to the experience. The only thing that disrupts the peace at this dargah are the oft-heard anguished cries and weeping of devotees who come to pray for their loved ones. This indeed holds true for all dargahs in Kashmir, as the social and political turmoil that the region finds itself in ensures that there is never a shortage of tragedy in the lives of its people.

Under the Nizams, Hyderabad saw many saints settle down in the city. The most famous dargah in Hyderabad is that of Maula Ali. The Maula Ali Dargah is dedicated to Hazrat Ali ibn Abi Talib.

According to Tuzuk-e-Qutb Shahi, a eunuch in the court of Ibrahim Qutub Shah (who was the fourth ruler of the kingdom of Golconda) dreamt that a man dressed in green told him to visit a hill where Maula Ali was waiting for him. The eunuch went there in his dream and found Maula Ali on top of the hill with his hand resting on a stone. The next day, the eunuch went up the hill and saw the rock with the imprint of a hand. He got the impression hewn out of it and built a masonry arch over it. On hearing about this, Sultan Ibrahim Qutub Shah visited the hill and ordered that a mosque be built there. Since then, that area has been known as *Koh-e-Ali* (Ali's hill). The rock is enshrined at the back of the dargah. It is covered by a cloth and flowers and is said to have healing powers. The 500 steps leading up to the dargah have in fact become a part of the city's heritage walks now.

The thousands of devotees are not deterred by the arduous ascent and make their way up motivated by faith in Hazrat Ali. And the first sight of that imprint is truly a moving and spiritual experience well worth the physical exertion.[2]

Even my mother with a severe heart condition wanted to visit the shrine while we were there for a wedding. We told her very firmly that she wasn't to even think of it. So while we were all asleep, she slipped out in the early hours of the morning and came back triumphant; she had done *haziri* and made her supplications to her Maula. Faith has strange and magical powers indeed. (I too once climbed the steps barefoot as I had made a vow to do so if my wishes were answered.) Spiritual strength keeps one going.

A testament to the fruit of such faith stands in the dargah's courtyard. A hollow stone shaped like a boat has been filled with sugar by devotees whose prayers are fulfilled.

Another dargah, popular amongst the Shia community in India, is Jogipura in Uttar Pradesh, where there is an imprint of Hazrat Ali's horse's hoof. It is said that the saint came here on his horse to rescue Syed Raju, a holy and son of a high-ranking official in Shah Jahan's court, who was expecting Aurangzeb to take some adverse action against him because of his dissent against his injustice.[3] He called out, '*Ya Ali, madad*' (O Ali, help me), and so Ali came to his rescue.

Najaf in Iraq, where Hazrat Ali's shrine is located, is a very popular pilgrimage place for Shias; Jogipura is therefore called *Najaf-e-Hind* (Najaf of India). Those who can't go to Najaf come here instead. There are some extremely grand replicas of the mausoleum of Hazrat Ali and Imam Hussain that have been erected in this village.

The mausoleum attracts many daily visitors from nearby villages and areas, who come with petitions in hand. During the month of Muharram devotees flock here in lakhs, and religious congregations to commemorate the sacrifice of Imam Hussain are held.

As is common in other dargahs of India, one can find mentally disturbed persons here as well: some are chained while others are free to move around under the supervision of their guardians, as they all await a cure from the spirits they feel have possessed the person. Whenever I visit it I wish people would realize that the best place for them would be a hospital where they could be cured.

In the nineteenth century, Mohammad Iftikhar Ali Khan Bahadur, the Nawab of Jaora, a principality in Ratlam, dreamt that he had seen a group of horsemen there next to a pond. They were the souls of the martyrs of Karbala. The very next day, a pond was also discovered. Crowds started gathering and wishes started being granted. Soon structures were built and today it is a magnificent complex. The Hussain Tikri Dargah attracts not only Shias but Sunnis and also Hindus. It is famous as a spiritual hospital, for many with mentally illnesses claim to have found a cure here.

Six shrines here dedicated to the sacred memory of Hazrat Ali, Hazrat Fatima Al Zehra (the Prophet's daughter and Hazrat Ali's wife), Imam Hussain (Hazrat Ali's son), Hazrat Zainab (Hazrat Ali's daughter and Imam Hussain's sister), Hazrat Abbas (Hazrat Ali's son and Commander of Hussain's forces at the Battle of Karbala), and Bibi Sakina (Imam Hussain's daughter).[4]

Once passing by Ratlam in a train I had pledged to visit if a particular wish of mine was fulfilled. In a year it was and I came to spend the day there in 2001. In the evening they perform special prayers inside these shrines, and I was fortunate to find space inside. The atmosphere is extremely emotional and electric as devotees supplicate.

The dargah of Shah-e-Mardan in Delhi's Jor Bagh is dedicated to Hazrat Ali. Ali was the epitome of knowledge, wisdom, generosity, and valour, and he was given the title of *Shah-e-Mardan* (King of Men). A very popular qawwali celebrates this:

*Shah-e-Mardan, Sher-e-Yazdan,*
*Quwwat-e-Parwardigar,*
*La fata Illa Ali,*
*La Saif Illa Zulfiqar.*

[King of men, Lion of Yazdan,
Strength of God,
There is no one unconquerable like Ali,
There is no sword like Zulfiqar.]

This dargah was built by Udham Bai, wife of the emperor Mohammad Shah. Udham Bai was given the title of Nawab Bai and then Nawab Qudsiya Sahib uz-Zamani during the reign of her son, Emperor Ahmed Shah. In 1724, she acquired a stone with the imprint of Hazrat Ali's footstep and got it fixed inside a marble tank.

The dargah receives many visitors daily, but there are huge crowds during Muharram and on the birthday of Hazrat Ali on the 13th Rajab (Islamic month). Many buildings have now been added to it. A building adjoining the Qadam-e-Ali, the room where Hazrat Ali's footprint is kept, is called Bibi ki Chakki and is dedicated to Hazrat Fatima al Zehra, the Prophet's daughter and Hazrat Ali's wife. Since she was very particular about *purdah*, only women go in there and a screen has been erected at the door shielding the building from the male gaze. I often go there to ask Bibi to intercede for me with Allah.

No visit to Lucknow is complete without stopping by the dargah of Hazrat Abbas, son of Hazrat Ali. This shrine is also called Chote Hazrat ki Dargah, as his father Imam Hussain is the *bade* Hazrat or elder brother. Hazrat Abbas was truly the Lion of Arabia and the bravest warrior of his time – his father having been the bravest of all time was called the Lion of God. In the battle of Karbala, Abbas was appointed the commander in chief. However, since Karbala was a war of ideology, and of good over evil, Imam Hussain did not give Abbas the permission to go to battle. In those days, battle was one-on-one and Hussain knew that Abbas could single-handedly rout the enemy. The only permission Abbas was given was to go to the river Euphrates and fetch water for his four-year-old niece Sakina. Since Yezid's forces had stopped water supply to Hussain's camp, the children had been thirsty with water bound to run out in a day. Abbas was surrounded, wounded, and finally martyred on the banks of the river. His shrine stands there, and all who go to Karbala visit his shrine before proceeding to the shrine of Imam Hussain.

The dargah of Hazrat Abbas in Lucknow came into existence during the reign of Nawab Asaf-ud-Daulah (1775–1797) and is one of the oldest shrines in the city. According to legend, a Lucknow resident named Mirza Faqeer Beg saw a dream in which Hazrat Abbas directed him to go to a particular spot and find his *alam* (standard). The man did so and found a large bronze *alam* in the shape of a hand (*panja*). He placed it, with utmost respect, in his house, but once its fame spread people started visiting to view it in huge numbers. Nawab Asaf-ud-Daulah also came to visit and gave orders for a shrine to be built there.

Hazrat Abbas is also called Bab-ul-Hawaij (a gateway of fulfilment of desires). Since his desire to protect Imam Hussain from his enemies by going to war and defeating them was not fulfilled, he was granted the power to grant wishes of his followers. It is believed that no follower has come away disappointed from his threshold – the only caveat being that the desires should be legitimate and for the better of the person asking it.

The Shah-e-Najaf, or Shahnajaf Imambara, as it is popularly called, dedicated to Hazrat Ali in Lucknow, is also universally popular.

*Ghalib nadiim-e-dost se aati hai bu-e-dost,*
*Mashghul-e-haq hun bandagi-e-bu-turab mein*

[Ghalib, from the confidant of a friend comes the smell of a friend; I am occupied with Truth/God, in the service/bondage of Bu Tarab.][5]

# 12

# Popular Dargahs of North India

I have visited many dargahs in cities and villages across India. Almost every big habitation in India will have one, even if it is just a small shrine under a tree or by a roadside. Everyone needs some extra help in trying times and dargahs offer devotees the solace they need.

I even found quite a big shrine amongst the churches and convents of Goa. It belongs to Hazrat Hamza Shah and has many devotees. This is not truly surprising though, for Sufi saints are considered spiritual authorities and are often referred to as 'Shah' (king), their *wilayat* (spiritual authority) being as important as that of a temporal king. In fact, many times it was believed that medieval rulers depended on them – on their *'barakah'* or blessings – to be able to perform their duties well. Hazrat Nizamuddin Auliya, whose blessings were sought by the rulers, is a case in point.

Writing about their power, historian Richard Eaton says, '[S]ince such saints possessed a special nearness to God, in reality it was they, and not princes or kings, who had the better claim as God's representatives on earth.'[1]

Even if this was not the case, rulers surely drew their authority from these saints, who could make or unmake kings. Apart from this:

> From a village perspective, after all, kings or caliphs were as politically abstract as they were geographically distant; and after the Mongol destruction of Baghdad in 1258, caliphs all but ceased to exist even in name. Sufi saints, by contrast, were by definition luminous, vivid, and very much near at hand.[2]

This sums up the experiences of modern world too, and the reason why many flock to them.

Though, there are no rulers in modern India, the dargahs continue to attract rulers and commoners alike. Even today, the president of India – as head of the state – sends a *chaddar* to the Ajmer Sharif Dargah, and local officials too vie to offer the first *chaddar* at their local shrines. It is thus important to examine these dargahs and their relevance in the lives of people who visit them.

With so many dargahs it was not possible for me – however much I wanted to – to visit every single one of them. So I am describing just a few – state-wise in this chapter. For some of them, I rely on oral traditions and the experiences of friends. Of those that I did visit, I am describing only a few important ones as it is beyond the scope of the book to describe every one of them.

Kashmir is also called '*pir waer*' (the valley of saints), and it is dotted with shrines sacred to Hindus and Muslims. Charar-e-Sharif and Amarnath are both in Kashmir.

However, in the past many decades, Kashmir has been racked by pain and violence which is also affecting the fabric of social, cultural, and religious life.

Poet, cultural theorist, and curator Ranjit Hoskote articulates the situation as follows:

> The Sufi tradition in Kashmir has been associated, for seven centuries, with the meditative and devotional practices of the Rishi order, with a focus on the achievement of a serene oneness with the Divine. The Sufis of Kashmir were drawn, especially in the fourteenth and fifteenth centuries, both from immigrant seekers from Central and West Asia – especially Samarkand, Bokhara and Hamadan – and from the forest-dwelling Brahmin ascetics of Kashmir. Through the dialogue between incoming Sufi Islam and indigenous Kashmir Shaivism and Pancharatra Vaishnavism, there

arose a syncretic set of practices in which *fana* and *moksha* were not far apart. A shared vocabulary emerged, as did a blending of values. The foundational figure of the Rishi order was Nund-resh, revered by Hindus as Nund Rishi and by Muslims as Sheikh Nuruddin Noorani, Alamdaar-e-Kashmir. He is regarded as the spiritual son of the great fourteenth-century transreligious mystic Lal Ded, known as Lalleshwari or Lal Arifa. The Sufis of the Rishi order chose a vegetarian diet, lived close to nature, and allowed in their shrines for an affective, votive form of worship that allowed people at large to express their relationship to the Divine in an intimate and personal manner, rather than a formal and stylized manner. This texture and tonality of Kashmiri Sufism is still in evidence in the *ziarat*s (visits) of the Rishis in the Valley, which is in fact called the Rishi-vaer, the Valley of the Rishis. However, this Rishi tradition is under threat today, due to several factors.

He goes on to add:

> The template of an austere global Wahhabism – which is a modernist turn in Islamic practice – looks with suspicion upon all practices that are seen to borrow from local sources, which emphasize the affective and the votive, and which foreground the sacred nature of place, monument, ritual or talisman. All this is central to Kashmiri Sufism – and anathema to Wahhabism. Another factor that has affected Kashmiri Sufism is the long-running situation of conflict in Kashmir, which has divided and polarized its people. In such a scenario, the more declarative ideology of Salafism – with its promise of a universal solidarity of Muslims suffering oppression – becomes more attractive to some, especially to the justly angered youth, than the Rishi path, associated with retreat, tranquillity, and quietism. When the Kashmir that produced the Rishi order is itself undergoing major and turbulent change, we wonder how the Rishi order will survive such a traumatic historical experience, keeping its redemptive teachings secure for a new generation that may benefit from such healing wisdom.[3]

This however, does not mean that Kashmiris don't visit dargahs. They do, and the shrines of Hazratbal, Shah-e-Hamadan, Dastgeer Sahib, and Makhdoom Sahib in Srinagar are full at all hours of the day and night.

> There is one God
> But with a hundred names.
> There is not a blade of grass,
> Which does not worship Him.[4]
>
> – Nur-Nama

In the village of Charar/Char-e-Sharif is one of Kashmir's holiest and oldest shrines: the shrine of Nund Rishi also known as Alamdar-e-Kashmir (flag bearer of Kashmir), and visiting it is a cherished dream for many. I visited it on one of my trips to Kashmir in the last few years and was struck by the influence it has on the lives of locals. Though, the original shrine was gutted in an encounter between militants and security forces in 1995, a new and beautiful wooden structure has replaced it, and once inside, one temporarily forgets the trauma that the area has witnessed.

As per legend, when the sheikh was born he would not accept milk from his mother's breast. Three days after his birth, Lalla, a celebrated Shaivite female ascetic of Kashmir, happened to come by. She spoke to the newborn baby saying, 'You are not ashamed of being born, why are you ashamed to suck?' Thereupon the baby immediately started drinking milk and Lalla kept visiting the house. In Kashmiri folklore, the personalities of Lalla and Nooruddin are so mixed up that it was impossible to separate them, but there seems little doubt that Nooruddin drew inspiration from Lalla, even if he did not become her disciple.

According to Prof. Abdul Qaiyum Rafiqi, in his book *Sufism in Kashmir*, 'The Rishi *silsilah* of Kashmir is an indigenous Sufi order developed amidst the traditions of Buddhist renunciation and Hindu asceticism. In fact, the very word Rishi is derived from Sanskrit.' He does not agree with some Muslim scholars of Kashmir who have tried to Islamicize the term, seeing it as a derivation of the Persian word *resh/raish* which means a garment made from the feathers of a bird, or abundance of means, or a beard. He proffers that from surviving sources one can say the order flourished in the first half of the fifteenth century and that

Shaikh Nuruddin, popularly known as Nund Resh (b. 1378), was largely responsible for its growth and popularity.

Nund Resh died in 1439 and was buried in the village of Charar. He was survived by his four disciples Bamuddin, Zainuddin, Latifuddin, and Nasruddin. One of the mourners was the Sultan Zainuddin.

The dargah of Hazratbal is a handsome white building with a lofty dome and is sacred because of the strand of Prophet Muhammad's hair it houses. It is known in Kashmir simply as 'the dargah'; the fact that no other description is needed signifies its importance.

Similarly, the Shah-e-Hamdani is simply known as the *khanqah*. It is an exquisite papier mâché and wood *khanqah*. (As a descendant of Shah Hamdani, it was a homecoming for me.)

The Dastgeer Sahib is named after Sheikh Syed Abdul Qadir Jeelani, popularly known as Dastgeer. It houses a Quran written by one of the companions of the Prophet and a single strand of Sheikh Syed Abdul Qadir Jeelani's hair.

A stiff climb on Hari Parbat takes you to Makhdoom Sahib Dargah. This is the shrine of the Sufi saint Hamza Makhdoom Kashmiri, popularly known as Makhdoom Sahib. He is also known as Mehboob-ul-Alam and Sultan-ul-Arifeen.

In the dargahs of Hazratbal, Dastgeer Sahib, and Makhdoom Sahib, the separate spaces reserved for women were full of heart-rending sights. Women of all ages were sitting there, praying and sobbing. In a state gripped by terrorism and unrest, I could only guess that they were crying for their loved ones. I sat there praying for them to find solace. Unlike my experiences in dargahs of other states, this was very traumatic for me as I came up – here more than anywhere else – against the real anguish of women who are often the collateral damage of any conflict.

The fertile land of Punjab in undivided India saw many Sufis settling down there. Today, the famous dargahs of Baba Farid in Pakpattan and Data Ganj Baksh lie in Pakistan, while the Indian territories of Punjab and Haryana have those of Sheikh Ahmed Sirhindi and Sheikh Jalaluddin Thanesari.

Haryana also houses the Char Qutub Dargah in Hansi, where Baba Farid's most senior disciple, close friend, and *khalifa* – Sheikh Jamaluddin Hansvi (1187–1261) – lived for many years. The Char Qutub Dargah is accessed through a medieval gateway; along with the main shrine and attached mosque; the shrine was built in the fourteenth century by Sultan Firoz Shah Tughlaq.

Apart from Sheikh Jamaluddin, Char Qutub is also the dargah of his son Burhan ud-Din (1261–1303), and descendants Qutb ud-Din Munawwar (1300–1354) and Nur ud-Din, also known as Nur-e-Jahan (1325–1397). They were the celebrated Sufi saints of their times and were together given the designation of Qutub (meaning polestar).

The shrine is named Astana-e-Jamal (shrine of beauty). Baba Farid himself stayed in Hansi for 12 years before leaving for Ajodhan. Sheikh Jamaluddin visited him frequently after he left.

Sheikh Jamaluddin wrote a few books during his time – of which two books have survived, the *Mulhimat* written in Arabic, and *Diwan* written in Farsi.

Sheikh Qutab ud-Din Munawwar, grandson of Sheikh Jamaluddin, was a disciple of Hazrat Nizamuddin Auliya. He spent many years in Mehboob-e-Ilahi's *khanqah* in Delhi.

I spent a few moments inside the dargah all alone, and the sounds of the late afternoon namaz being read in the small mosque attached to the shrine came wafting in. It is an extremely peaceful space and one can understand why Baba Farid spent so many years here. There is a small enclosure by the side of the shrines identified as his *chillahgah*.

Every dargah has people of every faith, caste, and class gathered to seek blessings and protection from the saint. In Thaneswar, I found petitions strung onto the small shrines and Hindu–Muslim devotees crowded in Sheikh Jalaluddin Thanesari's small shrine. One family had brought their newly wedded son and daughter-in-law to seek the Baba's protection against evil eye and future happiness.

Haryana is also home to the dargah of the famous medieval saints known as Bu Ali Qalandar (described in Chapter 9). The marvellous complex in Qalandar Chowk, Panipat is also very welcoming, and since there were no restrictions on the entry of women, I could go into the shrine and sit there for some time, absorbing the peaceful atmosphere. Qawwalis were being sung just outside the main shrine and added a mystical charm to the place.

Devotees of all faiths visit it in huge numbers and put a lock on the dargah grills as part of their vows. Once the wish is fulfilled, they return to open the lock and, as per their means, feed the poor.

This dargah was constructed by a Mughal noble Mahabat Khan, whose own red sandstone tomb is adjacent to it. The famous Urdu poet and writer Maulana Altaf Hussain Hali's marble tomb is also located in this complex.

One very interesting dargah is in Bathinda in Punjab. It is called Haji Ratan ki Dargah and it shares a wall with a *gurdwara* of the same name, Haji Ratan ka Gurdwara.

According to legend, Haji Ratan went to Mecca and Medina in the lifetime of the Prophet, converted to Islam, and witnessed the famous incident wherein the Prophet split the moon. He lived to be more than 500 years old, passing away in 1300.

This relatively not-so-well-known dargah is a repository of many legends and stories – one such story claims that Haji Ratan was a companion of the Prophet, and he was a nath yogi and he was connected to Goga Chauhan, a folk hero of Rajasthan. Even now, Goga's *naumi* (a day dedicated to worshipping Goga) is celebrated in the Hindu calendar month of Bhadra, during which a large number of Hindu devotees come and pay their respects at the saint's shrine.[5] The crowds there during that time are unbelievable. Yet, all supplications are heard, according to a devotee known to me who has for two decades been going to the dargah every year. Before Partition, the Haji Ratan Dargah was in the possession of Madari fakirs, who are known to have connections with nath yogis.

A small mosque in the compound of the dargah is said to have been built by Sultan Raziya (r. 1236–1240), the first female monarch of Delhi who visited the saint's grave during her imprisonment in the fort of Bathinda by Malik Altunia. It now functions as a mosque for women. A curiously shaped mound in the courtyard is said to be the grave of a camel in a sitting pose. The camel was supposedly gifted to the saint by the Prophet himself.

These days, the most famous story related to the dargah is about Guru Govind Singh, who visited it on his way to Talwandi and camped there for a night just outside. He was apparently dissuaded from doing so by the caretakers of the dargah because it is believed to be haunted, but the guru slept there to dispel the superstition. Another story says that the Guru released the saint from his cycle of rebirths and that the *gurdwara* was built on the spot where Haji Ratan attained *moksha*. This seems implausible because of the time period involved, but then faith stretches every boundary in people's minds.

Whatever the anecdotal histories might be, today the dargah and the *gurdwara* share a wall. The same *prashad* (offering) of salt that is offered in the dargah is offered in the *gurdwara*, and Haji Ratan is a symbol of Punjab's syncretism.

Punjab also has the distinction of being the state where the erstwhile princely state of Malerkotla is located. The state ceded to the Indian Union in 1947, and the city and area are famous for its communal harmony and for not witnessing a single incident of rioting during the partition of India when Punjab was a victim of unprecedented riots, looting and arson. This is commonly believed to be due to a boon granted by Guru Govind Singh.[6] In 1705 when Wazir Khan, the governor of Sirhind, ordered that the two *sahibzada*s (sons) of Guru Govind Singh be bricked alive, it was only Sher Mohammed Khan, Nawab of Malerkotla, who raised his voice in protest. He said that it was against the tenets of the Quran, and indeed Islam, and walked out of the court.

Malerkotla was established in 1467 by Sheikh Sadruddin Jahan (b. 1434) who hailed from Shervan in Afghanistan. He was the son of Sheikh Ahmed Zinda Pir and grandson of Sheikh Ali Shahbaz Khan. He is revered as Pir Haider Sheikh, and his dargah is visited by people of all faiths and religion.

There are a number of stories of the Sheikh's meeting with Bahlol Lodi, the Afghan who later went on to become the Sultan of Delhi. One goes as follows. On a stormy night in 1451, Sultan Bahlol Lodi who was on his way to conquer Delhi camped at Maler (the word Kotla meaning 'citadel' was added in the seventeenth century). The only lamp that was not extinguished was in Sheikh Sadruddin's house. Another version says that the entire area was destroyed in a flood while the sheikh's house was unharmed. Whichever one of the two is correct, they both converge in the part about how Bahlol Lodi was impressed and met the Sheikh who prophesied his victory over Delhi.

In 1454, after Bahlol Lodi had established his rule over Delhi, he visited the Sheikh while going from Multan to Lahore. 'While meeting with the *shaykh* he asked a second time that he take his daughter in marriage because he was a greatly pious and religious [person] and no one equal to the *shaykh* could be found.' Thus Hazrat ji married Lodi's daughter Taj Murassa Begum and was given 12 villages and 56 plots of land in a grant, and an annual grant of ₹3,00,000 from the Lodi government was thereafter assured.[7] These villages became the foundation of the state of Malerkotla.

The Sheikh and his Afghan wife had two children – a daughter, Bibi Mangi, and a son, Hassan. In 1458, Sheikh Sadruddin also married the daughter of Rai Bahram Bhatti, the Rajput ruler of Kapurthala, a nearby principality, and had two more sons, Isa and Musa.

Since Punjab is largely an agricultural state, the followers of Baba Pir Haider Sheikh are lovingly called to come on *Ekadashi* to celebrate the harvest season with the saint. A four-day event called the Pir Haider Sheikh fair is held annually in the June–July period. It is said that Baba grants every boon, especially to childless couples wishing for a child, and protection against evil eye and possession.

The dargah was humming with activity when I visited it and a Sikh couple was instructing their four-year-old son on the etiquette of offering a *chaddar* at the shrine.

One of the most famous dargahs of Punjab is that of Sheikh Ahmed Sirhindi in Sirhind. Its importance can be gauged from the fact that the locals call it Rauza Sharif (noble shrine). The dargah is close to the Gurdwara Fatehgarh Sahib, and the grand complex has, as was usual in medieval era, an imposing gateway for an entrance. The tomb made of red sandstone and marble was built in 1671. From Alexander Cunningham's (the first director General of ASI) description in 1863–64, we know that it originally was an octagonal building with open arches, surmounted by a pear-shaped dome, and the interior was covered by paintings of flowers. The dome was ribbed, like a melon, with the intervals filled by tiles. The initial tomb was built by Sheikh Sirhindi himself for his son Muhammad Sadiq who died in 1616 and was interred in it. The present structure was built in 1925 under the patronage of Haji Hashim and Haji Wali Muhammad from Saurashtra.[8]

He has a lot of international devotees, especially from Bangladesh and Afghanistan. Ahmad Shah Abdali visited it during 1734–35, with his grandson, Shah Zaman, and the latter's wife, who are buried in a tomb in the complex. It has a cemetery used even today, and it is considered a great honour to be buried there, guaranteeing those who are laid there a place in paradise!

Due to the pandemic I could not visit the shrine till October 2021, so I spoke to a couple of friends who had made it instead: Yusuf Shahab, a heritage enthusiast who works at the Rekhta Foundation and has written a book on Sirhind,[9] and Syed Mohammed Qasim, a passionate photographer who promotes the cultural and spiritual heritage of India.[10] Shahab, who visited it first in 2019, tells me:

> The Rauza Sharif is one of the popular attractions of Sirhind. It is like a second home to me. Although my affiliation [is] with the Chishti order of Sufism, I have a heartfelt attachment with the Naqshbandi [*silsilah*] because of Hazrat Shaikh Ahmad Sirhindi. Whenever I visit the dargah, I feel [at] peace and [sense] no discrimination amongst the devotees. Every person gets food on one *dastarkhwan,* [tablespread]. On one of my visits in 2020, I reached Sirhind at 3 a.m., the main entrance door was closed, but they opened it after just one knock from me. It feels as if the *khanqahi* culture is alive here which one doesn't see in the present times [at other dargahs]. I feel blessed in the dargah of Shaikh Ahmad Sirhindi.[11]

However, Prof. Syed Ali Nadeem Rezavi, former chairman and coordinator of the Centre of Advanced Study, Department of History, Aligarh Muslim University (AMU), who went to the dargah not out of any spiritual interest but as a historian, notes on his blog and in a conversation with me that the big shrine built over his grave and an annual *urs* held there, was in fact contrary to the Sheikh's teachings and that his dargah appears like any other dargah of a Sufi whose rituals he was critical about.[12]

And he added that, 'It provided me neither with spiritual solace or satisfaction as a historian: as the place is nothing but a modern structure – a whim of some modern disciple of the Naqshbandi *silsilah.'*

These conversations fuelled my desire to visit it myself. As soon as I could, I undertook a trip to the dargah of the saint who had invoked such extreme reactions in the people that I spoke to.

As someone who has been asked not to come near the shrine chamber on account of my gender in many other dargahs, I went in with a lot of trepidation. I was sceptical about how I, as a woman, would be treated in Sheikh Ahmad Sirhindi's shrine – the dargah of a man who was said to be such a strict and orthodox Sunni Muslim.

The Rauza is built on two levels, with the lower-level housing the main grave chamber and the upper level the cenotaph. I reached on a Friday afternoon, just as the Friday prayers were going on, and after a visit to the upper level, as the lower shrine chamber in the dargah was closed, I sat down in a corner waiting for the rauza to be opened. I tried to make myself as unobtrusive as possible because I didn't want to be scolded for coming too close to the Sufi shrine, though I could see many women around.

Immediately after the prayers, the caretaker of the shrine came and unlocked the door of the underground crypt. I had asked my husband to accompany me here so that he could go inside and take photographs for my reference and describe it to me since I was quite sure I would not be allowed. So, when the door was opened and he went in, I stood in a corner outside. To my surprise, the caretaker gestured and asked me to enter. There was a line of men waiting outside but he told all of them to wait and asked me to go inside. Again, I went and stood in a corner. He apologized that women could not enter the main grave chamber, but suggested I stand at the doorway to see it, study it, and anything else that I had come to do.

Afterwards, I introduced myself to him and told him that I was conducting research for a book. He told me about the dargah, about the people who come there (many come from Bangladesh). Since a group there was waiting for him, he gave me his number and his name.

Syed Muhammad Saifullah and his family have been hereditary caretakers of the shrine for over 300 years. He told me that qawwali or music of any kind isn't allowed, and even a loud recitation of the Quran can only be done in the mosque attached so as to not disturb anyone. If someone wants to come and sit there, they can meditate or read the Quran silently but nothing else is allowed.

For me it was surprising that I was treated with so much respect and affection, and that there was no one around to ask us for alms or even donations.

A friend who is clairvoyant had advised me to go there some months ago and said that my visit was awaited. I am being fanciful, but I could honestly feel welcome.

My other acquaintance Qasim,[13] on the other hand, has been going there for many years and said he finds solace in Baras village (23 km from Sirhind), where according to Naqshbandi sources, there are graves of prophets discovered by Sheikh Ahmed Sirhindi when he saw a *nur* (light) emanating from the place. However, he didn't identify either the names of the prophets or the exact location. He used to go to the mound there for his supererogatory prayers.

As per Islamic belief, there has not been any place on earth where prophets were not sent 'and to every people a guide'. (Quran: 13:7) So although Baras was inhabited by Sikhs post-partition in 1947, they returned it to the Muslims when they found a sweet smell emanating from it.

Now there is a mosque and a large compound, with nine simple kinds of grass covering inordinately long graves (people of that age are said to have been very tall). The spot is called Gulzar-e-Ambiya (Garden of Prophets). I visited it October 2021, and was also struck by the sheer size of the graves and the simplicity and sense of peace there.

Delhi is known as *baees khwaja ki chaukhat* (the threshold of 22 saints). There are of course many more saints now. This was the number under the first dynasty of the Delhi Sultanate. Of these, the most famous are Khwaja Qutubuddin Bakhtiyar Kaki (or Qutub Sahib as he's simply known in Mehrauli), Hazrat Nizamuddin Auliya, and Roshan Chiragh-e-Dilli Hazrat Nasiruddin Mahmud. As we have seen in previous chapters, their dargahs are always full of devotees from all walks, class, and faiths. The locals usually revere the saints whose dargahs are near their houses and offer jaggery, incense sticks, and flowers at the tombs of the Tughlaq-era, Lodi-era, and Mughal-era nobles in particular in their neighbourhood. Most of the locals call the nobles/kings buried in these tombs *Dada Pir*s (ancestral saints) and look after their tombs. They also celebrate Holi by applying coloured powder to the graves and celebrate Diwali by lighting diyas near them.

These shrines are as much a part of their daily lives as their own temples at home. If there is space, the courtyards see children playing in it, like they would at a grandparent's house. There are many dargahs in Delhi, but I have limited myself to a few popular ones.

The dargah of Hazrat Nizamuddin is the busiest in Delhi and full of devotees at all times. They come regularly from far and wide to seek redressals for problems – related to money, health, or children.

Qutub Sahib's dargah in Delhi's Mehrauli is one of the oldest in the city. It was visited by all the sultans and emperors of Delhi. It was also the place where Mahatma Gandhi made his last public appearance on 27 January 1948; he had gone to appeal for Hindu–Muslim amity and to put a stop to violence against Muslims in the wake of the partition riots.

In the dargah of Qutub Sahib, a Sikh businessman sits at the entrance on all important days such as *urs*, Thursdays, and *ghusl sharif*, and does *karsewa* (community service) by polishing the shoes of the devotees who go in. He considers Qutub Sahib his *Dada Pir*, as he was the *pir* of Baba Farid whom Guru Nanak revered. Sometimes his wife also accompanies him.

The dargah of Mehboob-e-Ilahi Hazrat Nizamuddin Auliya is one of India's most famous. It has been visited by almost every head of state – whether in medieval times or now. Whilst the temporal kings lie in oblivion, the spiritual king (also known as Sultan al-Mashaikh or the king of mystics) is visited by thousands daily. It is home to all those who come to pray. Everyone who comes, be they rich or poor, is a fakir or seeker in the saint's presence. People come to ask for children, prosperity, promotions, health and wealth, marriage (their own or of their children), relief from stress, and success in their endeavours. Some come to seek charms from the *pirzada*s (descendants of the saint), to protect them from black magic and the evil eye. Hazrat Nizamuddin Auliya's *karamat* (miracles) are famous and the most important of them is the sense of peace and inclusiveness that prevails in the dargah.

Gourab Ghosh is pursuing his PhD in theatre studies from Delhi's Jawaharlal Nehru University (JNU), besides teaching as a visiting faculty at the Narsee Monjee Institute of Management Studies (NMIMS) in Mumbai and working as a queer rights activist. Ghosh tells me:

> I am an atheist. I do not believe in any god or religion but I believe that to love and respect nature is important. It can be out of a spiritual belief or faith or from a sense of responsibility. I guess that is what Sufism also teaches us: to love all. Perhaps that's why I like going to dargahs and listening to qawwalis, looking at people tying strings [to the stone screens walls of the shrine] as they close their eyes and wish [for] something, cats moving around and crawling up to you as you sit on the marble floor of Hazrat Nizamuddin Dargah in Delhi. I have a few friends there who take me around, feed me – their families open their doors and hearts for me whenever I go. I am a queer man and for me this is like meeting my extended family. If there is any paradise, perhaps it is in the form of [the] acceptance, love and friendship that blooms in the courtyard of [the] Nizamuddin dargah. Sufism is soulful love and devotion to oneself, and to love yourself and the world is also what makes one a queer.[14]

Hazrat Roshan Chiragh-e-Dilli was Delhi's last influential Chishti saint and his dargah is a magnet to all those who stay nearby. The other popular dargahs are those of Mai Sahiba and Bibi Fatima bin Sam, described in Chapter 18 on women Sufis.

Patte Shah ki Dargah near Humayun's tomb is the shrine of a contemporary of Hazrat Nizamuddin Auliya. Hazrat Shamsuddin Utawala's dargah is called Patte Shah because of an ancient tree growing in the shape of the Arabic letters that spell Mohammad, the Prophet's name. It is very common for supplicants to go there and eat a few leaves of the tree with sugar candy.

An unusual and relatively unknown dargah is Hijron ka Khanqah in Mehrauli, a cemetery for *khwajasaras* (eunuchs). It is built on a land said to have been gifted by Qutub Sahib to a *khwajasara* he referred to as Apa. It is looked after by a local named Sripal Yadav who tells me that everything he has is due to the blessings of Apa, and that many come here to pray for children.

Shahid Sarmad Mansur-e-Sani, or the second Mansur al-Hallaj is a popular dargah at the foot of Delhi's Jama Masjid; it is a magnet for lovers and those praying for love. Sarmad was executed on the orders of Emperor Aurangzeb for blasphemy. He was buried in a simple grave next to his spiritual master, Syed Abul Qasim Hare Bhare Shah. Not much is known about Hare Bhare Shah, but it is commonly believed that he was the pir of Sufi Sarmad and had come from Subzwar to Delhi in 1654–55. Today, the portion with Sarmad's grave is painted a bright red as testimony to the fact that he was a martyr of love, and Hare Bhare Shah's side is painted green. A neem tree divides the two shrines. The contrast between the two colours is probably a mute testimony to their lives too. One lived a full and prosperous life as the name Hare Bhare suggests, while the other's life was cut short.

Sheikh Baqi Billah's dargah in Delhi's Paharganj area is a simple one. I had first visited it in 2013 and met Janab Salamatullah Naqshbandi, a direct descendant of Hazrat Baqi Billah and the *mujavir* (caretaker) of the dargah. Old and frail, Pir Sahab, as he is known there, looked very spiritual and serene, and I was very impressed by his personality. Though he was preparing for namaz, he very kindly took me around and patiently answered my questions. The mosque is stunning and well-maintained. There are no crowds of devotees or beggars, and it is a place of solitude and meditation. His shrine is in a small green building just outside the mosque, and again, very well kept. It is open from all sides and has a simple roof.

I saw cats there and when I casually remarked about having noticed them, Pir sahib told me a story. It is said that one night, after having offered his Tahajjud prayers, Hazrat Baqi Billah came to his bed to rest. To his great surprise, a cat was crouching on it. The kind-hearted saint did not want to disturb it so he quietly sat down on the floor and passed the rest of the night like that, despite the chilly winter. The cat, on the other hand, enjoyed its sound sleep till morning.

Another very popular dargah is of Sheikh Jamali in Mehrauli Archaeological Park. It is inside a small complex with a mosque and a compound wall that encloses a small square room. This room looks like a jewel box from the inside, with a glorious, incised plaster design. The shrine is kept locked but it attracts many visitors who come and pay their respects from outside the grill door of the compound.

As was very common in those days, the dwelling places of saints later became their tombs. Shaikh Fazlullah is said to have died in Gujarat and his body was brought here to be buried. It is very plain on the exterior but there's a burst of colour inside. It is adorned by ornamental tiles and immediately beneath the ceiling runs a long Persian verse inscription in Naskh characters that has been cut in plaster.

The tomb elicits tremendous curiosity for one other reason as well. A grave of an unknown male called Kamali, next to his grave, has led to many oral traditions and much speculation. Even though Kamali is described as 'unknown' in all archaeological records, the oral traditions and local lore lead us to believe that the two were lovers.

The tomb is, in fact, called Jamali Kamali by locals. A popular book by American author Susan Chase titled *Jamali-Kamali* has tried to construct their story. In her words: 'Seeing the beauty of their graves, hearing the tale that had been passed down, spurred me on to invent a story of love, sex, separation and death. It is not based on any historical record – there isn't one.'[15]

We only know that Sheikh Jamali had two sons Abdul Haq and Sheikh Gadai. The former was a poet and served the Afghan ruler Sher Shah, while the latter remained loyal to the Mughals. He was appointed as Sadrus-Sudur, chief judge, by Bairam Khan and his prestige was such that his *sama mehfils* were attended by Akbar himself. However, Sheikh Gadai, due to his revoking land grants to certain ulemas and Sufis who supported the Afghans, the previous dynasty, became extremely unpopular. Badauni, Akbar's chronicler and a staunch critic of Akbar's 'radical religious policies' had many scandalous comments to make about the Sheikh and his role in Bairam Khan's estrangement with Akbar.

When Bairam Khan, Emperor Akbar's prime minister, fell out of favour and was sent on a hajj pilgrimage, Sheikh Gadai went with him. Bairam

Khan was killed enroute, Sheikh Gadai decided to live in Jaisalmer for some years before returning to Delhi. In Jaisalmer, he lived on a small land grant. Abdul Haq has mentioned that Sheikh Gadai, despite his great age, 'loved the company of pretty-faced youth, probably boys'.[16]

There is no record, but some speculate that Kamali was a lover of Jamali's, or that he is none other than Sheikh Gadai, the saint's eldest son. Did Sheikh Gadai's unpopularity amongst the ulemas and Sufis and stories about his preference for the company of boys lead to the fictional same-sex lover story of Jamali and Kamali? Perhaps, we will never know.

The beautiful mosque attached to the twin graves is said to be the dwelling place of Jinn saints and continues to fascinate.

> Our restlessness in your love has passed beyond bounds,
> Our hope is that you will pity our weeping.
>
> – Sheikh Jamali

In the Rajasthani city of Ajmer is the most popular dargah of India, visited by celebrities, dignitaries, commoners – all lovers of the Khwaja – and especially the poor, earning him the title of Khwaja Garib Nawaz. One is just overwhelmed by the sheer number of people who come there on a daily basis.

On my trip to Ajmer and Pushkar, both holy cities in Rajasthan geographically close to each other, my love for praying to Allah at every religious shrine or place of worship that I go to is clear for all to see. The religious energy and miracles associated with each place of worship I visit instil in me a sense of spiritualism. I don't find anything odd about praying to Allah in temples, gurdwaras and churches, for ultimately there is one God. I believe that Allah is omnipresent and so listens to me everywhere. After all, it has been written: 'Verily! We have sent you with the truth, a bearer of glad tidings and a warner. And there never was a nation but a warner had passed among them.' (Faatir 35:24)

I was accompanied on this journey by my friends, Alka Mathur and Gayatri Manchanda. We first visited the Brahma temple in Pushkar and then performed the evening *arti* (prayer) on the banks of the river before leaving for Ajmer. Alka and Gayatri also share my philosophy; so the next day we sat in complete absorption and devotion in the dargah of Khwaja Garib Nawaz.

The dargah allows both men and women to enter. Jahanara Begum, Shah Jahan's elder daughter, came here often. She wrote a biography of the saint and built a covered platform next to the shrine, which is known as the Begumi Chabutra.

At the dargah, a daily *langar* of simple wheat porridge is cooked and distributed, reflecting the Khwaja's concern for the welfare of the poor. Taking into account the eating pattern of the local populace, the food served here has always been vegetarian.

Just above this dargah is another one, which also received royal patronage. It is the shrine of Meeranji or Meeran Shah, Syed Hussain Khingsawar Mashhadi (d.1201),[17] who is said to have been appointed by Sultan Qutbuddin Aibak as the garrison commander of Taragarh Fort, the Chauhan citadel that Aibak had conquered. As per the *khadims* who were present there and who described the history, Meeranji was born in Mashhad in Iran and was a descendant of the eighth Shia Imam, Imam Raza. He was ordered to go to Hindustan. Through a miracle, he and his horse were transported to Taragarh where he fought many battles on behalf of Aibak. As per the website of Indian dargahs:

> [H]e attracted a large number of devotees through his pious, simple but generous lifestyle. He served humanity by taking care of the medicinal needs of those stricken with leprosy and epilepsy. His noble deeds and bravery propelled Meerat, Cheeta and Deswali communities to embrace Islam. His growing popularity caused much heartburn among the non-believers. They twice made attempt[s to] recapture Taragarh Fort that was one by Shah Meeran (sic). But on both occasions their bid was foiled by Khingsawar. The raiders however succeeded in their attempt on [the] 18th Rajab and martyred Shah Meeran while he was offering 'Asr' prayers.[18]

He was buried in the Taragarh Fort, and his horse a little ahead of the main shrine; like every visitor there, we also offered flowers and gram at his grave before going up. The simple shrine with a domed structure was first added during Jahangir's reign. Over the centuries, many construction activities have been undertaken here, including that of a small water body attributed to Sher Shah Suri, a *buland darwaza* (lofty doorway) by Ismail Quli Khan on orders of Emperor Akbar, an apartment during the reign of Jahangir, and one set of apartments by Maratha chief Kumar Rao Scindia whose prayers for a son were answered in the dargah. Maharani Baiza Bai Scindia of Gwalior (1784–1863) has also contributed to the many edifices decorating the dargah. There are also contributions by the Nizam of Hyderabad, Rajput chieftains and a Sikh gentleman who resides in UK. These represent the syncretic traditions of the dargah in cold hard stone, not just emotions.

As in the neighbouring dargah of Khwaja Gharib Nawaz, there are three huge cauldrons for cooking and distributing *langar.* Two of these were gifts of Emperor Jahangir and one by an officer of Gwalior state.

While most shrines are covered in sandal paste during the *urs*, his columns of the shrine are covered in a henna paste, symbolizing his interrupted nuptials. According to some stories he was about to get married when he was given orders to go to Hindustan; others say he was martyred before the marriage could be solemnized and he died in his wedding dress. Visitors to the shrine pray for the marriage of their near and dear ones. The *khadim* gave me some dry henna paste too which I later added to the henna that was applied to my daughter's hands during her wedding ceremonies. I find such gestures sweet, and since they come from a place sanctified by prayer, they add to the blessings of the couple.

Apart from henna, 1¼ maunds of red thread (*kalava*) are tied to the shrine, and as per belief, during late afternoon prayers *asr* on the day of his martyrdom (Islamic date is 18th Rabi Awwal), the shrine shakes for 2 seconds and all the *kalava*s fall down. Devotees collect the thread as they are considered a safeguard against calamities, black magic and the influence of jinns.

During my visit I found out that according to a local legend, the famous Bhakti saint and poetess Meerabai is named after him. A few years ago my friend Meera Rizvi, whose father Prof. Mujeeb Rizvi was one of the foremost exponents of medieval 'Hindi' poetry, told me how the poetess had been named after a Sufi saint Miran Shah. I had filed away the story and after all that time I was pleasantly surprised to find that the legend connects communities, and is a reflection of our plural past.

The old berry tree in the compound of the dargah is said to be connected to the poetess. I was told that this tree is always green and full of leaves, and that whoever eats its leaves has their wishes fulfilled, especially if they desire to have children. Meerabai's mother is reported to have been one of those who ate it and prayed for an offspring and when the wish was granted, named her daughter after the saint. This legend is also mentioned in Seetaram Lalas' (1908–1986) dictionary of Rajasthani words, *Rajasthani Shabd (Sabada) Kosh*, where the entry under Meera's name says that no one knows how and why she got this name but Purohit Shri Hari Narayan ji Vidya Bhushan and a few other scholars suggest that before her birth, Meera's mother had visited the dargah of Miransah (Miran Shah) and prayed there. When she was blessed with a daughter she named the baby after the saint.

According to Prof. Imre Bangha, '[T]his story could have come to being because it is difficult to find a Sanskritic etymology for her name. The name is very often written in Hindi with a nasalized 'a' at the end, hence the Miran spelling, which is also a Persian word.'[19] He adds, 'The word figures several times in the Dadu-vani[20] in the sense of God, Lord, generous, etc. All these Rajasthani usages eventually go back to Persian. Moreover, Miransah is also used in a more general sense in Rajasthan.'

In answer to my query on the difference of the present-day spelling, where it is not nasalized, he replied, 'Most manuscripts and Hindi scholarships use the nasalized form, and it is mostly the inaccuracy of the English language to represent nasalization that मीराँ/ میراں has become Mira. Callewaert and Sharma's entry on Mira in the *Dictionary of Bhakti* cites Dadu and Kabir using the original word. However, while Lalas nasalizes, Callewaert [and Sharma] do not. Neither of them has the other version of the word hinting at the fact that nasalization does not make a difference. Both Callewaert and Lalas (though implicitly through the meaning) derive the word from Mir.'

Another attraction in Miran Shah's dargah complex is a recent addition – a replica of Imam Hussain's shrine in Karbala, Iraq. The devotees of

Hussain who can't afford to make a pilgrimage to Iraq come here. It is a very awe-inspiring sight to behold in the middle of the ruins of the erstwhile Taragarh Fort and the surrounding hillside.

In Nagaur, which is about 150 km from Ajmer, the dargah of Khwaja Garib Nawaz's *khalifa* Hazrat Hamiduddin Nagauri is very popular. Hazrat Hamiduddin Nagauri was sent by his master to live amongst the people of Nagaur, a predominantly Jain area. In deference to their religious sentiments, he never consumed non-vegetarian food. In fact, in its entire 800-odd-year history, meat has never been served even in the Ajmer Sharif Dargah, where *langars* are served daily.

The name Awadh (identified with Uttar Pradesh) was derived from the holy city of Ayodhya, famous as the birthplace of Lord Rama and the temple. It also houses two unique dargahs which draw in crowds from all over the subcontinent, if not the world.

One of them is the dargah of Shesh Paigamber, who is said to be the son of no less than Aadam himself! It is believed that he came and settled here after travelling the world.

Extremely popular locally, this shrine is surrounded by an old cemetery. The present edifice was built upon during the reign of Sultan Sikander Lodi (r. 1489–1517). The first thing that strikes the visitor is the dargah's length. Like the Baras village dargah near Sirhind, the graves (said to be of prophets from Syria, Iraq and Oman) here too are also extremely long, and again, as per local belief, this is because people from that age were very tall. At the entrance itself is a simple *mazar* (shrine) of Shesh Paigamber's *pir*, Hazrat Baba Jalil Naqshbandi. This grave, now in a grilled enclosure, is also long and is awe-inspiring because of its size. There are also the graves of his wife Bibi Hur and their four children.

Since the dargah is associated with the first man on earth, people of all faiths come here and supplicate for humanity and the well-being of the world.

The other famous dargah in Ayodhya is simply called Naugaza (nine-yard long), as it too is inordinately long. It is believed to be the grave of prophet Nuh (Noah). However, it is also believed, according to locals, to be only 1,000 years old. This indicates that it may perhaps, in reality, be a Sufi saint named Nuh who was customarily buried there along with his staff. Besides, the Quranic Nuh is more widely said to be buried in Najaf next to Hazrat Ali. This dargah is also popular with people of all faiths, and I was told that many newly-weds come here to ask for children.

Not very far from Ayodhya is Kichhauchha Sharif, the dargah of Sheikh Ashraf Jehangir Simnani (d. 1425)[21]. They say that if one wants to visit a holy place, one has to be called there. Unfortunately, my *bulava* (call) hasn't come for this dargah.

Sheikh Ashraf Jahangir Simnani is a very important saint in Sufism though, as he is the primary transmitter of *Wahdat al-Wujud* and the metaphysical teachings of Ibn al-Arabi in India. He was born in the Simnan, Khurasan. His father, Saiyed Muhammad Ibrahim, was a local ruler, while his mother, Khadija, was a granddaughter of Shaykh Ahmad Yasawi (1093–1166), founder of the Yasawiya order. At the age of 23, he left Simnan and travelled to India, settling ultimately in Kichhauchha in present-day Ambedkar Nagar of Uttar Pradesh. He gave it the name Ruhabad (city of the spirit). He travelled to many cities and countries from there. He travelled to Pandua during this time, where he became the disciple and *khalifa* of Sheikh Ala-ul Haq Pandvi, who instructed him to return to Kichhauchha. Islamic Studies expert Carl W. Ernst writes:

> He was a man of diverse talents, who dabbled in magic as well as mysticism. He is remembered as a well-travelled, highly esteemed saint who sought out the company of wise, famous, and powerful men, from the local rulers of Jaunpur to the Persian lyricist of Shiraz, Hafiz. He is even reputed to have once met the Mongol warlord Timur. Among his several literary monuments, only two have survived: his letters (*Maktubat-I Ashrafi*) and *Lata'if-i Ashrafi*.[22]

His dargah is set on top of a small hillock with a pond on one side. This pond is said to have been started with the water of the holy spring Zamzam from Mecca and is called Neer Sagar. It is alleged to have healing powers. At any given point of time, there are huge crowds waiting to bathe or wash themselves in its waters.

Since I could not visit it, I talked to Syed Mohammed Qasim, a friend who is deeply interested and invested in Sufism and has visited it a number of times. Qasim told me of a visit he made during the pandemic of 2020–21, when places of worship were closed to visitors. He set off with his brother Syed Misbahur Rahman, an engineer from Lucknow, along with a friend who was from the Ashrafi family (the *peerzada*s of the dargah). They knew that they would not be able to do *ziarat* but were content to go and present their *salaam* from outside itself, make their supplications and return. When they reached there, they met a *khadim* who recognized his brother who is an engineer and said that that the main member of the dargah committee (a *peerzada*) had been waiting for his visit as they wanted to consult him on some structural problems with one of the walls of the dargah. According to Qasim, it was a spontaneous visit and not a planned one, yet he found someone waiting for them. After the consultation, they were taken to the shrine and got a special *ziarat* and offered the *chaddar*s they had brought with them, just in case. They had a very peaceful *ziarat* all alone in the tomb chamber, where it is usually difficult to stand because of the crowds of devotees. This, he says, is just the power of the dargah that hears the call of a true devotee's heart.

This dargah is also a major centre of exorcism and will be discussed again in Chapter 16.

Another dargah in the region which I am still waiting to visit is the dargah of Sheikh Alauddin Ali Ahmad Sabir or Sabir Ali Piya as he is called. Sheikh Alauddin Ali Ahmad Sabir's splendid green and white dargah in Kaliyar is always full of supplicants and followers. A huge fig tree near it is the repository of petitions, which are tied to its trunk by those who seek the saint's intercession. His *urs,* marked on the 13th, 14th and 15th of the Islamic month of *Rabi Awwal*, is attended by lakhs of devotees from every faith and region. *Mehndi* (henna) and blessed red threads are distributed to his followers.

Lucknow, with its Nawabi past (Shia nawabs who ruled Awadh in eighteenth and nineteenth centuries), has many dargahs devoted to the *Ahl al-Bait* (which have been described in chapter 11) but one of its most frequented dargahs is that of a fifteenth century Chishti saint. Shah Mina (d. 1479), as he is called, rests in one of the busiest parts of Lucknow. This dargah is in the chowk near the King George Medical College and is a natural magnet for those who come there for treatment. Shah Mina's early spiritual master Sheikh Qiwam-ud-din is also buried in the same complex.

Sheikh Qiwam-ud-din had a son named Muhammad, whom he affectionately called Mina. Scholar Carl W. Ernst explains, 'In the dialect of that region "Mina" is a word that is used for the station of greatness and belovedness, that [in Hindi] we call "Miyan".'[23] The son incurred his father's displeasure as he joined the service of one of the kings to further his ambitions. He was forgiven once, but the second time the father ordered the son to never appear before him again. The son fell sick and died. The sheikh then adopted a dervish by the name of Qutb ad-Din who was in his service. He gave him his son's name Muhammad Mina;[24] the latter, receiving his master's favour, became famous and is known today as Shah Mina.

The dargah was built in the vicinity of Machchi Bhavan, the seat of power of the Shaikhzadas who governed Lucknow under the Mughals. After the Uprising of 1857, Machchi Bhavan was demolished by the British but the graves of the two saints were spared. Today, the dargah is in a very constricted space but it is always full of visitors – especially on the first Thursday of the Islamic calendar known as *Nauchandi Jumeraat*. Flowers, sweets, and *chaddar*s are offered here. The saint's annual *urs* is still celebrated, though not with the grandeur that it was celebrated with under the nawabs.

Dastango (oral storyteller) Himanshu Bajpai, who grew up very close to this dargah, has visited it often but has a special connection with the Khamman Pir Dargah near Charbagh Station in Lucknow instead. The saint who rests there is Shah Syed Qayamuddin, called Khamman Pir. Not much is known about the saint but he is alleged to have come to Lucknow nine centuries ago and was buried in this location in a simple grave, which locals revere.

The railway tracks running on both sides of this splendid dargah has an interesting story behind it. When Charbagh station was being constructed (the foundation was laid in 1914 and the work completed in 1923), the British engineers wanted to lay the tracks over the grave of Khamman Baba, but they found that every morning the tracks had been dug up. Eventually plans were made to circumvent it and the present structure built sometime after that, lies between the two tracks of an extremely busy railway line.

Bajpai recalls that he would go there often as his school was close to it. One of his class fellows was called Khamman; he had been so named by his parents who had prayed for a son at the dargah before he was born. As with all dargahs this one too sees a lot of visitors on Thursdays, with many coming to offer their respects, *chaddar*s, and flowers to the saint on this day.[25]

In the *takia* of Kakori Sharif near Lucknow, I found serenity and peace among its mango orchards. An old man who took care of the dargahs welcomed me and took me around, opening all the shrines and describing their histories. These shrines are normally busy on Thursday evenings and during the annual *urs*. Refreshingly, there was no segregation of women here. (More on this *takia* in Chapter 9. The dargahs of Dewa and Makanpur are described in Chapter 12.)

The city of Bareilly, also in Uttar Pradesh, is home to two vastly different dargahs. The first is the dargah of Ala Hazrat,[26] Ahmed Raza Khan Barelvi (1856–1921) the leader of the Ahl-e-Sunnat Movement – popular as the Barelvi school, and the second is the dargah of Shah Niaz Barelvi (1742–1834) who wrote poetry under the pseudonym Be-niaz (incomparable).

In her book *Born a Muslim: Some Truths About Islam in India*, Ghazala Wahab links the growth of the Barelvi movement, as a fallout of the failed uprising of 1857, against the background of retributive killings of Muslims and the fanning of a narrative of Hindu victimhood by the British.

The *ulema* were quick to draw on the disillusionment of the Muslims, who had become despondent and inward-looking – as defeated people often do. 'They [ulema] claimed that while the Muslims' cause was just, their faith was weak. Hence, the faith needed to be strengthened. The growth and eventual rise of Sunni Muslim sects like the Deobandi and Barelvi were the consequence of this new dependence of the ordinary Muslims on the ulema.'[27]

Ala Hazrat had taken an oath of allegiance with the Imam-ul-Asfiya, Shah Aale Rasul Marehrawi. His revivalist movement was based on the Hanafi school of jurisprudence with Sufi influences and is extremely popular the world over.

The dargah itself is inside a narrow lane and is a simple affair. As in other dargahs, when I went there I was told to go to the cloistered and suffocating ladies section. From there, I could see the male devotees, in the main chamber which houses the graves, praying and supplicating.

Elaborating on the situation and practices of the dargah, Ghazala Wahab, who researched the sect for her aforementioned book, wrote in response to my query about segregation:

> The irony of Dargah Aala Hazrat is that all his life Ahmed Raza Khan Barelwi campaigned against both the Sufis and the Deoband. He, and subsequently his followers, considered going [to] shrines Bi'dah and likened it to idol worship. Yet, after his death, his followers created a hereditary cult of Ahmed Raza Khan Barelwi, something which neither the Sufis nor the Deobandi [would approve of].
>
> His dargah is pretty nondescript, yet visitors to the dargah follow all the decorum/ rituals of Sufi dargahs, barring the *elaichi danas* (cardamom pods). Baskets of rose petals are bought from outside the dargah and are offered/sprinkled on the shrine. The segregation of women is akin to [the] Tablighi Jamaat; and the cultism is similar to the Bohras or the Ismailis.[28]

Ala Hazrat's annual *urs* brings the city to a standstill, and I have often witnessed the enormous crowds in Bareilly during the ceremony. People flock in from all parts of the world to participate. For the past many decades, it has also been used as an occasion to give lectures on Islamic teachings, methodologies, and the socio-economic issues of the followers.

Some 500 metres away is the Khanqah-e-Niazia. As a great admirer of the mystical poetry of its founder Shah Niaz Ahmed Be-niaz, I have visited it a number of times and always felt welcome in its huge courtyard surrounded by the marble shrines.

Shah Niaz Ahmed, the renowned saint and founder of the Khanqah-e-Niyazia and the Niyazia Sufi Order, was born in 1742 in Sirhind.

He was given the name Raaz Ahmed on his birth in the family of Alvi Saiyed (descendants of Hazrat Ali). His father was appointed the Qazi of Shahjanabad. His mother Bibi Lado was from the family of Sheikh Kalimullah Jehanabadi. He came to Delhi with his parents in 1748 and his early education was under his maternal grandfather, Maulana Saeeduddin Rizvi. Later he was educated in the Madrasah-e-Fakhriya under Maulana Fakhruddin Dehlvi Chishti, famous as Fakhr-e-Jahan.

After completing his education in the madrasah, he started teaching there. He took an oath of allegiance with Maulana Fakhruddin in the Chishti *silsilah* and the latter appointed him his *khalifa* and sent him to Bareilly to carry on his spiritual task. There he established the *khanqah* which became a centre of both traditional and spiritual knowledge.

He was later inducted into the Qadri *silsilah* by Hazrat Abdullah Baghdadi, who was a direct descendent of Ghaus-ul Azam Shaikh Abdul Qadir Jeelani, and then he finally started his own Niyazia *silsilah*.

His mystical verses convey the message of love and brotherhood. Each word is soaked in spirituality and it takes an age to grasp its entire meaning. One of his verses, for instance, embodies the meaning of *ishq-e-haqeeqi* (described in detail in Chapter 3) and the message that service and love for mankind is service and love of God:

> *Kafir-e-ishq hun main banda-e-Islam nahin,*
> *But-parasti ke siwa aur mujhe kaam nahin*
>
> [I am an idolator of love, not a servant of Islam;
> I spend my time worshiping at the altar of love.]

The pervasive feeling of inclusiveness prevails even today. As descendants of Hazrat Ali, the Niyazia *silsilah* observes the month of Muharram and the martyrdom of Imam Hussain with great solemnity. They organize *langar*s and commemorative functions. I have had the good fortune of attending a *majlis*, an assembly to commemorate Imam Husain's martyrdom and eat *langar* there. The memories stay with me because of the pervading feeling of love and affection with which they ensured that I stay back to eat the *langar* and seated me comfortably as I couldn't sit on the floor. Some years later I experienced that same love in the Dumduma Gurudwara in Delhi.

A relatively unknown dargah is that of Haji Harmain in Zafarabad (district Jaunpur); like many others, it is a symbol of pluralism and worth mentioning. Haji Harmain's name, Sheikh Sadruddin Chiragh-e-Shiraz-e-Hind, itself gives us a sense of the importance of the region and the saint.

In 1359, Sultan Firoz Shah Tughlaq stopped at a place called Zafarabad along the river Ganga on his way to campaign against the Ilyas Shahi rulers of Lakhnauti in Bengal. Zafarabad was a strategic point on the road to Bengal, and the Delhi sultans had long been fighting with the rulers of Lakhnauti. This probably prompted the sultan, a prolific builder, to think of building a new city near Zafarabad. The city was built on the river Gomti and was named Jaunpur after the sultan's cousin and predecessor, Jauna Khan, who had ruled as Sultan Mohammad bin Tughlaq.

Jaunpur later became the capital of the Sharqi rulers, under whom it prospered, and was called Shiraz of Hindustan after the famous Persian city. The name Harmain is a reference to the holy cities of Mecca and Medina, which is what Zafarabad was likened to.

The saint's *urs* is in the Islamic month of Zil-hajj and is attended by Hindus and Muslims alike. Men and women pray together, with the women standing at the back. There is a rush for the offering of the first *chaddar,* as it is said that the worries of the person who does this are over! Normally, it is the government officials who offer the first *chaddar*.

Apart from the regular ceremonies that occur in an *urs,* such as 'sandal', 'ghusl' and Quran recitation, a fair is held for enjoyment of the visitors.

The dargah of Sheikh Salim Chishti is of course very famous because of the Mughal emperor, Akbar's association with it. Akbar was 28 years old and did not have an heir for the empire he was busy consolidating. This was when he heard of a saint who lived a hermit's life in Sikri. Akbar visited the saint, often described in legends as a powerful emperor walking barefoot like a beggar to the saint's door. The saint promised him three sons, and Akbar promised to dedicate the first to the saint. True to his promise, when his wife Mariyam az-Zamani became pregnant, she was sent to the saint's *khanqah* and his son, named Salim after the saint, was born there in 1569. The emperor got the Rang Mahal built for his wife's confinement; later many other magnificent buildings and the city of Fatehpur Sikri were constructed by Akbar, starting in 1571.

The shrine of Sheikh Salim Chishti is in the magnificent Jama Masjid complex and is accessed through the imposing Buland Darwaza. The marble tomb itself is a pearl drop set in the red sandstone background and is one of the most exquisite monuments of the Mughal era. But to most visitors, it is the saint associated with childbirth and children who is the star attraction. The saint is a descendant of Baba Farid and was initiated into the Chishti *silsilah*. The dargah was built after his death in 1571/72, and the city of Fatehpur Sikri was an ode to his memory. Its marble eaves and lattice screens, with the light outside streaming in through them, are not only famous for their beauty, but also the spiritual quality – in fact, especially the latter. The sheikh was buried, as was the tradition, in mud brought from Mecca.

The windows of the tomb chamber, with their pierced, geometrical tracery, are world-famous; images of the red thread tied by supplicants has often flooded the internet. Brides from all faiths come here and tie a thread to ask for the saint's intercession for domestic happiness and children; women come here to pray for children and once the vow is fulfilled, offer a *chaddar*. Whenever I too have visited, it has been to make a wish for my children and family.

There are always devotees thronging the inner chamber and tourists flocking around the qawwali singers outside.

Ghazala Wahab who grew up in Agra describes her experience to me:

> This is one dargah that I have been visiting regularly since my childhood, and my experience has remained the same. It is one of the most unassuming and peaceful places where each visitor has the privacy of one's belief. Nobody forces anyone to do anything. Just as it was during my childhood, there is no gender segregation even today. The last time I went to the dargah was in February 2021. I went inside the shrine as I have done all these years. There were no minders and no fixed rituals. Visitors did exactly what they wanted to. Some offered a *chaddar*, some offered flowers, and some like me offered nothing except prayer.
>
> I wondered if this hands-off approach was because it was part of a historical monument – Fatehpur Sikri – and hence a tourist attraction. But this assumption was incorrect. I realized that most dargahs in Agra follow this non-obtrusive approach to faith. I

> visited the dargah of Sayyidna Shah Amir Abul Ala, famously known as Sayyidna Dargah, and found the same quietude there. Not a single *mutawalli* or *sajjada nasheen* asking for donation for various causes. All it had in the name of fund collection were few locked boxes in which devotees could drop whatever they wanted. Clearly, these dargahs still maintain the sanctity of the shrine in the spirit of Sufism, where each has to find her own path and destination.[29]

If the dargah of Sheikh Salim Chishti is associated with children, a famous one in Bahraich is associated with weddings. The dargah of Saiyed Salar Masud Ghazi, or simply Ghazi Miyan, or Bale Miyan as he is known, is one of the earliest dargahs in India. Ghazi Miyan has become famous as the nephew of Mahmud of Ghazni – surely a fictional and historically unverifiable connection, as history and hagiography both show that is far from the truth.

Ghazi Miyan, so popular amongst the Hindus and Muslims in precolonial India, and revered amongst the locals as a protector of cattle particularly cows and the downtrodden, and an enemy of oppressive landlords, became famous later as a religious fanatic who destroyed Hindu temples. How did this come to pass? Based on a critical evaluation of multiple sources, such as Indo-Persian texts, popular folklore, colonial ethnographic accounts, Urdu poetry and popular Hindi tracts, historian Shahid Amin describes the construction of the legend of Ghazi Miyan. If the invention of Ghazi Miyan as a virtuous nephew of Mahmud of Ghazni, who destroyed the temple of Somnath, was done from the fourteenth century onwards in Persian tracts, the image of a religious fanatic comes up in postcolonial literature. In his book, Amin establishes that the character of Ghazi Miyan, seen as a local hero in precolonial era was appropriated for communal mobilization later.[30]

Ghazi Miyan is said to have been martyred in the holy war against Hindu kings near Bahraich, in modern-day Uttar Pradesh, in 1034 and buried in a simple grave.

A milkmaid who was thrown out of her marital home by her mother-in-law, for her supposed failure to produce a child, is said to have found the then simple mud grave of Ghazi Miyan being tended by a few devotees. They advised her to pray there. Soon, she was joined by her husband, who also prayed and vowed to make an offering of sweets if their prayers were heard. She became pregnant almost immediately on going home, and the legend of Ghazi Miyan's powers was born.

The story of a miracle wherein a congenitally blind 12-year-old girl, Zohra Bibi, from a Saiyed family in Radauli (Barabanki district in Uttar Pradesh), regained her eyesight seems to have sealed the legend some decades later. In Shahid Amin's words:

> On hearing about the legendary Salar Masud, Zohra was consumed by a pining for the warrior saint. Blind and impetuous, the 12-year-old vowed that if cured (by the intercession of the Ghazi), she would devote her life to serving his shrine. One night, exhausted, she sensed the Ghazi approaching. 'If I be possessed of true love', prayed Zohra in her dream, 'may I regain my vision, so that I may be able to set my eyes on Masud'. Riding his favourite grey mare, the Prince of Martyrs appeared in her vision; the girl chased her dream: when she awoke she had gained sight, but Masud was lost from view.[31]

She became a staunch devotee, and being a lady of means, she built a grand tomb for him. She did not marry and spent her whole life there, ultimately being buried next to Ghazi Miyan's tomb. The fame and spiritual powers of Ghazi Miyan grew and it was visited by Sultan Muhammad bin Tughlaq.

As Zohra Bibi died on the same date, as per the Islamic calendar (14th Rajab), as Ghazi Miyan, the day is considered and celebrated as a double *urs*; since then, their metaphorical wedding is celebrated on the first day of the Indian solar month of Jeth. Their supposed reunion in the afterlife is understood as an *urs-i-ursiana* (marriage of all marriages) since it 'came to stand for the marriage-in-death of Zohra with the warrior saint of Bahraich, who had also embraced his death/bride on the day of his martyrdom.'[32] The tomb built by Zohra Bibi was thereafter considered a monument of love, and the celebration, called the Bahraich *mela,* falls roughly on the first Sunday of May, provided a Thursday precedes it in the same month.

After Zohra Bibi's death, her mother and other members of her family would visit the shrine with a trousseau, as if a wedding were indeed taking place. That tradition continues to date with the family's descendants.

The saint is now locally also addressed as Ghazi Dulha (bridegroom). A well-known song goes:

*Kya Hindi, kya Musalman,*
*Sab rakhat mohabbatiya, Ghaziaiyaa tumri.*

[Be it Hindu or Muslim,
Everybody harbours love for you, oh Ghazi Dulha.]

Anab Naiyer documents this in his MPhil dissertation and rightly adds: 'Such songs are symbolic of the cross-border and cross-cultural communication as a way to look for harmony in times of struggle and tensions amongst religions and beliefs.'[33]

The story of his birth, as memorialized in ballads, is as interesting as the story about his afterlife. The ballad suggests that he was born because of the blessing of Shah Madar. However, since his mother did not carry out all of his instructions, the saint cursed her son, saying he would die on the day of his wedding.

The balladeers describe Ghazi Miyan's mother, Mamula, getting her son ready for his marriage when the milkmaid Jaswa shouts that local chieftain Sohal Deo is attacking the groom's cows. Despite his mother's pleas to not get up from the ceremony, Ghazi Miyan goes to protect them and frees his cows from Sohal Deo. The ballad imagines him singing:

*Hum to lubhāvan byāh mein, apne lagāya ghāt!*

[Here I was engrossed in my nuptial rites and you ambushed my cows and cowherds!][34]

There are also many versions of how he died, but the most popular one is this: After his victory over Sohal Deo, he rests under a tree and an arrow pierces his heart; he dies unwed at the age of 19 and is celebrated as a martyr.

Innumerable songs and ballads – from Bahraich and Varanasi to Punjab – were composed in his memory. Contrary to the modern-day portrayals,

Ghazi Miyan is the protector of cows and cowherds. He is also remembered for having put an end to oppressive practices of the landlords such as human sacrifice and exploitation of women.

Ghazi Miyan's following cuts across social and religious groups. His cult was frowned upon by Sultan Sikander Lodi in the fifteenth century for its unorthodox practices, and by Muslim clergy for propagating grave worship, while the elite frowned upon the exuberance displayed by the lower classes. According to Amin, Ghazi Miyan's memory endured across religious divides, till 'the 1870s saw the beginning of a concerted attack from a narrowly sectarian view point on the life, shrine and cult of Masud'. Since his memory was mostly oral, the newly arrived print medium was used to counter it in Hindi books. Amin explains:

> These early attacks on Salar Masud were aimed at saving Hindu women from their [supposedly] blind adoration of the warrior saint. Often couched in the voice of the rational Hindu housewife, this rubbishing of Ghazi Miyan was of a piece with the construction of a common sense: the memory of 'Hindu defeat' at the hands of Muslims in India's medieval past. Such a remembrance was linked equally to the logic of colonial modernity: for the siring of communities through print and the affixing of history to a persistent memory, here as elsewhere, went hand in hand. It is within this new 'Hindu History', increasingly abrasive, yet unable to fully dislodge Masud from familial altars, that the contest over the devotees of the Ghazi played itself out.[35]

Today we see this scenario being played out on WhatsApp and social media, aimed at most of the Sufi saints. Yet, Ghazi Miyan's legend continues – thanks to his unfailing balladeers.

> *Saiyed ki sarguzasht ko Hāli se pūchiye,*
> *Ghazi Miyan ka hāl Dafāli se pūchiye.*
>
> [For Sir Syed's (the great educationist's), tale, ask Hali, his biographer,
> For Ghazi Miyan's story, ask Dafali, his balladeer.][36]

# 13

# Popular Dargahs of East and Northeast India

Sufis started coming to Assam from the fourteenth century onwards. Interestingly, available evidence shows that they were not linked to any *silsilah* but were wandering *fakirs* who settled down there and left behind the legacy of their own dargahs.[1]

The most famous dargah is that of Hazrat Shah Miran, who came to India from Baghdad in the seventeenth century and settled in the Sibsagar district. He taught the locals to pray and recite the *azaan* (call to pray), so he was given the sobriquet of 'Azan' and is widely known as Azan Pir aka Azan Fakir (Azan is sometimes spelt as *ajaan* since that is how the 'z' is pronounced locally). His dargah is at the confluence of two rivers, Dikhow and Brahmputra, in Saraguri. Azan Pir is credited with having introduced Islam in Assam, as he initiated many into the fold.

Another lasting contribution Azan Fakir made was to the genre of a musical tradition called *zikir* (described in Chapter 18), which was begun by a Vaishnavite saint Sankardev who preceded him by a century and a half. His *zikir*s are now an important part of Assamese poetic traditions.

Given this association with the local Vaishnav culture, his dargah is visited by people of all faiths but mostly by non-Muslims for, as Nahida Mumtaz puts it in her MPhil dissertation, 'The local people or the visitors did not seem to understand the tradition of syncretism or Sufism but are aware that Azan Fakir was a Muslim. But for them he is a *pir*, a *sadhu*, or *baba* and beyond religion.'[2]

He married a local Ahom lady and had three sons. His descendants are known as Suraguria Dewans, named after the place where they had settled. Azan Pir probably died sometime around 1690.

Another popular dargah in the region is the Poa -Mecca Dargah situated on a peak of the Garudachal Hill in Hajo, Kamrup district. It is the dargah of a fourteenth-century saint, Sheikh Ghiyasuddin Auliya. Not much is known about his origins, but his dargah was patronized by Ahom and Koch kings who 'granted land and endowments to the mosque complex and took keen interest in the administrative system of the sacred complex of Hajo.'[3]

The local Muslims believe that the sheikh brought a lump of earth from Mecca – apart from his 70 disciples – and built a *khanqah* upon it. Though the pluralistic traditions and culture of Assam are under threat from both Hindutva and Islamic forces, these dargahs still provide solace to people of all faiths. They bring together people of different communities. Nahida Mumtaz writes:

> Hindu pilgrims visit the shrine particularly on the full moon day of the month of Jaistha (May–June) when an *urs* is held. In fact Hajo is the meeting place of several religious and cultural streams. The process of assimilation gave the society and culture of the area a magnificent character in these days of communal disharmony and violence. The Hindu–Muslim unity is a single feature of the life of Hajo which is due to the co-existence of these shrines and temples.[4]

Though Nahida Mumtaz's dissertation is a decade old now, I am told by friends in Assam that it still holds true.

In Dhubri district of Assam is the famous Panch Pir Dargah (built in 1662), said to be the resting place of five *pir*s brought to the region by a Mughal commander when he attacked Assam to counter the magic of the people of Kamrup. The *pir*s were Shah Akbar, Shah Bagmar, Shah Sufi, Shah Sharan, and Shah Kamal. It is generally believed that the five of them stayed together and after death were buried next to each other at the Panch Pir Dargah (which translates as the dargah of five *pir*s).[5]

Nahida Mumtaz explains that this dargah, too, is like the previous one:

> The dargah is a centre for pilgrimage for both Hindus and Muslims of the locality; like most of such shrines they associate miracles and magical power with the dargah and offer prayer[s] to the saints. The devotees however do not attach any importance to the fact that it is

> a Muslim religious shrine where Hindus go. They feel it is normal after all neither God nor devotees have any religion.[6]

The culture of syncretism in this region is best captured in Azan Pir's *zikirs*, one of which reads, '*Hindu Musalman, ek Alar farman gorasthana kabar sari sari hinduk puriba monninak gariba.*' (Hindus and Muslims are bound by the same set of the divine rules – the rules of The Almighty. The act of cremating a Hindu and the entombing a Muslim both signify one end – death – for all.)[7]

When one talks of Sufism in Bihar, it is normally in connection with the Firdausi *silsilah* and the dargahs of the father and son who spread it there. Sheikh Makhdoom Yayha Maneri, the father is buried in Maner, a little way off Patna, in what is known as Badi Dargah. It is a simple dargah and very popular in Bihar. As has been mentioned in the *Baburnama*, Babur, the founder of the Mughal empire, visited and recited his midday prayers there during his visit to Bihar. He even circumambulated the shrine.

Just next to the Badi Dargah is its counterpart, the Choti Dargah, which is preserved by the Archaeological Survey of India. The Choti Dargah, immortalized in a Daniells painting from 1780s,[8] is a far more imposing monument, built on the edge of a large water tank. The body of Makhdoom Shah Daulat, a Firdausi saint who died in 1608, is interred in it. The dargah was built in 1616 during Jahangir's reign by Ibrahim Khan, one of the saint's disciples. A fine example of funerary architecture, with its projecting lotus brackets and small *chhatris*, cupolas, at the corners of the roof.

For anyone wondering about the size and nomenclature, the 'badi' (big) and 'choti' (small) dargahs refer to the saints' spiritual status and not their material aspects or size of the shrine.

Patna, the capital of Bihar, has a concentration of dargahs in an area that is often called the Sufi circuit in tourism circles. Apart from the Maner dargahs is the Khanqah-e-Mujibia in Phulwari Sharif, established by Hazrat Tajul Aarfin Makhdoom Shah Mujeebullah Qadiri (1688–1778). Entry to the complex is through an impressive gateway. The shrine itself is a pretty enclosure with a blue dome. The saint also established a madrasah, where students from all over came to study Persian and Arabic. Research shows that the founder of the Brahmo Samaj, Raja Ram Mohan Roy, studied the two languages, the Quran, the works of medieval Sufis, and the Arabic translations of Aristotle and Plato here.[9]

Phulwari Sharif also houses a dargah of Syed Minhajuddin Rasti (d. 1381) who is said to be the disciple of Sheikh Sharfuddin Yahya Maneri. The shrine of a Bibi Jamal, a female saint, is also inside this complex.

The dargah of Sheikh Sharfuddin Yahya Maneri, the son of Sheikh Makhdoom Yayha Maneri, in Bihar Sharif, is probably the most famous one of Bihar. It is huge and the dargah complex itself is quite well-maintained even though it exists in an otherwise shabby neighbourhood. The present complex is quite a modern structure juxtaposed against some medieval buildings.[10]

The saint's mother is buried next to him and the dargah receives a lot of female devotees. Like in other Firdausi shrines, women are allowed to go into the shrine chamber. A *khadim* there said: when the saint's mother sleeps next to him how can we stop women from coming here? Its simplicity is very appealing as it is covered with a simple roof on four columns.

The syncretic nature of dargahs and its importance in the lives of locals was emphasized for me when friends I was staying with friends in Tilauthu, a small town in Rohtas district, Bihar, took me to a dargah there. I found people of all faiths and religions praying there, and bonding with each other.

Odisha is the land of the Konark Sun Temple and Lord Jagannath temple. It is the land of the famous rath yatras of Lord Jagannath. But it is also the land of Pir Jalaluddin Bukhari Baba, or Bukhari Baba as he is fondly called, whose dargah is located in Kaipadar village some 30-odd kilometres from Bhuvneshwar. As is evident from his name, the saint came from Bukhara (Uzbekistan) – in the seventeenth century.

As I could not visit it myself, I requested my friend Hemant Sachdeva, a local businessman, for help. He in turn connected me to Hanif Khan, an insurance agent and a deeply religious man who has performed hajj and is a regular visitor to Ajmer Sharif. According to Khan, as relayed to me by Sachdeva, his wife was cured of an ailment after she started visiting Bukhari Baba's dargah and drinking water from the well there, and for the past 10 years she has been healthy.[11]

As with many dargahs, there are many legends attached to this one and its well too. It is believed that when Baba first arrived, it was a heavily forested area. He had reached in the afternoon and wanted to pray, so he needed water for ablutions. He met a long-bearded, matted-haired *sadhu* and asked him for water. The *sadhu* recognizing him as a *Siddha Purusha* (one who has transcended worldly pursuits) said there was no water available and asked him to generate it. Baba who had his staff in his hand struck the earth with it and water came gushing out. The well he created is still in the courtyard, and it was its water that cured Khan's wife. The water is considered to be healing and the well is said to never dry up. The sadhu then stayed on with Baba for many years.

Perhaps it is this legend that is responsible for the pluralistic traditions there. The *prashad* sold to all visitors and devotees is a jaggery ball and is always prepared by Hindu devotees at home, Muslim merchants sell the *chaddar*s and incense sticks along with *itr/attar* outside, says Khan. (I subsequently verified this from videos and articles on the dargah.)

The shrine itself is magnificent with its white and blue theme, but it is the grave which stands out. Unusually, it is a rather elevated hump. The reason for this, given by Khan, is as follows: The Baba used to sit and worship Allah for long hours every day. One day, while praying, white ants suddenly covered him with mud. Just then, a Hindu cowherd's child came to him and insisted on sitting on his lap. Though the saint told him to move away, the boy did not and the white ants covered him as well. The mound that was formed became his grave; it was not cemented and still remains an anthill.

Baba has a huge following among locals as well as people of Bengal. As in other dargahs, supplicants come to ask for his intercession and tie letters known as *arzi*s to a tree nearby and the screens of the shrine itself.

> 'In the country of Bengal, not to speak of the cities, there is no town and no village where holy saints did not come and settle down.'[12]
>
> – Richard Eaton

Bengal was one of the first regions to attract Sufi saints after the conquest by Bakhtiyar Khilji in 1204 on behalf of the Delhi Sultanate. This was a time when the spiritual authority of the Sufi saints was also being established. They played an important role for 'the most dramatic Islamization occurred, such as eastern Bengal or western Punjab, lay on the fringes of Indo-Muslim rule, where the sword was weakest, and where brute force could have exerted the least influence'.[13] The same is true of Kerala which also has a sizeable Muslim population. In the areas where there was Muslim rule in the Indo-Gangetic plains, the population of Muslims as per the first census of 1872 was 10–15 per cent, while in East Bengal, in the alluvial plains of the delta (present-day Bangladesh), it was 70–90. The reason for this, according to historian Richard Eaton, was not immigration, the sword, patronage, or social liberation of lower caste Hindus; it was linked to cultivation of fertile land. The people of this region followed local forest cults that focused especially on female deities such as Manasa or Chandi, and initially the Sufi saints were set up along with these deities. The main growth came in much after the establishment of the Mughal rule. Eaton links the growth of the Muslim population, as stated above, to the siltation and shifting cultivation of the Ganges river towards the sea. Eaton writes:

> From at least the sixteenth century, the arduous business of forest-clearing and land reclamation in the eastern delta was associated with the activities of enterprising men who were popularly – and often retroactively – identified as holy men. In local memory, some of these men swelled into vivid, mythico-historical figures whose lives served as metaphors for the expansion of both religion and agriculture. They endured precisely because, in collective memory, their careers captured and telescoped a complex historical socio-religious process whereby a land originally forested and non-Muslim became arable and mainly Muslim.[14]

Persian hagiographical sources seek to invest a violent past in the establishment of the hospices, and 'Persian biographies often depict early Sufi holy men of Bengal as pious warriors waging war against the infidel, such biographies were not contemporary with those Sufis,' Eaton says, adding:

> In sum, the more contemporary evidence of Sufis on Bengal's political frontier portrays men who had entered the delta not as holy warriors but as pious mystics or freebooting settlers operating under the authority of charismatic leaders. No contemporary source endows them with the ideology of holy war; nor is there contemporary evidence that they slew non-Muslims or destroyed non-Muslim monuments.

The most important early Sufi saints came to the capital of the Bengal sultans in Lakhnauti and later moved when the capital shifted to Pandua.

The city of Pandua lies in ruins now, but it was the capital of Bengal's Ilyas Shahi dynasty from the fourteenth to the fifteenth century, and it houses the famous Adina mosque as well as the Badi and Choti dargahs (not to be confused with the ones in Bihar with the same names).

Pandua's Badi Dargah is a shrine dedicated to Sheikh Jalauddin Tabrezi. He is not buried there, but the dargah where he spent a lot of time has many of his relics. As mentioned in a previous chapter, it also has a Qadam-e-Rasul (footprint of the Prophet on marble).

As with many dargahs, there is a special place here which is associated with fulfilment of wishes. A henna tree here is believed to have magical powers and one can find many men and women praying there. Henna, given its association with weddings, is a natural magnet for mothers and girls who come on their own to pray for a suitable match; I saw many bangles hanging there. The tree attracts people from far and wide and the dargah is popular with people of all religions and caste.

The Choti Dargah is a shrine of two famous Chishti saints, Sheikh Ala-ul-Haq Pandwi and his son Sheikh Noor Qutb-e-Alam (light and axis of the world). The father was a very learned man and scholar and greatly respected by Shamsuddin Ilyas Shah, the sultan of Bengal. The complex comprises a mosque, a reservoir, tombs, a rest house, and various other structures. It is also known as Shash Hazari Dargah (which means, the dargah endowed with ₹ 6,000).

Both father and son played a dominant role in the lives of the people of Bengal. The father set a very rigorous training schedule for the son – including fetching water, laundering clothes, and cleaning toilets for many years. Shaykh Nur ad-Din [Qutb-e-Alam] once said,

> The shaykhs of old had set 99 stages for the completion of the spiritual quest (this corresponded to the number of the names of God). The *shaykh*s of our *silsila* have fixed on 15 stages, of which this *faqir* has selected three. First: Taking account of yourself before God demands an account from you. Second: Whoever thinks he has been righteous for even a day has deceived himself. Third: The true worship of the *faqir* is to repel thoughts of other than God. Whoever acts according to these three principles – God willing – he will complete the work of the traveller.[15]

Sheikh Nur Qutb-e-Alam is one of India's best-known saints. 'He was a master of love, taste, and miracles.'[16]

Apart from his son, Sheikh Ala-ul-Haq Pandwi's other famous disciple is Sheikh Ashraf Jahangir Simnani (whom we have met in the last chapter). His shrine in Uttar Pradesh's Kichhauchha Sharif draws great crowds of devotees.

In Kolkata's busy Khidirpur area, which once upon a time used to be a hub of trading activities because of its proximity to the sea, is the dargah of Syed Ali Shah Baba, a saint of the Madariya *silsilah*. As mentioned in chapter 9, it used to be the place where all sailors came for blessings before sailing. It has so many devotees even today that the flyover nearby that had to be built in such a way that it would go around it, with an extra turn, so as to not disturb the saint. (See chapter 9 for more on this dargah.)

One of the other famous dargahs is that of Hazrat Syed Ghaus-e-Bengal Shamsuddin Shah Wali. He is said to be a descendant of Sheikh Abdul Qadir Jilani.

Another fascinating dargah is in Hooghly district. It is known as the Furfura Dargah. It was in the news recently because Pirzada Abbas Siddiqui decided to float his own political party, called the Indian Secular Front, for the 2021 West Bengal assembly elections and was much sought after by politicians. The dargah is held in great reverence by Bengali Muslims and is said to have been built in 1375. It is the tomb of a great social and religious reformer of the fourteenth century, Hazrat Abu Bakr Siddiqui, and his five sons. It is known locally as Punch Huzur Qibla.

India's landscape abounds with dargahs where people flock to pray for their needs and seek divine blessings. The dargahs listed above are just a few of the more major shrines, but there are many more which serve as a place for the distressed or devout to supplicate, pray and meditate.

> Pour upon us Thy Love and Thy Light,
> give sustenance to our bodies, hearts and souls,
> use us for the purpose that Thy Wisdom chooseth,
> and guide us on the path of Thine Own Goodness.
> Draw us closer to Thee every moment of our life,
> until in us be reflected Thy Grace, Thy Glory,
> Thy Wisdom, Thy Joy and Thy Peace.
> Amen. [17]

– Hazrat Inayat Khan

# 14

# Popular Dargahs of Central and West India

The town of Burhanpur in Madhya Pradesh was once an important provincial capital of the Faruqis and the Mughals. It was founded and named in 1399 by Nasiruddin Nasir Khan after Sheikh Burhanuddin Garib, who was the successor of Hazrat Nizamuddin Auliya. Nasiruddin Nasir Khan was the founder of the Faruqi dynasty in Khandesh, and Burhanpur was his capital. Though Sheikh Burhanuddin Garib is buried in Khuldabad, like most medieval capital cities Burhanpur also attracted many mystics. The city's imperial past is interwoven with its spiritual past, but while the former has been forgotten, the latter is thriving with devotees flowing in from all parts of the world.

Sheikh Nizamuddin Shah Bhikari is the most famous saint of Burhanpur and is known as Sarkar-e-Burhanpur (master of Burhanpur). His simple dargah, which of course has seen much better days under the royal patronage of the Faruqi Sultans and later the Mughals, is perched on top of a hillock overlooking the Utawali River. Eid prayers are said on the dry bed of the river.

The Chupwaali Dargah, also in the same place, is again simple and well maintained. It is the shrine of Shah Bahauddin Bajan, a tutor of the Faruqi royal family. He spoke very little and so became famous as Chup Shah (the silent saint; *chup* meaning silent).

In the town famous for its dargahs, the most popular one is the Dargah-e-Hakimi of Syedi Abdul Qadir Hakimuddin (1665–1730), a Dawoodi Bohra saint. His grave is visited by Bohris from all over the world. It is a beautiful complex spread over 125 acres, with mosques, gardens and international-class accommodation facilities for visitors. The Bohri pilgrims look after it themselves, considering service there an honour. In the evening, its pristine white marble shrines shine luminously against the black sky and give the impression of being pearl drops.

One of the most popular and peaceful religious places in Madhya Pradesh is the dargah complex of Ghaus Gwaliori. Muhammad Ghaus Gwaliori's tomb in Gwalior, built by his son and successor Sheikh Budh Abdullah, is beautiful and considered an architectural gem. It is very popular with both tourists and his followers. Tansen, the legendary musician of Akbar's court, lies buried in the same compound.

Then there is the dargah of Hazrat Peer Fatehullah Shah Baba in Raisen near Bhopal, which is extremely famous although comparatively small. Baba, as Hazrat Peer Fatehullah Shah Baba is known, is a Chishti saint related to Khwaja Muinuddin Chishti and popularly known as Shahenshah-e-Malwa. People from all the neighbouring areas visit this dargah. In fact, it sees more non-Muslim visitors than Muslims.

This dargah is popular not just with the locals but also with the police force. Every new car that is bought by the police department makes its first trip to this dargah, for protection from accidents. During the saint's *urs,* the District Magistrate and Superintendent of Police of the district present the first *chaddar* at his shrine.

When one of the hereditary caretakers of the shrine sat a group of us (belonging to different religions) down, to pray for us, the policeman on duty also joined. It was an extremely spiritual experience, as all of us who were praying unconsciously adopted the same pose we use in our personal prayers.

There is a belief that a tiger used to come and sweep this dargah's courtyard with its tail during the Baba's lifetime.

While Delhi is known as the threshold of 22 saints, Khuldabad near Aurangabad in Maharashtra is known as the garden of saints.

The relative peace offered by Delhi in the Sultanate period attracted the secular and religious people of Central Asia, which was being ravaged by the Mongols. They were welcomed by Sultan Iltutmish, who was a Sufi himself, and by subsequent rulers. Many believers attribute the safety of Delhi to the blessings of Hazrat Nizamuddin Auliya. Sultan Muhammad bin Tughlaq was a disciple of the saint and is said to have been one of his pallbearers.

When Sultan Muhammad bin Tughluq ordered, in 1327, that his capital be shifted from Delhi to Deogir, which he renamed Daulatabad, he instructed the elites, nobles, officers, common men, and even the saints to shift with him. The Sufi saints – 1,400 of them – decided to settle in an area near Daulatabad. The shrines of these saints dot the area, which is why the place was initially called Rauza (garden/shrine). After Aurangzeb's burial, it was renamed Khuldabad, after his posthumous title *khuld-makani* (He who resides in paradise). Famous saints such as Shah Raja Qattal, Sheikh Burhanuddin Garib, Sheikh Muntajibuddin and Sheikh Zainuddin Shirazi are buried there.

This led to the spread of the Sufism, especially with the Chishti *silsilah* growing its reach in the Deccan. Today, Khuldabad is just a dusty town visited by very few people, but once upon a time it was a thriving centre of spirituality. So important was the place, Aurangzeb willed that he be buried in the compound of Saiyed Zainuddin Shirazi in an open and simple grave.

Khuldabad is perhaps the most fascinating place for anyone who wants to spend time meditating and praying, though outside Sufi circles it is more well-known as the resting place of Aurangzeb. One experiences an immense sense of peace in Khuldabad, which perhaps also has something to do with the fact that it is not crowded by tourists or casual visitors and only supplicants and devotees visit it.

While, originally, Aurangzeb's grave built in the courtyard of Saiyed Zainuddin Shirazi's shrine was a simple one made of mud, in accordance with his wishes, the Indian National Trust for Art and Cultural Heritage (INTACH) and United Nations Development Programme (UNDP) board at the entrance states that the former British viceroy of India, Lord Curzon, decorated it with marble. As per oral history, however, Lord Curzon requested the Nizam of Hyderabad, under whose governance Aurangabad fell, to construct a marble railing around the grave in 1911. Later, a headstone with his name and titles was also placed there.

Aurangzeb's son Muhammad Azam Shah and his wife have an even more elaborate enclosure in the dargah.

Saiyed Zainuddin Shirazi (1302–1369), a Chishti saint, was the disciple of Sheikh Burhanuddin Garib. He was the 22nd descendant in the Chishti *silsilah* and this fact is inscribed on a tablet near his shrine. He did not anoint anyone as his successor and the Chishti order passed on to Hazrat Gesu Daraz in Gulbarga.

The dargah also houses the robes of Prophet Muhammad (*Pairhan-e Mubarak Muhammad Mustafa*). According to the caretaker of the dargah, they are the same robes that the Prophet wore on *Shab-e-Miraj* (night of the ascension) and are displayed on 12 Rabi Awwal, the Prophet's birthday.

The saint's adopted daughter Khwan Bibi was also a mystic. She is buried to the right of his shrine in a small enclosure.

The dargah of Hazrat Burhanuddin Garib (d. 1337) is situated opposite this complex, and as the *khalifa* of Hazrat Nizamuddin Auliya sent to the Deccan to propagate Sufism, he has the highest station of all in Khuldabad. His dargah complex is also the resting place of the first, second and third nizams of Hyderabad, along with other family members in separate enclosures.

Before Sheikh Burhanuddin Garib, his brother Sheikh Muntajibuddin (d. 1309) had been given the responsibility of the Deccan by Hazrat Nizamuddin Auliya. Sheikh Muntajibuddin came from Delhi to Daulatabad accompanied by 1,400 disciples. This was probably at the time when Sultan Muhammad bin Tughlaq ordered the transfer of the capital from Delhi to Daulatabad and ordered Sufi saints to move there as well. He came to Daulatabad and rested on a hill where he later made his *khanqah* in what is present-day Khuldabad.

His dargah is at a little distance away from the main ones on the small hillock. He was given the title of Zar Zari Zar Baksh (giver of gold) and gold is the dominant theme in his dargah. He is also called *dulha* or bridegroom, a name given to him by Hazrat Nizamuddin for when he left with his disciples behind him on horseback and palanquins, the master smiled and said, 'Muntajibuddin you are looking like a bridegroom today.' Sheikh Muntajibuddin however, died a bachelor.

And there are many legends regarding the origin of his title Zar Zari Baksh, too. One story suggests that once when he wanted his attendant to draw water from a well so he could perform his ablutions, the daughter of a local chief named Sona Bai who was passing by put forth the condition that he could only draw water from the well if the water turned to gold! In response, the saint gave his handkerchief to the attendant and told him to drop it into the well. When the attendant did so, the water turned into liquid gold. The princess, along with her family, later converted to Islam and became his disciple, even as he came to be associated with the title.

Another explanation for the origin of his title is that before setting off on a journey once he expressed his concerns about being able to meet their expenses to Hazrat Nizamuddin Auliya. The master went into meditation and said that gold [coins] for his expenses would appear every night under his prayer rug when he performed his supererogatory prayers. Even if there is no truth in this or other stories, the main thing to note is that people come from far and wide to pray for happiness and prosperity at his shrine.

His mother Bibi Hajira's tomb is adjacent to his, and that is where women gather to pray for their children (as did I.) He had five sisters known as Panch Bibiyan (five ladies), and the mother and sisters are revered in the Sufi circles in Khuldabad.

Close to his dargah, is the shrine of Hazrat Raju Qattal (d. 1331), the father of Hazrat Gesu Daraz. Hazrat Raju Qattal had come with his son and family in 1328. Later his son returned to Delhi and became the disciple of Roshan Chiragh-e-Dilli.

The last Qutub Shahi king, Tana Shah, is also buried in this complex. He had been imprisoned by Aurangzeb after his defeat in the fort of Daulatabad.

Next to this dargah is the mosque of 1,400 saints and the tomb of the famous Deccan general Malik Ambar. Amidst the spirituality of the dargahs, his tomb emanates a quiet strength and power.

A short drive through dirt roads from here leads to the fascinating dargah of Sheikh Shah Jalaluddin Ganj-e-Ravan (flowing treasure). He was a Suhrawardi saint and born in Khirkan near Bukhara. He was the first saint to come to the Deccan during 1300–01; he established his *khanqah* before the invasion of Alauddin Khilji.

As you enter the complex, you can see an object which looks completely out of place here. I was told that people believe it is a *yoni* (the base of a *Shivalinga*) that was used to trap a jinn. No one knows how or when it came to be here.

This dargah has a tree which is said to have miraculous powers. It is believed to have grown from the saint's staff, which he had rested on the ground. It is known as the tree of fertility.

The caretaker who told me about this legend attached to the dargah related another very interesting story, too. The story was about a eunuch who mocked the saint saying that if he indeed were a miracle worker, he should make him pregnant. The saint gave the eunuch a fruit and asked him to eat it.

There are two versions of what follows. The one I was told went as follows: The eunuch became pregnant after eating the fruit and died during childbirth. I was shown two graves, one of an adult and another of a baby in the dargah compound, and was told that the eunuch and baby were buried there.

The other version is that when the eunuch's belly started swelling up, he asked for forgiveness and became the saint's disciple for life.

If Delhi has the bard Hazrat Amir Khusrau, then Khuldabad houses the shrine of another famous medieval poet and writer. Amir Najm-al-Din Hasan Dihlavi ibn Khwaja Ala-al-Din Sistani, commonly known as Amir Hasan Sijzi or Hazrat Amir Hasan Dehlvi, is also buried there. He too had been ordered to leave Delhi for Daulatabad and was never to return. If Amir Khusrau captured Hazrat Nizamuddin Auliya's teachings in his songs and poetry, Amir Sijzi did the same in his famous compilation titled *Fawa'id al-Fu'ad*, which contains the literary discourses of Hazrat Nizamuddin Auliya. Unlike Amir Khusrau who became a disciple when he was around eight years old, Amir Sijzi became Auliya's disciple arrived quite late in life, when he was already an established poet and had already earned the title Saadi-e-Hind.

Amir Sijzi was born in Badayun in Uttar Pradesh in 1254 and died in Daulatabad in 1337.

Nearby is the shrine of Bibi Ayesha, the daughter of Baba Farid who is buried in a simple tomb along with her daughter. Hazrat Nizamuddin

Auliya had entrusted the responsibility of looking after her. 'Shaykh Burhanuddin dutifully paid his visit to her every Friday, and even prophesied that her grandson, who later came to known as Alauddin Ziya, would be a great saint.'[1]

Aurangabad, another city in Maharashtra, also has many famous dargahs, but the most popular among tourists is the one known as panchakki (water mill). However, most people know the mill but are not even aware that it is attached to a dargah. The dargah was once the *takia* (convent) of a famous Naqshbandi saint, Baba Shah Musafir, who studied in Bukhara under the celebrated Hazrat Palangposh Naqshbandi. He came to India in the sixteenth century and settled in Aurangabad. He ran a *langar* and ground wheat daily to feed the people. Eminent people of Aurangabad helped him build a travellers' inn, a madrasah, and a system of water cisterns and fountains. After his death in 1601/2, Turktaz Khan Bahadur, a nobleman under Nizam Asaf Jah, erected a shrine, mosque, and water mill in his *takia*. Twenty years later, Jamil Beg Khan added the reservoir and fountains that are an architectural draw for tourists.

The dargah of Syed Shah Nur Mohammed Hamvi Jeelani Qadriya in Aurangabad is also very popular. According to oral narratives, Aurangzeb went to the saint twice to repent – once for the execution of Sufi Sarmad, and on another occasion to summon the spirit of his father Emperor Shah Jahan, so that he could beg for his forgiveness.[2] In the first instance, the saint advised that Aurangzeb be buried in the dargah of Sheikh Zainuddin Shirazi; in the second, when the emperor came dressed in royal robes, he was turned away. It was only when he came in clothes of a fakir that the saint gave him audience and told him to return after reciting the whole Quran. When the emperor returned at dawn, Shah Nur drew the curtain and left the room telling him to speak. So Aurangzeb talked to Shah Jahan and asked for forgiveness.

> Aurangzeb was in his royal garments. He said, 'Salam alaykum,' and Shah Nur said, 'Wa alaykum salam and go away. I have nothing [for you].' So he [Aurangzeb] went away. The next day Aurangzeb went again in the same garments, and again Shah Nur said, 'Go away: I have nothing.' On the third day Aurangzeb came in the dress of a faqir and Shah Nur said, 'Sit down,' and asked, 'What do

> you want?' He said, 'I want to meet my father.' Shah Nur asked, 'For what reason?' Aurangzeb said, 'I want to request his pardon.' But Shah Jahan was dead. Aurangzeb had punished him a lot and imprisoned him, so he wanted to ask for his father's pardon. So Shah Nur said, 'Good. You should read Quran Sharif for the whole night and come to meet me at dawn (fajr).' Aurangzeb said, 'Good,' and when he came [again] it was dawn. Shah Nur was in the room and he left it and drew the curtain and said, 'Speak!' So Aurangzeb talked to Shah Jahan and asked for his forgiveness. Then he went back and said, 'Now I want to do something for you.' But Shah Nur said, 'I don't want anything from you.' So Aurangzeb left."[3]

One of the most iconic dargahs of India is also in this region in the city of Mumbai. Many will recall, thanks to Hindi films, the Haji Ali Dargah situated on an islet in the Arabian Sea and accessed by a causeway. It is the shrine of a wealthy merchant Haji Ali Shah Bukhari from Uzbekistan who is revered in India as a Sufi saint. It was constructed in 1431. He had settled down in the then city of Mumbai and, before going on the Hajj pilgrimage, gave away all his considerable worldly possessions.

According to legend, he was in his hometown when he saw a lady carrying an empty pot and crying. On being asked about it, she told him that she had spilled the oil that she had bought, and her husband would beat her when she reached home. Ali Shah Bukhari struck the earth with his finger and oil came gushing out. He told the lady to fill her pot.

Later he dreamt that the earth had been injured by his act. A remorseful man, he tried to make amends and eventually left his home and came to Bombay where he settled down near Worli, close to the area where his shrine stands today. He continued doing good deeds and spreading knowledge. He willed that after his death his body should be wrapped in a shroud and dropped in the sea, a wish that was obeyed by his followers. His shrine is built on the spot where his shroud came to rest on an outcrop of rocks.

The Haji Ali shrine sees an enormous number of devotees across faiths, religions, classes, and castes.

The other famous dargah in Mumbai is the Mahim Dargah of Hazrat Makhdum Ali Mahimi (1372–1431). He was a great saint and scholar of international repute. He lived during the time of the Tughlaq dynasty and that of Sultan Ahmed Shah of Gujarat, and was married to the Gujarat Sultan's sister.

An interesting aspect of the Mahim Dargah is that he is patron saint of the Mumbai police force, which started as a citizen's militia in the seventeenth century. This is apparently the reason why the local police station is built next to it, on the site where the saint lived. Whenever the *urs* takes place, the first *chaddar* is presented by the police. There is a steel cupboard in the office of the police inspector, which supposedly contains the saint's relics; during the *urs* this room is opened to devotees.

An interesting dargah that exists near Mumbai's busy Crawford Market is that of Pedro Shah Baba. He is supposed to cure eye ailments. There are many versions of his identity, but the most popular is that he was a Portuguese sailor who had converted to Islam. In another version, Pedro is supposed to have been a porter who revealed his miraculous powers to a Parsi family. He walked past them with a basket floating above his head. This Parsi couple had a blind daughter, who was later cured by the saint. Then there is a third version according to which his name was Abdullah Shah Qadri and he had come from Arabia, and the title Pedro, which is the name on the board of the shrine, was given to him by the Portuguese.

I visited his shrine with my friend Lubna, a resident of Mumbai, who described her experience to me as follows:

> As a child I had heard of the legend of Pedro Shah Baba, the eighteenth-century porter cum Sufi saint. Decades later, when I stepped into this shrine, I found myself embraced in a cool fragrant welcoming air. I find this shrine special; it is here that I find peace.
>
> When I first visited, a few years ago, I was suffering from severe eye problems – I didn't know then that this Sufi saint is known to heal those with visual impairment. It was perhaps Allah's will that led me to this serene shrine.
>
> As a Muslim, we worship only Allah, and Allah truly hears us. However, Sufi saints, in my view, provide us strong support. They help expedite our plea of help to Allah and shower their own blessings. Prayers and blessings including, I am sure those of Pedro Shah Baba, have helped me.

> Thursday nights, post the Maghrib prayers, is a special time when the entire neighborhood seems to congregate, *fatiha* (prayer) is held, and *mithai* (sweets) distributed.
>
> There is a courtyard in the area surrounding the shrine. Sitting beneath the stars, breathing in the cool fragrant air, listening to the soft swish of the leaves of the drumstick tree, calms me, like nothing else can. Even amid the crowd I continue to find myself at peace.
>
> This feeling of bliss is something that needs to be experienced and cannot be explained in words. Some time spent here ensures that my fears and worries fade away, almost as if the fragrant breeze which is always blowing has picked them and carried them far-far away. The shrine is well tended by Omer bhai, the Khadim and his family.[4]

Since the fishing community in Mumbai used to be very strong, and considering the risks they take, they definitely needed a lot of divine help. In Bandra just near the Mount Mary Church, tucked away among the houses of the people of the small fishing community, is the peaceful dargah of Hazrat Jafar Shah Mustan Qadri al-Rafai Baba. The posters of Jesus Christ nearby revealed that it is a mixed community living in harmony. An old woman was in charge of looking after the shrine when I visited, and there were no gender restrictions.

A nearby dargah of a Naqshbandi saint, patronized by rich Parsis and traders, was built on a larger scale and was of recent vintage – that is, it isn't more than a century old, as is the case with many dargahs.

Women, especially mothers, have always played a central role in Islam and this comes to be reflected in the next shrine. If Mumbai has the dargah of Haji Ali, it also houses the one of Ma Hajiani, the mother of a wealthy sea merchant. Her spectacular dargah is also situated in Worli – on the opposite side of Haji Ali. It was built in 1908. It was in a pretty bad shape a few years ago, but it is now being restored by conservationists. It is a hidden gem of the city and not many go there, so those who do can sit and contemplate in peace on the transitory nature of life.

My friend Lubna, whom I mentioned earlier in this chapter, looks after her mother, and described to me a beautiful incident, which takes us to the heart of what living Sufi practices are all about. Lubna wrote:

Our Prophet, PBUH, has said, 'Paradise lies at the feet of mothers,' and I was trying my best to take care of my loving Mum who is now bedridden.

Being a caretaker can take a physical and emotional toll, and my doctor was advising me to take a break – at least for a few days.

Even though Mum was in the hands of a good [professional] caretaker [in addition to me], I could not risk being far away from Mumbai. Places that otherwise would seem nearby like Goa, or even Lonavala, were ruled out. I needed something much closer, so that I could return in a jiffy, if need be.

Things just seemed to fall in place. A colleague recommended a seaside resort in Uran (an hour or so away from Navi Mumbai). So here, in mid-February 2019, is where I landed – unknowingly right in the middle of an *Urs* at the shrine of Hazrat Mukim Shah Baba.

I do find solace when I visit Sufi shrines; my worries melt away. Little did I know that my short five-day break will result in unexpected blessings.

This shrine is also known as Pirwadi Dargah and is located at one end of the Pirwadi beach. It is a picturesque site, with the sea as a backdrop.

According to the local folklore, the saint's casket landed at the shore, several hundred years ago, and he was buried at this site.

Colourful tents had sprung up on the open ground surrounding the shrine. There were carts serving food – be it omelettes, idlis or biryani, and other vendors were selling offerings to be made at the shrine (coconuts, flowers, attar and agarbattis). It was a proper mela (fair) replete with a giant ferris wheel. Kolis (community of the local fisherfolk) are ardent devotees and throng here with their offerings.

Most of the devotees were locals and were poor – in material terms. But the joy they radiated was infectious. I was sad and depressed when I had reached the shores of Uran and just hours later, caught up in the festive atmosphere of the *Urs,* I was smiling.

There is another shrine, just a few steps away – which is open to the sky. This is the shrine of Hazrat Jilani Shah Baba.

Was I called by Hazrat Mukim Shah Baba and Hazrat Jilani Shah Baba to pay a visit and get blessed? I would like to think that I was.[5]

The dargah of Sheikh Ahmed Ganj Baksh Khattu in Gujarat is famous as Sarkhej Roza. The word *sarkhej* is derived from the Persian word *zarkhez* which means 'fertile'.

The saint's devotees come from far and wide to drink water from the wells. There is a lake attached to the dargah, the waters from which were used for performing ablutions, but access to it is not so easy now.

The area was inhabited by indigo weavers and dyers when Ahmedabad was founded in the fifteenth century, and as a befitting tribute to their spiritual master, they painted the ceiling of his shrine with indigo. I have visited the dargah a couple of times and though like many other shrines women are not allowed inside, I have sat at its doorstep fascinated by the blue and the devotion of those who used a precious commodity (indigo being a prized crop in the medieval era) to colour their master's shrine.

This dargah is just on the outskirts of Ahmedabad city, and the saint is famous for his mediation with God and his healing powers. For instance, when I was visiting, I saw one lady in particular who was weeping softly. When I sat next to her and held her hand in sympathy, she told me that her name was Parul. Her husband had been paralysed for two years and no doctor had been able to help. On one of her numerous visits to the hospital, an auto rickshaw driver asked her to come to this shrine as he believed that no one returns empty-handed from this place. We prayed together for her husband's recovery that day. This is a typical phenomenon when the saints become a last refuge for devotees who either can't afford a physician's fee or have not found a medical cure.

Another very interesting dargah is the Pirana Pir Dargah, some 20-odd km from Ahmedabad in Gujarat. There are many legends about the saint and the dargah.

The dargah of Hazrat Pir Imamuddin Kufr-e-Shikan, or Imam Shah Bawa, is very popular and so also very crowded. Imam Shah Bawa established a unique sect called the *Satpanth* (True Path), which is a unique blend of Hinduism and Sufism.

The dargah of Pir Imam Shah Bawa is looked after by Kutchi Patels and the attendant in front of the shrine is a *pujari* (priest). The entrance to the complex itself is built on the lines of a temple and *dharmshala,* and it is only after one reaches the dargah that one realizes that the saint was a Muslim. In fact, the priest who was sitting there said that Imam Sahib was an avatar of Brahma. So we have the priests performing an *aarti* outside the Sufi saint's shrine, celebrating his *urs* in the month of Ramzan – reflecting India's living syncretic customs and beliefs.

Women are allowed to enter the shrine between 4 a.m. and 5 a.m. after a bath. If ladies go at any other time, like I did, they sit outside and supplicate with the saint silently.

The Kutchi Patels have great faith in him and come in large numbers. The chairman of the Pir Imamshah Bawa Roza Sansthan is a Kutchi Patel known as Kaka and the saint's descendants – the Saiyeds – are also part of the *sansthan* (organization). In the past two decades, though, this symbol of syncretism is under attack[6] and a wire fence has been erected between the dargah looked after by the Patels and the area with the mosque where the saint's descendants are in-charge. The dargah is looked after by the priests appointed by the Kutchi Patels, while that of his grandson is looked after by Saiyed Shabbir Hussain and family. Earlier, it was all one complex but following the riots in the wake of the Babri Masjid demolition, a wire has been stretched between the two. The difference is stark – the one looked after by the Satpanthis is very affluent, well-attended, crowded, and well-maintained. The other side hardly has any visitors.

I met Saiyed Shabbir Hussain too, but because of the fencing I had to access their dargah after walking through the village. According to the very affable and spiritual Saiyed Shabbir Hussain, the saint came to and settled in this village from Multan in the mid-fifteenth century. He preached what he called the *satpanth* or *sirat-e-mustaqeem,* as it's called in the Quran, both of which mean 'the right path to God'. He taught tolerance and universality of religions. He translated the *kalima* or Islamic creed into Sanskrit. His followers are called *Satpanthi* and it was only in the census conducted in the nineteenth century by the British that they were forced to declare themselves as Hindus or Muslims.[7] He also has a large following amongst the Imamshahi Nizari Ismailis.

Saiyed Shabbir Hussain said that his mission is to see how many people he could help or who could benefit from his presence, and to stay faithful to his country, his wife and people, and at all times to spread love and charity.

Pir Imam Bawa had prayed for rain for the Pirana village which was drought-prone and the villagers begged him to stay back. He settled in the nearby village of Girmatha during the reign of Mahmud Begada. It is here that his dargah is situated.

Unfortunately, communalism is rearing its ugly head here as well: there have been bitter allegations that the Kaka and the *sansthan* are erasing the Muslim past of the dargah and turning it into a temple. That this was once a symbol of syncretism makes it doubly tragic.

*Aa mil yaar saarley,*
*Meri jaan dikhaan ney gyheri*
*Ander khawab vchora hoya, Khabar na payndi teri*
*Soni ban wich luti saiyaan, Soor palang ney gheyri*

[Come my love take care of me,
I am in great agony.
Ever separated, my dreams are dreary,
Looking for you, my eyes are weary.
All alone I am robbed in a desert,
Waylaid by a bunch of way words.][8]

– Bulleh Shah

# 15

# Popular Dargahs of South India

The Bahmani Sultan (1347–1518) and later the Adil Shahi Sultans (1489–1686) saw as many as 300 Sufi saints settle down in the Bijapur area in Karnataka. Bijapur is therefore full of dargahs and graves. Many Chishti and Junaydi saints too migrated to the region from Asia Minor as well as other parts of India, particularly neighbouring Bidar. The Adil Shahi reign saw the coming of many Qadriya saints. The Shattari order also gained prominence here.

The more prominent ones there are the dargahs of Hazrat Khwaja Ameenuddin Ali, Hazrat Abdul Hameed Qadiri, Syed Shah Murtaza, Khwaja Abdur Razzaq Qadiri, and Syedna Roomi Chishti. The dargah of Syed Chanda Hussaini is in Gogi near Bijapur. In accordance with the custom of being buried near Sufi saints, the first two Adil Shahi kings are buried in Gogi too in the dargah's compound.

The most famous dargah, of course, is the Jod Gumbad, but it was the Syedna Roomi Chishti's shrine – said to be one of the earliest open air ones – that seemed the most peaceful with its small-walled enclosure. As in many other Chishti dargahs, women weren't allowed inside but there were many women offering their respects at the entrance. I too joined them and sat by their side in peace for some time. I can still smell the rose that the *khadim* brought from the shrine as a gift for us.

Another city in north Karnataka, Gulbarga, is home to the dargah of the Deccan's most famous saint with a huge following, Hazrat Banda Nawaz Gesu Daraz. The dargah complex is huge. As one walks the long distance to the steps leading to the gateway, one may find beggars, and not mendicants, lining up outside. This seems to have become a pattern in most dargahs and is encouraged by the sense of piety with which a person enters a dargah, compelling him or her to donate generously.

Sheikh Sirajuddin Junaydi too came to Gulbarga in 1347. Sultan Alauddin Hasan Bahman Shah became his *murid*. The Junaydis constitute another branch of Sufism and trace their origin from Sheikh Abul Qasim al-Junayd (830–910). Sheikh Sirajuddin Junaydi was his descendant. Sheikh Junaydi moved initially to Daulatabad when Muhammad bin Tughlaq made it his capital, but later came to Gulbarga. His dargah is called Rauza-e-Sheikh and is again very peaceful and popular with the locals.

Kerala is known to be a very modern state, with advanced literary rates and matrilinear practices followed in its Nair Hindu community. So it should not come as a surprise that the most famous dargah of Kerala is of a female saint.

The Beemapalli Dargah in Thiruvananthapuram is dedicated to Syedunnisa Beema Beevi, also affectionately called Amma, and her son Syed us-Shuhada Maheen Abubacker, who came from Arabia. She is said to be a direct descendant of the Prophet. Not much is known about her, but the fact that she is believed to have arrived in Kerala at the same time as Malik Ibn Deenar (d. 748) – one of the first Muslims to come to India – has no historical evidence. Though the date of her arrival maybe suspect, her powers and popularity are not.

Beema Beevi is said to have performed many *karamat* (miracles), and it is these miraculous powers that drew people of all faiths and caste to come to her. Though not a Sufi, her resting place is called a dargah and she is venerated by many – especially the fishing community.

I contacted Dr Mohammad Ismail in Calicut to find out more. He kindly got in touch with a relative in Thiruvananthapuram, who found out the following information from the dargah committee and relayed to me. Once again there is no historical reference for this information, but as it is an important part of the local cultural and religious experience, I am recording it here. He said:

> Beemapalli Dargah Sharif is an important pilgrim centre in Kerala, not only for Muslims but also for Christians as well as Hindus. This shrine advocates communal harmony and thousands of pilgrims coming from different parts of South India especially from Kerala and Tamil Nadu for the annual festival (*uroos/urs*) here. Apart from *uroos*, hundreds of people come rushing to this dargah on a daily basis to offer prayers to cure their diseases, or for thanksgiving. The devotees have a firm belief that this lady saint has miraculous powers to cure diseases, especially mental illnesses. There are hundreds of living examples, according to the dargah administration. One can see many a number of such cured patients in and around, most of whom have been abandoned by relatives and are taken care of by the dargah administration.

The history of the dargah, in Ismail's words, is this: Beema Beevi, a descendant of the Prophet, and her son came to Tamil Nadu some three hundred years ago for dawah (preaching Islam), and later settled down in Kerala. She came from a family of hakims (traditional physicians) and the mother-son duo treated and cured many patients, simultaneously preaching Islam. Many people embraced Islam and stayed in and around her place of residence and gradually that place became a Muslim settlement. Ismail says:

> As per belief of her followers, some envious local clergy decided to put an end to the increasing popularity of the Beevi and her son. Upon their instigation the local king imposed a heavy tax on them. But Sayyid Maheen Abubakkar refused to pay. He said that since the country belongs to God he would pay it directly to God. This resulted into a conflict, and he was killed in action, becoming a *shaheed* (martyr). The bereaved mother died on the 41st day of the demise of her son, and both were buried on the same premises. Thereafter, her devotees have had many miraculous experiences and gradually her tomb became a pilgrim centre. People of all faiths come to offer prayers at Beemapally. The majority who come to pray here are women.

Interestingly, Thiruvananthapuram has two other pilgrim centres which also belong to lady saints/deities; one is Vettukad St. Mary's Church, where the Perunnal (annual festival) is very famous, and the other is Attukal Temple, where goddess Parvathy is the principal deity. The Attukal Ponkala (annual festival) here, is purely a women's festival and is referred to as the Kumbhamela of women.

Beema Beevi's miracles continue even today. Lawyer Chandrasekhar Tampi told me an interesting story about her. His mother left Kerala in the 1970s when she married his bureaucrat father. Neither he nor his mother were aware of the Beemapalli Dargah. In Tampi's words:

> As a child, living in Kolkata, I would, for a long time, see an apparition of a woman with a child every night standing outside my door. One day, it suddenly stopped.
>
> Many years later, probably... probably in my second year of graduation... I learnt from my grandmother [...] that my mom had spoken to her about it, and someone back then had suggested to my grandmother that an offering be made in Beemapalli. My grandmother tells me that it is roughly around the same time that I stopped complaining about the apparitions. To clarify, it is not that I knew that offering was made and hence the apparitions disappeared.

Thampi doesn't remember who his grandmother had spoken to, as he was too young then (in the eighth standard), nor whether the offering was subsequently made.

Bema Beevi's annual *urs,* called the Chandanakkudam Mahotsavam, attracts huge crowds who come to offer pots, *chaddar*s, sandalwood paste, incense sticks, and oil.

The highlight of the festival is the earthen pots (*kudams*), covered with sandalwood paste and flowers, filled with coins as offerings.

The offerings are later distributed as prashad. It is held for 10 days, starting on the first of the Islamic month Jamad ul-Awwal.

The two wells in the compound are also said to have healing powers, and are considered capable of curing any disease. One is said to contain hot water and the other cold; they don't dry up even in the most severe drought.

A beautiful mosque, with soaring minarets and domes, began to be constructed in 1960 and the construction took 18 years to complete. Govindan Gopalakrishnan, who though not a trained architect, has so far designed around a hundred mosques, including this one, and feels that it is a talent bestowed to him by God. Gopalakrishnan fasts during the months of Ramzan and Lent and takes off for the Sabarimala pilgrimage every year. He keeps copies of the Quran, Gita, and the Bible in his house.[1]

The *urs* ceremony is led by the imam of the mosque. The imam leads the devotees as they do the 'Pattana Pradakshinam' (circumambulation of the tomb), and it ends with an Annadanam (feast).

Special buses are deployed in the state to ferry devotees, and a local holiday is declared in Thiruvananthapuram.

The festival is also a time to see several art forms like Daharamuttu (done with a sword) performed within the mosque.

Tamil Nadu is home to some of the most beautiful religious monuments including the rock architecture of Mahabalipuram and the magnificent Meenakshi temple. It is also home to some very popular dargahs. The dargah of Hazrat Syed Shahul Hameed, a Qadriya saint and direct descendant of Sheikh Abdul Qadir Jilani, is revered by people from all over.

Syed Shahul Hameed was born in 1491 in Uttar Pradesh. As a young man well versed in the scriptures, he felt a spiritual inclination to becoming a disciple of Sheikh Ghaus Gwaliori.

As per legend, he visited Thanjavur and cured the local king of a grievous ailment. The grateful king gifted him 30 acres to establish his *khanqah*. The saint passed away in 1570 and was buried on that land in Nagore.

The shrine was deeply integrated into the local history and it was:

> [C]closely tied to the state-making ambitions of the seventeenth and eighteenth-century Maratha rajas of Tanjore. The shrine's official histories commemorate the Maratha ruler Pratab Singh (1739–63) as the builder of one of the site's five great *minar*s (minarets): under the patronage of these officially Hindu rulers, the shrine became one of the most celebrated sacred sites in south India.[2]

These pagoda-like minarets are very distinctive and have inspired many architects. The shrine is popular not only in South India but also Sri Lanka.

His *urs* is celebrated on the first day of the Islamic month of Jamad ul-Aakhir and is called the Kanduri Festival. Popular and acclaimed music director, A.R. Rahman is a regular visitor to the *urs*.

An enquiry I made on Twitter had a friend from Tamil Nadu respond. Admitting that she has never been there herself, Hyderabad-based Natasha Ramarathan who works for an education non-profit, interested in heritage and heritage preservation says, 'My paternal grandmother, S. Seethalakshmi would make a pilgrimage of all the major holy places once a year. Nagore was always on that list. When my mother was a new bride, she was also taken to [the] Nagore dargah.'

'My mother, Padma Ramarathnam, says she vividly remembers my grandmother in a blue *Kanjeevarammadisar* (a nine-yard saree), carrying her youngest grandson with his freshly-shaved head into the dargah [...] and she did a head-shaving ceremony for all her grandsons,' she concludes.[3]

Her grandmother would also get her head shaved ritually at a nearby temple.

What she has heard of the place, she adds, is that there were equal number[s] of Hindu and Muslim pilgrims, all with equal faith (the word she used was *bhakti*).

The other popular Tamil Nadu dargah in the same region is that of the saint Tamim ibn Zayd al-Ansar, a *sahabi* (companion of the Prophet), in Kovalam. He is said to have been born in Medina and was introduced to Islam by the Prophet himself, alongside whom he fought in the Battle of Badr. As per the instructions of the Prophet, he lived in the world of the jinn (*alam-e-jinnat*), teaching them the Quran and about Islam. He was gifted a precious ring, which contained the *asma-ul-husna* (secret name of Allah), and was once in the possession of prophet Solomon. When he returned to the earthly world, it was the time of the second caliph and he left for Hindustan, reaching and living in the Sindh. He lived in Sindh for 18 years as the Amir-ul-Mumineen (leader of the believers).[4]

An interesting legend is attached to the saint, who willed that he should be thrown into the sea instead of being buried. Accordingly, he was given a send-off from Karachi in a coffin after all the rituals connected with burial were completed. His body was guarded by fishes for 400 years, it is said, before washing ashore at this village near Mahabalipuram. The body of the *sahabi* had not decayed and there were documents identifying him inside the coffin. Some stories suggest that the local ruler built the mausoleum for him. Some legends have it that in the eighteenth century, the Nawab of Arcot, Muhammad Ali Khan Wallajah, allegedly had a dream where the saint asked him to find his body which had been washed ashore at Kovalam and to bury him there.

Whatever be the truth, the dargah remains extremely popular.

A famous dargah of Hyderabad (the current joint capital of the Telangana and Andhra Pradesh states) is called Yusufain. Two prominent saints Syed Shah Yusufuddin and Syed Shah Sharifuddin are buried there. They were the disciples of Hazrat Kalimullah Jahanabadi of Delhi.

It is located in the centre of the city and sees a significant number of people come not just to pay respects to the saint and petition him, but also for regular prayers at the daily prescribed times. The courtyard is usually full, and beyond that is a graveyard where many of Hyderabad's famous people are buried, including the poet Dagh Dehlvi who had migrated there in his later years. The custom of being buried within the precincts of a dargah is very old, as it is believed that the area near saint's shrine is blessed.

Another very popular dargah close by is that of Hazrat Shah Khamosh, which was built in the late nineteenth century. Hazrat Shah Khamosh was a Sufi of the Chishti Sabri order and his real name was Syed Muinuddin Hussaini. He received the title *khamosh* (silent) because he spoke very little. He once had an altercation with his *pir bhai* (disciples of the same *pir*) and when he took the matter up with his *murshid,* Hafiz Mohammed Musa Manakpuri, he was told to be silent. Obeying his master's command, he never uttered another word after that for the rest of his life.

The dargah has a beautiful and imposing domed structure and it is very well maintained. In 2007, it was one of six structures to be awarded the INTACH heritage award for being 'probably the first among the few religious structures to have incorporated classical European elements within its architectural inheritance to produce an arresting blend of two very distinct and diverse styles'. It has an open shrine with railings around it and there is no segregation for women. A sense of peace prevails all around.

There is also a *Bahishti Darwaza* (Heavenly Gateway) which was brought from the shrine of Baba Farid, as Shah Khamosh was his spiritual successor. The dargah has a tradition of playing music.

Though not as much of a climb as Maula Ali's dargah, there are a number of steps leading up to the Pahadi Sharif Dargah in Hyderabad. It is the dargah of Syedna Baba Sharfuddin Suhrawardi and is one of the oldest in Hyderabad. He had come to the Deccan via Delhi from Baghdad in 1190 and settled in a place called Balapur, which is some five kilometres away from the dargah. He first came to this spot on a hillock for prayers and meditation, eventually deciding to stay on. While Aurangzeb built the structure over his grave, Nizam Mahbub Ali Khan added a big hall. The complex houses many other dargahs, of relatives and disciples, including one of Hazrat Syedna Phikhi Bibi Sahiba Suhrawardi. In May 2018, his 752nd *urs* (death anniversary) celebrations were held.

During my visit, I climbed up the hillock with a young mother, Jyoti, who was carrying her child to seek Baba's blessings for her child. She told me that he was born after she prayed here, so it's a personal practice to bring him to the dargah at least once a month. She is not alone in doing so. Since the shrine is associated with fertility and well-being of children, many women like her, go to it to either to pray for children, or for their long and healthy lives. There is no restriction on entering the main shrine, and there is anyway a separate space for women to sit and pray within the large dargah complex.

The dargahs of Maula Ali, Hazrat Shah Khamosh, and Pahadi Sharif all welcome women, but in Yusufain there are restrictions on women entering.

Another small dargah in Kadapa (formerly Cudappa) district of Andhra Pradesh has also become famous because of a famous follower, music director A.R. Rahman. He came to offer his grateful thanks after winning an Oscar for his music in the *Slumdog Millionaire* movie in 2009. It is the shrine of Khwaja Syed Shah Ameenullah Muhammad Mahmoodul-Hussaini Chisti-ul-Qadiri. It is also known as Ameen Peer dargah, Peerullah dargah, and Peda dargah (as the popular offering made there are the sweet called *peda*). Since I couldn't visit it, I am relying on various articles written about it and are available online. Ameen Peer, was born in Bidar, Karnataka sometime in the sixteenth century. He went to Mecca for the Hajj pilgrimage and on his return he visited various Sufi shrines in India, including the Ajmer Sharif dargah. Here he is believed to have received divine instructions to shift to the Kadapa region. He was given the title Khwaja (master).

> Ameen Peer Dargah (Asthana-e-Maqdoom Ilahi Dargah complex) (Badi Dargah, Pedda Dargah) in Kadapa City is an example of the communal harmony preached by great saints and sages in ancient days. Come Thursday and Friday, scores of pilgrims cutting across religious faiths, throng [to] the the 300-year-old shrine seeking blessings of saints Peerullah Hussaini and Arifullah Hussaini II who lie buried here. Followers of the ameenpeer dargah believe that any wish that one makes at the shrine is always fulfilled. A large number of Hindus, Muslims, and people of different faiths are disciples of the shrine. The family's descendants identify themselves with a saffron dress and the disciples wear a saffron cap.[5]

On a recent visit to Bangalore, while I was following the Tiger of Mysore Tipu Sultan's trail I was told to visit the dargah of Baba Hasan Tawakkul Mastan Shah Suhrawardy (d. 1777). Since I was on my way to the Bangalore Fort and this was on the way, I stopped here first. The dargah painted a bright green can be seen from afar, with an imposing mosque behind it. The mosque has replaced a smaller and older building. The dargah was full of devotees and I was greeted very politely by the *khadim* Tabrez Ahnmed Muzavar who told me about the saint. Baba's family, he said, were horse traders who had come from Iran and he was one of three brothers. One of the brothers, Manik Mastan, is also buried in Bangalore and is venerated as a saint, while the third, Tipu Mastan, lies in Arcot, where his shrine is very popular.

According to Ahmed, when Hyder Ali was rebuilding the Bangalore Fort, and converting its walls from mud to stone, he noticed that one man involved in the construction had refused his salary. This piqued Hyder Ali's interest and he asked for more information on him. And two soldiers were sent to find him. They came to the present Cottonpete locality and found that his body was lying in three pieces and was guarded by two dogs. The soldiers returned and informed Hyder Ali that the man had been slaughtered. To their surprise the next day the man returned to work, making them realise that he was no ordinary man. When he was asked about his renumeration he requested that a mosque and *khanqah* be built in the place where he lived. The mosque as mentioned before is newly-built but the shrine is said to be original and to my untrained eye looked as if it had been added to and embellished along the years.

Hyder Ali was childless, according to Ahemd, and Tipu was born as a boon from Tawakkal Mastan Shah and named after his brother. However, this story doesn't seem true since Hyder Ali's reign started in 1761 and Tipu Sultan was born in 1751.

The first thing that met my eyes was a huge flyer with the words 'all are welcome'. On enquiry I found out one of the most beautiful customs. In the flyer was Haji Mohammad Ghouse Muzavar and a Veerakumara. I found out that during the *karaga* festival, the deity Draupadi visited the dargah to give her blessings to the saint. The nine-day mahotsava, organised by Tigalas or the Vanni Kula Kshatriyas, concluded just a few days before my visit. I was told it was never complete without 'Draupadi Devi' giving 'darshan' to Hazrat Tawakkal Shah Mastan. The Baba in his lifetime would take the *karaga*'s blessings.

Karaga, a folk dance, is literally the lime-topped clay pot in which the deity resided during the festival celebrated in Karnataka. It originated as a ritual dedicated to Draupadi as known in these parts as Droupadammaand, and 'included processions with *ter*s and *capparam*s, wheeled chariots and handheld platforms on which the deities were brought out from their shrines and paraded through their worshippers' residential quarters.'[6]

The nine-day festival starts with the establishment of the *Hasikaraga* or holy pot. The contents of this flower decked pot is a secret and is carried on the head by devotees without their hands touching it.

In Bengaluru it is installed at the Sampangi Tank. On the ninth day, the *karaga* is taken in a procession to the Dharmaraya Swamy temple. A priest dressed as Draupadi leads the procession. Bare-chested, dhoti-clad, turbaned devotees known as Veerakumaras, bear unsheathed swords, take the *karaga* to the Dharmaraya temple, and one of the stops on the way is the dargah of Baba Tawakkal Mastan Shah, so that Draupadi amma can give *darshan* to the saint. They do *pradakshina* (circumambulation), and exchange sacred lemons with the Muzavars (priests) of the shrine. 'The decision by the organisers to uphold the fair's syncretic tradition came despite alleged appeals by Hindutva workers to skip the dargah halt. [They] described the traditions of inter-faith unity as crucial.'[7]

The Karaga Utsava Samithi (Karaga Festival Committee) has stated that no matter what, all the traditions would be continued during Karaga festival.[8]

And may our glorious syncretic customs continue. Ameen.

# 16

# The Possessed and the Dispossessed

The village my ancestors come from was established by Sultan Jalaluddin Khilji in the thirteenth century and has a mosque dating back to that time. We also have a *jinn wala imambara* near our ancestral home, and of course, many tales. As children, we would be fascinated by their stories, especially of the *Ahl al-Bait*-loving jinn who would observe Muharram and do *matam* (self-flagellation) in memory of Imam Hussain. We would hear stories of Jafar Jinn who was a devotee of Hazrat Ali and during the battle of Karbala, described in Chapter 2, offered to come to the Imam's aid, though the latter did not accept as he wanted the fight between good and evil to be fought between humans. Of course, we grew up loving them, (though always scared of their anger) and were told to respect their spaces and to always address them as Jinn Mamu and chant the *Naad-e-Ali* (discussed in Chapter 2) for protection.

Our childhood was peppered with many other stories of Jinn Mamu, and to date I call them respectfully by this name, adding the appellate Mamu or uncle, for it is ingrained in me that if they are happy with us, like the proverbial lamp, we get wishes fulfilled, and we if we anger them, the consequences can be bad.

Most children, like me, grow up on that story of Aladdin and the magic lamp, and wish they too had a friendly genie who would grant their wishes. I, like all children, was fascinated by the supernatural, though it isn't children alone who are drawn to such stories.

These don't remain just stories for many as 'the belief that jinn can cause mental illness in humans through affliction or possession is widely accepted among Muslims, meaning this belief is a crucial, but a frequently overlooked aspect of mental health problems with Muslim patients in psychiatric care,' according to Prof. Rasool.[1] He has described the Islamic perspective on mental health in his book, *Evil Eye, Jinn Possession, and Mental Health Issues*. However, in India, as I found out, this is not limited only to Muslim patients, as belief in the healing power of shrines, especially in relation to mental health, is prevalent across faiths.

Instead of medical treatment for psychiatric disorders, many patients with mental health issues (and often their relatives on their behalf) seek out the services of people who are said to be experts in removing the effects of the evil eye, and jinn and witchcraft possession, and visit shrines said to heal such problems. There is a need to understand this belief in order to deal with the issues that they raise.

Dargahs are sanctified spaces and are believed to be blessed with healing powers. The premises constantly ring out with the recitation of the Holy Quran and other invocations to Allah. Apart from humans, it is believed that even some angels and jinn participate in the recitation of the Holy Quran here. These sacred spaces attract men and women, rich and poor, the powerful and the powerless, who come to avail of this goodness, whether it is for physical or mental healing, a better life, solutions for problems, or for spiritual upliftment. There is a belief that anyone with bad intentions is sent scurrying out because of the miraculous powers of the saint who is buried there, and that is why, combined with the healing powers of the saint, dargahs see many visitors who come seeking succour. It is believed that the saints have a divine gift known as *karamat* (miracles of saints), and they are able to continue exercising it even from beyond the grave, through their shrines. Dargahs are thus a source of *barkat* (blessing), for that power is believed to be embodied in the saint's shrine or in their successors who have continued the religious and spiritual practices of the saint. These powers are also perpetuated through popular stories of miracles that are connected with the saints and recounted by many a grateful devotee. This reinforces the image of a saint as powerful – as someone who not only grants wishes but can counter sorcery and witchcraft, which are condemned by Islam. It is said that for the casting of spells and evil acts, '[T]hey knew that the buyers of (magic) would have no share in the happiness of the Hereafter.' (Quran 2:102).

In this chapter, I seek to understand this belief, and how dargahs came to be associated with mental health, by describing my personal encounters with afflicted persons in various dargahs across the country.

But first, we need to understand what are the jinn. Are they the boon-granting genies conjured by the Western imagination? The Quran mentions three creatures made by Allah. The first are angels, who are made out of *nur* (light). However, angels do not possess free will and can only worship and obey Allah. The second are jinn, and the third are humans.

In the Quran, the jinn are described as akin to humans – except where humans were made of clay, the jinn have been created from smokeless fire and can take any form they want – animal or other. The word 'jinn' (plural) means hidden, concealed from the eye, and is similar to the Arabic word for heaven, *Jannah*. According to Bruce Lawrence, professor of religion, 'jinn' is derived from the *Jannah* as they both inhabit the world between Allah and man and are deemed to be closer to heaven than earth.[2] The singular 'jinni' is close to the English word genie.

Jinn were the first to inhabit the earth, 'and it were the jinn, who caused corruption there and spilled blood.'[3] Thus they predate human civilization and are frequently mentioned in the Quran (appearing 32 times). *Surah* 72 is named after them. The *Surah* was revealed at a time when a group of jinn, hearing the Prophet recite the *Surah al-Rahman*, stopped to listen to him, and later embraced Islam.

In Islam, Lucifer – known as Iblis in Arabic – is also a jinn. His original name was Azazil, and he was a jinni whose piety, obedience, and virtues had placed him at a par with the angels. He was always to be found among them, busy worshipping God. However, unlike the angels, he had the capacity to disobey and choose to do good or evil. He rebelled against Allah's order to prostrate before Aadam, the first man, and was thus banished from paradise. Azazil then became Iblis or one who despairs (of God's mercy) and *al-shaitan* (the devil – its Christian counterpart is Satan), the one who leads men astray.

As mentioned above, like humans, jinn are also intelligent, have free will, can be good and bad, and they also have the right to choose their religion. Like humans, they too live and die, marry and procreate, and will face consequences on The Day of Judgement. But unlike humans, they have been given certain special powers. They are shape-shifters and can take on any physical form they want; they have the power to move quickly and travel huge distances, along with the ability to take over the minds and bodies of humans – which is what we are concerned with in this chapter. In fact the word *majnun,* an epithet used for someone enraptured by ecstatic love, means to be possessed by a jinn, or an evil spirit.

A famous hadith says: 'There is none amongst you with whom is not an attaché from amongst the jinn (devil). They (the Companions) said: Allah's Messenger, with you too? Thereupon he said: Yes, but Allah helps me against him and so I am safe from his hand and he does not command me but for good.'[4]

The idea that the jinn possess miraculous powers can be seen in the story of Prophet Sulaiman, (Solomon) who was the master of jinn and had powerful jinn doing his bidding. 'And there were jinn that worked in front of him, by the leave of his Lord,' (Quran 34:12) building him palaces, statues, and basins as large as reservoirs and fixed cauldrons (Quran 34:13). One jinn with knowledge of 'the Book' (the books revealed before the Quran) brought the Queen of Sheba's throne to Solomon in the 'twinkling of an eye' (Quran 27:39–40).

In the pre-Islamic era, human mages, sorcerers, and cunning practitioners of the secret arts were believed to have formed pacts with mighty jinn who would grant them a jinn guardian called a *re'ya*.

It is also believed that jinns have been given certain powers which can help them do magical things. These powers are a test for them – for if they use it to oppress anyone, they will be held accountable for it.

Bruce Lawrence says, 'Jinn can work good or ill but they are always at work. One cannot live without the interference of the jinn. To understand and control them is to prosper. To ignore or try to avoid them is to invite defeat, loss of health and even death.'[5]

It should thus come as no surprise that men and women have long been using special incantations and *wazifa*s (special prayers) for a stipulated period of time, which can give them power over the jinn. It is believed that '[t]he jinn used for sorcery by their controllers are said to be the heretic jinn who refused to submit to the new religion [Islam].'[6]

The Quran mentions only *jinn*, *marid*, and *ifrit*, but Islamic literature and folklore differentiates between 10 types of jinn: *hinn* (close to animals and often appear as dogs), ghoul (shape-shifter evil beings), *jann* (shape-shifters who live in deserts and appear as white camels), *marid* (large and powerful jinn; almost giant-sized, in the Qur'an, the *marid* are said to be 'an unruly force always striving to predict the future by means of astrological hearsay'[7]), *ifrit* (powerful and cunning creatures; in fact, it was an *ifrit* who offered to bring the Queen of Sheba's throne for Prophet Solomon), *shiqq* (half-formed creatures who look like monsters), *nasnas* (offspring of *shiqq*; also half-formed, they live away from urban centres), *palis* (they live in deserts and drink blood of sleeping humans by licking their feet), *silat* ('resembles the ghoul in many aspects. Like the ghoul, she, too, is a temptress, a first-class trickster. She likes dancing relentlessly with men and playing with them as a cat plays with a mouse. People in medieval Islam told stories about how the *si'lat* would attract a man to her by imitating a woman's voice and screaming [that] a wolf is eating her!'[8]), and then, of course, there are the *shaitans* (the devil and his offspring who are out to tempt humans to sin).

Though *bhoot-pret* (a kind of ghost or soul of dead) are sometimes conflated with jinn by those unaware of the Islamic perspective, it must be clear by now that there is a difference between the two. Jinn are intelligent and subtle beings, with agency by nature, while *bhoot-pret* are 'liminal, illegitimate, and therefore dangerously manipulatable'.[9]

Muslims and non-Muslims, the illiterate and the literate, seek protection and favours from jinn. Though Islam places importance on holistic healing, 'connecting it [health] to the well-being of the mind (*aql*), body (*jism*) and spirit (*ruh*)',[10] there is no direct connection between *al-Shaitan* and mental illness in the Quran, and in it, madness is not linked to sin and misguidance. Kinesiology and health researchers, F. Islam and R.A. Campbell bring this to light, saying:

> The most explicit example of the connection between possession and mental illness in the Qur'an comes from the disbelievers replying to Hud, saying 'All we can say is that one of our gods may have inflicted some harm on you'(11:54). Pickthall translates this as 'our gods hath possessed thee in an evil way', even though the phrase does not contain any words with the j-n-n root. The

> unfortunate consequence of this is that the concept of jinn-possession is being read back into the text, perhaps on the basis on later theological developments, rather than reflecting the implications of the text at the time it was produced. None of the other translations reflect this interpretation.[11]

Islam and Campbell go on to say:

> Our search of the text of the Qur'an for themes related to the terms jinn, Satan and madness yielded no direct connection between spirit-possession and mental illness. When people were spoken of as jinn-possessed or crazy in the text, this was done so in reference to the ignorance of pagan insults or to spiritual insanity, as a result of sin. No person of spiritual authority in the Qur'an ever expresses this belief.[12]

It should also be noted that the Prophet himself emphasized the use of medicine for diseases, saying: 'Take medicine, O servants of God. For every illness He gave medicine';[13] and the study of medicine was encouraged by him. Another researcher, Amira el-Zein, says:

> Classical Islam stressed that Muslims should strive to find cures for diseases. Islamic physicians built up a huge and intricate medical corpus. This all-embracing literature was not confined to strict medical knowledge in the sense that modern medical literature is. Rather, it was blended with philosophy, natural science, mathematics, astrology, alchemy, biology, spirit healers, charms and religion. In this sense, it was what we call today 'interdisciplinary'.[14]

Ignorance of mental illnesses continues to result in people with mental health conditions chained or locked in parts of dargahs. In some, I have seen heart-rending scenes where these patients are shackled or tied to the railings of the shrine, left to thrash about in acute distress – sometimes with the 'guardians' of the afflicted standing guard nearby to prevent escape. As they are confined to only small portions of every dargah compound, not everyone notices them. The dargah of Hazrat Nizamuddin Auliya is a case in point; few are aware of what is hidden behind the marble *jaali*s of Princess Jahanara's tomb.

Princess Jahanara, the elder daughter of Shah Jahan, was a mystic herself and she is buried, as per her will, in the dargah of Hazrat Nizamuddin Auliya in Delhi. One can often find women sitting there in various states of mental agitation and anxiety – some wailing, some quiet and subdued, others thrashing about with their male and female relatives standing outside. The families have faith that the *shahzadi* (princess) will cure them, and attempts to persuade them, through offers of logical advice, and to get them to seek the help of a psychiatrist don't work before that faith.

Rehan Asad, a medical doctor and heritage enthusiast, tells me about the time he visited the dargah of Sheikh Alauddin Ali Ahmad Sabir near Roorkee (Uttarakhand) in 2018. On my request, he described his experience via email, which I now share with his permission:

> As I reached the capacious courtyard outside the main tomb, I saw [a] number of mental patients who seek *ziyarat* (visit) of the revered saint. I was surrounded by loud growls, wails, [and the] pleadings of these visitors while some of them are in state of convulsive actions flexing their postures with abnormally dancing eyeballs. It's difficult to exactly diagnose their illness that might range from split personalities to epilepsy. But for their families, they were occupied by jinn and here they find solace and treatment at the blessed shrine of their beloved Sabir Piya.
>
> In the same compound, one can find innumerable handwritten letters on an old heritage Ficus tree. These are the *arzi* (request letters) fixed by the attendants for the saint. The cure of these patients might be hidden in their beliefs. Though evidence is lacking for these approaches in medical science.
>
> Here, there is no demarcation between caste, creed, religion, and gender. You can find supplicants from diverse faiths. Even with [the] bulk of such [a] great number of mental patients, the general environment of the compound is soothing and full of positive vibes.

These practices are always in the compound, and are in stark contrast with from the main tomb where, as Asad says, 'Inside the tomb, it's a different world that is filled with serenity, silence, and [a] soul-enriching environment.'

Though the link made between mental illness and evil spirits predates Islam, today people mainly flock to dargahs to find the cure to such ailments.

Cures for two main types of maladies are sought in the dargahs. One, of course, is for possession and the other is for *kala jadoo* (black magic) also known as *sihr*. *Sihr* is said to involve people casting spells out of jealousy, enmity, or envy. As a child, I was told never to accept any food that was white in colour, such as milk or kheer, as it is believed that these are the favourite mediums used for casting spells. Other objects used to cast spells are (stolen) underclothes and (slyly acquired) cuttings of the corners of *dupatta*s (scarves); evil spells are said to be tied into these objects with the intention of bringing harm to their owners. At weddings, the *dupatta* of the bride is closely guarded to prevent its (mis)use through such magic, by jealous exes and former suitors, envious relatives, and so on. Every day of the wedding ceremonies, burn red chillies to ward off the evil eye.

Both those who feel that they have fallen prey to the evil machinations of their enemies, and those wanting to hex them, may visit *pir*s, *amil*s, and *tantrik*s (practitioners who are believed to help in removing the effects of black magic and the evil eye) to have spells removed or cast. The latter often charge a lot of money and exploit the persons afflicted by the *sihr*, so for the desperate and needy there are the dargahs, which are especially popular with those who think they have been possessed by an evil jinn or spirit. The *barakat* of the dargah is said to force the evil spirit to leave the host in peace. (It must be remembered here that according to widespread belief not all jinn are bad for the host; there are good jinn too who are said to help the host prosper in life and look after them.)

During the research for this book, I met a couple of men and one woman who were mediums. One hosted a very old Jinn Baba, who gave solutions to problems and prayers for recitation on Thursday evenings. The host would be in what seemed like an unconscious state, while the Jinn Baba would answer questions, and give solutions – mostly Quranic verses, *zikr* and at times very practical advice on steps to alleviate sufferings. I had a few meetings with Baba, as he's popularly called, and his advice to me, among other things, was to be stop being impatient and to submit myself to Allah's wishes. Once again, it is Allah and His word that is considered final. The *amil*s and practitioners who make predictions, or who say that they can achieve anything, are fake or worse, frauds, and should be avoided; this was the advice given to me by an ordained Sufi. According to him, these aren't practitioners but unscrupulous men out to make money by charging exorbitant sums from the distressed.

This perception that erratic behaviours and mental illnesses are a result of possession by evil spirits must have started many centuries ago when there was less understanding and treatment for mental illnesses, but unfortunately it continues till today. The reasons for this are not very hard to imagine. This belief persists because mental illness is still considered a taboo in many houses, and medical intervention can be an expensive affair. Coming to the dargah, especially after having heard of someone having a miracle cure, may seem like an acceptable – even attractive – option. (This is not to deny the fact that many dargahs abound with cynical *amil*s who think nothing of exploiting another's distress for their monetary gain.)

Many of those who come to these dargahs for a cure are from the lower socio-economic strata of society and of the female gender. The word '*pagal*' (mad), with all its negative connotations, is used for people with mental health conditions. Saying that an evil spirit has possessed someone takes away the onus of blame from them and makes the illness and them socially acceptable. In the case of young girls, in particular, mental illness is perceived to affect their marriage prospects so all efforts are made to 'heal' them in dargahs.

The most interesting relevant case study of possession is the dargah of Hazrat Ashraf Jahangir Simnani in Uttar Pradesh which is famous for its exorcism. There is a tree just below the steps leading up to the dargah, under which afflicted people sit. The saint calls the malevolent spirit that supposedly possesses the person to manifest itself and then asks it to leave the host body; the word *haziri* is used for the manifestation of the spirit[15] (This is different from the *haziri dena* described in Chapter 10 where devotees go to pay respects to the saint.) There are *adalat*s (courts) held thrice a day where these people assemble and the malevolent spirit is interrogated.

> 'To an outside observer, interrogation of the malevolent spirit appears to be a one-way conversation, since no one but the spirit can hear the voice of the saint. The saint's statements and actions can only be inferred by the statements made by the malevolent spiritual presence. Thus, for example, if a spiritual presence said, "I'll never tell who did the magic that sent me, no matter how much you beat me!" and then the body of the person in *haziri* was suddenly thrown onto the ground, an outside observer would understand that the saint was interrogating the spirit, attempting to elicit the information necessary to render a *faislā,* or judgment.'[16]

The duration of the *haziri* depends on the severity of the 'possession'. It can be anywhere from 1 day to 40 days. The 'possessed' person, who is accompanied by a guardian, is first made to have a bath and come and sit under the tree, and then they attend one of the *adalat*s daily. The evil spirit is eventually exorcized and given a punishment, which could even be orders for its execution.

The Husain Tikri dargah complex described in Chapter 11 also has similar customs. When I visited it in 2001, I found crowds of mostly women and a few men in a state of acute distress thrashing about in front of the dargahs. Regular *haziri* and *adalat* as described above are also held here. A point to remember is that not all dargahs have *adalat*s, and *haziri* of this kind is discouraged.

The *peerzada*s who help perform the exorcism are said to be aided by *muwakkil*s. The idea of *muwakkil*s is a popular one in the subcontinent; the term refers to those jinn or angels appointed to guard the names of Allah and letters of the Quran. They are made of half *nur* and half smokeless fire. *Muwakkil*s, though in possession of free will, will only perform good deeds and are more powerful than ordinary jinn. *Muwakkil*s can be attracted/conjured up by pious men and women who constantly do *zikr* and chant the names of Allah, especially the *ism-e-azam* (the greatest name of Allah, known to Prophets and the *wali*s). They then do the 40-day *chillah,* where they say *wazifa*s (special prayers) and perform other devotional rituals in a state of ritual purity. As per this concept, the *muwakkil*s will in turn assign good jinn (*ruhani*) who are spiritually inclined to help these pious humans.

As per Islam, these *muwakkils/khodam* will not participate in any activity that can harm a person and will only help in lawful and beneficial acts.

Ali A. Olomi, historian of the Middle East and Islam, tells me:

> *Muwakkil* are a class of spirits which developed in the medieval tradition. *Khodam/ Muwakkil/ Ruhaniyya* are all ambiguous beings and were defined occasionally as jinn and other times as angels. They emerged as part of cosmographic and esoteric work interconnecting the celestial and natural worlds. So they are associated with sacred letters, names of God, astrological/planetary attributes, elements, virtues, and minerals. For example, Azrail is the Angel of the letter 'ta' and the planet Saturn.[17]

This reminded me of my mother-in-law, Sultan Jahan Begum, who would always tell me to take out the *sadqa* (propitiatory offering) for the *muwakkil* when I would sit down to read a *tasbih* (rosary) of *zikr*.

A Sufi practitioner that I spoke to told me on conditions of anonymity[18] that every *muwakkil* has hundreds of minor *muwakkil*s working under him. Men, and at times women, seek to make them obedient to their commands through 40-day retreats and *zikr*, and use them to get various tasks accomplished. These retreats or *chillah*s are very difficult as it includes absolute seclusion, purity of place, clothes, thoughts, and mind. They only eat whatever necessary for bare sustenance (no meat, onions, garlic or anything that has a strong smell) and concentrate on the prayers and *zikr*. They need the permission of the owner of the place that they occupy. However, he emphasized that whatever happens is in accordance with the wish and command of Allah; men or jinn can only strive according to His will in these matters. As he put, '*Na tab kuch insaan ke haath mein thaa, naa aj kuch hai. Bas yeh hai ke jitney qareeb jaaoge Khuda ke, utne* powers *Khuda deta hai. Jitna nafs ko maaroge utna* power *milega. Lekin utne hi imtihan Khuda leta hai.*' (There was nothing in man's hand then [at the beginning of time] and there is nothing in his power now. It is just that the closer you go to God, and the more you control your ego, the more powers he bestows on you, but he also tests you more.) However, he adds that these *chillah*s are done for God and to gain His pleasure. Everything else, including having any *muwakkil* who obeys you, are just a bonus.

Peerzada Altamash Nizami, a descendant of Hazrat Nizamuddin Chishti, described the two types of *haziri*: One is the *haziri* (attendance) of the devotee at any dargah, the second is the *haziri* of the *bala* (evil spirit) in a dargah, where the spirit, possessing some person, becomes visible (not physically) to the practitioner and can then be removed. Like the practitioner I spoke to, he also emphasized that whatever happens is only because of God's command. He told me that all spirits avoid sacred places and in case they do come there, their presence within the possessed person becomes obvious as they either start thrashing around, screaming or being physically violent. This is called *haal khelna*.[19] These spirits become visible in the dargahs of very pious saints. Once the evil spirit has made itself visible to the practitioner, they use the help of the junior *muwakkil*s to remove and punish them. Some spirits are so well entrenched that the host person has to go to a number of dargahs for *haziri* before s/he can be rid of them.

There is a gendered angle to all of this. Young boys were told not to relieve themselves on trees as they might have *jinn mamu*s resting in them. The girls would get scolded if they ever went out into the garden at dusk with open hair, especially near certain flowering bushes which were the believed to be favourite haunts of jinn. The jinn that live on trees are said to result in *saaya* (influence of an evil spirit), especially on young women, as discussed below.

As a young girl myself, I remember a Baba who had come to our house in Bareilly (UP) to meet my father. He held just such an aseembly in a nearby village called Baheri. He was famous as the Baheri Wale Baba. He would gather people in a dark room and chant some Quranic verses, then address each of the spirits one by one and supposedly force them to leave the host body. I was very curious, but then young girls would never be allowed to go to such a place. Luckily, a relative who had gone, described the scene to me. I must add the disclaimer that the relative who described it also said the room was very dark and they could only hear a deep-throated voice and see the shadowy shape of the person said to be possessed, and the description could well be just his imagination at work. There was a young girl who was allegedly possessed by a jinn. When the Baba questioned the jinn and asked him to leave the girl, he is supposed to have said that he was from Russia and that there weren't such pretty girls in the jinn community so he had lost his heart to her. Anyway, he was forced to leave with much difficulty, according to my relative.

Al-Damiri (1341–1405) tells a similar story about the Sufi Abdul Qader al-Gilani (1078–1166), known for his power over the jinn:

> A man from Baghdad came one day to the sheikh 'Abdul Qader al-Gilani and informed him the jinn abducted his daughter, and asked for his help. So, the sheikh told him to do the following: 'Go this night to the ruin of al-Karkh. Sit at the fifth hill and draw a circle on the floor and say while drawing it: "In the name of God and according to 'Abdul Qader's intention." When the night becomes pitch black, you will see tribes of jinn passing by you in different shapes. Don't be afraid! None among them can enter the circle where you sit. When their king comes, he will approach you and enquire about your presence among them. You ought to tell him your story.' The man followed exactly the orders of 'Abdul Qader al-Gilani. As the Sufi sheikh told him, none of the jinn was able to enter the circle where he was sitting until came the king of the jinn who questioned him, and then brought his daughter back to him. She was abducted by one jinni from China! He fell in love with her and carried her away.[20]

Though the number of female Sufi saints is very low, the number of female visitors to a shrine is very high. They come there to pray for intercession for the many problems of their day-to-day life, for which they seldom get succour anywhere else: these include the ill effects of the evil eye on their children, husbands, and themselves. They come to pray for deliverance from wayward husbands and oppressive in laws, for the health of their children, and for protection from black magic, which results in erratic behaviour otherwise.

The night of no moon, *Amavasya*, and full moon, *Purnima*, are both very important in Hindu culture. *Purnima* is considered auspicious, and *Amavasya* is considered equally inauspicious. As per tradition, on the night of *Amavasya,* evil spirits roam around unchecked, and it is on this night that *tantra* and black magic can be done. In the Deccani dargahs, an *Amavasya* day is reserved for the exorcism of evil spirits.

I visited the dargahs of Bijapur during *Amavasya* and found a sense of urgency in most of them, especially the dargahs of Khwaja Abdur Razzaq Qadiri and Khan Muhammad in the Jod Gumbaz complex. In fact, the corridors of the latter were full of people with mental health conditions waiting for their turn to give *haziri* at the dargah in the hope of being cured by the powers of the saint on an *Amavasya* day. The devotees and their attendants there believed that their condition was due to possession by spirits – and not a mental illness, and that they can be exorcised in these dargahs.

There, I met Shanta Bi, a woman in her 60s and resident of Bijapur, who had been 'cured'. She had been visiting the dargah for the past five years, ever since, according to her, she had fallen prey to evil spirits. After she started visiting the dargah, she found relief, and now she came every *Amavasya* to do service in gratitude. She was also all alone and found solace and companionship in doing service here.

The dargahs of Sheikh Aleemuddin Ala, Sheikh Abdur Razzaq Qadiri, Khan Muhammad, and Hazrat Shah Murtaza Qadriya were extremely crowded with devotees who had travelled long distances to come in from many parts of Karnataka, Maharashtra, and Andhra Pradesh for the occasion of *Amavasya*. There were Muslims and non-Muslims amongst them.

It is believed that *saaya* is easier to cure, but *aaseb* (misfortune, trouble, calamity, especially such as is the consequence of the shadow of a jinn or demon having fallen on one) is a major issue and these are the cases we see more often in dargahs.

At the dargah of Sheikh Ameenuddin Aala, I met Ambuja, who had come with her daughter Saujanya and relative Nagamma. With the help of my friend Abdul Aziz Rajput, a Sufi practitioner who lives in Bijapur, I asked them a few questions. Rajput translated their answers for me. Ambuja's aunt used to come to the dargahs on Thursdays and *Amavasya* to pray for her daughter who was having marital problems. After a few visits, the daughter's problems were sorted out, and she is now living in domestic bliss, according to Ambuja.

The daughter had thus recommended that Ambuja too start visiting the dargah for the speedy disposal of her personal problems. Saujanya had been feeling restless, and according to the mother, was often in a state of unconsciousness. Fearing that some evil spirit may have possessed her, they started visiting and very soon Saujanya felt better too. Now they are regular visitors and return on other days too, in case Saujanya isn't feeling well.

The ways to counter these spirits and force them to leave are many and vary as per the practitioner, but most rely on the healing power of the verses from the Quran – especially the second *Surah*, *Surah Baqarah*, of which Ayat-ul Kursi is often recited for protection.

This makes sense as the Prophet has said, 'Truly Satan leaves a house when he hears Sūrat al-Baqarah recited in it,' and 'Learn al-Baqarah. Holding to it is a blessing, leaving it is an affliction, and falsehood has no power over it.'[21]

Amulets with the Ayat-ul Kursi and *Surah* 114 inscribed on it are also very popular and worn by many Muslims, especially in infancy, to ward off the evil eye. *Surah*s 113 and 114 are known as *al-mu'awwidhatan* (Verses of Refuge) and are the last verses of the Quran; they provide protection from the evil eye, evil spirits, magic, enemies, and jinn. They read:

> Say: I seek refuge with the Lord of the Dawn,
> From the mischief of created things;
> From the mischief of Darkness as it overspreads;
> From the mischief of those who practice Secret Arts;
> And from the mischief of the envious one as he practices envy.
>
> (113:1–5)

> Say: I seek refuge with the Lord
> And Cherisher of Mankind
>
> (114:1)

> And:

> From the mischief of the Whisperer (of Evil) who withdraws
> (After his whisper), – (The same) who whispers into the hearts of Mankind,
> Among Jinn And among Men.
>
> (114:4–6)

The other Quranic verses considered effective in warding off spirits and jinn, known as *ayat al-hifz* (verses for protection), are 12:64, 13:11, 3:7, 33:3, 33:48, 4:81 and 15:17. The *Surah Yasin* (no. 36) is also considered very effective against all diseases, afflictions, and problems and many, including me, recite it daily. The words of the *bismillah* are said before the start of anything and in times of trouble.

Water with various Quranic verses and names of Allah breathed over them are very popular with devotees, who even sprinkle it in their houses to ward off evil and keep the house purified for blessings to descend on them. In the *takia* in Kakori Sharif I saw a mother and son who had come to take consecrated water from the *peerzada*s sitting in the two antechambers in what must have been the *jamatkhana* of the saint, dispensing water and amulets to ward off evil spirits and cures for ailments.

In West Bengal's dargah of Sheikh Nur Qutb-ul-Alam, I found a young girl in her early teens doubled over the side railings of his shrine. Nothing except her arched back and two small hands were visible. It was quite a forlorn picture and one that touched my heart. Her mother was sitting behind her in one corner with a group of women. On my asking, she said her daughter was suffering from severe stomach pain for the past few months and they could not afford a doctor's fees so they came here where everyone is cured free of cost. To say the truth, I was horrified. For while one can and should pray in dargahs if they find it brings them comfort and peace, it should not be blind faith and never in lieu of medical treatment. (I gave some money to the mother and asked her to go to a doctor. I don't know if she did, but I do hope that the girl is cured.)

Possessions aren't the only reason why people visit dargahs. The dispossessed also find solace in the welcoming and friendly environment of a dargah. Since everyone is asking the saint to intercede with God for something or the other, no one feels alone in their sorrows here. This is one place where everyone comes with outstretched hands and feels they are greeted with open arms by the saint, and their religion, caste or class don't matter.

In every dargah there are devotees praying for things as varied as success in legal cases, increase in prosperity, cure for physical illnesses, children's well-being, promotions, success in present and future endeavours, marriage of near and dear ones, better marital relations, better relations with in-laws, and much more. The saints are believed to intercede on behalf of the devotee, after which the devotee offers a cloth chaddar and flowers. I am describing just a few that struck me but I have come across them in thousands.

In the dargah of Shah Murtaza Qadri in Bijapur, I once saw a courtyard full of people. I met Amina Bi among them. She had come from Sholapur and had been visiting the dargah for the past 50 years, spending a night here on the 28th of every Islamic month. She said that these visits ensured that there was peace, prosperity, and health in their houses. The months in which they didn't visit, they would suffer losses and fall sick.

Dargahs are not used for the sick and troubled alone, though. In the Shah-e-Alam Dargah in Ahmedabad, apart from the usual fare, I found a kind of marriage bureau! I met a lady whose job was match-making and had set up her work station in the dargah where people come to pray for good matches for their children. She operates from the courtyard and corridors of the dargah and is very successful. I even met a couple of people who vouched for her.

Another common problem is fertility. I know this because, given the segregation in most dargahs, my interlocutors were often female.

In Khuldabad, I found many women in the shrine of Sheikh Shah Jalaluddin Ganj-e-Ravan, which is connected to fertility, described in Chapter 14. The women had come with their husbands and in-laws or parents. One lady had come with her baby to offer thanks for his birth. At the entrance of his shrine, baskets containing fruits and other symbols of fertility are sold. The women bring offerings to the saint's shrine where they pray and later go and have a bath in a small pond below the shrine called the *pariyon ka talab* (the pond of the fairies). Only women are allowed there and I saw many women going there to take a bath.

It is not just ordinary folks who need the intercession of saints. We know emperors pray for offspring as was the case of Akbar and Sheikh Salim Chishti and sultans have prayed for victory in battle. In 1478, when Sultan Hussain Shah of Jaunpur attacked Delhi with numerous troops Sultan Bahlol Lodi is reported to have prayed at the dargah of Qutub Sahib, standing bare-headed the whole night like an ordinary supplicant.

At dawn he returned, filled with the hope of gaining success against his rival, and since the attack failed, his hopes weren't misplaced.[22]

In the dargahs of the *Ahl al-Bait* I have seen a system called *girvikarna*. Though the word literally means 'mortgage' it is actually a system whereby one of the caretakers in the dargahs tie a thread to the *alam* (the hand-shaped standard Hazrat Abbas described in Chapter 11) and its other end to the devotees wrist. That is supposed to offer security against all trouble. It is also something my family and I have followed throughout our lives at the Hazrat Abbas dargah in Lucknow.

If there are jinn who torment people, there are many others who help, and there are multiple stories of that. One of them is set in a medieval fortress. In the fourteenth century, Sultan Firoz Shah Tughlaq built the fifth major city of Delhi, called Firozabad, on the banks of the river Yamuna. Its ruins, now called Firoz Shah Kotla, lie on Bahadur Shah Zafar Road in Delhi. The Jami Masjid in this fort was so grand that Timur offered prayers there and ordered a similar one to be made in Samarqand. Even today, the ruins are magnificent and it is a functioning mosque. It was in front of this mosque that Sultan Firoz Shah embedded an Ashoka Pillar, which had impressed the antiquarian sultan so much that he took to calling it Minar-e-Zarrin (golden minaret). The fort itself became a prototype for Mughal forts later, as it introduced the concept of public and private royal spaces which became the Mughal Diwan-e-Aam (public court) and Diwan-e-Khas (special court) with a separate area for the seraglio.

However, today Firoz Shah Kotla's local claim to fame is the resident spirits who grant wishes to the dispossessed and needy in and around Delhi. The cells and rooms under the mosque and the pillar are full of letters to these jinn, asking for the fulfilment of needs, *diya*s (oil lamps) as mark of respect, and flowers after the fulfilment of wishes. At any time of the day, you will find incense sticks, *diya*s, and candles burning in the nooks and corners of the Kotla. These serve as small dargahs to the jinn saints believed to be living there. Written petitions – mostly in Hindi but some also in Urdu and English – are stuck on to the walls of these nooks. They contain varied pleas – from seeking financial or legal help to protection from the evil eye and scheming in-laws. Wedding invitations are first brought here by the devotees to offer to these jinn saints. On Thursdays, those whose wishes have been fulfilled distribute pots of biryani and sweet rice.

In his book *Jinneology*, Anand Vivek Taneja writes that these petitions in the Tughlaq ruins are reminiscent of *shikwa*, a Perso-Islamic legal form of addressing one's complaints to the sovereign, practiced in the Delhi Sultanate. 'The letters written to the jinn-saints enact an intimate sovereignty,' writes Taneja, 'A paternalistic government whose justice reaches far beyond the categories of the care imposed by the post-colonial state on its subject population.'[23] That has also been my experience. Those who despair of justice in law courts or don't have the wherewithal to fight cases, and those whose emotional needs are not taken care of, come to the father figure that the jinn-saint is and present their *shikwa*.

Here one needs no money, no caste status or contact in the echelons of the government. Here, the powers that be treat everyone equally, and they bond with them in their despair and in their happiness. In a country threatened by narrow religious and sectarian divides, this free mingling of men and women, Muslims and non-Muslims, sharing of bread together without worrying about each other's caste or religion, petitioning together, is heart-warming to say the least.

How did the jinn suddenly populate this abandoned city? Taneja traces the history of the jinn-saints and links it to the disenchantments of the post-Nehruvian era and the atrocities of the Emergency in 1975–77. Many of the persons who came to pray here were from the areas worst affected by eviction, demolition drives, and the forced sterilization campaigns of those years: mainly working class Muslims and Dalits.

Through oral histories, Taneja fleshes out how the tradition of petitioning the saints emerged and the fascinating story of Laddu Shah, a black-marketeer-turned-healer. He was a gifted flute player and often played near the Ashoka pillar. The Laatwale Baba, as the pillar is known today, pleased by his sweet melody, granted him the gift of healing and helping people in distress.

There are very few visitors to the place except on Thursdays, when after 2 p.m. entry is free as people coming to pray, supplicate to the jinn, or make good their pledges after the fulfilment of their prayers – usually by distributing biryani and sweets.

A conversation with the imam and his friend in the Jami Masjid there reinforced my notions about the benevolent jinn. According to the imam, every masjid has a jinni, and they guard the citadel and in fact Delhi as a whole lot. As long as the jinn live in Delhi, no harm can come to it!

Jinn-saints aren't the only ones receiving letters. Similar petitions can be found in a *mandir* (temple) in Almora (Uttrakhand) called Chitti Mandir (Temple of Letters). These days with rising expenses and the stress of modern-day life, the dispossessed find that the most accessible places are the dargahs, temples, and churches. One can go and unburden ourselves, ask and hope for redressal – without having to spend or take favours.

Ultimately, we are all one in the court of Allah!

*Ai madad-gar jinn-o-insan ke,*
*Bigdiyon ko meri bana jaana*

[O helper of jinn and humans,
Solve my problems.]

– Jamila Khuda Baksh

# 17

# Expressing the Divine

*Nami danam chi manzil bood shab jaiy ki man boodam;*
*Baharsu raqs-e-bismil bood shab jaiy ki man boodam.*

[I wonder what was the place where I was last night,
All around me were half-slaughtered victims of love,
tossing about in agony.]

– Hazrat Amir Khusrau

The minute one thinks of Sufism, the two strong images that come to mind are qawwalis and Mevlana Jalaluddin Rumi's mystical verses. The power of music and poetry to convey a mystical experience is unparalleled; they are art forms that are very much a part of Sufi culture and dargahs and *khanqah*s. But there were many other mediums too that propagated the Sufi message and help in the union with the Divine. This chapter will deal with them.

'Sufism is the soul of Persian poetry, especially ghazal. In fact, ghazal has grown and developed with the rise of Sufistic ideas,' Maulana Shibli says. 'Sufism appeared in the third century AH (ninth century CE). But it reached its consummation in the fifth century AH (eleventh century CE), which is the first New Year Day of ghazal.'[1]

The early Sufis used Persian *rubayi* (quatrain) for their poetic expression. These are a kind of mystical epigrams which, according to Professor of Persian de Bruijn, is 'the terse formulation of a poetical idea, suitable to serve as a brief interruption in a conversation, a sermon or a prose composition. Because of the great variety of its uses, it is impossible to delimit the subject matter of the quatrain.'[2]

The first Sufi poet whose quatrains are known to be authentic is the eleventh-century dervish Baba Tahir Uryan Hamadani. His verses were full of his love for God whom he saw everywhere. For him life was 'a continuing fight against the soul that clings to this world; this struggle can only end in the final destruction of the "self", the most formidable obstacle on the path towards the Beloved.' In one of Baba Tahir's quatrains, physical death is welcomed as the delivery of the soul from its bondage to this world:

The great day when this grave shall hold me tight,
My head will rest on tiles and mud and stones.
The feet turned to the Qiblah, the soul set free,
My body will be in a fight with snakes and ants.[3]

The concept of *fana* and *baqa*, and the *nafs* or ego which prevents the self from a union with the Beloved was a very popular one in Sufi poetry:

Thus, moth to candle spoke: Be my Beloved!
The candle said: If you so madly love me,
Enter my flame; and be consumed by it
If you so badly want to be embraced.[4]

– Fariduddin Attar

*Qasida*s (panegyrics) were the next form to be used by Sufi poets, but it was the Arabic ghazal, which was passed onto Persian, Turkish, and Urdu, that transformed the mystical scene with its outpouring of love. In the thirteenth and fourteenth centuries, great ghazal writers such as Amir Khusrau of Delhi, Hafiz, and Sheikh Saadi of Shiraz took the ghazal form to dizzying heights as a form of mystical lyrical poetry. Today, ghazals are the most popular form of Urdu poetry in India, used more to express earthly rather than divine love and a genre that was once a way to express love of god is now often associated with expressions of romance.

The metaphors and tropes used for earthly love were used for the Divine Beloved, and perfect beauty became a reference to the perfect beauty of the poet's Beloved; the nightingale pining for the rose became a symbol of love and yearning of the Lover and Beloved; if spring was joy, autumn was decay, reminding the poet and readers of an ephemeral world.

Ghazals were the ideal vehicle to express the dominant theme in Sufism: love for the divine, with layers of meaning to each word which opened only for the initiated.

The famous Sufi, Mevlana Jalaluddin Rumi, is said to be the best-selling poet in America today, and one can commonly find quotes attributed to him on social media. The reason for Rumi's popularity is the universality of Islamic teachings, which were lost in the time between when he wrote it and us reading it.

Nizami's *Leyli Majnun* too has deep Sufi overtones and depicts the pain and obstacles that have to be overcome to be united with the beloved. The love that is shown is unconventional and 'stories talk about love that contravenes the social, sexual and religious convention'. Further,

> These repeated metaphors are analogical to the life of a Sufi. The Sufis, having been initiated to the esoteric world, perceive in a way incomprehensible to the ordinary man, and hence Sufis have been doubted upon through [the] ages. Their understandings and ways of life are not that of the ordinary people, and the Sufis do not tread on the known path. Afraid of the unknown as the human nature is, the society shuns the Sufi path, and so the stories reflect the discomfort and questions Sufis face every day in their life.[5]

So it comes as no surprise that the imagery used was also unconventional – with wine, the drunkard (*rind*), cupbearer (*saqi*), and intoxication used to express love or *ishq-e-haqiqi* for the divine. The lover destroys his ego for the ultimate union (*visaal*) with the Divine Beloved when all else is annihilated and the lover achieves *baqa*. These are all Sufi practices, as discussed above, understood on different levels as per different levels of sensibility and consciousness. An example of this is below:

> O cupbearer, brighten our goblet with the light of wine!
> O minstrel, tell how the world has succumbed to our desires!
> We have seen in the cup the reflection of the face of the Friend,

> O you who know nothing of the joy of our eternal wine-drinking! He whose heart has been made living by love never dies; our permanence is recorded within the pages of the cosmic text.[6]
>
> – Hafiz

Non-conformism was attractive, while authority became objects of derision and detestation.

Saiyid Naqi Hussain Jafri writes that Persian poetry '[f]rom Rumi onwards to modern times has been anti-establishment and non-conformist, an essential part of the teachings of Sufis.' He goes on to say:

> Persian poets explained Islamic doctrines in a mystical manner that was often seen as heretical and non-conformist... In the process, *shaikh, waiz* [preacher], *muhtasib* [keeper of public morals], *mimbar* [pulpit], *sajjada* [prayer mat], *tasbeeh* [rosary] and *zunnar*[sacred thread worn by Hindus] became the images that were targeted and censured while images like *rind* [drunkard], *maikada* [tavern] and *pir-emurghan* [tavern keeper] were celebrated and glorified.[7]

Thus Hafiz writes:

> Where is the pious doer and I
> The estray'd one, where
> Behold how far the distance, from
> His safe home to here.
> My heart fled from the cloister,
> And chant of monkish hymn.
> What can avail me sainthood,
> Fasting and punctual prayer.
> What is the truth shall light me
> To heaven's strait thoroughfare.[8]

The masnavi form of poetry (written in rhyming couplets) was made popular by Amir Khusrau, Attar, and of course Rumi.

Attar's *Manṭiq-uṭ-Ṭayr* (*Language of Birds*) with its allegorical references is a popular masnavi. The name itself is from Quran (27:16), where there is a reference to the favours bestowed by Allah on Prophet Solomon, one of which was to understand the speech of birds.

*Manṭiq-uṭ-Ṭayr* describes the journey of the soul in search of its true essence by using the symbol of the bird for the human soul. The birds gather to choose the worthiest of them as their sovereign and the hoopoe (*hud-hud*) describes a miraculous bird named Simurgh who lives at the end of the world. It was the *hud-hud* who brought the news of the magical throne of the Queen of Saba (Sheba) to prophet Sulaiman (Solomon) in the Quran.

The birds decide to make this thrilling journey only to realize how arduous it would be. Eventually, a small group, each representing a human fault, sets out with the hope who symbolizes the *pir*. The journey entails going through a desert with seven valleys, which represent the seven stations that a Sufi has to cross in life on his spiritual quest: these are search, love, knowledge, detachment, unity, bewilderment, and finally poverty and annihilation. Only 30 birds manage to reach, while the rest fall prey to the human weakness they represent.

The *Encyclopaedia Iranica* entry on the story concludes:

> [As they wait for an audience with Simurgh, they realize its] inaccessibility and self-sufficient majesty.Only after they have apprehended the vastness of the gulf between their own dependence and the Sīmorḡ's independence are they granted admission for an audience. ʿAṭṭār then consummates the epic with an affirmation of his cherished belief that man will find the sought supreme being, within himself, and he expresses his meaning through an ingenious pun: The 30 birds (sīmorḡ) find to their amazement that the Sīmorḡ is none other than their own selves.[9]

They have thus found their essence.

When I sit in the Yaarani Chabutra, listening to the rhythmic verses of *namidanam* reverberate throughthat pious courtyard, I am transported to the thirteenth and fourteenth century and compelled to imagine myself in the company of the saint's favourite, dancing, and singing about love for his *pir*. The chabutra, saturated with the feeling of divine love (*ishq-e-haqeeqi*) is occupied by disciples of the saint, who surrender themselves to Allah.

Today, qawwalis have become extremely popular and are being sung in films, parties, weddings and, of course, Sufi shrines. But does it serve the same purpose of 'hearing chanted verse (with or without accompanying instruments) in the company of others also seeking to participate in the dynamic dialogue between a human lover and the Divine Beloved'[10] that it was originally meant to? To understand this, we have to understand what *sama mehfil* (assembly of listening) and qawwali actually mean.

'*Sama* is the glue which binds diverse people, diverse practices and diverse beliefs and invites them to enter a shared space [the shrine] and in fact in that shared space it becomes the vehicle of deliverance.'[11] This description given to me by Sufi singer Dhruv Sangari (also known as Muhammad Bilal Chisty) offers us a precise description of *sama mehfil*s. The word *sama*, derived from Arabic, literally means listening and refers to the act of listening to sacred/mystical words accompanied by music.

The Sufi seeks to connect with Allah in a direct and intimate way and is willing to go out of their way to achieve the state whereby it is possible; *zikr* (remembrance) through music is one of the preferred paths to achieve this state. Elaborating on this, Regula Burckhardt Qureshi writes:

> Through the act of listening – *sama* – the Sufi seeks to activate his link with his living spiritual guide, with saints departed, and ultimately with God. At the same time, in opening himself to the powerful message of qawwali, he hopes for a spiritual experience of intensity and immediacy that transcends his conscious striving. The music serves to kindle the flame of his mystical love, to intensify his longing for mystical union, and even to transport him to a state of ecstasy and to sustain him there to the limit of his spiritual capacity.[12]

A lover likes nothing better than the constant remembrance of his beloved and direct communion with God is easy to establish through *sama mehfils* (acts of listening or hearing). These often involve the rhythmic chanting of Allah's name that induces *wajd* (state of religious ecstasy where direct communion with God is established). These *sama mehfils* were always conducted under the guidance of a sheikh. However, the emphasis should be on 'listening', which is the literal meaning of the word *sama*– and not on the singing itself. The listener should be spiritually attuned and morally purified for the music to produce the state of ecstasy or *wajd*.

Amongst the most popular *zikr* used to induce ecstasy are the words *Allah hu* (He is God).

The name Allah itself is the most perfect as it is composed of four Arabic letters, which is believed to correspond to the four elements, the four cardinal points, the four seasons.[13]

*Hu* is one of Allah's names. Omid Safi explains a point made by Ahmad Sam'ani in his commentary on divine names:

> Within the Islamic tradition, there is a notion that the sacred names of God have a grace beyond the mere meaning of them. There is an intimate and organic connection between the sacred sound, which may be said to possess a mantric quality. A beautiful examine of this is in the sound and meaning of Hu, the Divine name 'He', that indicates the Divine essence. The great sage Ahmad Sam'ani wrote an exquisite commentary on the Asma al-Husna (Beautiful Names of God). In it, he brings out something powerful about breath, prayer, and the Names of God. In Rawh al-arwah, Sam'ani mentions that the reason the name Hu is mentioned first in the litany of names mentioned in the Qur'an is that every other name (al-Malik, al-Quddus, al-Salam, al-Mu;min, al-Muhaymin, al-;Aziz, al-Jabbar, al-mutikabbir, etc.) is made through moving the tongue and the lips. However, Sam'ani says that the First name, Hu, is simply the breath coming from the chest. So he says that there is something about Hu that has to come from that realm beyond sound, beyond words, beyond language, and only from the heart. We are to call on God from that place before language.[14]

Music and *sama mehfils*, as a way of stimulating ecstasy, have been part of the lives of Sufi saints, and started gaining popularity from the ninth century onwards, and reached a peak in the thirteenth century under Mevlana Jalaluddin Rumi. It is said that he heard the words '*La ilaha Ilallah*' in the rhythmic beating of the goldbeaters' hammer and started dancing with one hand raised upwards, to receive, and the other pointing downwards, to give. This gave rise to the establishment of the whirling dervish of the Mevlavi order.

In India, *sama mehfils* were popularized by the Chishti saints who used music as a way of inducing trance or *haal*. They were established in Ajmer by Khwaja Muinuddin Chishti as a means for *zikr o fikr* (remembrance and meditation) and by the time the Chishti *khanqahs* were established in Delhi, they were in regular practice.

Khwaja Qutbuddin Bakhtiyar Kaki is known as *Shaheed-e-Muhabbat* (martyr of love) as he went into a state of *wajd* (spiritual ecstasy) induced by a couplet of Sheikh Ahmad Jam and died a few days later, as described in Chapter 5.

Hazrat Nizamuddin was extremely fond of *sama mehfils* and he considered them a source of spiritual enlightenment and sustenance. Even today the sound of qawwalis resonates in his dargah. Nizami records that 'When the Sheikh heard the mystic songs he went into ecstasy and tears flowed endlessly from eyes.'[15] He would sometimes gesture one of his disciples to dance in ecstasy.

It was in the dargah of Hazrat Nizamuddin Auliya that the qawwali as we know it today was developed by Hazrat Amir Khusrau, who is credited with composing the first-ever qawwali. It is said that the credit goes to him for creating a soulful fusion of Turkish, Arabic, and Persian influences with the north Indian Hindustani music traditions. The traditional qawwali is based on Indian *ragas*.

There are two versions of the story of how the first qawwali was composed. Here I discuss both, with the disclaimer that this is all hearsay passed down through generations and no documentary evidence regarding the validity of either could be found.

According to the first version, which I heard at the dargah of Hazrat Nizamuddin Auliya, once Hazrat Amir Khusrau was at the *khanqah* of the famous Chishti saint Hazrat Bu Ali Shah Qalandar in Panipat. The latter asked him to sing something in praise of the Amir-ul-Momineen (leader of men), Hazrat Ali. Hazrat Amir Khusrau obeyed Hazrat Bu Qalandar and set Rasul-e-Khuda's *qaul* to music. '*Qaul*' literally means 'a saying' and it refers to the sayings of the Prophet.

The most popular *qaul* of the Prophet is:

*Man kunto maula,*
*Fa haza Ali-un maula.*

[Whoever accepts me as a *maula* (master),
Ali is his master too.]

It was set to music by the genius Amir Khusrau, who did it on the spot. To give body and soul to the music and help induce a trance, he added the meaningless mystic chants of the famous *tarana* (a form explained later on in the chapter):

*Dara dil-e-dara dil-e-dar-e-daani*
*Hum tum tanana nana, nana nana ray*
*Yalali yalali yala, yala ray.*[16]

Be that as it may, the *qaul* or saying of the Prophet was put to music and developed into qawwali by Hazrat Amir Khusrau. This is documented in his own book *Ijas-e-Khusravi*. Many people wrongfully attribute the saying to Hazrat Amir Khusrau, although he merely set it to music.

The 800-year-old tradition of qawwali continues till date.

Dhruv Sangari, who was given the name Muhammad Bilal Chisty by his *pir-o-murshid*, Syed Najm-ul Chisty of Ajmer Sharif, took an oath of allegiance with him when he was 19 or 20 years of age. Sangari had already read the *kalima* and accepted Islam before he met his *pir o murshid* in Ajmer. Dhruv, as he is still popularly called, trained under Ustad Meraj Nizami and later under Ustad Nusrat Fateh Ali Khan. He was the maestro's last student, and as a 16-year-old, spent a year with him in USA, Pakistan, and India. He later returned to India and resumed his singing under the famous Ustad Meraj Ahmed Nizami, a descendant of the original qawwal *bacchas* trained by Hazrat Amir Khusrau. He had become Ustad Meraj's student in 1995–96, before he met Ustad Nusrat Fateh Ali Khan.

According to Dhruv:

> The legends connected to the origin of qawwalis are part of oral intangible culture; so, unless some scholars sift through hitherto untapped archival material it is difficult to differentiate between facts and traditions. We normally rely on oral traditions that we have assimilated unquestioningly from our ancestors and we pass it on to our children. There is no doubt that Hazrat Amir Khusrau gave it the present shape and taught it informally to his coterie, disciples and friends.

He adds that there is a group that raises questions over the Hindi verses attributed to Hazrat Amir Khusrau as these are not found in any of his *diwans*.

Dhruv, who has a huge collection of oral traditions, shared an interesting anecdote about him as well. Once Hazrat Amir Khusrau was asked why he had never penned down his vast collection of Hindi poetry. The poet replied that it was said for his friends and was created informally as an experiment. Dhruv points out that these organic experiments of that age gave rise to a rich and vast treasure of poetry and music.

There are different sub genres in qawwali: *qaul, qalbana, tarana, naksh,* and *gul.* The last two have lapsed into obscurity, but the rest remain. The qawwali includes *hamd* (poems in praise of Allah), *naat* (poems in praise of Prophet Muhammad), *manqabat* (poems in praise of Ali ibn Abi Talib and Sufi saints), *madah* (poems in praise of eminent personalities), and ghazals (poems set in a particular poetic structure and suited for emotions of love, loss and longing). All qawwals will begin with a *hamd*, then go on to a *naat* and *manqabat* and so on.

The word *tarana* itself means a song in Persian. Ustad Amir Khan (1912–1973) devoted a great part of his life to studying the *tarana* and deciphered the meaning of seemingly meaningless words and syllables followed sometimes by the *bols* (words coined to denote the various sounds of instruments) of tabla and sometimes by Persian poetry. According to Ustad Amir Khan, some of the *bol*s and their meanings are as follows:

*Tanan Dar Aa*: Enter my body.
*O Dani*: He knows.
*Tu Dani*: You know.
*Na Dir Dani*: You are the Complete Wisdom.
*Tom*: I am yours; I belong to you.
*Yala*: Ya Allah
*Yali*: Ya Ali[17]

Other musicologists have also tried to explain their meanings; for example:

*Dar*: *Bheetar*, *Aandar* (inside)
*Dara*: *Andar Aa* (get in or come inside)
*Dartan: Tanke Aandar*(inside the body)
*Tanandara*: *Tanke Aandar Aa* (Come inside the body)
*Tom*: *Main Tum Hun* (I am you)
*Nadirdani*: *Tu Sabse Adhik Janata Hai* (You know more than anyone else)
*Tandardani*: *Tanke Aandarka Jannewala* (One who knows what is inside the body)[18]

Qawwalis were traditionally sung in the classical genre of *khayal,* which was developed in north India in the Mughal era. One of its famous exponents was Niamat Khan, also known as Sadarang, who was the court musician under Mohammad Shah (r.1719–48). This classical genre also became the medium for qawwalis being performed in Sufi dargahs.

A modern qawwali involves a performance by a lead singer and a group of secondary singers and those who clap and sing the refrain. Clapping is an important part of the rhythmic experience as it energizes and elevates the mood of the listener. The lead singer or singers will sit in the centre in the front row. The lead singer normally plays the harmonium himself, and there may be one more harmonium player, and a couple of percussionists as well as other instrumentalists such as dhaf, sarangi, and rabab players. The harmonium players are in the front row, while the percussionists and other instrumentalists will sit at the back. The whole party sits cross-legged in two rows. The success of the lead singer or singers depends on their ability to induce a trance, and their interaction with the audience. There is direct communion with the audience, and the lead singers exhort them to get involved and will often ad-lib verses to do that.

The tempo in the middle becomes faster as it proceeds, and towards the end, the qawwal will repeat mystical chants that are very often meaningless and only aimed at inducing a trance.

As a child, I remember hearing the great qawwal Habib Painter, who had been given the title *Bulbul-e-Hind* by Prime Minister Nehru. There were many other real qawwals, but in recent times, it was Ustad Nusrat Fateh Ali Khan who brought great popularity to this form amongst the masses.

Qawwali is still a male bastion in dargahs. Though Abida Parveen is very popular, she sings more *sufiana kalam*s (devotional verses steeped in mysticism sung in *sama mehfil*s) and kafis (a kind of short poem) that don't require such a big group of backup singers.

The qawwali starts with an *alaap* that is usually without musical instruments and sets the tone. This is followed by some verses which, though not part of the main song, also help set the tone. Very often these are kafis or dohas. The lead singer often adds additional verses (from other poems apart from the main one) to the main song, which is called *girah lagana* (tying a knot) to enhance the mood of the listener. *Girah* verses become especially important when the main lyric text is short as in the qaul, *man kunto maula*. These verses would be thematically the same as in the case of the qaul, praises of Ali.

In 2013–14, as part of the Basant celebrations in a dargah, I had the good fortune to listen to Ustad Meraj Ahmed – one of the foremost exponents of the qawwali in the twenty-first century – a year before he died. Though by that time he was very frail, he would lead the singing in the procession, often adding Persian *girah* verses to his recitation. Listening to any qawwali is always a joyful experience but when one hears a master qawwal adroit in the art of *girah lagana,* it has the ability to transport the listener into a whole other world.

> *Girah* verses are usually sung in recitation while the beat of drums recedes to the background. Sometimes the lines of the girah are sung by the leading vocalist alone, but he is frequently lent vocal support by at least part of the group. The last line of the *girah* acts as a punchline leading musically and emantically back to the salient text and it forms an exception to this practice. All the members of the group join in singing it, and it is usually repeated only once. Entire *girah* verses can be repeated after briefly returning to the salient text.[19]

*Takrar* (repetition) and *dohrana* (repeating) are a very important part of qawwali and the side singers will keep doing the repetition in a certain sequence, to increase the tempo and 'give the listeners enough time to grasp the meaning of the verse.' On the other hand, *takrar* 'is resorted to when some listener is deeply affected by the performance or undergoes a mystical state. Such states are by Sufis attributed to the combined effect of musical and poetic phrase, and upholding them requires repeating the phrase in question until the state abates.'[20]

The length of a qawwali depends on how well it is received and if the qawwal has managed to get his audience into a trance. It can be anywhere from 15 minutes to an hour.

The lead singer and second lead are very sensitive to the audience and will pick out the most spiritually attuned listener and address the words and refrain to him. They know exactly what to emphasize, repeat, or improvise with the *girah*.

At a Delhi college in 2015, I saw the popular qawwali singers from Pakistan, Farid Ayaz and Abu Muhammad[21], sway an entire audience of college students more attuned to Western pop than Indian semi-classical. They chose songs and interspersed its *girah* verses that they knew would resonate with them. They sang from their hearts and seemed to intuitively know how to touch the heart of the listener. They not only transported the listener to another world but they seemed to have reached there too.

The qawwali has a classical and semi-classical base and its structure is more that of folk music. When sung in a dargah, the listeners shower the qawwals with money called *vel*. The etiquette for this is that it is first offered to the *sajjada nasheen* (hereditary successor) present in the gathering and only then to the qawwals.

Today qawwali has become very popular in films, but it is important to remember that this is devotional music meant to touch our inner core and bring about a state of trance, or at least an enhanced feeling of spirituality, something that songs in movies never do.

When I had the good fortune to visit the Masjid-e-Nabvi, the Prophet's mosque in Medina (Saudi Arabia), I found myself in a daze, singing the words of the famous qawwali sung mentioned above:

> *Bhar de jholi meri Yaa Muhammad*
>
> Fill my bag [physical and spiritual] O Muhammad.[22]

In 2001, we had been going through a financial crisis and I prayed fervently to Allah for relief. One night I dreamt that a veiled lady was beckoning me to follow her in a huge hypostyle hall with striped marble arches. When I related this dream to my younger sister, who had lived in Saudi Arabia, she identified it as Masjid-e Nabvi. A year later my husband got a job in Saudi Arabia and I joined him and immediately went for umrah. [Was it Bibi Fatima once again who had heard my pleas?]

A very unique aspect of devotional music in India is the adoption of relatable Indian idioms and symbols, particularly those connected with brides and wedding ceremonies. This can be seen in the *marsiya* (elegiac poetry to commemorate Imam Hussain's sacrifice) of Mir Anis or the qawwali of Hazrat Amir Khusrau. In the Indian milieu, there is ample imagery of a bride and her ornamentation. Her bangles symbolize her married state, and there are many qawwalis that talk of green bangles on the bride's arms. The quest for the beloved, the longing, separation, and the union were mostly conveyed through such metaphors in the feminine voice. Maternal bonding and love was another popular metaphor.

The music and structure itself are a blend of Arabic, Persian, Turkish, and Indian elements, which combine into a glorious whole. Take for instance:

*Gori gori bayyan, hari hari churiyan,*
*Bayyan pakar dhar leeni ray mosay naina milaikay.*
*Bal bal jaaon mein toray rang rajwa,*
*Apni see kar leeni ray mosay naina milaikay.*

[My fair arms full of green glass bangles,
You have held my hand and trapped me withjust one glance.
May I give my life over you, O cloth dyer,
You have dyed me in your hue with just that one glance.]

*Khusrau Nijaam kay bal bal jayyiye,*
*Mohay Suhaagan keeni ray mosay naina milaikay,*
*Chhap tilak sab cheeni ray mosay naina milaikay,*
*May Khusrau's life be sacrificed over Nijam.*

[You have made me your bride with just that one glance;
You have stolen my identity with your glance.]

The symbolism and allegorical references of Sufi poetry often escape the uninitiated. Here, wine is a symbol of devotion to God, with God Himself being the *saqi* (cupbearer). The *rind* (drinker) who is intoxicated is the seeker of the divine. The Beloved (God) can intoxicate the seeker with just one glance, and the seeker loses his identity in the identity of his beloved – to become just a reflection of the divine. Although wine is forbidden as per Islamic law, 'the Qur'an depicts the inhabitants of paradise with "a full cup" (78:34) or "a pure drink, sealed with a seal of musk" (83:25–26). This paradisal imagery is in part the source of the extensive wine symbolism employed in later Sufi poetry.'[23]

In many *sufiana kalams*, there is a reference to the *ghoonghat* (veil). The veil represents the distance between the Sufi lover and the Divine Beloved. For instance Baba Bulleh Shah writes:

*Ghoonghat chuk le sajna.*

[Lift thy veil, O beloved]

The ultimate goal is the revelation (lifting the veil) by the Divine Being to the lover. The night journey of the Prophet known as the *Miraj* is described by using the metaphor of the lifting of veils.

Since the lover seeks a union with the beloved, it was but natural for bridal references to creep in. The lover becomes the shy young bride and, as is common in north Indian households, green glass bangles become a symbol of her marriage.

This imagery is further strengthened by Hazrat Amir Khusrau's Persian verses, which describe a scene where lovers are in the presence of God and are writhing and tossing around in the agony of love:

*Nami danam chi manzil bood shab jaiy ki man boodam;*
*Baharsu raqs-ebismil bood shab jaiy ki man boodam.*
*Pari paikar nigaar-esarw qadde laala rukhsare;*
*Sarapa aafat-edil bood shab jaiy ki man boodam.*
*Khuda khud meer-emajlis bood andar laamakan Khusrau;*
*Muhammad shamm-emehfil bood shab jaiy ki man boodam.*

[I wonder what was the place where I was last night,
All around me were half-slaughtered victims of love,
tossing about in agony.
There was a nymph-like beloved with cypress-like form
and tulip-like face,
Ruthlessly playing havoc with the hearts of the lovers.
God himself was the master of ceremonies in that heavenly court,
oh Khusrau, where (the face of) the Prophet too was shedding light
like a candle.]

(translated by S.A.H Abidi)[24]

When Hazrat Nizamuddin Auliya left this world, Hazrat Amir Khusrau was in Bengal on an official mission. He rushed back on hearing the news and in a state of acute sorrow is reported to have said this doha:

*Gori sovay sej par, mukh par daaray kes,*
*Chal Khusrau ghar aapnay, saanjh bhayee chahu des.*

[The fair maiden sleeps on her bed, with her curled lock hiding her face;
O Khusrau, return home, the whole world is now dark.][25]

The bed here is a reference to the marital one, as the bride is now about to be united with her beloved, while the *kes*, curled lock refers to divine mysteries. Hazrat Amir Khusrau predicted his death and passed away within six months of his master's death, as he was unable to bear the separation from his *pir-o-murshid*.

Baba Bulleh Shah expresses his anguish at the separation from his *pir*, who was angry with him, and wishes to win back his trust through music knowing Shah Inayat's love for music:

*Tere ishq nachaya*
*Kar ke thaiya ve thaiya*
*Cheti bawdi ve tabiba*
*Nahi te main mar gayiaan*

[Your love has made me dance;
In sacred ecstasy
Come soon, O physician of my heart,
Or I will surely die.]

My favourite remains the famous Pakistani qawwal Aziz Mian (1942–2000). He was a rarity amongst modern qawwals as he wrote his own lyrics. His raspy voice and lost-in-devotion style were very conducive to producing a *haal* or trance. He wrote more than 3,000 verses presenting intoxication as closeness to God. His *Main sharabi* (*I'm a drunkard*) resulted in thinly veiled criticism from the very popular Sabri Brothers in their qawwali, *Sharab chod di maine* (*I have left wine*).

Aziz Mian replied by writing one of his immortal qawwalis:

*Hai kambakht, tu ne pii hi nahin.*

[O unlucky one, you have never drunk.]

The lyrics are evocative and equate drinking with love of the Divine, intoxication in that love via *sabr* (patience) and *tawakkul* (faith in Allah) – both high virtues. As he goes on to sing:

*Mere sher'on ke haqeeqat mein naa maa'ni samjha,*
*Baada-e-haq ko tu angoor ka paani samjha.*

[You didn't understand the truth in the meaning of my verse,
Don't confuse
The wine of truth with the water of grapes.]

Music and dance were not the only metaphors of divine ecstasy. Each poet saint used idioms and metaphors from their own life or from society around them.

This fondness for *sama mehfil*s and qawwalis in the Chishti dargahs was frowned upon by the ulemas and orthodox Muslims; the ulemas deemed them un-Islamic. Maulana Jamali in Siyar-ul-Arifin has described a famous incident regarding this. He writes that some plaintiffs who were jealous of Hazrat Nizamuddin complained to Sultan Ghiyasuddin Tughlaq that the saint had no other work except to spend time in *sama mehfil*s and listen to music and the sarod, which is forbidden for the followers of Imam Hanafi (a sect of Sunni Muslims). They further complained that this was the saint's pastime and thus the sultan should summon the learned men of the city, form a *mahzar* (an assembly) and summon the saint along with all those companions of his who participated in these music assemblies that were against shariah. The sultan made arrangements for such a *mahzar* to be held and Sheikh Jamali writes that 253 exceptional, distinguished, and learned men of the city were invited. The saint came with his followers and mendicants. Accompanying him was also Maulana Fakhruddin Zarradi who too participated in the *sama mehfil*s and was a scholar who could interpret (the Quran) at his own authority.[26]

The sultan himself started the debate and turned towards Qazi Ruknuddin Walwaji, the chief judge of the kingdom and the saint's biggest opponent.

The *qazi* challenged the saint, asking him to produce evidence that could justify his activities – listening to music and the sarod. The saint presented a hadith of the Prophet where the Prophet himself had permitted his wife Ayesha to listen to singing and instruments – once at a wedding, and another time on the occasion of Eid.[27]

The *qazi* insisted on being given some proof from Imam Hanifa. This angered the saint who said, 'All praise is for Allah! Despite there being a saying of Mustafa (*Sallallaho Alaihai wa Sallum*), you demand something from the sayings of Hanafis!'[28] He further said that he would be dismissed from his post for the disrespect he was showing the friends of Gods (the Auliyas).

While this conversation was taking place Maulana Alemuddin Allama, son of the daughter of Hazrat Sheikh-ul-Islam Bahauddin Zakaria, arrived. The sultan ran to welcome him, but the sheikh first turned towards Hazrat Nizamuddin and honoured him and paid his respects.

He was curious as to why the saint had been summoned here. The Sultan replied that a *mahzar* had been summoned so that the question over the legality of *sama* in Islam could be solved, and he had been sent by God at just the right time so that he could reveal the truth.

The sheikh replied,

> I have wandered in Mecca, Medina, Misr (Egypt) and Sham (Syria). Despite the presence of the great magnitude of the learned men, the illustrious spiritual guides listen to sama. None forbids! Without any doubt, the sama is permissible for one who is worthy of it! Hazrat-i-Sheikh and his companions are the men of Allah, men of accomplishments and the men of state, due to whose blessings this thing has an effect in the group of mendicants and they have proved sama from Hazrat Rasul Allah Sallallaho Alaihai wa Sallum and even the wajd (ecstasy).[29]

On hearing this, the sultan got up and with great deference and respect allowed the saint to leave.

Qawwalis are a feature of all Chishti dargahs, especially on Thursdays and during the *urs* celebrations. To prevent a division amongst the people, Hazrat Roshan Chiragh-e-Dilli, discouraged the singing of qawwali during his time and even today, qawwalis aren't regularly performed in his dargah. According to Siyar-ul-Arifin, he didn't like musical instruments and preferred clapping in his *sama mehfil*s. He got into a state of ecstasy at this couplet:

Sight in the eyes has become defective
Otherwise my beloved is not hidden from anyone.[30]

As in *sama mehfil*s, when qawwali is performed in a dargah, it is always with the *peerzada/sajjada nasheen* sitting and guiding. No qawwal will begin without taking their permission.

It will follow a particular order, beginning with a *hamd* (praise of Allah) followed by a *naat* (praise of the Prophet) and then a tribute to Hazrat Ali from whom the Chishtis claim descent. After that it will focus on the particular occasion.

Arman Ali Dehlvi, a young and popular Sufi singer in Delhi, says:

> Music is the sacred medium to reach the divine or to attain self-realization. It has been used forever in all places of worship such as temples, churches and dargahs. In the Indian subcontinent, qawwali emerged in the *khanqah*s and dargahs to elevate the spiritual state of the Sufis, as they too need music after a certain point of meditation to take them into deep trance. These days, thanks to Bollywood and Facebook, qawwali is at the height of its popularity and people are flocking to Hazrat Nizamuddin's *dargah* for qawwali and kebabs.[31]

Hazrat Amir Khusrau's immortal verse describes Sufism in just a few lines:

*Chhap tilak sab chheeni ray mosay naina milaikay,*
*Chhap tilak sab cheeni ray mosay naina milaikay,*
*Prem bhati ka madhva pilaikay,*
*Matvali kar leeni ray mosay naina milaikay.*

With just one glance you have snatched away my looks and identity,
With just one glance you have snatched away my looks and identity,
By serving me the wine of love,
You have intoxicated me with just that one glance.

In the eighteenth century, Sufi poets such as Mir Dard, Mazhar Jan-e-Janan wrote mystic Urdu ghazals that became very popular.

Sufism not only gave us a new genre of Hindustani music, it also helped propagate it. Hazrat Amir Khusrau (1253–1325) gave us the genres of *qaul*, *qalbana*, *tarana,* and many new *raga*s, while Pir Bodhan of Barnawa (near Baghpat in Uttar Pradesh) became a centre for music to flourish where musicians from Delhi, Deccan, and Jaunpur gathered at his house. Indian classical music in the fifteenth century got a fresh impetus under Sultan Hussain Sharqi (r.1461–79) of Jaunpur and Pir Bodhan (d. 1497–98). Musicians from the Deccan came to Pir Bodhan's *khanqah* and qawwali and *tarana* flourished there.

Apart from *qaul* and *tarana,* Hindu devotional songs were also sung in *khanqah*s as is evident from the incident given below, described by Professor Saiyid Zaheer Hussain Jafri at a conference.

> We come across similar examples from the Chishti centres. We had the occasion to examine some data from the Upper Gangetic valley, which requires a proper perspective. It has been recorded about the *khanqah* of Shaikh Nur Qutb-I Alam (d. 1415) that during the *sama* gatherings even the vishnupadas (devotional songs from the Vaishnavite tradition) were recited, when it was objected to, the Shaikh is reportedly said to have replied that 'even Qur'an has the stories of Fir'au, Haman and Namrud. These verses are recited with equal reverence and nobody object to that'. Hence, he seems to have justified the singing of the vishnupadas in the *sama* gatherings at his *khanqah*.[32]

Muhammad Ghaus Gwaliori, the Sufi master and the writer of *Bahr ul-Hayat*, influenced Tansen, the famous singer in Akbar's reign. Today, Tansen sleeps in eternal bliss next to his master's shrine in Gwalior.

In the reign of Mughal emperor Muhammad Shah 'Rangeela' (r. 1719–48), music reached its zenith in Delhi.

Khwaja Mir Dard (1720–85), a Sufi saint of the Naqshbandi Majdudi *silsilah*, was a mystic poet. His greatness lay in translating his mysticism into verse.

*Tujhi ko jo yaan jalwa farma na dekha,*
*Baraabar hai duniya ko dekha na dekha..*

[If I did not see you here,
It's irrelevant whether I saw the world or not]

He was also skilled in music and 'considered *khayal* as an impressive composition, which gladdens the heart and elevates the soul. For this reason most of the Sufi orders have included it in their worship', according to the famous nineteenth century Urdu scholar, Muhammad Hussain Azad.[33]

Under the last Mughal emperor, Bahadur Shah Zafar, qawwali and *khayal gayki* (style of Indian classical singing) received great patronage, and the famous singer Tanras Khan (a descendant of the qawwal *bachhe*) flourished. The emperor, himself being an ordained Sufi who enjoyed the qawwali experience, often visited the dargahs of Hazrat Nizamuddin Auliya and Qutub Sahib.

A very popular qawwali sung in dargahs is *Kanhaiya yaad hai kuch bhi hamari* (*O Kanhaiya, do you remember us at all*?) written by Nawab Sadiq Jung Bahadur Hilm of Hyderabad.

*Haqaiq-e-Hindi*, a dictionary written in 1566 by Abdul Wahid Bilgrami, explained the meaning of Hindi mystical words used in *dhrupad* songs in the first section, the second section allegorically explains the words used in Vaishnavite songs in Braj Bhasha of the Mathura region, while the third gives the Sufi explanation of words used in Hindi Sufi tradition.[34]

Bilgrami writes that Krishna and his other Hindavi names are used to indicate the perfect man or insan-e kamil. According to him, all the symbols and names used in Krishna songs are indicative of some Sufi theme: the *gopi*s are angels or sometimes the reality of life in relation to the unity of Being, the flute indicates the appearance of existence out of void, Kans is the *nafs* (ego), while Yashoda is divine mercy, which God has appointed to the worldly. Bilgrami also considers Mathura to be the temporary station in the road to *marifa* while Dwarka is the permanent station of Sufis.

In fact, such allegories were not unusual, for:

> In Khusrau's Hindavi poetry, his pīr is called the *jag ujiyāro* (world illuminator) and mahārāj (emperor) along with a number of other

> epithets that were shared among devotees of different faiths in India. While literature produced at the royal courts was meant for the international, cosmopolitan audience of the broader Persianate world. By contrast, the works found in Sufi *khānaqāhs* had a more local and socially inclusive audience. The entire body of Khusrau's Hindavi poems is based on oral traditions and has been inextricably merged with other folk songs and poems.[35]

The tradition of mystical music gave rise to some beautiful genres and among them are the Assamese *zikir* (also called *jikir*) and *zari* (*jari*).

I came to know of this thanks to Teresa Rahman, the editor of the magazine *Thumbprint*. She introduced me to 58-year-old Samsuddin Ahmed as 'a man on a mission – to keep the age-old tradition[s] of zikir and zari alive.'

While *zikir*, as the name suggests, is the remembrance and praise of Allah, *zari* is in the tradition of the north Indian *marsiya* and commemorates the martyrdom of Imam Hussain. In Utpola Bora's words:

> Zikir, took root in Assam during the seventeenth century within the socio-cultural framework instituted by Bhakti movement of Saint Srimanta Sankardev (1449–1568) and under the patronage of Ahom (1200–1800) kings.
>
> Zikirs were mainly composed and popularized by the seventeenth-century Sufi saint and poet Hazrat Shah Miran, popularly known as Ajan Fakir.[36]

As was a common practice of the Sufi saints, they steeped their language in the idiom of the locals and many a times borrowed from them, too. *Zikir* was oral and transmitted orally and was only written down in the last century. The language used was the local language and dialects with a few Arabic and Persian words.

Azaan Pir was greatly influenced by the Vaishnavites and the teaching and music of Sankardeva. It is in this genre that he composed praise of Allah, thus building a bridge between communities. This bridge was reinforced by Samsuddin Ahmed, who says that he is often invited to the *naamghar* (prayer houses of followers of the Vaishnavite saint Sankardev) and even at celebrations in honour of the local festival of Bihu. This Islamic musical tradition is also a fine example in communal harmony, and singers and the accompanists on table and dotara are from other communities.

In fact, over the past decade, Ahmed has been facing opposition from the clergy who deem singing un-Islamic, especially since the *ijtima* (religious gatherings) organized by the Jamaat-e-Islami Hind actively preached against it. I am sure the fact that his *zikir* and *zari*, a combination of Sufi and Vaishnavi cultures of Assam, must be exacerbating the opposition further.

A beautiful verse that embodies the intertwining of the Sufi and Vaishnavite traditions in *zikir* is:

*Mur Monot Bhed Bhav Nai, O Allah;*
*Mur Monot Bhen Por Nai, O Allah;*
*Hindu Ki Musolman, Ekei Allahar Farmaan,*
*Gorethane kabar sari sari*
*Hinduk puribo Mominal garibo.*

[There is no discrimination in my mind, O Allah
Hindus and Muslims are bound by the same set of divine rules;
The act of cremating a Hindu and the entombing of a Muslim only signify one end – Death for all.]

Hearing Ahmed sing the verse was a sublime experience.

Ahmed, with Teresa Rahman as the translator for me, described the verse's similarities to local folk songs. These similarities are made even more conspicuous by the fact that it is often accompanied by a dance akin to the well-known Bihu dance of Assam, which is usually performed during marriages with the men forming a circle before they begin. Even in this, the lyrics are in praise of Allah.

Ahmed picked up this tradition from singers in his village.

While *zikir* itself does not take the listener into a trance, Ahmed tells me that during the *urs* of Azaan Pir and Langar Shah Mazar in Golaghat, there are some *fakir*s who sing and go into a kind of trance by repeating the word 'Allah'. This very similar to the state of ecstasy produced in a qawwali where the words 'Allah Hu' are chanted repeatedly.

*Sufiana kalam* refers to mystical devotional poetry. It is mostly written in vernacular languages, popularly from Punjab, Sindh, and Gujarat. Of this, the most popular is kafi (a genre of classical Sufi poetry in Punjabi or Sindhi), ghazals, dohas, *sakhi*s (stories about Guru Nanak ji), and masnavis.

These verses are meant to be sung, and in recent years Abida Parveen, the legendary Pakistani singer, has done much to popularize them. Popular poets from the past such as Baba Farid, Baba Bulleh Shah, Shah Hussain, Shah Abdul Latif Bhittai, Kabir, Shaikh Hamiddudin Nagauri, Sachal Sarmast, and Surdas wrote in the vernacular.

In a qawwali, the lead singer will often incorporate many of the poetic forms and very often qawwals begin their performance with a kafi or doha and then go on to a ghazal. The vishnupadas of Surdas and Kabir were also popular in *sama mehfils*.

In a kafi, the first and second lines act as a refrain either singly or together. The word is derived from the Arabic language and means a group, though it requires just a single vocalist, and harmonium, tabla, and dholak players. In it, the emphasis is on the words not on the music.

The *Qadriya silsilah* is blessed with some of the most outstanding and popular poets in today's times. Sultan Bahu and Bulleh Shah are the two most popular ones. Bulleh Shah expressed his love for his master Shah Inayat Qadiri and his rejection of religious orthodoxy through his kafis, which afforded him great flexibility. One of his most popular kafis is:

*Makkay gayaan, gal mukdee naheen,*
*Pawain sow sow jummay parrh aaeey.*

[Going to Mecca is not the ultimate,
Even if hundreds of prayers are offered.]

*Ganga gayaan, gal mukdee naheen,*
*Pawain sow sow gotay khaeeay.*

[Going to River Ganges is not the ultimate,
Even if hundreds of cleansing[s] (baptisms) are done.]

*Gaya gayaan gal mukdee naheen,*
*Pawain sow sow pand parrhaeeay.*

[Going to Gaya is not the ultimate,
Even if hundreds of worships are done (sic).]

*Bulleh Shah gal taeeyon mukdee*
*Jadon mainu dillon gawaeye*

[Bulleh Shah the ultimate [thing to do] is
When the 'I' is removed from the heart!][37]

In Kashmir, mystical verse found expression in the *vaakh* (speech) of the Shaivite devotee Lalla and in the *shruk*s (poems) of her disciple and Sufi saint, Nund Rishi. You may remember that the latter was born and raised as Sheikh Nuruddin Wali before he went on to become mystic who founded the Rishi order in Kashmir in the fifteenth century. Syed Affan Yesavi, a Sufi scholar from Kashmir, says:

> Nund Rishi is considered the symbol of Kashmir and the guiding light of its people. He wrote in Kashmiri, the common man's language, and used his poetry as a tool to spread the knowledge of the Absolute. He says in one of his shruks:
>
> *Laila ilallah sahi kauram*
> *Wahi kauram panun pan,*
> *Wajood trawith maujood saurum,*
> *Her maukh wuchum panun pan.*[38]
>
> [No sooner did I proclaim the unity of God
> Than I surrendered myself to His jurisdiction,
> Diffused my being in His Omnipresence –
> I remained reflecting on His Omnipotence!]

'Mystical thought was at the core of all the arts, including poetry, as creative activity was seen as a way to comprehend the complexities of the universe and the role of the divine. This was a powerful metaphor that permeated both Sufi and courtly spheres of society.'[39]

– Sunil Sharma, Professor of Persianate and Comparative Literature, Boston University

Sufi saints were very learned themselves and encouraged learning. They and their disciples produced some high-quality mystical literature, which acted as guides for others on the path of Sufism – be it Data Ganj Baksh's Persian treatise on Sufism and its doctrines and practices, the *Kashf al-Mahjub,* or *malfuz* literature.

*Malfuz* literature originated in Iran but here we look at it in the context of medieval India. It not only records the lives and the utterances of the Sufi saints, but is also a valuable record of the times more broadly. Court chronicles contain a record of the political and administrative triumphs, failures and problems of kings then, in addition to the solutions they employed, but *malfuz* literature describes the life and problems of common people. The first example of *malfuz* literature that was written in India is *Fawaid al-Fu'ad*, a record of the life and utterances of Hazrat Nizamuddin Auliya, compiled by Amir Hasan Sijzi.

According to Delhi University's History professor, Saiyid Zaheer Hussain Jafri, *Fawaid al-Fu'ad* was the first book of its kind in India. No one before had ever written about the day-to-day interactions, reactions and teachings of a Sufi Sheikh in his *khanqah*.[40] He says:

In this book, you find the principles of Sufism being talked about in the simplest of terms by the great sheikh, and we also see that every section of society is represented. The sheikh is not only talking to the elites but to the common man as well. It's not that sheikhs didn't speak earlier, but a mature scholar, recognizing the value of these discourses, recorded it for posterity. The entire book is in the form of conversations supported by examples. It is a lively speech that captures the reader's imagination.[41]

Very simply written, this book is an important historical, social, and literary document as it records contemporary life and society and is a great gift to Sufis and students of Sufism. In fact, Amir Khusrau offered to exchange all his works for it. It is also important because the saint himself checked the account's veracity.

However, these *malfuz*s and spiritual treatises were not accessible, because of their language and complexity of thought, to the common man who came to the *khanqah*s and later dargahs. What influenced them instead were folk literature and music.

Hazrat Nizamuddin Auliya encouraged his disciple Amir Khusrau to use the local language Hindavi, which is now called Urdu. This was to connect to the common masses and speak to them in their language.

Under the Sur dynasty, when poet Shah Muhammad Farmuli was asked why he wrote in Hindavi, and not in the court language of Persian, he replied that his beloved were Hindi (Indians) and they could not understand Farsi (Persian).

In fact, Sufi saints adopted local dialects and languages everywhere they settled as a means of communication with the local populace. Nizami writes:

> They invested the local languages with the dignity they deserved and prescribed devotional practices in them. Their aim was emotional integration and they did not consider language an impediment in the realization of that objective. Their motto was: To be of one heart is better than to be of one tongue.[42]

This gave rise to a beautiful body of music and literature that symbolizes Sufi thought for us.

Sufi literature was important not only for its mystic content but because they also captured the spirit of the age – the zeitgeist. They described a society where people were living compatibly in some part due to the Sufi saints.

> Their broad and tolerant outlook paved [the] way for the liquidation of social and linguistic barriers between the various

> culture groups of India; while their pantheistic approach brought them very close to the treasures of ancient Hindu religious thought, particularly the Upanishads, and created an atmosphere favourable for the exchange of ideas at a higher level. One of the most significant elements in their thought was their concept of religion, which was not merely catholic and humanitarian but also dynamic and revolutionary.[43]

Sufi literature in India also included *maktubat*– a collection of letters written by the saints on various issues including Sufi doctrines and political issues, *tazkira* (Sufi hagiographies), treatises such as *Kashf al-Mahjub* and commentaries on Sufism.

The *maktubat* of Khwaja Gesu Daraz, in particular, offer us valuable insights about life in that period. While most of the literature meant for the Sufis was in Persian, literature aimed at common people was in the local dialect – Khari Boli, Braj Bhasha, Marathi, Bangla, or Dakhani, depending on the target audience.

Sufi saints not only wrote many books, they also translated Sanskrit texts. The most important text is the *Bahr-ul-Hayat*, a translation of *Amrit Kund* by the Shattari saint Syed Muhammad Ghaus. Nizami has this to say about it:

> 'What is most striking about this book is the way Syed Muhammad Ghaus has used Muslim mystic terminology to communicate Hindu mystical concepts. He was in a way a precursor of Dara Shukoh whose *Majmua'ul Bahrain* is an expression of the same attitude which inspired Syed Muhammad Ghaus.[44]

Abdur Rahman Rudaulvi, a prolific Chishti writer of the seventeenth century, made an attempt in his Mir'at-ul-Makhluqat to adapt and approximate Hindu legends to Muslim concepts.

Another popular Sufi genre of literature was mystical love stories. The stories were ostensibly about love between a man and a woman but metaphorically describing the relationship between a Sufi and the divine, known as *ishq-e-haqeeqi*.

It is *ishq-e-haqeeqi* that is portrayed in Persian literature through the widely known story of Layla–Majnun. Today, Layla–Majnun stories are thought of as tales of tragic love but originally it was a mystical story. Majnun saw absolute beauty only in Layla and was oblivious to everything else but her. Majnun becomes, thus, the mystical lover who sees God everywhere and has found him not outside himself but in the innermost corner of his own heart.[45]

With their emphasis on universal brotherhood, service, and tolerance, the *khanqah*s became gathering places for people of all religions, class, and cultural backgrounds. And this started a process of interaction in language, social life, religious thought, and behaviour. The earliest sentences of Hindavi discovered were in fact uttered in these *khanqah*s.[46]

A new genre called *premakhya* was developed under the Chishti Sufis that was in line with the Persian *Mathnavi* tradition. The characters in these poetic compilations and their progressive narrations of the storyline are invariably 'the heroes/cult figures of local caste groups'. This new genre was used to propagate, ultimately, the Islamic-Sufi ideology of 'attaining the Truth (*ma'arifat*) through the medium of mortal love'.[47]

According to author Aditya Behlin,[48]

> They also drew on local languages of asceticism and devotion, drawing symbolism and imagery from Gorakhnathi yogis and worshippers of Krishna. These Sufi poets produced a sophisticated Indian Islamic literary tradition, employing a set of desi (indigenous) literary and religious terms and a romantic narrative universe to express their distinctive spiritual agenda in the local landscape of Avadh and Bihar.

These *premakhya*s include the *Chandayan* composed by Mulla Daud, Qutban's *Mrigavati*, Manjhan's *Madhu Malati*, and *Padmavat* by Malik Mohammad Jayasi. These writers were all Sufis themselves. Mulla Daud and Jayasi belonged to the Chishti *silsilah*, Qutban was a Suhrawardi, while Manjhan was a follower of the Shattari *silsilah*.

The heroine was described in passages known as *nakh-sikhvaranana* (head to toe descriptions), with the object's loveliness symbolizing divine beauty. The meeting of the two lovers signifies the meeting of the soul with the divine. The first wife represents the material world. These are allegorical poems based on the premise of the Sufi's journey to his/her ultimate destination, which is divided into the four stages described previously in this book: *shariah* (religious law), *tariqah* (path), *haqeeqah* (truth) and *marifah* (gnosis, or being one with the beloved). They described the obstacles faced by the *salik* (traveller) on his journey of piety and devotion, through the continuous remembrance of the divine and control of *nafs* (ego). The writers used Hindi terminology as well as Sufi symbols.

*Chandayan* was the first of the *premakhya*s and served as an inspiration for the ones that followed. Chandayan is based on a local folk tale from Dalamau (present-day Uttar Pradesh).

Similarly, Qutban's *Mrigyavati* was also based on a folk tale and describes the love of a prince of Chandragiri named Raj Kunwar for the titular protagonist. Mrigyavati is a reflection of eternal beauty and a symbol of the divine as only those willing to annihilate themselves in its quest can see the beloved through love. His true beauty, as Saiyid Athar Abbas Rizvi, in his volume on the history of Sufism, writes, 'Love is the embodiment of affliction and only the stupid expect an eternity of happiness in love.'[49]

Malik Muhammad Jayasi's *Padmavat* is about the imaginary island of Sinhaldvip – a land where an ideal woman, a young princess named Padmavati, resides. Once again, all the familiar tropes of Sufism are employed here, with Padmavati being the beloved; a parrot who guides the lover Ratansen is the *pir*. There is *nafs* (ego), the material world, the spiritual world, *fana* and *baqa,* all explained to the audience through these allegories.

Sufi poetry, music, and literature is a vast ocean, of which I, with my very limited vision and capacity have only been able to present a few droplets. If I have been able to merely arouse a curiosity in my readers to search further, I will feel blessed.

*yaar ko humne ja-ba-ja dekha*
*kahin zahir kahin chhupa dekha*
*kahin mumkin huwa kahin wajib*
*kahin fani kahin baqa dekha*
*yaar ko humne ja-ba-ja dekha*

I saw my beloved in all I saw,
At times revealed, hidden at times.
Been familiar with the issue of faith,
I saw the face of my beloved in all I saw.[50]

– Shah Niaz Be-niaz

Another expression of love for the Divine is seen in the architecture of Sufi buildings. My fascination for architecture started by falling in love with the red sandstone city built by Mughal emperor, Akbar to honour Sheikh Salim Chishti whose blessing he believed had given him a son. In fact, my interaction with Sufi dargahs started with my interest in architecture and monuments. The pristine beauty of the Sheikh Salim Chishti dargah in Agra with its exquisite serpentine brackets were already engraved in my heart as was the grandeur of the Shahnajaf dargah dedicated to Hazrat Ali in Lucknow. I was just as fascinated by the stone *jaali*s (perforated stone screen) of Sheikh Yusuf Qattal's simple domed dargah in Delhi as I was by the inspired by the entire dargah complex in Ajmer. These were sacred spaces and built by devotees to express their devotion inspired by the Divine and a human being's articulation of it.

Architecture did not spring out of nowhere. On one level, it's an expression of divine beauty and on the more mundane one, of how we engage with our environment and especially our faith, whether it's the rock cut temples, grand mosques, or exquisite dargahs. There is a strong relationship between architectural works, history, faith, and society.

Artists find inspiration in nature, in the universe created by God and juxtapose freedom and discipline, light and darkness, in their creative composition as a homage to the Divine. It symbolizes the harmony within and without us.

Reflecting on the various ways in which Sufis have tried to follow the path of Sufism, Seyyid Hossein Nasr writes:

> In order to express its truths Sufism can make use and has made use of every legitimate means, from weaving to archery, from architecture to music, and from logic to traditional theosophy (*hikmat-heart ilâhi*). The goal of Sufism is to lead man from the world of form to the world of the Spirit; but since man lives in the world of form and at the beginning of the spiritual path is not detached from it, by means of this very world of form Sufism turns his attention towards the spiritual world.[51]

In the eighth and ninth centuries, translations of Greek and Sanskrit works, amongst many others, brought about intense developments in science and technology in Iran, the Middle East, and Central Asia. The Persian polymath Khwarizmi's (whose name was latinized as Algorithmi) writing on mathematics, astronomy, and geography led to many scientific and technological advancements, including in the art of building.

The Pythagoreans had already imbued numbers with a mystical quality, and this was now linked to Islamic spirituality. Just as in everyday life, Islamic philosophical concepts were reflected in the architectural forms created by Muslims and gave birth to the term 'sacred architecture'.

The architect 'stressed "arguments from design" to prove God's existence'.[52] The Islamic world was a pioneer in mathematics during early and medieval times and this showed in their geometric prowess. Thus, right from the beginning of Islam, there was a tendency to build geometrically ordered, symmetrical spaces around a central point. Referred to sometimes as sacred geometry, the patterns symbolize the cosmos – timeless and universal. Constructing religious spaces became a meditation. What better way to express the mystery of life than through shapes that display the realities of life that are ephemeral and at the same time eternal?

An architect was thus creating an 'image of the cosmos or of man taken in this cosmic dimension'.[53] Architecture in the Islamic world was inspired by the sense that it is sacred, and therefore also a replica of the cosmos and the locus of the encounter of man and the Divine Word or Logos.'[54]

Everything led to the 'Oneness' of the Divine: squares reflected the Holy Kaaba, octagons called *hasht bahisht* were inspired by the Divine Throne (referred to as *arsh*) which is supported by eight angels, and the dome was a reminder of the vault of heaven, beyond which is infinity.

Architect Dr. Hakim Sameer Hamdani describes it thus:

> In his *Iḥyā' 'Ulūm al-Dīn* (*The Revival of the Religious Sciences*), Imam al Ghazali, the theologian, jurists, and mystic of medieval Islamic world, draws an interesting parallel between the work of an architect who draws (*yusawwir*) an exemplar (*nuskha*) and then brings the exemplar into existence and the creation of Allah who has a *nuskha* of everything and for all times in the Preserved Tablet (*al-lawha al mahfuz*), which he then brings into existence. The creative choice of marking the empty *nuskha* with a starting point – the origin of everything, and then sub dividing a form into a myriad of patterns and motifs is what defines the sacred geometry of Islamicate art. It is something we witness in the *fann* (craftsmanship) of the *khusnivais* (calligrapher) as he brings into a visual form the sacred text of Allah's speech from a single starting point – the *nukta*; something we see in the craft of the artisan as he gives life to an unending series of vegetative decorative motifs-the *islim* (arabesque) visually echoing the unending *zikr* of divine remembrance, and the *tarah* (design) that inspires the *mimar* (the architect-builder) to interpret and creates the shapes and forms that define our human desires to manifest the divine design.[55]

Further, Islam with its monotheism placed restrictions on the use of images and sculptures; thus, buildings were ornamented with calligraphy, geometrical designs, arabesque patterns, beautifully shaped domes and minarets, and *jaali*s (perforated stone screens). Geometric ornament emerged as a multi-layered sign system adaptable to a wide variety of shifting contexts, rather than as a static mould of timeless forms detached from historical memory and context-bound cultural codes of recognition.[56] Domes and minarets soaring into the heavens can be seen in mosques and *hasht bahisht* is seen in the tomb patterns set in Charbagh, but what is interesting is the *jaali*s seen in the dargahs of saints in India.

*Jaali*s created space and a sense of light – both important Islamic concepts. This architectural feature was already flourishing in India, where Hindu artisans especially of Gujarat were renowned for their *jaali*-making skills. *Jaali*s were used to ornament dargahs and mosques, palaces, and tombs. *Muhajjar* (screen enclosures around the graves) were also constructed using them.

A favourite Gujarati design of small square panels fitted together to form a large screen can be seen in Sarkhej Rauza in Ahmedabad, at the tomb of Sheikh Ghaus Gwaliori in Gwalior, and the Nizamuddin Parisar in Chanderi, amongst many others. These square panels were patterned in three ways: geometric, curvilinear, or a combination of both. Stylized floral motifs were also used to heighten the sense of being in a garden – as that is how paradise is also described. In the tomb of Sheikh Ghaus Gwaliori, there are over a hundred panels with one screen comprised of both geometrical and stylized designs.

Gireh-sazi, with *girah* literally meaning a 'knot', refers to geometric designs in woodwork and architectural decorations. It is a technique employed in the sublime *girah* marble screens at the dargah of Sheikh Salim Chishti in Fatehpur Sikri. It is bliss to sit in the mixture of light and shade produced by the screens, contemplating the favours of the Almighty.

In the tomb of Sheikh Ghaus Gwaliori, the first thing that strikes visitors is the light scattering through the beautiful *jaali*s that settles on them and the lightness of spirit that characterizes the ambience! There is no one to disturb them, no one asking for donations or preventing women from going in...just the saint in his shrine, and devotees streaming in. It is a very intimate experience, making visitors feel spiritually uplifted.

Shrines of saints were also important markers of Muslim spaces and remain at the centre of community life. In most cities, some of the finest architecture is found in and around shrines. Not just the dargah but the surrounding area was believed to be sanctified and the rich and poor, famous and unknown Muslims wanted to be buried in its vicinity. It is no coincidence that Delhi's famous architectural monument Humayun's Tomb is next to a shrine or that Urdu's most famous poet Ghalib is also buried next to a shrine. It is believed that the *barakat* of the shrine spills over and the soul of the deceased blesses the spirit of the saint.

These shrines are not only an expression of devotion towards a particular saint but also repositories of history and culture and became a permanent point of collective memory and in many cases rulers and noblemen used it to perpetuate their power. Nile Green explains:

> The most visible ways in which this dialogue of kingship and sainthood transformed the landscape of India was through the stylistic overlapping of the architecture of sultans and Sufis and the shared ritual actions of the adab etiquette that brought these spaces to life. The architectural splendour of many Indian shrines is testament to the fact that the power of the Sufis was more than merely religious or symbolic. Styles of shrine architecture seem always to have mirrored the fashions of the court. The tomb of Baha al-Din Zakariya (d. 1267) at Multan is perhaps the earliest grand example. Later styles of shrine architecture encompassed the brooding basalt solemnity of the shrine of Muhammad al-Hussayni Gesu Daraz (d. 1422) at Gulbarga and the delicate marble and sandstone tents comprising the resting place of Muhammad Ghaws (d. 1562) at Gwalior.[57]

Whether it was Sultan Muhammad bin Tughlaq building a dome over the grave of Sultan al-Mashaikh Hazrat Nizamuddin Auliya, disregarding the saint's instructions for a simple grave, Firoz Shah Tughlaq decision to build a domed shrine for the Roshan Chiragh-e-Delhi, Emperor Akbar's show of gratitude by constructing a marble shrine for Sheikh Salim Chishti, or the simple pavilion of Choti Dargah at Pandua, rulers, rich and poor devotees alike have expressed their piety by making architectural offerings to the saints they revered.

The imposing Sarkhej Rauza, for instance, was started by Sultan Muhammad II (r. 1442–51) after the saint's death in 1445 but completed by his son and successor Sultan Qutbuddin Ahmed II (r. 1451–8). It was embellished by the indigo workers who lived near the shrine. This shrine is remarkable for its large size as well as design. The Qutub-e-Alam dargah in Vatawa, outside Ahmedabad, was built by Sultan Mahmud I (r. 1458–1511 ). Its soaring arches and vaults symbolize the upliftment of the senses one is expected to experience there. The Rauza Sharif in Sirhind owes its present structure to two businessmen from Saurashtra while

Jahanara Begum (1614–81) built a *khanqah* for her spiritual preceptor Mulla Shah Badakshi in Srinagar.

These shrines are described in Chapters 14, 15, 16, and 17.

> 'This visible world was made to correspond to the world invisible and there is nothing in this world but is a symbol of that other world.'[58]
>
> – Muhammad al-Ghazali

Love for the Divine was reflected not only in word, verse, or stone but also in paint. Sufi allegorical literature was illustrated with some of the most beautiful paintings. Art in itself is a reflection of 'truth', as the artist perceives it, and for the mystical mind there is no higher truth than Allah, the Al-Haq (The Truth). The Divine is the source of their inspiration.

Art historian Ursula Weekes in response to a query by me on impact of Sufism on art writes:

> Sufism also influenced Mughal painting at a systemic level because it offered a Neoplatonic justification for the relationship in art between *surat* (outward form) and *ma'ni* (inner meaning) within the Islamic tradition. This conceptual outlook encouraged Mughal artists to explore aesthetic hybridity, including ideas of naturalism and verisimilitude, which in turn played a significant role in the development of a distinctive Mughal style. The idea of the 'archetype' in Neoplatonic Sufism meant that Mughal albums were often compared to the diverse celestial painting of God himself in creation. Mughal albums were called *Muraqqa*, meaning 'that which is patched' and in a beautiful parallel, Sufi *pirs* wear patched robes to signify their spiritual authority, patched because they pass them down through the generations from one master to the next. Somehow, therefore, Mughal albums, as material repositories, are almost like Sufi cloaks themselves.[59]

The art of illustration was first developed under the Timurid dynasty in Herat and flourished under the Safavid rulers of Persia, who descended from the fourteenth-century Sufi Sheikh Safi ad-Din. In India, this was taken to greater heights under the Mughal rulers who combined the Persian art forms with prevailing Indian style.

Lavishly illustrated manuscripts were produced under Mughal Emperor Akbar (r. 1556–1605), the first of these being the Hamzanama. Painted on cloth and large in scale, these 1,400 paintings were based on the *Dastan-e Amir Hamza/Hamzanama*. The *dastan* (an ornate form of oral history) has been transmitted orally as tales of courage and morality through the ages, and illustrations – of which now only a few remain. They were used to reinforce oral storytelling. This was the only large-scale illustration, with the rest being made for books. The miniature paintings made as a form of instruction for the young princes are important testaments of that era and its mystical expression.

Apart from the *Hamzanama* illustrations, some illustrated texts were also made. They were Maulana Jami's *Yusuf Zuleika*, Sheikh Sadi's *Gulistan* and *Bustan*, the illuminated copies of Mevlana Jalaluddin Rumi's *Masnavi*, Nizami's *Leyli Majnun* and *Khamsah,* and Amir Khusrau's *Khamsah*. *Yusuf Zuleikha* and *Leyli Majnun*, though famous as heterosexual human love stories, were written by Maulana Jami and Nizami respectively as Sufi romances depicting *ishq-e-majazi* and *ishq-e-haqeeqi,* as discussed above. Mevlana Rumi's illuminated copies also contained a few illustrations. Sheikh Sadi's books of wisdom too – *Gulistan* and *Bustan* – were very popular.

Paintings were also used to depict famous saints and one of the most popular is Khwaja Khizr, known as the Green Saint. Blessed with immortality, Khwaja Khizr's mystical knowledge and wisdom is legendary, and it was to him that Musa, known as Moses in the Bible, is directed to go to in the Quran to acquire true wisdom – wisdom that is accompanied by humility and has defeated the ego. The famous verse in *Surah Kahf* is said to refer to Khwaja Khizr: 'One of our servants, on whom we had bestowed mercy from ourselves and whom we had taught knowledge from our own presence.' (Quran 18:65)

Dervishes were another favourite subject of miniature art, and we find them in the north of India and the Deccan. Royal visits to Sufi saints were painted, as were saints with their disciples giving discourses and scenes depicting stories from the Quran, such as Nuh's Ark (Noah), the birth of Isa (Jesus). (Interestingly, Mariyam known as Mary in the Bible is the only lady to be not only named but with an entire chapter dedicated to her.)

Reflecting on these developments, Weekes notes:

> The impact of Sufism is suffused through much of the art produced in the imperial Mughal painting atelier from the sixteenth to the eighteenth centuries. Mughal emperors understood their encounters with Sufi ascetics, both real and imagined, to be an important part of their imperial image. Mystical meetings were thus materialized in paint, bringing Jahangir into dynamic meetings across the centuries with figures such as Mu'inuddin Chishti, founder of the Chishti *khanqah* of North India, and the famed poet of Shiraz, Sa'di. Observed portraits of Sufi dervishes were cherished by elite Mughal viewers, and generalized paintings of Sufis whirling in ecstasy fill their albums. The open, mystic stance of Sufism meant that Mughal paintings frequently expressed ideas of confluence between religions. The earliest illustrations of hatha yoga asanas, for example, occur in a Mughal manuscript commissioned in c. 1602 of the *Bahr al Hayat* written by the Shattari Sufi Muhammad Ghauth of Gwalior.[60]

An exquisite painting which is part of the Petersburg album, for example, depicts Jahangir sitting on an hourglass throne, symbolizing time. In front of the emperor is a Sufi saint – a symbol of spirituality – and the emperor is handing him a book. Jahangir is shown preferring the company of the saint to the Ottoman Sultan and King James I of England – both also portrayed in the painting. This painting was made around 1614–15 by Mughal artist Bichitr. In 1614, the emperor was seriously ill and had vowed to pierce his ears in honour of Khwaja Muinuddin Chishti. Is his illness and recovery depicted here by showing human mortality and sovereign immortality? Is the book in the painting an allegorical representation of the emperor's *naama-e-amal* (register of deeds)?

The cherubs under the hourglass throne, where the sand is mostly at the bottom, are praying that the emperor gets to live for a thousand years (inscribed in Persian). There are two cherubic angels hovering above the emperor. Could they be the two *kiraman kitabin* (honourable scribes) called Raqib and Atid, who record the good and bad deeds of every individual? Paintings offer a lot of layered meanings indeed.

There are innumerable miniatures of Mughal emperors, princes, and princesses visiting Sufi saints. They are shown sitting with utmost humility while the saint bleeses them.

A famous painting made between 1630–40, by the Mughal painter Govardhan, now on display in the Met Museum of New York, shows a *qalandar* leading a bear. The Arabic word *nafs* is mentioned many times (295 times) in the Quran and has several meanings. In one way, it is the self (what could loosely be the soul in English) and the other is in the sense of base instincts, lower self sometimes also called ego. An oft-repeated phrase is *nafs pe qaboo* (control over one's baser instincts).

There are a number of classifications of *nafs,* of which I will describe two. *Nafs al-ammara*, the *nafs* which commands us to do as it wishes and has a negative impact on us, is often portrayed as a wild animal. It is referred to in the Quran (12:53) as follows: 'Indeed the nafs that overwhelmingly commands a person to do sin.' The other one is opposed to be *Nafs al-ammara* and is mentioned in the Quran as *nafs al-mutmainnah. Mutmain* (content) are those people who are content to submit to the will of Allah. Amongst the multitude of things, a Sufi strives to control the baser *nafs* and cultivate the *nafs al-mutmainnah*.

There are many rigorous exercises a Sufi uses to control *nafs*. In the aforementioned painting from the Met Museum, the dervish/*qalandar* has controlled the *nafs* represented in the form of a bear. The bear is now willing to do his masters bidding and not the other way round.

There is another famous painting from 1630, again in the Met Museum, of a dervish and a lion. In Indian Sufism, there is often a symbolic equivalence between '*qalandar*' (questor) and '*haidar*' (lion). The *qalb al-nimr*, the 'heart of the lion', indicated a step in the initiatory process of the Sufi, and of course, Hazrat Ali, is Asadullah, the Lion of God.

Calligraphy is the art of ornate handwriting, using a harmonious and elegant arrangement of characters. In Islamic culture, the written word became of paramount importance, as it was used to transmit the word of God in the Holy Quran. Over time, calligraphy evolved into an exquisite art form, with ornamental writing achieving its peak under the Timurid, Safavid, and Mughal dynasties.

Written from right to left, the earliest calligraphic script in Arab culture was *kufic*. Typified by angular, bold lettering, the *kufic* style was well-suited to transcribing the Quran, for engraving coins, and for inscriptions on stone. Other scripts needed to be developed for daily use. Among them were *naskh*, characterized by rounded letters, and *thuluth* (literally, 'a third', referring to the ratio of straight to curved lines in the lettering). *Nastaliq*, which Khwaja Mir Ali Tabrezi is credited with inventing in the Timurid era, has since became the form used most commonly in literature.

*Muraqqa*s (albums) were commissioned, with verses written in the most exquisite of calligraphic styles. Since calligraphers were also making copies of the Revealed Word of Allah, the Quran, they were steeped in spirituality, and that showed in their work. Calligraphers were valued highly, and this can be seen from the fact that the only artist who signed his name on the Taj Mahal is the calligrapher Ustad Amanat Khan. The calligraphic panels in the upper cenotaph chamber bear his name.

> Helplessly practice tracing pain's rending alphabet
> For in love's ledger
> a line's nothing
> but an incision on plain paper.[61]

– Bedil Dehlvi

# 18

# Celebrating with the Saint

*Hori khelungi, kah Bismillah.*
*Naam Nabi ki ratn charrhii,*
*Boond padi Allah Allah.*

[I start playing Holi with a Bismillah.
Covered with the light of Prophet's name,
Showered by blessings of Allah.]

– Baba Bulleh Shah

The Sufi saints who settled in India had a deep sense of appreciation of the land's multicultural and plural heritage. For them, every inch of land was a creation by God and thus pious. They became 'the key mediators between the new Muslim communities that emerged in early modern India and the rural landscapes and urban spaces of the settlement and home making.'[1]

It wasn't long before the dargahs adopted Indic customs and locals gathered to celebrate with the saint. A devotee needs no excuse to celebrate with the saint, and there is always a reason and a season to do so, as we will see in this chapter.

As Hazrat Nizamuddin said:

*Har qaum rast rahe,*
*deen wa qibla gahe.*

[Every people has its right path and right faith and the direction (towards which it faces when) it worships.]

(The qibla is the direction to Mecca, towards which Muslims turn to pray.)

Most people are familiar with the term *urs*, which is celebrated with great enthusiasm in all dargahs and sees huge crowds of devotees congregating there. In South Asia, *urs* (an Arabic word meaning 'wedding') is the death anniversary commemoration of a Sufi saint, usually held at the saint's dargah.[2]

The concept of a death anniversary as an *urs* (associated as it is with weddings) has been taken from the hadith of the two angels Munkir and Nakir – who will question the soul on their faith and deeds in the grave, and if they pass the test will tell the pious to sleep with restfulness and comfort just like a bride, who will not be awakened by anyone except for the person who is most beloved to her[3]. The word for a bride is *uroos* in Arabic and *urs* or marriage ceremony becomes 'a religious ceremony celebrating the union of the soul of a deceased pīr or saint with the Supreme Spirit (the saint's disciples gather round his grave and read the fātiḥa').[4]

'At the most basic level the *urs* celebrations form part of a wider tradition of pilgrimage to the shrines of Sufi and other Muslim saints that developed in Iran and Iraq during the tenth and eleventh centuries before spreading to India through the migration of such Sufis as Hujwiri (d. c. 1072),' Nile Green explains.[5] This was subsequently integrated with local customs.

An example of this integration is the sandalwood paste that covers the shrine. This is clearly an indigenous custom as sandal is considered auspicious in the subcontinent. Just as sandal is normally applied on the bodies of brides in this part of the world, the shrine of the soul going to meet the Divine Beloved is smeared with sandal paste. The shrine becomes the wedding chamber and is filled with the heady scents of flowers and *attar* and decorated with colourful *chaddar*s.

Sufi poet Manjhan describes one such wedding chamber, which is an 'important marker of the transference of the bridal spiritual symbolism from the Persian to the vernacular register in India.'[6] Manjhan describes the wedding chamber where 'two of his poem's [*Madhumalti*'s] allegorical characters are about to be united'. He says:

> Sandalwood and saffron were crushed together,
> Mixed with perfume and the chamber anointed.
> Inside and out and all around,

Lengths of red silk were draped.
Then the wedding bed was brought in.[7]

The *urs* celebration of any dargah is an important day for every follower of that saint and is usually marked as such on their Sufi calendar. It is celebrated differently in every *silsilah*, in a Chishti dargah it can go on for up to five days and involves daily recitation of the Quran, *sama mehfil*s, food distribution and prayers for the saint. The *shajara-khwani*, or reading the saint's genealogical tree, is also an important part of a Chishti *urs*. The *urs* of Sheikh Ahmed Sirhindi lasts for three days and involves the recitation from the Quran and food distribution. The recitation and food distribution (*langar*) are universal so they are seen in every *urs*.

An *urs* is attended by people of all faiths and from many countries. In many cases the head of the state, or local administration will offer the first *chaddar*s. The *urs* at Ajmer Sharif receives *chaddar*s from the President of India and other state dignatories. As mentioned in a previous chapter, the Mahim police station in Mumbai shares its premises with the dargah of Hazrat Makhdoom al Mahimi and consider him their patron saint. A green steel cupboard in the police station is said to contain the saint's possessions. During the 10 days of the *urs* celebration at the dargah, the office is thrown open to devotees.

Similarly, the dargah of Zafarabad in Jaunpur described above is also respected by the local administration; local police officers competeto offer the first *chaddar* on the shrine during the *urs* ceremony. These are just a few examples, for in every region the state and saint have a interactive relationship.

The birth anniversary of a saint is known as *ghusl sharif*. The shrine is washed on this day and once again there are recitations from the Quran, serving of *langar*s and prayers.

While every festival is celebrated in all the dargah by the devotees, Shab-e-Miraj – the night of the Prophet's ascension to the heavens – and Eid-e-Miladun-Nabi (also known as Barawafat), his birthday, are special occasions. Both occasions will see special prayers and distribution of *langar*s in almost every dargah. The dargahs are brightly lit and special qawwali sessions are held.

The most popular qawwali on Shab-e-Miraj is of course the multilingual *Balaghal-Ula Bi-Kamalihi* (he reached the highest place through his perfection), based on the words of Sheikh Saadi (1210–1292) with Urdu additions, made famous by the Sabri Brothers of Pakistan.

The original Persian verse by Sheikh Saadi is:

*Balaghal-ula bi-kamaalihi, kashafad-duja bi-jamaalihi*
*Hasunat jamee'u khisaalihi, Sallu alaihi wa aalihi*

[He reached the highest place through his perfection;
He dispelled darkness through his beauty.
Beauteous are his characteristics,
Blessings on him and his family.][8]

While researching this verse, I discovered many references to the Prophet having written the last line. Since there is a gap of at least five odd centuries between them, I was surprised. Then I found that there is a beautiful tradition in which Sheikh Saadi started writing the verse, but after writing the first one and a half lines in praise of the Prophet, he couldn't write the verse. While working on it, he slept. In his dream, he saw the Prophet Muhammad along with his companions. He asked Saadi why he was looking troubled. Saadi replied that he didn't know how to finish his verse. The Prophet asked him to recite it for him and added the finishing touch by reciting:

*Sallu alaihi wa aalihi*

The Urdu additions are:

*Suhani raat thi aur pur sukoon zamana tha*
*asar mein dooba hua jazb-e-aashiqana tha*
*Unhein to arsh pe mehboob ko bulaana tha*
*hawas thi deed ki Miraj ka bahaana tha*
*sar-ela-makaan se talab hui*
*soo-e-muntaha wo chale nabi*

[It was a beautiful night, and a tranquil time;
The world was lost in a trance of love.
He [Allah] had to call his beloved to the heavenly throne,
Miraj was just an excuse He longed to see him/
A command was sent from the *la-makaan* (a place without limit or origin),
The Prophet set off for the final boundary (of the universe).]

In north India, particularly the Hindi belt, *sohar* is a genre of folk song sung at the birth of any baby and associated with the birth of Lord Rama. In a perfect adaption of Indic traditions the my favourite *sohar*, made famous by Ustad Jafar Hussain Badayuni, is in praise of the Prophet's birth sung in dargahs of Eid-e-Milad-un-Nabi

*Baaro ghee ke diye na*
*Bhayile Amina ke laalna*

[Fill the lamps with ghee and light them
For Amina has been blessed with a boy.]

In the Ajmer Sharif Dargah of Khwaja Garib Nawaz, on Barawafat (12th Rabi Awwal), a door known as Jannati Darwaza or heavenly door is opened. This door marks the spot where Baba Farid had a vision of the Prophet, and is kept locked. It is opened only on this one day.

In Delhi's Hazrat Nizamuddin Auliya Dargah, on Barawafat, relics of the Prophet are shown to devotees. These include a *moi-e-muqaddas* (beard hair) and an imprint of his foot. These were in the possession of the Mughal emperors who had inherited them from their Timurid ancestors and given for safe keeping to the *sajjada nasheen* of the dargah in September 1857, by Emperor Bahadur Shah Zafar. When Bahadur Shah Zafar knew that the fall of his empire was imminent, he wanted to ensure that these relics were kept in safety in the dargah.

The 13th Rajab, the birthday of Hazrat Ali, is another joyous occasion celebrated by the followers throughout the world. Since most Sufi *silsilah*s claim descent from him, it is a special occasion in these dargahs too. Special mention must be made of the celebrations in the dargahs associated with

Hazrat Ali such as Maula Ali ka Pahad in Hyderabad, Shahnajaf Imambara in Lucknow and Shah-e-Mardan dargah in Delhi. Special assemblies called *milad* are held where Hazrat Ali's birth, his bravery, and chivalry are valorized and *manqabaat*s are sung. The dargahs are brightly lit and food is distributed. I once happened to be present in Shah-e-Mardan dargah in Delhi, where a group of Hazara refugees from Afghanistan had gathered to celebrate. They brought a cake with green icing and amidst joy and laughter cut it. Seeing me in a corner they invited me, shared their food with me, and said these were rare occasions of joy for them amidst their struggles as emigres.

In other Sufi dargahs, qawwali sessions, illumination and *langar*s are arranged.

*Dum Mast Qalandar* and *Ali Da Malang* are the popular qawwalis that are performed. The following *manqabat* or praise of Hazrat Ali, reverberates in many dargahs:

*Ali Imam-e manasto manam ghulam-e Ali*
*Hazaar janan-e girami fida-e naam-e Ali*
*Ali da malang main te Ali da*

[Ali is my imam and I am his slave.
May a thousand lives be sacrificed on the name of Ali,
I am intoxicated by his name, I am his dervish.][9]

Dargahs are places where all are welcome and the saint becomes part of the devotee's family. So it makes perfect sense for devotees to celebrate their festivals with the *pir* and for the dargah to celebrate with them. The followers of the saints thus flock to the shrines to celebrate not only the saint's *urs*, but their own festivals too with them, sharing their sorrows, asking for boons and offering *chaddar*s and flowers when their requests are fulfilled. Holi, Diwali, Basant, and Eid are all celebrated in dargahs with great enthusiasm and inclusiveness.

Fareed Ayaz and Abu Mohammad, famous qawwals, in a conversation with Affan A. Yesvi for the magazine *Wajd: Chronicling Ecstasy*, relate an anecdote from the time of Hazrat Nizamuddin Auliya. The story is based on oral history; even if not historically correct, for me, it captures the essence of what religion should be.

Some Muslims were once passing through an area where Holi was being celebrated.

Perhaps as a *shararat* (mischief), perhaps unwittingly, the Muslims got Holi colours on their clothes. This led to a fight among Hindus and Muslims. The news reached the *darbar* (court) of Hazrat Nizamuddin Auliya. The Muslims complained that they had been defiled. 'How would they offer namaz now?' said Fareed Bhai.

Hazrat Nizamuddin Auliya told them: my people, all colours come from Allah. Which colour is that, that does not come from Allah?

Then Hazrat Nizamuddin Auliya told Hazrat Amir Khusrau to capture this in a couplet. And Hazrat Khusrau wrote the [following] lyric:

*Aaj rang hai ri*
*Mere khwaja ke ghar rang hai ri, aaj rang hai.*

[The house of my Beloved is swirled in colours today.]

Fareed Ayaz continues, 'These differences between Hindus and Muslims, they are so sad. Our message is one of peace. Instead of fighting, find peace.'[10]

*Khanqah-e-Karimia* (a major Sufi centre at Salon, the present Rae Bareili district) holds an interesting ceremony called *gagar* ceremony.

As per tradition[11], this ceremony originated during the time of Sheikh Husam-ul-Haq (d. 1470), another Chishti-Nizami Sufi of Manikpur. He was in a state of wajd in a *sama mehfil* when he asked for water and was informed that there was no water in the *khanqah* kitchen. In that same state of spiritual intoxication he took a *gagar*, earthen pot, and moved towards the Ganges river to fill it with water. All those present along with the qawwals accompanied him. Everyone filled whatever utensil they had. The event left such a deep impression on everyone's mind that they asked for a repeat the following year. It was adopted as a regular ceremony in many dargahs/*khanqahs* of the Chishti-Nizami order. In Salon, since there is no river, they go to an old well. The current *sajjada nasheen* Syed Jafri took me to the well tracing the path of the *gagar* bearers.

During the *urs* ceremony, the '*murids* indulged in *raqs* (dance) in the state of *wajd* (ecstasy), keeping earthen pots filled with water on their heads.'[12] A procession is led by the *sajjada nasheen*; the disciples accompanied by musicians follow. The participants, singing Awadhi songs, carry empty *gagars* (earthen pots) on their head, and walk to the nearby shrine of *Piran-i Paratha*. They recite the *fatiha* on water in bigger earthen pots there, and with that water, fill their *gagars*.

The Awadhi songs are rich with local imagery taking from Quranic sources:

> *Kou aaye sughar panihar, kuana umand chala*
> *Ke tum gori sanjhe ki dhari, ke tumhe gadha re sunar*
> *Na mein gori sanjhe ki dhari, na mohe gadha re sunar*
> *Mai baap ne jana diyo hai, roop diyo kartar*
> *Kou aaye sughar panihar, kuana umand chala*
>
> [Who is this Accomplished water feature at whose approach
> the water in the well rises to the surface?
> Greatly in armoured by the beauty of the dame,
> the bystander asks, 'Are you made of gold?
> Which goldsmith has created you?'
> The dame replies, 'Neither am I made of gold
> nor is any goldsmith my creator.
> I am born of a mother and a father and my looks are the gift of God Almighty.'[13]

Jafri quotes Khwaja Hasan Nizami Sani (1931–2015), who once attended the *gagar* ceremony that the song is in praise of the Prophet and that it perceptively describes the Quranic revelation, 'This day I have perfected for you your religion and completed My favor upon you.' Quran 5:3. The well had always been there; the water was also there; only the coming of the accomplished water-fetcher was awaited by the thirsty. She arrived and such was a perfection and overwhelming mercy that everyone was satisfied."

Jafri goes on to say,

> Taking a cue from Khwaja Hasan Nizami Sami, we can say that the well symbolises the eternal grace of God that had been waiting for the perfect man to come and fetch water from it. The well got so enamoured of the beauty and perfection of the water-fetcher that it began to well up, keen to shower all his glory and plenty on him. The people were so struck by the charisma of the man that they and unhesitatingly attributed divinity to him. The last line depicts the Prophet's response which in Surah Kahfof the Quran is recorded in the following words, *Say: "I am but a man like yourselves, (but) the inspiration has come to me, that your Allah is one Allah: whoever expects to meet his Lord, let him work righteousness, and, in the worship of his Lord, admit no one as partner.* Quran 18:110

The Quranic message about prophethood and divinity was given in an Awadhi song, sung during a *urs* ceremony to the congregation and spread around the countryside.

Despite objections from the orthodox – going back to Saiyed Ahmed of Bareilly in the nineteenth century, the practice continues.

This ceremony has been captured in verse by a poet of a later period, Ishtiyaq Ahmad Mushtaq:

> *Ghairat-e-saghar-e-Jamshid Husami gagar;*
> *Mae 'Irfan sey hai Labrez ye nami gagar..*
>
> [The bowl of Jamshid[14] is envious of Husamul Haq's *gagar*;
> It is filled with the wine of *irfan* (gnosis).][15]

> *Sakal ban phool rahi sarson,*
> *Umbva boray, tesu phulay,*
> *Koyal bolay daar daar,*
> *Aur gori karat singaar,*
> *Malaniyan gadhwa lay aayin Karson.*

[Every field is filled with yellow mustard blooms,
Mango buds open, flame of the forest trees blossom,
Every branch echoes with the koyal's call.
The lovely maiden dons her make up;
The garden ladies bring fragrant bouquets.]

These Purbi lyrics, sung in the Bahar Raga, herald the beginning of Basant (on the eve of Basant Panchami) festivities at the dargah of Hazrat Nizamuddin Auliya.

Pirzada Altamash Nizami, a direct descendant of Nizamuddin Auliya who is part of the dargah committee, shared a story with me about the origin of Basant celebrations there.[16] Hazrat Nizamuddin Auliya did not have children and was very attached to his sister's son, Khwaja Taqiuddin Nuh. The attachment was deep and mutual. Alas, their time together was short for Khwaja Nuh fell fatally ill. His death was a deep blow for Mehboob-e-Ilahi; he grieved over the loss and was depressed. His followers, particularly Hazrat Amir Khusrau, longed to see him smile once again.

One day Khusrau saw a group of village women dressed in yellow, carrying mustard flowers and singing on the road near the Khwaja's *khanqah*. He asked them where they were going dressed like this. The women replied that they were going to the temple to offer flowers to their God. Amir Khusrau asked them whether this made their God happy? On hearing an affirmative answer, he immediately dressed up in a yellow sari and carried mustard flowers to his *pir*, singing the aforementioned line '*Sakal ban phool rahi sarson*'. The Khwaja, recognizing his favourite disciple, smiled, amused by his get up and song.

This was an occasion to rejoice, and since then, the tradition of dressing up in yellow, carrying mustard flowers, and singing qawwali on Basant Panchami has continued.

On the Basant Panchami day I visited it, the atmosphere in the dargah was electrifying, with a *langar* being held in the complex and various qawwali groups singing in the courtyard. After the *asr* (afternoon) prayers, all the qawwali singers gather in a lane near the dargah and celebrations start from a small by-lane there with a ceremonial prayer and the lighting of incense sticks and singing. Young and old, everyone joins the procession which goes through the by-lanes of Nizamuddin Basti, stopping at the grave of Khwaja Tajuddin Nuh and then entering the dargah. Inside, a yellow *chaddar* is held above their heads and offered on the shrine. This is apparently the only occasion on which the qawwali singing is done inside. On all other occasions, it happens outside in the courtyard. After this, they all assemble outside and encouraged by the *sajjada nasheen,* the various qawwals sing and rejoice. The qawwali session lasts for a few hours, after which everyoneproceeds to the Choti Dargah (Hazrat Amir Khusrau's grave) to make offerings there. The shrine's courtyard is full of people from different areas, regions, and faiths – all dressed in yellow, united by their shared love for the people's saint, to celebrate the occasion when he smiled once more on the eve of spring.

*Aaj Basant Manaley Suhangan*
*Aaj Basant Manaley*
*Anjan Manjan Kar Piya*
*Lambay Neher Lagaaye*
*Tu Kya Sovay Neend Maasi*
*So Jaagay Teray Bhaag, Suhagan*
*Aaj Basant Manalay.*[17]

[Rejoice, oh loved one, rejoice,
Spring is here, rejoice.
Don your make-up, put kohl on your eyes,
Braid your long tresses.
Oh, wake up from your sleep,
Your destiny too has woken up;
It's spring here, rejoice.]

Although today Basant celebrations by Muslims are restricted to the dargah of Hazrat Nizamuddin Auliya, this was not always the case. According to Dargah Quli Khan, a senior officer in the entourage of Nizam-ul-Mulk, Asaf Jah from Hyderabad, who had visited Delhi and stayed there for three years (1739–41), *basant* was celebrated in all the major Delhi dargahs. He describes the Basant celebrations *Muraqqa-e-Dehli* in his diary from that time. The festivities, as he describes them, are colourful and liberal.

They would start in Qadam Sharif, the dargah of Fatah Khan (son of Sultan Firoz Shah Tughlaq) in Paharganj. From there, the singers and dancers went to the dargah of Qutub Sahib in Mehrauli to offer salutations. The next stop was the dargah of Hazrat Chiragh-e-Dilli (in present-day South Delhi near Greater Kailash), and on the third day they gathered at the dargah of Hazrat Nizamuddin Auliya.

'In the courtyard and surroundings of this place of felicity, everyone waits impatiently for the qawwals, dancers and pilgrims,' he writes. Further, he says:

> The qawwals and singers pay their tribute[s] by reciting their compositions in a delightful manner and the pilgrims present colourful bouquets and pray for the pious soul of the Prophet pbuh [peace be upon him]. The celebrations went on for seven days. On the sixth day they would go to the Emperor's palace and it would culminate on the grave of Azizi in Ahadipura [a colony of gentlemen troopers], which they would wash with wine and take turns to dance. They feel their dancing and singing will provide peace and pleasure to his soul.[18]

*Phoolwaalo'n ki Sair* has been an annual fixture in the Delhi calendar from the early part of the nineteenth century. So popular was it that many moons ago the poet Ghalib had this to say about his beloved city Delhi:

> The existence of Delhi is dependent on many spectacles: The fort, Chandni Chowk, the daily crowds at Jama Masjid, the weekly jaunt of the Jamuna bridge, the annual fair at the Phool Waalo'n ki Sair – now that these five things are not there, then Delhi isn't Delhi.[19]

The Red Fort is now a shell of its former self, Chandni Chowk is a traffic nightmare, the crowds that assembled on the steps of Jama Masjid to watch *dastangoi* performances, cockfights, enjoy conversations, have been converted into either tourists or those who go to offer prayers, the

Jamuna has gone far away, but the Phool Waalo'n ki Sair still continues, though in a much restricted form.

It was a week-long fair in which the emperor, his queens, royal princes, princesses, nobles, and inhabitants of Shahjahanabad would go to Mehrauli every year. There would be fun and frolic, stalls would be put up, diving competitions held in the Jharna building and swings put up in the mango orchards; oil would be heated in huge woks, and piping hot sweets and savouries would be served; *malharragas* (monsoon songs) would be sung, and dancing girls would show off their skills.

The entire area from the Yogmaya temple till the Bagh-e-Nazeer (now Ashoka Mission) would be lit up, and various vendors would sell jewellery, food, or artefacts.

It has a very interesting history: Mughal Emperor Akbar Shah II (1808–1837) had wanted to nominate his younger and favourite son Mirza Jahangir as his heir, in lieu of the eldest (who later succeeded him as Bahadur Shah Zafar) – a move not liked by British Resident Sir Archibald Seton. Mirza Jahangir, a hot-headed youth, mocked the resident and later took a pot-shot at him from one of the buildings in the Red Fort. Though Sir Archibald was unharmed, Mirza Jahangir was exiled to the Allahabad Fort. This led to great consternation and grief to his parents particularly his mother, Mumtaz Mahal Begum.

Mumtaz Mahal Begum made a vow that if he came back safely, she would offer a *chaddar* at the dargah of Hazrat Qutubuddin Bakhtiyar Kaki in Mehrauli. When Mirza Jahangir was released, his mother fulfilled her vow with great pomp and show.

When the floral canopy and *chaddar* for the shrine were being made, the flower-sellers made a floral *pankha* (fan-shaped banner on a pole), and offered it at the shrine. Keeping her vow, Mumtaz Mahal walked barefoot, but the flower-sellers spread flowers in her path to act as a cushion.

The emperor and the queen shifted to Mehrauli for the *sair* (fair) and there was great merry-making. The emperor, for whom all subjects were alike, also sent a floral offering to the ancient and nearby temple of Yogmaya Devi, the sister of Lord Krishna.

Every year after this, the emperor ensured he and his courtiers went to both the dargah and the *mandir* (temple). If he could not go to the temple for some reason, he would not go to the dargah either.

When Akbar Shah II started Sair-e-Gul Faroshan, Bahadur Shah Zafar was heir apparent, but not in the emperor's good books. In order to please the emperor, Zafar had composed a poem in praise of the *pankha*:

*Yeh bana iss Shah-e-Akbar ki badaulat pankha*
*Aaj rangeen hai raiyyat se laga Shah talak*
*Zafranzaar hai ek baam se* dargah *talak*
*Dekhne aayi hai iss rang se khilqat pankha*

[To that great King Akbar do we owe this coloured fan;
From prince to pauper, all bedecked to the last man,
From the bower to the dargah, a wondrous saffron hue –
A blessed Pankha all creation has come here to view.]

The Mughal Family would come and stay in Zafar Mahal for the duration of the festival.

After the fall of the Mughal Empire in 1857, it was stopped an interval of a few years. Later, the British Commissioner of Delhi resumed the practice. In 1942, during the Quit India Movement, the British government put a stop to the *sair* as part of efforts to prevent all kinds of mass gatherings. Yogeshwar Dayal and Jawaharlal Nehru restarted it in 1961 as a symbol of secular, modern India.

It is a unique festival that truly symbolizes India's syncretic culture and Ganga-Jamuni *tehzeeb*. The Sair-e-Gul Faroshan or Phool Waalon ki Sair that was traditionally held in the month of Bhado'n (August/September) is now held after the monsoons and sees participation of people from all walks of life and faiths.

Though the Mughal Empire is no more, the tradition of the head of state being represented continues. Every year, the president and lieutenant governor of Delhi send a *pankha*, which is carried in a procession from the Town hall in Chandni Chowk to Mehrauli.

On the first day, which is a Thursday, a joyous procession goes to Qutub Sahib's dargah and offers floral *chaddar*s. Here it is the Hindu brethren who take the lead. On Friday, the procession goes to Yogmaya Temple, and offers the floral *chaddar* there with the Muslim brethren taking the lead.

On Saturday, there is a cultural function at Jahaz Mahal, a building from the Lodi period that may have been built for the use of pilgrims visiting Qutub Sahib's dargah. Cultural troupes representing the various states of India come in procession holding *pankha*s and perform on the stage.

A fair is held and people come from far and wide to sell and buy wares. There is a general air of festivity and gay abandon, and buildings such as the Jharna and Jahaz Mahal are decorated and spruced up.

The popular legend that prevails in Sufi lore is that Hazrat Nasiruddin Mahmud got the name *Chiragh-e-Dilli* (lamp of Delhi) because his *pir* Hazrat Nizamuddin Auliya asked him to take water in the palm of his hand and use that as oil to light lamps for the workers who were constructing the *baoli* in his *khanqah* when Sultan Ghiyasuddin Tughlaq had forbidden the sale of oil to discourage the construction. Though most historians feel that this is just a legend, the legend has grown, and to date locals call him the lamp of Delhi. Needless to say, who better than this saint to celebrate *jashn-e-chiraghan* (the festival of lights) with!

Every Diwali, all the families from the neighbouring villages – be they of any faith – come to offer jaggery and sweets to the shrine; only then do they go home and do their pooja. New brides too are brought to the dargah for the saint's blessings.

*Diya*s are also lit in the courtyard of Hazrat Nizamuddin Auliya's dargah on Diwali.

*Hori khelungii, kah Bismillah.*
*Naam Nabi ki ratn charii,*
*Boond pari Allah Allah.*

I start playing Holi with a Bismillah.
Covered with the light of Prophet's name,
Showered by blessings of Allah

– Baba Bulleh Shah

The eighteenth century Punjabi mystic Bulleh Shah's words above provide the perfect frame for the subcontinent's centuries-old syncretic culture, our Ganga-Jamuni *tehzeeb* that is under threat from fundamentalists of both religions.

Basant Panchami signals the onset of the festivities and people carry squirt guns with colours and smear *gulaal* (red powder) on each other's faces. Mustard flowers are offered in temples and *abiir/gulaal* would be flying in the air.

Flowers from the *Tesu/Palash/Dhaak* plants (aka flame of the forest) are immersed in earthen water pots. It is believed that Lord Krishna played Holi with Radha using colours made from the red Tesu flower, which blooms during the spring season. All colours used were natural and plant extracts. There were neither chemicals nor hooliganism.

Holi is one of the most delightful and colourful festivals of India. It is aimed at uniting people, helping them forget their complaints, and embracing one another.

'In a lyrical song, Nizāmuddīn Auliyā asks the Chishti Sufis to come out in their ecstatic state and join the celebrations of the Hindu spring festival of Holi, which is an occasion for great revelry and playfulness.'[20]

Amir Khusrau (1253–1325) is said to have written many verses in celebration of Holi. One of them reads:

*Kheluungii holi, Khaaja ghar aaye,*
*Dhan dhan bhaag hamare sajni,*
*Khaaja aaye aangan mere.*

[I shall play Holi as Khaaja has come home,
Blessed is my fortune, o friend,
As Khaaja has come to my courtyard.]

If you were to visit Ajmer Sharif on Holi, you'd see huge the crowds of people who come to celebrate with the Khwaja. It is common in some of the dargahs of Delhi for locals to visit the saints on Holi and put some colour on their shrines as part of celebration. It is, however, a relatively circumspect affair with people mainly coming to pay respects.

If one wants to see how Holi is really played in a dargah, one has to visit Dewa Sharif (near Barabanki in Uttar Pradesh). The patron saint there is Hazrat Saiyed Waris Ali Shah (1817–1905), the founder of the Warsi *silsilah*. Like all Sufi saints, Hazrat Waris Shah also believed that the basis of religion is love and devotion, and he started the tradition of playing Holi with his devotees – a tradition that has remained intact.

The colourful visuals that unfold against the background of the white dargah building are spellbinding. The entire courtyard is a riot of colours, with people of all religions and classes smearing, sprinkling, and spraying each other with the bright colours, apart from throwing them up joyously into the air.

Contrary to popular belief, Islam does not prohibit colour; it's just that when devotees perform our ablutions for namaz, water should touch the skin – so there should be no layer of colour on the skin. Washing the coloured powders away before praying is all that needs to be done – critics need to understand that it's as simple as that.

Celebrations didn't always take the shape of festivals. Sometimes, it was also a joyful sharing of age-old tradition and celebrating the craft of the community with the saint. We see this in the Sarkhej Rauza in Ahmedabad where the indigo workers have painted the ceiling of the shrine with indigo.

Before the founding of the city of Ahmedabad in 1411 by Sultan Ahmed Shah I, it was inhabited by indigo dyers and weavers. Indigo was one of the most sought-after commodities by the colonial traders. It was the only plant from which the colour blue could be extracted, so it was rightly considered a treasure. Since it was very expensive, it came to be associated with royalty and aristocracy – the few people who could probably afford it in the medieval ages. In fact, this association was one of the reasons for devotees to offer it to the saint.

The regions where it grew before the British came were the northern Gangetic plains, Sindh, Sarkhej, the Deccan region, and along the east coast. In fact, Sarkhej is a corruption of the word *zarkhez*, which means fertile.

Sufi saint Sheikh Ahmad Ganj Baksh Khattu came to Ahmedabad and settled in the area. (He was the spiritual advisor of Ahmed Shah I.) It was but natural that the locals started flocking to his *khanqah* and became his disciples. The dargah's association with these indigo farmers is manifested in one of its prominent features today: the blue indigo painting on its ceiling.

This blue connection was further reinforced by the devotees' love of Krishna; there is a 500-year-old tradition of celebrating Janmashtami. But this changed over time. A news report from 2014 tells us:

> Janmashtami celebrations were suspended after the riots that followed the demolition of Babri Masjid in December 1992 and then again after the post-Godhra riots. During the communal violence in 2002, Makarba villagers led by their sarpanch had guarded the Roza complex from rioters. Five years later, in 2007, the SRC had held a low-key Janmashtami fair for local people in the Makarba village, as was the tradition.[21]

Janmasthami is also celebrated in the dargah of Sharif Hazrat Hajib Shakarbarat at Narhat village in Rajasthan and in Kakori Sharif.

In fact, there are many such non-Islamic festivals held all over India in dargahs. This chapter has given only a peek into some facets of the syncretic existence of religions in the culturally diverse country that we call India.

> *Khalik Khalak Khalak mein Khalik,*
> *Sab ghat rahya samai.*
>
> [God is in the world and the world is in God,
> He permeates everything.][22]

# 19

## Separated by the Screen

When a wild lion comes into an inhabited area from the forest, no one asks: 'Is it male or female?' Similarly, the sons of Adam, whether they be men or women, must devote themselves to obedience and piety.[1]

– Hazrat Nizamuddin Auliya, *Fawaid al-Fu'ad*

Women holding on to stone screens and peeping through them into the shrine chamber is a common scene in most Indian Sufi dargahs. I have often done the same and felt hurt by this separation.

Considering the important roles played by Khadija, the Prophet's first wife and first person to accept Islam, Fatima, his daughter who not only carried his lineage forward but is said to be his spiritual heir, and Rabia al-Basri's contributions to Sufism, why is there a gender bias? Why is there a lack of representation of women in the history of Sufism? As Sa'diyya Shaikh writes, Sufism neither presents a monolithic position on gender nor 'a historical panacea for all things beneficial for women'.[2]

Whenever there is a discussion on Sufism, it's about the men. The women are cast in the role of mothers, sisters, and daughters. Does this mean that such a role was or is forbidden to them, and there were no women Sufis?

This chapter discusses the position of female Sufis and women in dargahs.

Women have been sharing the workload of men from the beginning of time. They not only cooked, looked after the children, and fetched water and firewood; they also worked in the fields, and carried food and water for their menfolk. They held positions of power in the past and are in leading positions globally today.

In the Islamic world too, there have been many women – starting with Khadija bint Khuwalid – who were successful businesspersons. Some of them were: the Prophet's youngest wife and important transmitter of hadiths, Ayesha; the first Sufi to vocalize an ecstatic love for Allah, Rabia al-Basri; and the famed Egyptian queen, Shajar al-Darr (d.1257) – the wife of the last Ayubid, who after her husband's death defeated the Crusaders and took King Louis IX captive. In this part of the world, there was also Sultan Raziya of the Delhi Sultanate, who was the first female monarch of South Asia.

Islamic history is full of famous women scholars, scientists, and teachers who shaped the intellectual world and left their mark for ages to come. Schimmel mentions a Bubu Rasti (d. 1620), living in Burhanpur, India, who 'was an expert in interpreting medieval Persian mystical texts, especially the works of Fakhruddin Iraqi whose *Lamaat* (flashes) – a small book of poetry mixed with prose,it charmingly elucidates several Ibn al-Arabi stories and ranks amongst the finest works we have a mystical love.'[3]

Hussain mentions three women Sufis of the seventeenth century who were made *khalifa*s by their spiritual masters. Shaikh Ilahbadi Sambhali Naqshbandi (d. 1650) appointed his *murid* Bibi Dola his *khalifa*. Saiyed Shah Abdul Hasan Qadri Kankali gave *khilafat* to Bibi Asmatun Nisa, while Bibi Khaki Shan became the *sajjada nasheen* of her brother Shair Ali Shah Darwaish, who gave her all his responsibilities.[4]

There may have been others, but their records are lost to us, for women had to face obstacles then just as they face them now.

Let us see study these obstacles in the light of the Quran. The Quran does not discriminate between men and women in matters of faith. All that is required is a 'sound heart'. (Quran 26:89) Further, it says: 'O mankind! We [Allah] created you from a single (pair) of a male and a female.' (Quran 49:13) Men and women were created from a single soul (Quran 4:1), and both are responsible for their own morals.

The Quran not only recognizes women's equality as far as spiritual prowess is concerned, it also endows women with the right to inherit property or dowers from their husbands, and sees them as capable of negotiating marriage contracts.

The verse where the Quran differentiates between men and women in *Surah Baqarah*, verse 228, says, 'And women shall have rights similar to the rights against them according to what is equitable; but men have a degree (of advantage) over them. And God is Exalted in Power, Wise.'

In this verse the preceding lines are regarding divorce, and Amina Wudud, the American Muslim theologian, argues that this advantage is given in regard to divorce alone. She writes:

> In the Qur'an, the advantage men have is that of being individually able to pronounce divorce against their wives without arbitration or assistance. Divorce is granted to a woman, on the other hand, only after intervention of an authority (for example, a judge).[5]

Wudud points out that instead of restricting this verse to the subject of divorce, it has been taken as a blanket statement, contradicting 'the equity established throughout the Quran with regard to individuals'. Allah has commanded that 'each *nafs* [literally means self and has been used for ego and soul] shall have in accordance to what it earns'; yet, as Wudud adds, '[T]he verse is presumed to state what men have believed and wanted others to believe: that society operates hierarchically with the male on top.'[6]

The fact that two of the Prophet's wives were highly educated women and exerted their agency freely was also ignored, and female education was frowned upon, leaving many women unaware of or confused about their own rights.

The *Surah Baqarah* (2:187) has another verse regarding the relationship between a husband and wife, 'They are your garments. And ye are their garments.' Reflecting on these lines, German Orientalist and scholar Annemarie Schimmel writes, 'The phenomenology of this religion interprets this to mean that one is technically always the alter ego of the other, simply because a garment (being a portion or an aspect of a person) is frequently used *pars pro toto* to represent the whole person.'[7]

If interpreted correctly, Islam's egalitarian credentials are evident. In keeping with the egalitarian ideas of Islam, women Sufis could inherit lands and get grants (*madad-e-maash*), even if they unfortunately were never considered equals. They were also benefactors and endowed Sufi hospices.

To study all this, one of the places we have to go to is literature and folklore. Sufi poetry and terminology use many feminine traits as metaphors. Annemarie Schimmel has this to say about these metaphors:

> The equation and the subsequent identification of the woman with the soul, plays an important part in the literature of the movement. *Nafs*, soul or self, is a feminine noun that appears three times in the Quran in three specific senses: Once as the 'soul inciting to evil', (Sura 12:53), once as the accusing soul (Sura75:2), and once as the 'soul at peace' (Sura 89:27–28). Though conceptually *nafs* has no gender, it is usually compared to a woman, who as the ascetics thought, incites evil. To a certain extent then, the feminine *nafs* in this role can be seen as a mirror image of the secular world (*duniya* likewise a feminine noun), and Muslim writers have made remarks and observations about the 'mistress world', who seduces and swallows up men and children, in terms almost as uncomplimentary as those of Christian theologians of the Middle Ages. With them too, the 'mistress world' seeks to divert the man from his intellectual or religious striving, which is just another expression of the typical ascetic male fear of the power of the female.[8]

The theme of women as seducers is an ancient one; even though the Quran places the blame for the sin of disobeying God and giving in to Satan's temptation on both Aadam and Huwwa (Eve), woman has been considered a distraction for men striving to achieve their goals in life. As Schimmel notes, 'Islam has no conception of original sin as being passed on by biological gender,' yet this theme of a woman leading a man astray was adopted.

In the chapter on marriage and celibacy in first Sufi treatise *Kashf al-Mahjub,* written by Sheikh Ali Hujweri Data Ganj Baksh, he cites the Quranic verses as well as hadith on marriage as being desirable and goes on to say that some sheikhs married 'as a means of quelling lust, and acquisition (of sustenance) to be desirable as a means of freeing the mind from anxiety', while others for procreation.

He adds the rider that since marriage is ideally one where husband and wife are congenial, and can provide companionship and serenity to each other, an uncongenial wife can be a torment. 'Therefore, the dervish must, in the first place, consider what he is doing and picture in his mind the evils of celibacy and of marriage, in order that he may choose the state of which he can more easily overcome the evils.'

He advocates marriage for those who 'prefer to associate with mankind' but recommends celibacy. He writes, 'In our time it is impossible for anyone to have a suitable wife, whose wants are not excessive and whose demands are not unreasonable. Therefore many persons have adopted celibacy and observe the Apostolic Tradition: The best of men in latter will be those who are light of back, i.e. who have neither wife nor child.'[9]

Despite such views among early (male) authors, in the initial stages of Sufism, we know many women were admitted as members in the order, though the number serving as *fakir*s or dervishes was significantly lower. There was also a tradition of elevating them to the ranks of men or comparing them to men, thereby subsuming their female identity.

Needless to say, their lives weren't always well-documented; in fact, until the discovery of As-Sulami's tenth-century book *Early Sufi Women*, which contains short biographical sketches of 82 women Sufis, only the names of a few women were known. In his book, 'As-Salami portrays Sufi women [as] full equals of their male counterpart[s] in religion and intellect, as well as in their knowledge of Sufi doctrines and practices.'[10]

In the early stages of Sufism, the emphasis was on ascetism and subduing and conquering the base instincts. We find that the same ascetism practised by men is followed by Umm Talq, who was one of the first to articulate it, 'The lower soul is a king if you indulge it, but it is a slave if you torment it.'[11] As-Sulami describes her as 'one of the female devotees and specialists in the ways – of self-denial and gnosis.'

Another female Sufi, Fatima of Nishapur (d. 838) explained the meaning of Sufism to Dhul-Nun (d.861), who considered her his teacher. She 'taught him such subjects as the doctrine of truthfulness (*sidq*), and the exegesis (*ta'wil*) of the Quran'. Dhul-Nun gave her the same praise he would have given a male Sufi, while Bayazid al-Bistami said of her, 'In all of my life, I have only seen one true man and one true woman. The woman was

Fatima of Nishapur. Whenever I informed her about one of the stages of spirituality, she would take the news as if she had experienced it herself.'[12]

If we go back further into time and consider Muhammad as the first Sufi, then we can also take the example of his family, many of whom were considered saints, particularly his daughter Bibi Fatima.

Bibi Fatima, 'perpetuated his lineage through her sons, Hasan and Husayn and deserved to inherit his property. Many also believe that she inherited some of the Prophet's spiritual and temporal authority. Rather than representing severing or detachment, she symbolized abundance.'[13]

Bibi Fatima is someone many call on often for intercession in Allah's *darbar*, as she is endowed with intercessory grace (*baraka*). Bibi Fatima's other name Zehra (the radiant one) 'reflects her mystical, transcendent and intercessory eschatological roles and is based on her emanation of the *nur Muhammadi* [Muhammad's light[14]], through which the prophets and imams descend.'[15]

'It is said that when she stood for prayer, the *mihrab* would reflect the light of her countenance. She was also called al-Batul (the virgin/the devoted one) because of her asceticism.'[16] Her title *Sayyidatu Nisa al-Alamin* (Leader of Women of The Worlds) reflects her piety, ascetism, patience, fortitude, and hours spent in devotion, making her an example for all Muslim women.

It is believed that the Ayat-e-Tathira in the Quran (33:33) – that reads, 'And God only wishes to remove all abomination from you, ye Members of the Family, and to make you pure and spotless' – was revealed for her and the *Ahl al-Bait*.

The famous Hadith-e-Kisa (hadith of the cloak) refers to an event when the Prophet brought his family members – Ali, Fatima, Hasan, and Hussain – under a cloak with him. In the hadith, they are identified as Bibi Fatima's father, Bibi Fatima's husband and Bibi Fatima's sons. This hadith was narrated by Bibi Fatima herself and the Prophet's wife, Umm-e-Salamah. In the words of Hassan Abbas, biographer of Ali Ibn Abi Talib:

> Fatima narrates that later the archangel Jibraeel also joined them under the cloak. When Umm Salamah asked to join, the Prophet reiterated that it was to be the five of them only, and that this was not upto him. He comforted her, though, by adding, 'you are on

> the path of righteousness and goodness'. This led to the five of them being known as Ahl al-Kisa, meaning 'people of the cloak', and in Persian and Urdu, the Panjtan Pak, 'the holy five'.[17]

In *Surah* 3:61, where the Prophet is asked, 'Come! let us gather together our sons and your sons our women and your women ourselves and yourselves: then let us earnestly pray and invoke the curse of God on those who lie,' it is generally believed that the woman referred to here is Fatima Zehra.

Her contribution to mysticism can be seen in the fact that a famous *zikr*, where one recites *Allahu Akbar* (God is Great), *Alhamdu-lillah* (Praise be to God), and *Subhan Allah* (Glory be to God), is known as Tasbih-e-Zehra. Jibraeel taught the Prophet to do *zikr*, and the Prophet in turn taught it to Fatima. This *tasbih* (rosary) is recited after every namaz.

'In many ways, Fatima's prominent role is encapsulated in Ja'far al-Ṣādiq's interpretation of the renowned 'Light Verse' of the Qur'an (24:35), as set forth by the prominent scholar Muhammad ibn Ya'qūb al-Kulaynī (d. 941), author of Al-Kāfī, the earliest of the 'four books' forming the Shi'i hadith canon. The verse, omitting commentary, reads as follows:

> God is the Light of the heavens and earth. His Light is like this: there is a niche, and in it a lamp, the lamp inside a glass, a glass like a glittering star, fuelled from a blessed olive tree from neither east nor west, whose oil almost gives light even when no fire touches it – light upon light – God guides whoever He will to His Light; God draws such comparisons for people; God has full knowledge of everything.

In his exegesis, Ja'far al-Ṣādiq explains that Fatima is the niche who holds within her Hasan (the lamp) and Husayn (the glass); she is also the 'glittering star, fuelled from a blessed olive tree (Abraham)'. In his brilliant exposition on this commentary, contemporary scholar David Pinault observes,

> [T]hat in this womb-like metaphor [Fatima] is described as the birthplace and source of the light of the Imāms... She is a celestial

> being...linked in a kind of mystical genealogy with her spiritual forefather Abraham: starfire kindled from olivewood. Fāṭima the Radiant, conveyer of illumination to her future offspring, unites celestial hierarchies, light upon light, with their earth-origins from the Abrahamic past.
>
> Once again, this interpretation graphically illustrates that Fatima, though female, is able to convey her prophetic lineage, which extends back to Abraham. She is both the hollow enveloping the light (the niche) and the light itself (the glittering star). Purified of menstruation, this unearthly being transmits illumination rather than blood as her inheritance.[18]

The Prophet not only loved his daughter very much but gave her great respect and would stand up if she entered a room in his presence. There is a very famous hadith in which the Prophet has said: 'Fatima is a part of me, and he who makes her angry, makes me angry.'[19]

Bibi Fatima is also identified as the 'generative source of prophecy and imamate. Fatima is the *majma' al-nurayn*, or the confluence of exoteric prophecy, and the esoteric source of mystical knowledge of the Koran and the cosmos,'[20] and is considered 'by some Sufis and theologians as the first spiritual head (*qutb*) of the Sufi fellowship,' according to Camille Adams Hemlinski, author and co-founder of the Sufi non-profit The Threshold Society. Hemlinski adds:

> The Prophet extolled her as one of the four most exemplary women in history along with Mary, mother of Jesus; her own mother, Khadija; and the wife of Pharoah, who rescued and raised Moses. These four women are considered the four holiest women of Islam.[21]

The Prophet's first wife, Khadija, was another important female figure. She was a successful entrepreneur in Mecca and one of the leading traders of her age. She hired the 25-year-old Muhammad as manager of her caravan going to Syria for trade; so impressed was she by his honesty, acumen, and intellect that on his return, she proposed marriage to the man 15 years her junior. After their wedding, he moved in with her and it was her money that was used to fund the initial spread of Islam. She comforted him when the Quran was revealed to him and he thought he was going mad; she helped him understand and reconcile to the fact that Allah had indeed chosen him as the next prophet. She was also the first person to convert to Islam at the Prophet's call.

After the battle of Karbala and the martyrdom of her brother Hussain, the Prophet's granddaughter Zainab was responsible for spreading the message of Islam as revealed by her grandfather. She was called Sani-e-Zehra (the second Zehra) as she resembled her mother closely.

After the martyrdom of all the male members of her family, including a six-month-old nephew (with the one exception being Imam Hussain's ailing son), it was Zainab who led the surviving women and children. They were taken captives and paraded through Iraq and Syria as a family of rebels who had been punished. However, Zainab left no stone unturned to give sermons and talks at every place they halted in an attempt to acquaint people with her brother's sacrifice for Islam and their legacy.

She even reprimanded Yazid in his court in Damascus. Today, if we follow Muhammad's Islam and not Yazid's version, it is because of the courage and resilience Zainab showed, refusing to be cowed down by personal losses, tragedy, humiliation, and imprisonment.

Women from the Prophet's family apart, there were many women Sufis in the initial years of its spread, for 'mysticism was the only religious sphere where women could find a place'.[22]

You may remember Rabia al-Basri, said to be the first true saint of Islam[23] and one of the most celebrated Sufi saints. She was the one to give expression to the concept of pure love. Mysticism scholar Margaret Smith writes,

> The high position attained by the women Sufis is attested further by the fact that the Sufis themselves give to a woman [Rabi'a al-Adawiyya] the first place among the earliest Islamic mystics and have chosen her to be the representative of the first development of mysticism in Islam.[24]

Historians see medieval Indian society as a patriarchal society and Islam as a 'male religion'.[25] It was in this very rigid society that Sufism gave women a space to vent their grievances. They could become *murids*, take oaths of allegiance, visit and serve the *khanqah*s and dargahs and at times even become *shaykha*s. There were women circles within the *khanqah*s and dargahs. For instance, it has been reported by Sheikh Nasiruddin Chiragh-e-Dilli's chief disciple, Saiyed Muhammad Gesu Daraz, that before his death, the master had distributed his spiritual *wilayat* among four disciples, one of whom was a woman.[26]

But a woman could not become a *pir*; Baba Farid famously said that he would have given the *khilafat nama* (spiritual succession) to his daughter Bibi Sharifa had it been permitted.

Even though women were not allowed to assume leadership, they were given the respect they deserve. The *Fawaid al-Fu'ad* records many incidents of Hazrat Nizamuddun Auliya's concern for women and his interactions with them.

In her dissertation, research scholar Priyanka Chanana in her dissertation describes the process of initiation (called *bai'a*) in Sufism. She writes that the process for women was different from that for a male *murid*. The latter were asked to hold the *pir*'s hand while facing Mecca during the initiation, but a woman held one end of a scarf while the *pir* held the other end.[27]

The *pir* would also generally give his male disciple a *khirqah* (a four-edged cap and coat) or a *chaddar*, and advice like not to rob or beg and also to follow the shariah. The *murid* gave something as a fee – clothes, money, parched rice, sweet meats, etc., after which the initiation feast was finally given. Carl Ernst writes that in the early centuries, the initiation took place in a special manner for women:

> Following the directive of a passage in the Qur'an [60:12] women could take initiation with a male Sufi shaykh just as women had taken the oath of allegiance to Muhammad. The procedure, derived from a hadith from 'Umar, was for a woman to place her hand into a cup of water, after which the shaykh (again following the example of the Prophet) would also put his hand in the water, and then the oath of initiation would be administered.[28]

This was the process adopted by Sheikh Nasiruddin Chiragh-e-Dilli for his female disciples.[29]

Sadia Dehlvi, author of the book *Sufism*, who took an oath of allegiance with her Sufi master, Shah Muhammad Farooq Rahmani, a few decades ago, confirmed during an interview with me that she held the edge of her *pir*'s scarf during her initiation. He asked her to be regular in her daily ritual prayers, which she followed. She also spent a lot of time in doing *zikr* and reading the *durood* (a special Arabic phrase which sends salutations to the Prophet and his family).[30]

Hazrat Nizamuddin Auliya once narrated a story to his disciples regarding his teacher Maulana Alauddin Asuli, who had come to live in Badayun after the establishment of the Delhi Sultanate there. A Hindu woman was brought in captive for rebelling against the sultan. The village woman was sold as a slave to a Maulana. One day, the Maulana found her crying and asked her the reason for her grief. She said that she missed her son. The Maulana enquired if she would be accepted back by her family and on hearing an affirmative answer, took her back to her village. Hazrat Nizamuddin Auliya commented that from the point of view of Islamic canon law he could be accused of abetting apostasy, but his association with Sheikh Jalaluddin Tabrezi had taught him the value of humanism.[31]

In the *khanqah* stage, as is apparent from the *Fawaid al-Fu'ad*, women played a rather active part; their presence is visible as disciples, mothers and wives. 'What is worth noticing is the fact that the women were also initiated as the disciples to the saints just like their male counterparts. The Sufis were generally regarded as men and women who adopt the ascetic mode of life. Therefore, women were no exception on the path.'[32]

However, as described above, women could not become *khalifa*s and their role in the hieirarchy was diminished. Once the institution of dargahs, as spaces where the saint's body was considered the source of *barakat*, developed, women were content to stay in the roles of wives, mothers, and daughters. The role of the Sufi woman as a mother has always been celebrated and eulogized, and mothers of the Sufi saints have always been accorded great respect – the *urs* of Mai Sahib, the mother of Hazrat Nizamuddin Auliya, is celebrated with much ceremony.

When I visited the shrine of Sheikh Burhanuddin Garib in Khuldabad (Aurangabad), I saw another shrine close by where many women were sitting. This was the shrine of his mother and I was told that women go and pray for her intercession in all their supplications to God. In fact, the word *'rahma'* is from *'rahim'* (Arabic for womb), referring to God's maternal love. There is also a famous hadith that claims that paradise lies beneath the mother's feet.

'Be grateful to Me and to both your parents.' (Quran 31:14)

According to the famous hadith, a man came to the Prophet and said: 'O Prophet of God! Guide me, to whom should I be good in order to benefit completely from my good deed?'

The Prophet said: 'Be good to your mother.'

He asked: 'Next to her?'

The Prophet repeated: 'Be good to your mother.'

He said again: 'And next to her?'

The Prophet answered: 'To your mother.'

The man said: 'To what other person should I be good?'

The Prophet said: 'To your father.'[33]

Mystic women themselves have not penned their stories; their biographers were limited but not entirely missing. Abdul-Haqq Muhaddis Dehlawi, for instance, included a chapter on women saints in his book *Akhbaru'l-Akhyar* (*Stories of the Chosen Ones*). *Rawdat al-nazirin wa khulasat manaqib al-salihin* (*The Garden of the Guardians and the Extract of the Deeds of the Upright*) by Abu Muhammad al-Witri (d. 1512) also recorded the lives of some of the Sufi women of later centuries. Many of the later Sufi luminaries too, like Ibn al-'Arabi in his *Sufis of Andalusia*, refer to radiant women who had a strong influence on their development and the continuation of their Sufi teaching.[34] As-Sulami's book has been referred to before.

Just as men stayed in *khanqahs*, women stayed in convents known as *ribats*. Aleppo alone had seven *ribats*, and there is mention of some of them being in Cairo and Baghdad.[35]

There are also some like the Betakshi *silsilah* of Turkey, which allow equal participation to men and women in all mystical experiences. Many orders gave women admission and offered them a religious sphere, little recognized in the legal religious set-up. However, while they could be enrolled as associates and even appointed as leaders to organize women circles, their religious roles were limited to visitations to the shrine on Fridays or festival days. Helminski says:

> The dualism between male and female religion was brought out on Fridays when the men went off to the Jami [Jama Masjid] to display their communal solidarity by participation in ritual prayer, whilst the women were at the saint's tomb or graveyard making their offerings, petitioning, or communing with the spirit of the tomb.[36]

Even today, some women take the oath of allegiance, and the Naqshbandi *silsilah* in India has *shaykha*s who are spiritual masters.

Apart from their important role as mothers who supported their saint sons, or were saints themselves, women were key in conveying the message of the Sufis to the masses. If women in the centuries following the advent of Islam had been active in the collecting and transmission of hadiths, now we have simple village women transmitting the message of the Sufi saints via their songs.

Richard Eaton searches for a satisfactory explanation for how 'an essentially esoteric mystical tradition might have filtered down to commoners in some sort of comprehensible and appealing form,' and how this could have led to conversion. According to him, this was facilitated by folk literature written by local Sufis in the Deccan who adapted the 'simplest elements of Sufi doctrine to the already existing vehicles of folk poetry'.[37] Written in the seventeenth and eighteenth centuries, and preserved as oral traditions amongst the Dakhani-speaking villagers of the Deccan plateau, this folk poetry of Sufi origin played an important role in the folk culture of the villages there, until they were replaced by radio and cinema.

These were sung by women as they engaged in their household chores and included *chakki-nama* (songs sung while grinding food grains), *charkha-nama* (songs sung while spinning thread), *lori-nama* (lullabys) *shadi-nama* (wedding songs), *suhaga-nama* (married woman's songs), and the *suhaila* or eulogistic songs. Eaton concludes, 'The few studies that have been made of Dakhani folk literature trace it to the efforts by Sufis to expand their teachings among the unlettered folk of the Deccan plateau.'[38] These were also adapted in Marathi and Kannada languages for the villagers of those areas. One such song goes:

> First was God's name,
> And then His qualities.

In my mind I keep the name, And with each breath
(refrain): Say 'La-illah' [There is no god],
Dwell in 'il-Allah'.
God Himself from the hidden treasure
Has created the whole world artistically.[39]

This *chakki-nama* written by Shah Hashim Khudawand Hadi then goes on to establish the ontological link between God, the Prophet, the *pir,* and the woman at the grindstone, simplifying the essential elements of the Chishti theory of creation and of God's relationship to the material world. Esoteric knowledge as well as *zikr*, an essential Sufi practice, was thus disseminated by the women spinning the wheel to other women and the children in the easiest of terms and in the most popular of ways.[40]

Eaton writes that in his view, 'The dominant role played by women in this Indian folk Islam cannot be underestimated.' He continues, 'One seventeenth-century account of a Sufi's conversations (*malfuzat*) noted that women were allowed to enter even the inner circle of a Sufi's followers. This would mean that at one time women, along with men, were instructed in the religious exercises of living Sufis.'[41]

## Some Famous Indian Women Sufi Saints

The most well-known female saint in Indian Sufism is Bibi Fatima, also called the Rabia of Delhi after Rabia of Basra, the famous mystic of the eighth century.

On a Friday evening in December 1308, an unknown woman devotee presented herself to Hazrat Nizamuddin Auliya and professed allegiance to him. He began to comment on the numerous benefits that accrued from the virtues of women and recalled a woman from Indraprastha called Fatima. 'She had been such a model of chastity and virtue that Shaykh al-Islam Farid ad-din – may God sanctify his lofty secret – used to repeatedly say of her: "That woman is a man whom the Creator has sent down in the bodily form of a woman."'[42]

Popularly known as Bibi Fatima Sam or Samina, she was the *pir-bahen* (spiritual sister) of Baba Farid and his brother Sheikh Najibuddin Mutawakkil. Bibi Fatima Sam reposed great faith in Sheikh Najibuddin

Mutawakkil; in fact, she was a devotee. When there was nothing in the house for him to eat, she would send him some bread. She would say, 'The saints will cast away both worldly and religious blessings to give a piece of bread or a drink of water to someone in need. This state is something one cannot obtain by one hundred thousand fasts and prayers.'[43]

Hazrat Nizamuddin Auliya would often visit her dargah for peace and solace after her death. In *Fawaid al-Fu'ad* he says,

> She had memorized many verses pertaining to every circumstance of life. I especially remember these two lines from her:
> For love you search, while still for life you strain.
> For both you search, but both you can't attain.[44]

Her dargah is one of the few where women can come into the shrine chamber and sit near it. I go there very often to pray for my children, for it is not very crowded and a great sense of peace pervades the shrine. The caretaker of the dargah once told me that at night jinn come and pray at the shrine too. And anyone who comes is only able to do so because Bibi wills it; no uninvited person can visit her.

'God purify their graves, repaired to the next world on the first of Jumada II in the year 648 Hijra (31 August 1250),' reads the inscription on the northern wall of the grave chamber of Bibi Zuleikha. Known as Mai Sahib, she was buried in the room where she lived.

Like many other families of Central Asia, Bibi Zuleikha's father and father-in-law, Khwaja Arab and Khwaja Ali, migrated to India during the Mongol invasions of Bukhara. They settled down in Badaun, then an important town in Awadh (now Uttar Pradesh). Khwaja Arab gave his daughter Bibi Zulekha in marriage to Khwaja Syed Ahmad, the son of Khwaja Ali.

There are many legends associated with her. One famous legend refers to her act of choosing her son over her husband. She once had a dream in which she was asked to make a choice between her husband and son, as only one was destined to live. She chose her son and her husband passed away soon after. Bibi Zuleikha felt very remorseful and was only comforted by the realization that she had no control over her dreams, which are involuntary experiences, and life and death are a matter of God's will.

Her influence on her son is deep and profound. She was a very devoted mother who ensured her children received the best of everything despite the severe financial and other hardships she had to face. She made sure that her son was educated by the best scholars of Badaun and once she felt her son had outgrown them at the age of 16, she moved to Delhi so that he could pursue his education.

Whenever there was no food in the house, Mai Sahib would tell her son, 'Nizamuddin! Today, we are guests of God.'[45]

She had total faith in God's will, and she taught her children that what mattered was that He would send them spiritual nourishment, which differed from worldly food but was more fulfilling.

The saint records in the *Fawaid ul-Fu'ad* that his mother was a remarkable lady in many respects, pious, inured to suffering, and resigned to the will of God. She was born in a wealthy family but when circumstances changed, she bore all her misfortunes with a smile. Her son's personality was a reflection of her upbringing, and her personal example teaches us that endurance and moral excellence are possible even in the midst of adverse circumstances. She provided her son with the best possible education but her health was compromised by her continuous fasting and struggles, and she did not live long enough to see her son at the height of his glory.

Every month, on sighting the new moon, the young Nizamuddin sought the blessings of Mai Sahib, placing his head on her feet. The *Fu'ad*, records that just before Mai Sahib left the world, she was ill for a few days and would often weep.

On the new moon night that month, when he presented himself before her and kissed her feet, she asked her son tearfully, 'Nizam! At whose feet will you put your head next month?' The Sheikh burst into tears. 'To whose care will you entrust me?' he asked. 'Tomorrow I will tell you,' replied the mother. She then directed him to go and sleep at the house of Sheikh Najibuddin.

In the small hours of the morning, the male servant came rushing to him and said that his mother had called him. Nizamuddin hurried to the house. 'Where is your right hand?' asked his dying mother. He stretched out his hand. She took it in hers and said: 'O God, I entrust him to Thee.' So saying Bibi Zulaikha breathed her last.[46]

Hazrat Nizamuddin says that he felt a state of contentment after these words and 'throughout his life he felt himself to be living under the protection and care of God'.[47]

Hers is another one of the few Delhi dargahs where women can go inside and pray for as long as they want. It is said that Mai Sahiba cannot bear to see anyone sad and helps fulfil wishes. The dargah sees a lot of women and young girls, supplicating, praying, or just meditating.

The twelfth century Bibi Amma, as she is popularly known, possessed great spiritual powers obtained through her rigorous devotion and prayers.

She was the daughter of Sufi Makhdoom Shahabuddin Pir Jagjot, who had come from Central Asia and settled in Bihar. Her husband was a Sufi saint, Hazrat Suleiman Langar. Her sister was married to Makhdoom Yayha Maneri.

Her simple dargah is in Jehanabad in Bihar and sees a great crowd of devotees every Friday. A stone tablet inscribed with verses from the Quran is installed next to her tomb. It is believed that if one pours oil over it, the oil acquires miraculous healing powers. People of all faiths come and collect such oil in bottles, using it to anoint the bodies of the unwell, and even for cooking. Devotees swear by its powers. As in other dargahs, many mentally ill people believed to be possessed by jinn are also brought here. Many of her Muslim devotees come and read the Quran in her presence, while the non-Muslims and Muslims sing *munajat*s (supplicatory hymns) asking for her intercession.

Princess Jahanara (1614–1681) was the eldest daughter of Emperor Shah Jahan and his favourite child. After her mother's death, she was made the First Lady and was given the titles of Sahibat al-Zamani (Lady of the

Age), Padishah Begum (Lady Emperor), and Begum Sahib (Princess of Princesses). Her power was such that, unlike the other royal princesses, she was allowed to live in her own palace, outside the confines of the Agra Fort. However, she considered herself a *fakir* in search of the Divine.

She aligned with Dara Shukoh in the battle of succession and gave up her preeminent position in the court after Aurangzeb's victory, retiring to look after her father in the Agra Fort, where Aurangzeb had imprisoned him. After Shah Jahan's death, she reconciled with Aurangzeb and regained her position in court.

Together with her brother Dara Shukoh, she was a disciple of Mullah Shah Badakhshi, who initiated her into the Qadriya Sufi order in 1641. Jahanara Begum made such progress on the Sufi path that Mullah Shah would have named her his successor in the Qadiri, except the rules of the order did not allow a woman to succeed a *pir*. She wrote a biography of Mullah Shah, titled *Risālah-i-Ṣāḥibīyah*, in which she also described her initiation by him.

She was also a devotee of Khwaja Muinuddin Chisti and wrote his highly acclaimed Persian biography titled *Mu'nis al-Arwāḥ*. Whenever she visited the dargah of Khwaja Muinuddin Chisti, she would offer prayers of gratitude at every step – all the way from the gateway to the shrine. She got a beautiful Begumi *dalan* (Begum's courtyard) added to the shrine.

She died in 1681 and is buried in a simple marble enclosure in the dargah of Hazrat Nizamuddin Auliya. She built the structure for herself during her lifetime. It is ornamented with embossed traceries, is hollow at the top, and exposed to the sky, as per her will. She had a tablet placed in the enclosure that bears a beautiful couplet written by herself:

*Huwal Hayyul Al Qayyum*
*Baghair subza na poshad kase mazar mara*
*Ki qabr posh ghariban hamin gayah bas-ast*
*Al faqeera, Al faaniya Jahanara mureed Khajgaana Chist,*
*Bint-eShah Jahan Badshah Ghazi Anar Allah Barhana*

[He is the Living, the Sustaining;
There cannot be any other curtain of my tomb except the humble covering of grass.

> Grass alone is sufficient to cover the grave of a poor person,
> As I am a disciple of Khwaja Moinuddin Chishti,
> Daughter of Shah Jahan, the Conqueror,
> May Allah illuminate his proof.]

Known by the male title of Babajan (beloved father), this Sufi saint was an Afghan woman who relocated to Pune when she was very old. Born in Afghanistan in an aristocratic family in the early part of nineteenth century and named Gulrukh, she died in Pune in 1931. She came to Pune when she was almost 100 years old and sat under a neem tree on Dastoor road.

A young nineteen-year-old named Mervan would often cycle down that path. One day she called him to come near; the young boy was entranced by her spiritual aura and the love emanating from her. She embraced him as her beloved son. He went on to become the saint Meher Baba.

She had many followers who would bring her gifts, but she would immediately give them away, leading a simple and almost ascetic life. Her only indulgence seems to have been hot cups of strong chai. Her generosity towards the poor and love for them also earned her the title Khwaja Sultana.

The Sufi matriarch being called Babajan, or father, is another confirmation of the inferior status given to women. According to Abdul Ghani, in his book *Hazrat Babajan of Poona*, she would respond negatively to the name 'Mai', which means 'mother' in many Indian languages. She would retort, 'I am a man and not a woman.'

She was buried under the same tree that she lived under and her funeral was attended by her followers from all faiths. Even today, her roadside dargah is very popular.

Raziuddin Aquil, historian and author of *The Muslim Question* and many books of Sufism says in an email to me,

> Women being barred from entering certain Sufi shrines is part of the usual strategy to segregate and remove them from public spaces, even if it's about deriving some simple spiritual satisfaction from visiting a Sufi's *mazar* [shrine]. We know that in large parts of the

> country women are not being allowed to enter mosques or even community graveyards. This is wicked and arbitrary.
>
> The history of attempts at such segregation in India goes back to late-fifteenth/early-sixteenth century, when Sultan Sikandar Lodi issued some *farmans* [orders] to this effect – those *farmans* are not extant now, but reports about them are available from late-sixteenth century.
>
> [...]
>
> In his own time, Hazrat Nizamuddin whose life is very well documented would just not have said anything discriminatory against women. Indeed, in the Chishti circles and in Sufi traditions everywhere – Punjab, Bengal, and Deccan included – women are seen as present sometimes even as primary audience throughout the medieval and early modern eras. The reference to Sikandar Lodi apart, attempts to invisibilize or remove women from the shrines is a new, modern, dubious exercise – emerging as part of Islamic reform of puritanical kinds with some prehistory in older times, in seventeenth–eighteenth century reformist movements, for instance. Hazrat Nizamuddin would not have prevented any woman from visiting his jama'atkhana when he was alive or paying *ziyarat* to his mazar subsequently.[48]

Attempting to make sense of when inegalitarian practices crept into Sufism, Schimmel writes that women were stopped from entering dargahs as early as during the reign of Firoz Shah Tughlaq (r.1351–1388), and again in the reign of Sikander Lodi (r.1489–1517). It was believed that doing so would mean avoiding the practice of 'unreligious' customs near some of the graves.[49]

The reason often given for the prohibition of women from visiting graves is a hadith that says, 'May Allah curse women who visit graveyards'.[50] Since a dargah is actually the grave of the saint, this is the argument used. However, scholars have argued that the above hadith was abrogated. 'Aishah narrated that the Messenger of Allah (ﷺ) (PBUH) gave permission for visiting the graves.[51]

Ayesha, the youngest wife of the Prophet, even said, 'The Holy Prophet taught me the manner of visiting the graves.' The method was described by her as follows:

> My Lord commanded me to come to Baqi' and seek forgiveness for them. Ayesha says: I asked him how one should seek forgiveness, to which the Holy Prophet replied: Say Peace (*salaam*) be upon the people of this place from the believers and Muslims; May God have mercy on those who have left and those who are to follow. We shall join you all very soon.[52]

Historically, women were allowed to visit dargahs at least in the Delhi sultanate till the fourteenth century. Quoting Futuhat-e Firoz Shahi, I.H. Siddiqui writes that Sultan Firoz Shah Tughlaq is said to have banned women in dargahs in Delhi and other places for it provided location for 'promiscuous meetings'.[53]

Today, the argument often given is that shrines are very confined spaces and women will be pushed and jostled around, which will be disrespectful towards them. But there are exceptions; the dargah of Ajmer Sharif, for instance, allows women to enter the main shrine along with men. In Mahim, in the very popular dargah of Hazrat Makhdoom al-Mahimi (1372–1431), in response to my request, the *khadim*s asked me to wait while they made arrangements. They then closed the door through which men were entering and opened a door in the women's section, allowing us to spend time inside.

So the rules are flexible and much of it is definitely made up to suit the convenience of the caretakers.

Author Annie Zaidi also questions why arrangements for the comfortable entry of women can't be made in all dargahs. She visited the dargah of Beema Beevi in Thiruvananthapuram in 2019, at the behest of a street-side astrologer, unaware of where she was going.

> Later in my hotel room, I ran a google search to figure out whose dargah it was and why it was pink. There was some information about a saint called Beema Beevi– a healer of diseases and pain and one of the earliest Arabs to have migrated to India. Her spiritual

> and medicinal powers attracted people to her and, ultimately, it led to the building of a dargah. So this is a woman saint's dargah. I began to think that it was funny how I could not go right up to the grave and place the *chadar* [*chaddar*] on it myself – not even on a woman saint's tomb. There are some dargahs where men are allowed right in but women are not, under the pretext that a certain kind of proximity is not allowed, not even when the material body of the saint has long ceased to be. I have always been irritated that there is no rotation system whereby sometimes men could be barred from entering so that women may approach the grave instead. Now here was a woman of great spiritual renown buried at Beemapally, yet there was no reversal of roles. True, male devotees can also not cross the barrier leading to the grave, but then nor can women. The caretakers were still all men, as far as I could see.[54]

Of the many dargahs I have visited, the ones that allowed me inside were that of Khwaja Muinuddin Chisti in Ajmer, Taragarh dargah in Ajmer, the Dewa Sharif dargah, Choti and Badi Pandua dargah, the Haji Ali Dargah in Mumbai, the Mahim Dargah, the dargah of Hazrat Sharfuddin Suhrawardi on Pahadi Sharif in Hyderabad, and of course, the ones of the two women Sufis in Delhi – Bibi Zulaikha and Bibi Fatima Sam. The dargahs of Haji Ratan and Hazrat Miran Shah in Bathinda were also open for women to enter and pray, as were the dargahs in Kakori near Lucknow. I seek forgiveness in case I have forgotten a few names. Of course, the status quo may change as it did in the dargah of Haji Ali in Mumbai, and one can only hope it does.

In 2012, the Haji Ali Dargah Trust imposed restrictions on the entry of women into the main shrine chamber, though they could enter the premises. The Bharatiya Muslim Mahila Andolan (BMMA) challenged the decision in 2014. In 2016, the Bombay High Court lifted the ban on the entry of women into the shrine chamber.

In 2015, when the case was going on, historian Raziuddin Aquil wrote about the issue in the *Economic and Political Weekly*:

> If that thing called soul does exist, the Prophet of Islam, who must have been one of the finest figures of his time and a role model for Muslims for all time to come, must be turning in his grave over what is wrong with the communities of people claiming to be his true followers. As lovers of God and followers of the righteous path shown by the Prophet, Sufis and other Muslim holy men would never ever discriminate against women in the manner in which the current guardians of Islam seek to bar them even from such spaces as a dargah – a place where they have historically been allowed to have a corner of their own as a sanctuary of relief from the oppressions of a patriarchal order that wants to subjugate women as a toy or a trophy as well as reproductive machine, mainly for a feudal society's fancy for the male child.[55]

The irony is that this is the situation although most of the Sufis, as discussed earlier, consider Prophet Muhammad as the first Sufi and trace their lineage from Hazrat Ali. In the Masjid-e-Nabvi in Medina, where the shrine of Prophet Muhammad is located, there are separate sections for men and women and all are allowed to come up to the rails of the enclosed grave. In Najaf too, in the shrine of Hazrat Ali, men and women are both allowed; they just have to stay in separate sections. This was the rule for the shrines of all the Shia imams as well – be it in Karbala, Iraq, or Mashhad in Iran.

Yet, today, in many dargahs in India, women are not allowed to enter the shrine for fear that they will pollute it. Separate sections/arrangements can and should be made for women, for Allah established a just social order through His Holy Word in the Quran and both men and women are equal in their spiritual endeavours in His eyes – to be rewarded or punished as per their individual deeds.

Meanwhile, Sufi saints continue to attract thousands of visitors, devotees, and disciples all across the world, irrespective of misunderstandings, misconceptions, propaganda against Sufi saints, accusations of innovation, and may they continue to do so. I would like to end with Amir Khusrau's famous verse,

*Ghar naari ganwari chaahe jo kahe,*
*Main Nijam se naina laga aayi re.*

[Let the women say whatever they want,
I have stolen a glance from Nizam's eyes.]

– Hazrat Amir Khusrau

# Appendix

## Important Dates in Islam

| | |
|---|---|
| 610 CE | First revelation of the Quran to Prophet Muhammad (pbuh) |
| 613 CE | The Prophet arranges *Dawat Dhul-Ashira* ('summoning the family') to introduce the message of Islam, with the help of the young Ali ibn Abi Talib |
| 621 CE | *Al-Israwal-Miraj* ('the night journey and ascension to heaven) |
| 622 CE | Prophet Muhammad's *hijrat* (migration) from Mecca to Medina |
| 622 CE | Beginning of the Islamic Calendar (known as Hijri, after the *hijrat*) |
| 632 CE | Death of Prophet Muhammad |
| 632–61 CE | Rashidun Caliphate (The four rightly guided caliphs appointed after the death of the Prophet) |
| June, 632 CE | Appointment of the first Rashidun caliph, Abu Bakr |
| August, 634 CE | Appointment of second Rashidun caliph, Umar ibn al-Khattab |
| November, 644 CE | Appointment of third Rashidun caliph, Usman ibn Affan |
| June, 656 CE | Appointment of fourth Rashidun caliph, Ali ibn Abi Talib |

| | |
|---|---|
| 661–750 CE | Umayyad Caliphate |
| 661 CE | Muawiah I becomes caliph |
| 680 CE | Yazid I becomes caliph; demands allegiance from Hussain, son of Hazrat Ali; when Hussain refuses to accept him as his spiritual leader, Yazid wages war against him; Hussain, along with all the male members of his family, martyred in the Battle of Karbala |

# Acknowledgements

Some special people have helped me on this journey, chief of them being Asif Khan Dehlvi who introduced me to the dargah of Qutub Sahib in Mehrauli. Since then, Qutub Sahib has become my patron Sufi saint. Peerzada Altamash Nizami has guided me through the intricacies of the dargah of Hazrat Nizamuddin Auliya, explaining not only the physical but also the mystical aspects of Mehboob-e-Ilahi's life.

When I started on this journey of exploring the world of Sufism, Faraz Ansari not only held my hand as I proceeded, but he also blessed me, advised me and adopted this project. Without his help this book would not be.

When we were studying together in Aligarh Muslim University, doing our postgraduation in history, I was unaware of the way our paths would meet again in the future – Saiyid Zaheer Hussain Jafri has been a pillar of strength for me as I journeyed into the world of history, writing and researching. I am forever grateful to him for reading the first draft of this book and correcting errors. He and his family are forever in my prayers.

Far away in Canada, Prashant Keshavmurthy has also become a source of strength for me. I look forward to our exchanges on subjects as varied as Persian, Urdu and Sanskrit poetry, the similarities between Persian metres and Sanskrit epics, and reflections on mysticism and *tasawwuf*. Prashant has an apt verse for every situation and his immense knowledge, so lightly worn by him, has been a great source of help to me. I have, I know, taken advantage of his amiable nature by asking for much more information than I should have, but he has never demurred or refused. I wish Prashant every success in this world.

Prof. Hassan Abbas's input was key to furthering my understanding of the relationship between Shiism and Sufism, which I explore in this book. I am grateful to him for his valuable suggestions.

Sarthak Malhotra, a research student at the University of Cambridge whose Ph.D is an ethnographic study of the Taj Mahal and Taj Ganj (also in Agra), has been a fellow traveller and explorer of some of the dargahs and Sufi concepts. I am extremely grateful to my young friend for reading some of the chapters and offering valuable insights. My book has been enriched by his various suggestions.

Many others have helped me along the way in understanding many aspects and I am especially grateful to Prof. Sunil Sharma, Prof. Raziuddin Aquil, Dhruv Sangari, Ranjit Hoskote, Shams Ur Rehman Alavi, Dr Muhamad Ismail, Dr Ursula Weekes, Prof. Ahab Bdaiwi and Prof. Omid Safi. I must also thank Prof. Ali A. Olomi, whose twitter threads and personal communication were very helpful to furthering my understanding of the role of jinn and angels in Islamic cosmology.

Annie Zaidi, Natasha Ramanathan, Chandrashekhar Tampi, Ghazala Wahab, Gourob Ghosh, Lubna and the numerous people who shared their experiences with me in various dargahs – you all have enriched my prose.

I would like to thank all the very special people who took out time to read and endorse this book. My book has been blessed by: the grace and erudition of Supriya Gandhi; Hassan Abbas's love for the *Ahl al-bait* and his knowledge; the mystical traditions that Zaheer Jafri is steeped in; the contemporary scholarship of Aanchal Malhotra; the expertise and ability to challenge the traditions of being 'born a Muslim' that Ghazala Wahab brings with her; the spirituality of Omid Safi and his generosity; and the knowledge and elegance of Moin Mir.

Kanishka Gupta, my literary agent, is always there to support and inspire me if I falter. Thank you for everything and for being my family.

Above all, I would like to thank Poulomi Chatterjee for her faith in me, for holding my hand throughout and to all my editors at Hachette, especially Sonali Jindal for making my pedestrian prose so beautiful. I owe you!

# Endnotes

## PREFACE

1. John T. Platts, 'A Dictionary of Urdu, Classical Hindi and English,' *Digital Dictionaries of Southeast Asia*. Web. July 2022. http://dsal.uchicago.edu/cgi-bin/app/platts_query.py?qs=tasawwuf&matchtype=default.
2. Carl W. Ernst, *Sufism: An Introduction to the Mystical Tradition of Islam*, Colorado: Shambhala, 2016.
3. The word *tasawwuf* along with the word *Sufi* are taken from the root word *suf*, which means a coarse woollen cloak, as explained in the chapters that follow.
4. Ernst, Sufism.
5. 'The Great Divide: How Westerners and Muslims View Each Other,' *Pew Research Center*, 22 June 2006. Web. July 2022. https://www.pewresearch.org/global/2006/06/22/the-great-divide-how-westerners-and-muslims-view-each-other/.
6. Raziuddin Aquil, 'Music and Related Practices in Chishti Sufism: Celebrations and Contestations.' *Social Scientist*, Vol. 40(3/4): 17–32, 2012.
7. Francis Joseph Steingass, 'Steingass Online Dictionary,' *Digital Dictionaries of Southeast Asia*. Web. July 2022. https://dsal.uchicago.edu/cgi-bin/app/steingass_query.py?qs=shaikh&matchtype=default.
8. Ibid.
9. Raziuddin Aquil, Email to author, 23 November 2021.

## CHAPTER 1

1. 'Thursday night is a very bright night and Friday is a shining day.' Baihaqi transmitted it in *[Kitab] ad-Da'awat al-kabir*, Mishkat al-Masabih 1369. 'Prayer,' *Sunnah.com*. Web. July 2022. https://sunnah.com/mishkat:1369.
2. When a child is born in a Muslim household, the first sound it hears traditionally is the *azaan*, recited in its right ear by the father or an elderly relative. This is to ensure that the first name the child hears is that of Allah and knows of his majesty.
3. Michael Lipka, 'Muslims and Islam: Key findings in the US and around the world,' *Pew Research Center*, 9 August 2017. Web. July 2022. https://www.pewresearch.org/fact-tank/2017/08/09/muslims-and-islam-key-findings-in-the-u-s-and-around-the-world/.

4. Seyyid Hossein Nasr, *The Study Quran: A New Translation and Commentary*, USA: Harper One, 2015.
5. Abdullah Yusuf Ali, trans., *The Holy Quran*, Lahore: Shaikh Muhammad Ashraf, 1937.
6. Nasr, in *The Study Quran*, writes: 'Several verses refer to different periods of gestation as a sign of God's creative power. The *blood clot* appears to be the third stage in the most extensive Quranic account of gestation: *O mankind! If you are in doubt concerning the Resurrection, [remember] We created you from dust, then from a drop, then from a blood clot, then from a lump of flesh, formed and unformed, that We may make clear for you. And We cause what We will to remain in the wombs for a term appointed* (22:5).'
7. H. Sahin, *The Qur'an: An Encyclopedia*, Ed. O. Leaman, London: Routledge, 2006.
8. Sheikh Safi-ur-Rahman al-Mubarakpuri and Ar-Raheeq Al-Makhtum, *The Sealed Nectar: Biography of the Noble Prophet*, Maktaba Dar-us-salam: Riyadh, Generic, 2016.
9. Ibid.
10. Ibn Ishaq, *The Life of the Prophet*, Trans. A. Guillaume, Karachi: OUP, 1998.
11. Ibid.
12. Al-Mubarakpuri and Al-Makhtum, *The Sealed Nectar*.
13. This is also known as the first *kalima*. There are six *kalima*s in all, which are the basic beliefs of all Muslims.
14. William C. Chittick, *The Sufi Path of Knowledge: Ibn al-Arabi's Metaphysics of Imagination*, Albany: State University of New York Press, 1989.
15. Carl W. Ernst, *Sufism: An Introduction to the Mystical Tradition of Islam*, Colarado: Shambhala, 2016.
16. Ibid. Ernst traces the use of the word *Islam* as used by followers of the religion: 'The use of the term *Islam* by non-Muslim scholars coincides with its increasing frequency in the religious discourse of those who now call themselves Muslims. That is, the term *Islam* became popular in reformist and protofundamentalist circles at approximately the same time, or shortly after, it was popularized by European Orientalists.'
17. Ishaq, The Life of the Prophet.
18. Nasr, The Study Quran.
19. Hassan Abbas, *The Prophet's Heir: The Life of Ali Ibn Abi Talib*, Yale: Yale University Press, 2021.
20. Ibid.
21. The minor pilgrimage which can be performed throughout the year is known as *umrah*, while the major one performed in the month of Zill Hajj is known as *hajj*.
22. Ishaq, The Life of the Prophet.
23. Ibid.
24. Abbas, The Prophet's Heir.
25. Ibid.
26. Lesley Hazleton, *After the Prophet: The Epic Story of the Shia-Sunni Split in Islam*, New York: Doubleday, 2009.
27. Ibid.

28. The three caliphates that succeeded each other were: the Rashedin or rightly guided caliphs (r. 632–61), the Umayyads (r. 661–750) and the Abbasids (r. 750–1258).
29. Kamran Scot Aghaie, *The Martyrs of Karbala: Shi'i Symbols and Rituals in Modern Iran*, Seattle and London: University of Washington Press, 2004.
30. 'The Definition of 'Ismah,' *Al-Islam*. Web. July 2022. https://www.al-islam.org/infallibility-prophets-quran-sayyid-muhammad-rizvi/definition-ismah#f_14a35a07_1.
31. Hassan Abbas, Email to author, June 2021.
32. Hadiths are a collection of traditions containing sayings of the Prophet Muhammad.
33. Called *shahada,* which means 'bearing of witness'.
34. Hadith of the Prophet, Sahih al-Bukhari, 4777.
35. Shaikh Mohammed Bin Yaqoob Bin Ishq Kulaini, *Kitab al-Kafi*, trans. Muhammad Sarwar, *Holy Books*. http://www.holybooks.com/al-kafi-shia-divine-text/. The excerpt describes an example:

    A group of our people, as narrated from Ahmad ibn Muhammad ibn Khalid from Ahmad ibn Muhammad ibn abu Nasr from Abu al-Hassan al-Muwsali from abu 'Abdallah (a.s.), said, 'Once a rabbi (hibr) came to Imam Ali (a.s.) and asked, "O Amir al-mu'minin, have you seen your Lord when worshipping Him?"'

    Imam Ali (a.s.) replied, 'This is not a proper question. I would not have worshipped a Lord whom I could not see.'

    He then asked, 'How did you see Him?'

    Imam Ali (a.s.) said, 'This is not a proper statement. Eyes can not see Him in eye-witnessing process but hearts see Him in the realities of faith.'
36. For Sufis, *ihsan* is a high goal reached when they are so absorbed in their prayers that they feel the presence of the divine with every breath they take.
37. Ernst, Sufism.
38. Tanvir Anjum, 'Sufism in History and Its Relationship with Power', *Islamic Studies*, Vol. 45(2): 221–268, 2006.
39. Ernst, Sufism.
40. Ibid.
41. Ibid.
42. This group comprised people from various parts of the world who accepted Islam and wanted to know more about it. While the *muhajirs*, or the emigrants from Mecca, busied themselves with commerce and the *ansars*, or friends of Islam in Medina, practised their traditional agriculture, the *Ahl-al-Suffa* worshipped during the night and fasted during the day. They lived ascetic lives in the Prophet's mosque and spent their time fasting, praying and in self-mortification. They also memorized the Quran as it was revealed and acquired religious knowledge, often from the Prophet himself and his companions. This tradition continued for many centuries with Sufi saints occupying themselves with religious studies, worshipping at night and fasting and praying through the day.
43. This hadith is not found in the canonical collections but quoted by many Sufi authors such as Ibn Arabi. See: James Winston Morris, 'The Spiritual Ascension: Ibn 'Arabī and the Mi'rāj' *Journal of the American Oriental Society*, Vol. 107: 629–652, 1987.

44. Rabi'a al-Adawiyya, *Doorkeeper of the Heart: Versions of Rabia*, trans. Charles Upton, Putney: Threshold Books, 1988.

## CHAPTER 2

1. John A. Subhan, *Sufism Its Saints and Shrines: An Introduction to the Study of Sufism with Special Reference to India*, Lucknow: Lucknow Publishing House, 1938.
2. Bevan Jones, *The People of the Mosque: The Study of Islam*, London: Student Christian Movement Press, 1932.
3. Alternative spelling of *Ahl al-Bait.*
4. Hassan Abbas, Email to author, 2 June 2021.
5. Omid Safi, *Radical Love: Teachings from the Islamic Mystical Tradition*, Yale: Yale University Press, 2018.
6. Rana Safvi, *Tales from the Quran and Hadith*, Delhi: Juggernaut Books, 2017.
7. Ibn Ishaq, *The Life of the Prophet*, trans. A. Guillaume, Karachi: OUP, 1998.
8. Sheikh Safi-ur-Rahman al-Mubarakpuri and Ar-Raheeq Al-Makhtum, *The Sealed Nectar: Biography of the Noble Prophet*, Maktaba Dar-us-salam: Riyadh, Generic, 2016.
9. Ishaq, The Life of the Prophet.
10. 'Sahih (Al-Albani), Book 14, Hadith 273,' *Sunnah.com*. Web. July 2022. https://sunnah.com/urn/2302710.
11. Ibn al' Arabi, *The Bezels of Wisdom*, trans. R.W.J. Austin, New York: Paulist Press, 1980.
12. Annemarie Schimmel, *Mystical Dimensions of Islam*, Chapel Hill: University of North Carolina Press, 2011.
13. Seyyid Hossein Nasr, *The Study Quran: A New Translation and Commentary,* USA: Harper One, 2015.
14. 'Made beloved to me from your world are women and perfume, and the coolness of my eyes is in prayer.' – Ahmad and An-Nasa 'i
15. Lesley Hazleton, *After the Prophet: The Epic Story of the Shia-Sunni Split in Islam*, New York: Doubleday, 2009.
16. Ibid.
17. Nasr, The Study Quran.
18. The earliest recorded hadiths are found in the *Life of Muhammad*, a biography of the Prophet written by Ibn Ishaq (704–767) and in Malik ibn Anas' compilation of Islamic laws known as *Al Muwatta*. By the third century AH (816 – 913 CE), these hadiths were compiled into six canonical collections known as *sahih* (which literally means authentic). The two most popular ones are *Sahih Bukhari* compiled by al-Bukhari (810–870) and *Sahih Muslim* compiled by Muslim ibn al-Hajjaj (817–875). The other four, also compiled around the same time, are: *Kitāb al-sunan* (Book of Traditions) of Abu Daud al-Sijistani (817–889), *Jami al-Sahih* of Al Tirmizi (824–892), *Kitāb al-sunan*of Al-Nasai (830–915) and *Sunan ibn Majah* of Ibn Majah (824–887).

    The Shias started compiling hadiths from the fourth and fifth centuries AH (913–1106 CE) and since these traditions emanate from the *Ahl al-Bait*, they consider them authentic and give preference to them over the *sahihs*. The most prominent books followed are *Nahj al-Balaghah* compiled by Sharif al-Radi (970–1015) and Kitab *al-Kafi* by al-Kulayni (864–941).

19. Omid Safi, 'Sheath Your Sword: The Man Who Spat on Saint Ali', *On Being*, 26 March 2015. Web. July 2022. https://onbeing.org/blog/sheath-your-sword-the-man-who-spat-on- saint-ali/.
20. Schimmel, Mystical Dimensions of Islam.
21. Muhammad Legenhausen, 'The "Irfan of the Commander of the Faithful, Imam Ali (a)"', *Religious Inquiries*, Vol. 3(5): 5–20, 2014.
22. Carl W. Ernst, *Sufism: An Introduction to the Mystical Tradition of Islam*, Colarado: Shambhala, 2016.
23. Rebecca Masterton, 'A Comparative Exploration of the Spiritual Authority of the Awliyā' in the Shi'i and Sufi Traditions', *American Journal of Islamic Social Sciences*, Vol. 32: 49–74, 2015.
24. Rana Safvi, 'How Interpretation of the Word Maula Caused the Shia-Sunni Schism', *dailyO*, 7 September 2017. Web. July 2022. https://www.dailyo.in/lifestyle/prophet-mohammad-muslim-world-shia-sunni-19373
25. Hassan Abbas, *The Prophet's Heir: The Life of Ali Ibn Abi Talib*, Yale: Yale University Press, 2021.
26. Nasr, The Study Quran.
27. Abbas, The Prophet's Heir.
28. Ibid.
29. Seyyed Hossein Nasr, *Living Sufism*, Srinagar: Gulshan Books, 2008.
30. Ahab Bdaiwi, Email to author, 25 May 2021.
31. Mohammad Ali Amir Moezzi, *The Divine Guide in Early Shi'ism: The Sources of Esotericism in Islam*, Trans. David Streight, New York: State University of New York Press, 1994. This is called Hadith Saluni and is verified by Sunni and Shia sources. The wordings may differ in different translations of the original Arabic but the gist remains the same.

    Also see:

    i. Abu 'Abd Allah Muhammad b. 'Abd Allah al-Hakim al-Naysaburi, al-Mustadrak 'ala al-Ṣahihayn, Beirut: Dar al-Kutub al-'Ilmiyyah; 1st edition, 1411 H) [annotator: Mustafa 'Abd al-Qadir 'Ata], vol. 2: 506, # 3736.

    ii. 'ALI'S ANNOUNCEMENT OF SALUNI (ASK ME) AND THE REPORTS OF THE SUNNIS', *Makarem*.ir. Web. July 2022. https://makarem.ir/main.aspx?reader=1&lid=0&mid=83517&catid=0&pid=72246
32. 'Many great Persian poets influenced by Imam Ali (AS): scholar,' *Tehran Times*, 27 June 2016. Web. July 2022. https://www.tehrantimes.com/news/403769/Many-great-Persian-poets-influenced-by-Imam-Ali-AS-scholar.
33. Keshavmurthy, Email to author, 3 September 2019.
34. In the commentary in *The Study Quran*, Nasr writes, 'Similar statements regarding faith are also found in: [the Quran's Surah] 10:99–100 "And had thy Lord willed, all those who are on the earth would have believed all together. Wouldst thou compel men till they become believers? It is not for a soul to believe, save by God's leave"; and 18:29 "It is the truth from your Lord! So whosoever will, let him believe, and whosoever will, let him disbelieve."'

35. Ikram Al-Waleed, *Bin Al-Waleed: Sword of Allah*, UK: Maktabah Publications, 2007.
36. Omid Safi, 'Sheath Your Sword.'
37. Sahih Bukhari, Volume 4, Book 56, Number 668.
38. The Kharijites were a group of people who had been Ali's supporters, but they rejected him when he accepted the arbitration with Muawiya I in the matter of succession to the caliphate after the Battle of Siffin. The Battle of Siffin fought between the armies of Muawiya I and Ali had been over the succession. Ali was winning when Muawiya asked his army to raise the Quran on their lances and ask for arbitration. Ali agreed. One group disagreed with Ali, who felt that success in battle was bestowed by Allah and no one could go against the Divine Will. By accepting arbitration and giving up a victory which had seemed certain then, they felt Ali had gone against the Divine Will. Under their leader, Abdullah ibn-Wahab, they left Kufa and settled a little distance away. They put their faith only in the Quran. As their insurrection grew, Ali went into battle against them, and in the Battle of Nahrwab ibn-Wahab was killed. As revenge, a Kharijte Abdul Rahman ibn-Muljim assassinated Ali.
39. Hazleton, After the Prophet.
40. Sayyid Abd al-Razzaq al-Muqarram. *Maqtal al-Husayn*, trans. Yasin T. al-Jibouri. Al-Kharsan Foundation for Publications. https://www.al-islam.org/maqtal-al-husayn-sayyid-abd-al-razzaq-al-muqarram.
41. This village was originally called Nainawa, but was renamed Karb o bala (Karbala), as *karb* means anguish and *bala* means calamity.
42. al-Muqarram, Maqtal al-Husayn.
43. Number nine of *The Fifteen Whispered Prayers* from: Willian C. Chittick, 'Introduction and annotation.' In *Al-Saheefah Al-Sajjadiyyah Al-Kaamelah*. Qum, The Islamic Republic of Iran: Ansariyan Publications, 2009.
44. Ibid.
45. Ibid.
46. Ali B. Uthman Al-Jullabi Al-Hujwiri, *Kashf al-Mahjub*: *The Oldest Persian Treatise On Sufiism*, trans. Reynold A. Nicholson, London, Leyden: E. J. Brill, Imprimerie Orientale, 1911.
47. Ibid. Most sources mention 702 as his birth year, although it has also been recorded as 699 and 705 in some places.
48. Al-Jullabi Al-Hujwiri, Kashf al-Mahjub.
49. John B. Taylor, 'Ja'far al-Sādiq, Spiritual Forebear of the Sufis', *Islamic Culture*, Vol. 40(2): 97–113, 1966.
50. Ibid.
51. Shaikh Mohammed Bin Yaqoob Bin Ishq Kulaini, *Kitab al-Kafi*, trans. Muhammad Sarwar, *Holy Books*. http://www.holybooks.com/al-kafi-shia-divine-text/.
52. Arthur Buehler, 'Overlapping Currents in Early Islam: The Sufi Shaykh and Shī'Ī Imam', *Journal of the History of Sufism*, Vol. 3: 1–20, 2010.
53. Hassan Abbas, Email to author, 2 June 2021
54. Allamah Sayyid M. Tabatabai, *Shiite Islam*, Trans. Seyyid Hossein Nasr, New York: State University of New York Press, 1979.
55. Masterton, 'A Comparative Exploration.'

## CHAPTER 3

1. Saiyid Athar Abbas Rizvi, *A History of Sufism in India, Vol. 1*, New Delhi: Munshiram Manoharlal Publishers Pvt Ltd, 1978.
2. Carl W. Ernst, *Words of Ecstasy in Sufism*, State University of New York Press, 1985. There are many dates given for ibn Adham's death, but I am going with the date given by Ernst.
3. Ibid.
4. Rizvi, History of Sufism, Vol. 1.
5. Amira Shamma Abdin, 'Love in Islam,' *European Judaism: A Journal for the New Europe*, Vol. 37(1): 92–102, 2004.
6. Muhammad ibn al-Husayn al-Sulami, 'Foreword,' In *The Way of Sufi Chivalry: When the Light of the Heart is Reflected in the Beauty of the Face*, trans. Sheikh Tosun Bayrak al-Jerrahi, New York: Inner Traditions International, 1983.
7. Ibid.
8. Ibid.
9. Bipan Chandra and Sucheta Mahajan, *Composite Culture in a Multicultural Society*, New Delhi: Pearson India, 2007.
10. Tara Chand, *Influence of Islam in Indian Culture*, Allahabad: The Indian Press, 1922, reprint 1936.
11. Ibid.
12. Susan Bayly, *Saints, Goddesses, and Kings: Muslims and Christians in South Indian Society, 1700–1900*, New York: Cambridge University Press, 1989.
13. A fifteenth century Tamil – and Malayalam-speaking community spread along the coast of Tamil Nadu, Kerala and Sri Lanka – descendants of the early Muslim seafaring people who married women from the coastal Mukkuvar community.
14. Bayly, Saints, Goddesses, and Kings.
15. Nizam ad-din Awliya, *Morals of the Heart*, trans. Bruce B. Lawrence, recorded by Amir Hasan Sijzi. Mahwah, New Jersey: Paulist Press, 1992.
16. Generally translated as 'the conference of the birds', but according to Prof. Prashant Keshavmurthy the correct translation is 'language'.
17. Shahid Amin, *Conquest and Community: The Afterlife of Warrior Saint Ghazi Miyan*, New Delhi: Orient Black Swan, 2015.
18. Rozina Ali, 'The Erasure of Islam from the Poetry of Rumi,' *The New Yorker*, 5 January 2017. Web. July 2022. https://www.newyorker.com/books/page-turner/the-erasure-of-islam-from-the-poetry-of-rumi.
19. Jawid Mojaddedi, 'Introduction', In *The Masnavi: Book One,* Jalal al-Din Rumi. Oxford: OUP, 2004.
20. Omid Safi, 'Rumi Without Islam: The Cultural Appropriation of Rumi,' *Bayt al Fann*, December 2021. Web. July 2022. https://www.baytalfann.com/post/rumi-without-islam-the-cultural-appropriation-of-rumi.
21. Rabi'a Al-Adawiyya, *Doorkeeper of the Heart: Versions of Rabia*, Trans. Charles Upton, Putney: Threshold Books, 1988.
22. Seyyid Hossein Nasr, *Ideals and Realities of Islam*, Chicago: ABC International Inc., 2000.

23. Fatima Bilgrami, 'History of the Qadiri Order in India: 16th–18th Century.' PhD diss., Aligarh Muslim University, 1982.
24. Ëric Geoffroy, *Introduction to Sufism: The Inner Path of Islam*, United States: World Wisdom Books, 2010.
25. Omid Safi, *Radical Love: Teachings from the Islamic Mystical Tradition*, Yale: Yale University Press, 2018.
26. 'Rumi's Masnavi,' *Masnavi*. Web. July 2022. http://www.masnavi.net/1/10/eng/1/34/.
27. Rizvi, A History of Sufism in India, Vol. 1.
28. Ibid.
29. Robert Frager and James Fadiman, *Essential Sufism*, San Francisco: Harper, 1997.
30. Rizvi, A History of Sufism in India, Vol. 1, 58.
31. Rizvi, A History of Sufism in India, Vol. 1.
32. A.J. Arberry, *An Introduction to the History of Sufism*, Oxford: Longmans Green and Co. Printed in University Press, 1942.
33. Rizvi, A History of Sufism in India, Vol. 1.
34. Al-Qāḍīal-Quḍā'ī, *A Treasury of Virtues: Sayings, Sermons, and Teachings of Ali, with the One Hundred Proverbs Attributed to al-Jahiz*, trans. Tahera Qutbuddin, New York: New York University Press, 2013.
35. As-Sulami, *Early Sufi Women: A Bilingual Critical Edition of as Sulami's Dikr An-Niswa Al-Muta 'abbitdat As-Sufuyyat*, trans. Rkia Cornell, US: Fons Vitae, 2001.
36. Ibid.
37. Ibid.
38. Carl W. Ernst, *Sufism: An Introduction to the Mystical Tradition of Islam*, Colarado: Shambhala, 2016.
39. Khwaja Khizr, who has drunk from the fountain of life and is thus immortal, is also said to be ever at hand to answer the calls of those in trouble and to rejuvenate the faith of the wavering. He is a dominant figure in a Sufi's quest for knowledge and realization of the Absolute Reality. He is also the patron saint of travellers. Sufis invoke him when they embark on their mystical journey, whereas laypersons like me never fail to call on him at the start of a physical journey.
40. Seyyid Hossein Nasr, *The Study Quran: A New Translation and Commentary*, USA: Harper One, 2015.
41. 'Dua Kumayl/The Supplication of Kumayl,' *Qul*. Web. 30 August 2021. http://www.qul.org.au/library/duas-supplications/399-dua-kumayl-the-supplication-of-kumayl.
42. 'Forty Hadith Qudsi,' *Sunnah.com*. Web. July 2022. https://sunnah.com/qudsi40.
43. Ibid.
44. Ibid.
45. *Hadith-e-Qudsi* are said to be those sayings of the Prophet through which Allah Himself is addressing the people, as opposed to the simple hadiths which are the Prophet's own words.
46. Faqir Zulfiqar Ahmed Naqshbandi, *Love for Allah*, Chicago: Faqir Publications, 2001.

47. Rizvi, A History of Sufism in India, Vol. 1.
48. William C. Chittick, 'Rumi and Wahdat Al Wujud,' In *Poetry and Mysticism in Islam: The Heritage of Rumi*, eds Amin Banani, Richard Hovannisian and Georges Sabagh, Cambridge: Cambridge University Press, 1994. 70–111.
49. Ibid.
50. Alexander Treiger, 'Monism and Monotheism in Al-Ghazālī's Mishkāt al-Anwār□,' *Journal of Qur'anic Studies*, Vol. 9(1): 1–27, 2007. □□□
51. Let's Talk Religion, 'The Unity of Being (Wahdat al-Wujud),' YouTube video, 24:25, 10 May 2020. https://www.youtube.com/watch?v=F_MIw4KG7Qk. I have greatly benefited from the videos of Filip Holm who explores the world of religion and philosophy through academic source in his series called Let's Talk Religion on Youtube.
52. Ibid.
53. Umi Sumbulah. 'Ibn 'Arabī's Thought on WahDahAl-Wujīd and Its Relevance to Religious Diversity.' *Journal of Islamic Studies Publish by State Islamic Institute Mataram* 20, no. 1 (2016): 53–73.
54. Let's Talk Religion, Youtube, 'The Unity of Being (Wahdat al-Wujud).'
55. Chittick, 'Rumi and Wahdat Al Wujud.'
56. Seyyid Hossein Nasr, *Three Muslim Sages*, New York: Caravan Books, 1976.
57. Schimmel, Mystical Dimensions of Islam.
58. R.A. Nicholson, *Studies in Islamic Mysticism*, Delhi: Idarah-I Adabiyat-I Dehli, 1921, reprint 2009.
59. Yohanan Friedmann, *Shaykh Aḥmad Sirhindī: An Outline of His Thought and a Study of His Image in the Eyes of Posterity*, Oxford University Press, 1966.
60. Rizvi, *A History of Sufism in India, Vol. 1*. The theory that *Wahdat al-Wujud* was tantamount to pantheism has been now rejected.
61. Aishah Al-Bauniyyah, *The Principles of Sufism*, eds. and trans. Th. Emil Homerin, New York and London: New York University Press, 2014.

## CHAPTER 4

1. Omid Safi, *Radical Love: Teachings from the Islamic Mystical Tradition*, Yale: Yale University Press, 2018.
2. 'Color,' *Iranica Online*. Web. July 2022. https://www.iranicaonline.org/articles/color-pers-rang.
3. Sir Syed Ahmad Khan, *Asar-us Sanadid*, trans. Rana Safvi, New Delhi: Tulika Books, 2018.
4. The Mongol invasion of Central Asia started in 1206 and was completed with the conquest of the Khwarazmian dynasty by Genghis Khan in 1221.
5. Raziuddin Aquil, *The Muslim Question: Understanding Islam and Indian History*, New Delhi: Penguin Random House, 2017.
6. Saiyid Athar Abbas Rizvi, *A History of Sufism in India, Vol. 1*, New Delhi: Munshiram Manoharlal Publishers Pvt Ltd, 1978.
7. Aquil, The Muslim Question.
8. Omar Khalidi, 'Qawwali and Mahfil-i-Sama', In *Muslim Shrines in India*, eds. Christian Troll, India: Oxford University Press, 2002. 257–261.

9. Raziuddin Aquil, Email to author, 25 January 2022.
10. Ute Falasch, 'Regulating Rapture: The "Malang" in the Madāriyyah,' *Oriente Moderno*, Vol. *92(2): 369–92, 2012.*
11. Rizvi, A History of Sufism in India, Vol. 1.
12. Khaliq Ahmed Nizami, *State and Culture in Medieval India*, New Delhi: Adam Publishers and Distributors, 1985.
13. Ibid.
14. Nizam ad-din Awliya, *Morals of the Heart*, trans. Bruce B. Lawrence, recorded by Amir Hasan Sijzi. Mahwah, New Jersey: Paulist Press, 1992.
15. Aquil, The Muslim Question.
16. Sunil Kumar, 'State Formation and Social Integration in Pre-modern South and Southeast Asia: A Comparative Study of Asian Society,' Paper presented at a conference in Toyo Bunko, Japan, 8–9 March 2014.
17. M. Zameer Uddin Siddiqi, 'Shaikh Abdul Quddus of Gangoh and Contemporary Rulers,' *Proceedings of the Indian History Congress*, Vol. 31, 1969.

## CHAPTER 5

1. Raziuddin Aquil, *Lovers of God: Sufism and the Politics of Islam in Medieval India*, Delhi: Manohar Publishers and Distributers, 2017.
2. S.A.H Abidi, *Memorial Volume: Amir Khusrau*, New Delhi: Publications Division, Ministry of Information and Broadcasting, Government of India, 1975.
3. Khaliq Ahmed Nizami, *State and Culture in Medieval India*, New Delhi: Adam Publishers and Distributors, 1985.
4. Saiyid Athar Abbas Rizvi, *A History of Sufism in India, Vol. 1*, New Delhi: Munshiram Manoharlal Publishers Pvt Ltd, 1978.
5. Bruce Lawrence, *Notes from a Distant Flute: The Extant Literature of Pre-Mughal Indian Sufism*, Tehran: Imperial Academy of Philosophy, 1978.
6. Rizvi, A History of Sufism in India, Vol. 1.
7. Ibid.
8. The language from which Hindi/Urdu is derived.
9. Lawrence, Notes from a Distant Flute.
10. Rana Safvi, *Where Stones Speak: Historical Trails in Mehrauli, the First City of Delhi*, New Delhi: Harper Collins India, 2015.
11. Sheikh Jamali, *Siyar-ul-Arifin* (*Biographies of Mystics*), Trans Ishrat Hussain Ansari, Hamid Afaq Qureshi and al-Taimi al-Siddiqi, Delhi: Idarah-I Adbiyat-I Delli, 2015.
12. Ibid.
13. Lawrence, Notes from a Distant Flute.
14. Rizvi, A History of Sufism in India, Vol. 1.
15. Haroon Khalid, 'Despite Mughal-Sikh conflicts, inclusion of Muslim poets in Guru Granth Saheb is proof of close tie', *Scroll*, 1 September 2017. Web. July 2022.
16. Rizvi, A History of Sufism in India, Vol. 1.
17. Khaliq Ahmed Nizami, *The Life and Times of Shaikh Nizamuddin Auliya*, Delhi: Oxford University Press, 2007
18. Nizami, State and Culture in Medieval India.

19. Nizami, Life and Times of Shaikh Nizamuddin Auliya.
20. This reinforces the Sufi concept that there are *rijal-ulghaib* (saints hidden from the human gaze).
21. Nizam ad-din Awliya, *Morals of the Heart*, trans. Bruce B. Lawrence, recorded by Amir Hasan Sijzi. Mahwah, New Jersey: Paulist Press, 1992.
22. Ibid.
23. Mohammad Habib, *Hazrat Amir Khusrau of Delhi*, New Delhi: Cosmo Publications, 2004.
24. Nizami, State and Culture in Medieval India.
25. Rizvi, A History of Sufism in India, Vol. 1.
26. Habib, Hazrat Amir Khusrau of Delhi.
27. Ibid.
28. Jamali, Siyar-ul-Arifin.
29. Ibid.
30. Ibid.
31. Rizvi, A History of Sufism in India, Vol. 1.
32. Ibid.
33. Jamali, Siyar-ul-Arifin.
34. Rizvi, A History of Sufism, Vol. 1.
35. Sunil Sharma, *Amir Khusraw: The Poet of Sultans and Sufis (Makers of the Muslim World*), Oxford: Oneworld Publications, 2005
36. Translated by Avinash Pandey.
37. Habib, *Hazrat* Amir Khusrau of Delhi.
38. Nizam ad-din Awliya, Morals of the Heart.
39. Sunil Sharma and Paul Losenky. *In the Bazaar of Love*. New Delhi: Penguin India, 2011.
40. Anna Suvorova. *Muslim Saints of South Asia: The Eleventh to Fifteenth Centuries*, Moscow: Institute of Oriental Studies, 1999.
41. I often go to his dargah called the Choti Dargah, to prayer for inspiration for my writing and seek his blessings for my pen.
42. Nizam ad-din Awliya, Morals of the Heart.
43. Telephonic conversation in February 2018 for an article I wrote for *The Hindu* on Hasan Sijzi on 4 March 2018. 'Sufism in the simplest terms', *The Hindu*, 4 March 2018. Web. July 2022.
44. Ibid.

## CHAPTER 6

1. Saiyid Athar Abbas Rizvi, *A History of Sufism in India, Vol. 1*, New Delhi: Munshiram Manoharlal Publishers Pvt Ltd, 1978.
2. Ibid.
3. Ibid.
4. Sheikh Jamali, *Siyar-ul-Arifin* (*Biographies of Mystics*), trans. Ishrat Hussain Ansari, Hamid Afaq Qureshi and al-Taimi al-Siddiqi, Delhi: Idarah-I Adbiyat-I Delli, 2015.
5. Rizvi, A History of Sufism in India, Vol. 1.
6. Sheikh Bahauddin died in 1262 having lived in Multan for around half a century, so one may estimate that he may have come to Multan around 1212.

7. Farida Khanum, *Sufism: An Introduction*, Delhi: Goodword Books, 2009.
8. Anna Suvorova, *Muslim Saints of South Asia: The Eleventh to Fifteenth Centuries*, Moscow: Institute of Oriental Studies, 1999.
9. To date, the older part of Mehrauli is said to be haunted by jinns, and many heritage enthusiasts organize jinn walks at night in the Mehrauli Archaeological park.
10. 'Shaikh JalaluddinTabrizi', *Banglapedia*. Accesssed on 6 June 2022. https://en.banglapedia.org/index.php/Shaikh_Jalaluddin_Tabrizi_(R)
11. Rizvi, A History of Sufism in India, Vol. 1.
12. Bruce Lawrence, *Notes from a Distant Flute: The Extant Literature of Pre-Mughal Indian Sufism*, Tehran: Imperial Academy of Philosophy, 1978.
13. Translation from Lawrence, Morals of the Heart.
14. Rizvi, A History of Sufism in India, Vol. 1.
15. Maulvi Zafar Hasan, *Monuments of Delhi Volume 3*, New Delhi: Om Books, 1997.

## CHAPTER 7

1. Robert Frager and James Fadiman, *Essential Sufism*, San Francisco: Harper, 1997.
2. Rana Safvi, *City of My Heart*, New Delhi: Hachette India, 2018.
3. Saiyid Athar Abbas Rizvi, *A History of Sufism in India, Vol. 1*, New Delhi: Munshiram Manoharlal Publishers Pvt Ltd, 1978.
4. Ibid.
5. Khaliq Ahmed Nizami, *State and Culture in Medieval India*, New Delhi: Adam Publishers and Distributors, 1985.
6. Saiyid Athar Abbas Rizvi, *A History of Sufism in India, Vol 2*, New Delhi: Munshiram Manoharlal Publishers Pvt Ltd, 1992.
7. Ibid.
8. Supriya Gandhi, *The Emperor Who Never Was: Dara Shukoh in Mughal India*, United States: Harvard University Press, 2020.
9. Avik Chanda, *Dara Shukoh: The Man Who Would Be King*, New Delhi: Harper Collins India, 2019.
10. Gandhi, The Emperor Who Never Was.
11. The kalimah La ilaahaillallah starts with a negation and then goes on to affirm: There is no God but Allah.
12. Translation by Kartar Singh Duggal from the Internet, 'BullehShah : Enough of Learning, My Friend!' *Random Musings*, 10 December 2015. http://sathyu-sathyu.blogspot.com/2015/12/bulleh-shah-enough-of-learning-my-friend.html.

## CHAPTER 8

1. Faqir Zulfiqar Ahmed Naqshbandi, *Love for Allah*, Chicago: Faqir Publications, 2001.
2. Basheeruddin Ahmed Dehlvi, *Waqeat-e Darul Hukumat Dehli*, Delhi: Urdu Academy, 2012.
3. Muzaffar Alam, 'The Mughals, the Sufi Shaikhs and the Formation of the Akbari Dispensation,' *Modern Asian Studies*, Vol. 43(1): 135–174, 2009.
4. Ibid.

5. Carl W. Ernst and Bruce Lawrence, *The Sufi Martyrs of Love: The Chishti Order in South Asia and Beyond*, US: Palgrave Macmillan, 2002.
6. Alam, 'Mughals, Shaikhs and the Akbari Dispensation.'
7. Ibid.
8. Khaliq Ahmed Nizami, *State and Culture in Medieval India*, New Delhi: Adam Publishers and Distributors, 1985.
9. Ibid.
10. Hamid Algar, 'The Naqshbandī Order: A Preliminary Survey of Its History and Significance,' *Studia Islamica*, (44): 123–52, 1976. https://doi.org/10.2307/1595445.
11. Nizami, State and Culture in Medieval India.
12. Saiyid Athar Abbas Rizvi, *A History of Sufism in India, Vol. 1*, New Delhi: Munshiram Manoharlal Publishers Pvt Ltd, 1978.
13. Muhammad Hisham Kabbani, *Classical Islam and the Naqshbandi Sufi tradition*, Washington: Islamic Supreme Council of America, 2004.
14. Ramita Udayshankar, 'Naqshbandi Silsilah in Mughal India', *Academia.edu*. Web. July 2022. https://www.academia.edu/33081247/Naqshbandi_Silsilah_in_Mughal_India.
15. Kabbani, Classical Islam and the Naqshbandi Sufi Tradition.
16. Saiyid Athar Abbas Rizvi, *A History of Sufism in India, Vol. 2*, New Delhi: Munshiram Manoharlal Publishers Pvt Ltd, 1992.
17. Kabbani, Classical Islam and the Naqshbandi Sufi Tradition.
18. Ibid.
19. Annemarie Schimmel, *Mystical Dimensions of Islam*, Chapel Hill: University of North Carolina Press, 2011.
20. Shah-Kazemi, *The Spirit of Tolerance in Islam*, London: I.B. Tauris in association with The Institute of Ismaili Studies, 2012.
21. Yohanan Friedmann, *Shaykh Aḥmad Sirhindī: An Outline of His Thought and a Study of His Image in the Eyes of Posterity*, Oxford University Press, 1966.
22. Nizami, State and Culture in Medieval India.
23. Irfan M. Habib, 'The Political Role of Shaikh Ahmad Sirhindi and Shah Waliullah', *Proceedings of the Indian History Congress* 23, Indian History Congress, 1960
24. Ibid.
25. Friedmann, Shaykh Aḥmad Sirhindī.
26. Prashant Keshavmurthy, Email to author, 20 June 2021.
27. Yohanan Friedmann, 'Medieval Muslim Views of Indian Religions', *Journal of the American Oriental Society*, Vol. 95(2): 214–221, 1975.
28. Kabbani, Classical Islam and the Naqshbandi Sufi Tradition.
29. Rizvi, A History of Sufism in India, Vol. 2.
30. Rizvi, A History of Sufism in India, Vol. 2.
31. Nizami, State and Culture in Medieval India.
32. Friedmann, 'Medieval Muslim Views of Indian Religions.'
33. Ibid.
34. Rizvi, A History of Sufism in India, Vol. 2.

## CHAPTER 9

1. Saiyid Athar Abbas Rizvi, *A History of Sufism in India, Vol. 1*, New Delhi: Munshiram Manoharlal Publishers Pvt. Ltd, 1978.
2. Simon Digby, 'Qalandars and Related Groups: Elements of Social Deviance in the Religious Life of the Delhi Sultanate of the Thirteenth and Fourteenth Centuries,' In *Islam in Asia, Vol. 1: South Asia*, eds. Yohanan Friedmann, Boulder: Westview Press, 1984. 60–108.
3. Rizvi, A History of Sufism in India, Vol. 1.
4. Ibid.
5. J. Spencer Trimingham, *The Sufi Orders in Islam*, London: Oxford University Press, 1971.
6. Rizvi, A History of Sufism in India, Vol. 1.
7. Since *urs* are celebrated according to the Islamic calendar, which is based on a lunar system, the Gregorian dates keep shifting.
8. Z. Ali, 'In All Its glory, Qalandar's Urs Culminates in Sehwan,' *Tribune*, 18 May 2017. Web. July 2022. https://tribune.com.pk/story/1412392/glory-qalandars-urs-culminates-sehwan
9. Anna Suvorova, *Muslim Saints of South Asia*, London: Routledge, 2004.
10. Carl W. Ernst and Bruce Lawrence, *The Sufi Martyrs of Love: The Chishti Order in South Asia and Beyond*, US: Palgrave Macmillan, 2002.
11. Rizvi, A History of Sufism in India, Vol. 1.
12. Tariq Khan, *Sufi Saints and Their Contributions*, New Delhi: Raj Publications, 2015.
13. Moin Ahmad Nizami, 'Abd al-Quddus Gangohi', *Encyclopaedia of Islam 3*, 2012. Web. July 2022. https://www.academia.edu/33421800/Abd_al_Quddus_Gangohi
14. Moin Ahmad Nizami, *Reform and Renewal in South Asian Islam: The Chishti-Sabris in 18th–19th Century North India*, New Delhi: Oxford University Press, 2017.
15. Rizvi, A History of Sufism in India, Vol. 1.
16. Farida Khanum, *Sufism: An Introduction*, Delhi: Goodword Books, 2009.
17. Rizvi, A History of Sufism in India, Vol. 1.
18. Sadia Dehlvi, *Sufism: Heart of Islam*, New Delhi: HarperCollins, 2010.
19. M. Ishaq Khan, *Kashmir's Transition to Islam: The Role of Muslim Rishi*, Delhi: Manohar Books, 2002.
20. Abdul Qaiyum Rafiqi, *Sufism in Kashmir*, Kashmir: Gulshan Books, 2015.
21. Ibid.
22. For me the visit to the *khanqah* was a kind of sweet homecoming as my paternal ancestors descended from Sheikh Hamdani. One of Hamdani's grandsons came to Jalali, a small town near Aligarh in Uttar Pradesh. We are his descendants, and some family members use the surname Hamdani even today.
23. Rizvi, A History of Sufism in India, Vol. 1.
24. Adil Mehdi, 'Radical Renunciation and Love: Haji Sahib of Dewa,' In *A Leaf Turns Yellow: The Sufis of Awadh*, eds. Muzaffar Ali, New Delhi: Bloomsbury Publishing India Private Limited, 2012.

25. Ananda Bhattacharya, 'Madariya Sufi Silsila: Distinctive Characteristics and Relations with the Indian Powers,' *Economic and Political Weekly*, Vol. 46(21): 384–402, 2011.
26. Ibid.
27. Meer Hassan Ali, *Observations on the Mussulmauns of India*, London: Humphrey Milford, 1917, reprint 2008.
28. Ute Falasch, 'Regulating Rapture. The "Malang" In The Madāriyyah,' *Oriente Moderno*, Vol. *92(2): 369–92, 2012.*
29. Bhattacharya, 'Madariya Sufi Silsila.'
30. Ibid.
31. Ibid.
32. A version of this fakir–sannnyasi revolt is described in Bankim Chandra's book *Ananda Math*.
33. A booklet published by the dargah itself. A copy was given to me by the *sajjadanashin* (caretaker).
34. Alexander Cunningham, *Archaeological Survey of India Vol. 17, Report of a Tour in the Central Provinces And Lower Gangetic Doab In 1881–82*, New Delhi: Archaeological Survey of India, Government of India, 1884, reprint 2000.
35. Ibid.
36. Masud Anwar Alavi, 'Kakori: Piety's Mass Appeal,' In *A Leaf Turns Yellow: The Sufis of Awadh*, eds. Muzaffar Ali, New Delhi: Bloomsbury Publishing India Private Limited, 2012.
37. Ibid.
38. Ibid.
39. Translation from C.M. Naim, 'The Maulana Who Loved Krishna', *Economic and Political Weekly*, Vol. 48(17): 37–44, 2013.
40. Personal communication over phone and email, 20 June 2021.

## CHAPTER 10

1. 'Mishkat al-Masabih 1369', *Sunnah.com*. Web. July 2022. https://sunnah.com/mishkat:1369.
2. 'Al-Adab Al-Mufrad 61', *Sunnah.com*. Web. July 2022. https://sunnah.com/adab:61.
3. Quran 7:156
4. Al-Qāḍīal-Quḍā'ī, *A Treasury of Virtues: Sayings, Sermons, and Teachings of Ali, with the One Hundred Proverbs Attributed to al-Jahiz*, Trans. Tahera Qutbuddin, New York: New York University Press, 2013.
5. 'Hadith 1, 40 Hadith Qudsi,' *Sunnah.com*. Web. July 2022. https://sunnah.com/qudsi40:1/
6. Shahab Ahmed, *What Is Islam? The Importance of Being Islamic*, Princeton and Oxford: Princeton University Press, 2016.
7. Faraz Arif Ansari, WhatsApp message, 26 September 2020. While talking of visits to dargahs.
8. William Chittick, *Sufism: A Beginner's Guide*. England: Oneworld Publications, 2007.

9. Saiyed Salman Chishti, Personal communication, 24 January 2019.
10. J. Spencer Trimingham, *The Sufi Orders in Islam*, London: Oxford University Press, 1971.
11. Richard Maxwell Eaton, *Sufis of Bijapur 1300–1700: Social Roles of Sufis in Medieval India*, New Delhi: Munshiram Manoharlal Publishers Pvt. Ltd., 1978.
12. Carl W. Ernst and Bruce Lawrence, *The Sufi Martyrs of Love: The Chishti Order in South Asia and Beyond*, US: Palgrave Macmillan, 2002.
13. Ibid.
14. Ibid.
15. 'Sufism in Turkey,' *Religion and Public Life, Harvard Divinity School*. Web. July 2022. https://rpl.hds.harvard.edu/faq/sufism-turkey.
16. Khaliq Ahmed Nizami, *State and Culture in Medieval India*, New Delhi: Adam Publishers and Distributors, 1985.
17. Ibid.
18. Ahmed, What Is Islam?
19. Nizami, State and Culture in Medieval India.
20. S.M. Azizuddin Hussain, *Sufis of Punjab: A Biographical Study*, Delhi: Kanishka Publishers, 2021.
21. Ibid.
22. Ibid.
23. Ibid.
24. Nizami, State and Culture in Medieval India.
25. Ibid.
26. Nizam ad-din Awliya, *Morals of the Heart*, trans. Bruce B. Lawrence, recorded by Amir Hasan Sijzi, Mahwah, New Jersey: Paulist Press, 1992.
27. Ibid.
28. 'Sahih al-Bukhari and Muslim, Riyad as-Salih 844,' *Sunnah.com*. Web. July 2022. https://sunnah.com/riyadussalihin:844.
29. Harbans Mukhia, Email to author, 10 May 2021.
30. Asghar Gondvi, 'ye ishq ne dekhahai ye aql se pinhanhai', *Rekhta*. Web. July 2022. https://www.rekhta.org/ghazals/ye-ishq-ne-dekhaa-hai-ye-aql-se-pinhaan-hai-asghar-gondvi-ghazals.
31. Nile Green, *Making Space: Sufis and Settlers in Early Modern India*, New Delhi: Oxford University Press, 2012.
32. Nile Green, *Sufism: A Global History*, N.P.: Wiley–Blackwell, 2012.
33. Annie Zaidi, Email to author, 21 May 2021.
34. Z.A. Desai, 'The Major Dargahs of Ahmadabad', *In Muslim Shrines in India*, eds Christian W. Troll and Marc Gaborieau, New Delhi: Oxford University Press, 2003.
35. Made famous by Ustad Nusrat Fateh Ali Khan.

## CHAPTER 11

1. Originally a ghazal by Purnam Allahabadi, it was popularized as a qawwali by the Sabri brothers and is sung with lyrical variations by various qawwals. I have used the qawwali words used by Sabri Brothers.
2. A short 10 folio Persian-language manuscript dating from 1858.

3. 'About Us', *Dargah Jogipura*. Web. July 2022. https://www.dargahjogipura.com/index.php/about-us/
4. I had an interesting experience when I visited it some two decades ago. I was going through some personal turmoil and so one day just took the night train to Ratlam, spent the following day there and returned that night. Not many knew of my visit. When I was there, I prayed for a sign that my prayers had been heard. The same night my younger sister had a dream, in which she saw Hazrat Ali giving her something in her hand to pass on to me. She didn't know I had gone there. That dream, when she related it to me, reassured me that my troubles would be taken care of and I am forever grateful to Allah that they have now passed.
5. Alternative translation from Frances Prichett's website A Desertful of Roses:

    Oh Ghalib, if I follow and obey Hazrat Ali, then it's as if in reality I obey the Lord,

    Because the aroma of a friend is certainly present with the companion of the friend

    – Bekhud Dehlvi.

## CHAPTER 12

1. Richard Maxwell Eaton, *The Rise of Islam and the Bengal Frontier, 1204–1760*, Berkeley and Los Angeles: University of California Press, 1993.
2. Ibid.
3. Ranjit Hoskote, Email to author, 16 May 2021.
4. Translated by Prof. Abdul Qaiyum Rafiqi in *Sufism in Kashmir* (2015).
5. A day dedicated to worshipping Goga.
6. Anna Bigelow, 'Saved by the Saint: Refusing and Reversing Partition in Muslim North India', *The Journal of Asian Studies*, Vol. 68(2): 435–64, 2009.
7. Anne Bigelow, 'Narratives of the Life of Haider Shaykh in Punjab', In *Islam in South Asia in Practice*, eds. Barbara D. Metcalf, Princeton: Princeton University Press, 2009.
8. Subhash Parihar, *Islamic Architecture of Punjab (1206–1707)*, Delhi: Aryan Books International, 2015.
9. Syed Yusuf Shahab, *Sirhind: A Monumental Example of Oblivion*, OrangeBooks, 2021.
10. Yusuf Shahab, Email to author, 18 May 2021.
11. Ibid.
12. 'A Date with Mujaddid Alf-i Sāni, Shaikh Ahmad Sirhindi', *Blast From the Past*, 24 May 2021. Web. July 2022. https://rezavisblastfromthepast.co.in/2021/05/24/a-date-with-mujaddid-alf-i-sani-shaikh-ahmad-sirhindi/
13. Syed Mohamad Qasim, Telephonic conversation (confirmed over email), May 2021.
14. Gourab Ghosh, Email to author, 15 May 2021.
15. Karen Chase, 'Jamali and Kamali in History,' *TheBestAmericanPoetry.com*, 19 November 2014. Web. July 2022. https://blog.bestamericanpoetry.com/the_best_american_poetry/2014/11/jamali-and-kamali-in-history.html.
16. Saiyid Athar Abbas Rizvi, *A History of Sufism in India, Vol. 1*, New Delhi: Munshiram Manoharlal Publishers Pvt Ltd, 1978.

17. *Khwing* is a dappled horse, and *sawar* is a rider. So his name literally means rider of a dappled horse.
18. 'Dargah Miran Sahib', *Dargah Info*. Web. July 2022. http://dargahinfo.com/Dargah_History.aspx?HID=157
19. Imre Bangha, Email to author, 22 Jan 2022.
20. Poetry of the sixteenth century Bhakti saint Dadu Dayal (1544–1603).
21. Carl W. Ernst and Bruce Lawrence, *The Sufi Martyrs of Love: The Chishti Order in South Asia and Beyond*, US: Palgrave Macmillan, 2002.
22. Ernst and Lawrence, Sufi Martyrs of Love.
23. Ibid.
24. Ibid.
25. Himanshu Bajpai, Voice note on WhatsApp, 21 May 2021.
26. Though Ala Hazrat is not technically a Sufi, his dargah is extremely popular and his annual *urs* sees devotees in the thousands, so I have included it here.
27. Ghazala Wahab, *Born a Muslim: Some Truths About Islam in India*, New Delhi: Aleph Book Company, 2020.
28. Ghazala Wahab, Telephonic conversation (confirmed by a Word document), 17 May 2021.
29. Ghazala Wahab, Telephonic conversation (confirmed by email), 17 May 2021.
30. Shahid Amin, *Conquest and Community: The Afterlife of Warrior Saint Ghazi Miyan*, New Delhi: Orient Black Swan, 2015.
31. Ibid.
32. Ibid.
33. Anab Naiyer, 'Songs and Supplicants at a Sufi Shrine,' MPhil diss., Jamia Milia Islamia, New Delhi, 2017.
34. Amin, Conquest and Community.
35. Ibid.
36. Ibid.

## CHAPTER 13

1. Nahida Mumtaz, 'Sufis and Their Contribution To Cultural Life of Medieval Assam in 16–17th Century, ' MPhil diss., Aligarh Muslim University, 2010.
2. Ibid.
3. Ibid.
4. Ibid.
5. Ibid.
6. Ibid.
7. Nahida Mumtaz. 'Sufis and Their Contribution'.
8. 'The Mausoleum of Mucdoom Shah Dowlut, at Moneah', *British Library*. Web. July 2022. https://www.bl.uk/onlinegallery/onlineex/apac/other/019xzz000004321u00012000.html
9. Ziya Us Salam and M. Aslam Parvaiz, *Madrasas in the Age of Islamophobia*, India: Sage Publications, 2019.
10. During my visit to the dargah, I was given an extensive tour of the entire complex by a *khadim* (caretaker) who was most gracious and generous with his time and knowledge when he heard I was conducting research for a book; he was the one

who pointed out some of the changes that had been made over time. I spent a day there in the calm and peaceful surroundings. As it was a non-*urs* period, and not a Thursday, there were very few people around. One elderly woman had brought her son to be blessed by the *khadims*, as the boy was not keeping well and she suspected that it was because of someone having cast *nazar* (the evil eye).

11. Hemant Sachdeva, WhatsApp message, 15 May 2021.
12. Richard Maxwell Eaton, *Sufis of Bijapur 1300–1700: Social Roles of Sufis in Medieval India*, New Delhi: Munshiram Manoharlal Publishers Pvt. Ltd., 1978.
13. Ibid.
14. Ibid.
15. Carl W. Ernst and Bruce Lawrence, *The Sufi Martyrs of Love: The Chishti Order in South Asia and Beyond*, US: Palgrave Macmillan, 2002.
16. Ibid.
17. Omid Safi, *Radical Love: Teachings from the Islamic Mystical Tradition*, Yale: Yale University Press, 2018.

## CHAPTER 14

1. Kashshaf Ghani, 'Tomb Complexes in Khuldabad', *Sahapedia*, 16 Nov 2016. Web. 3 June 2022. https://www.sahapedia.org/tomb-complexes-khuldabad.
2. This story was told by Abdul Hamid Khan, a *khadim,* to Nile Green. It is also a story I first heard many years ago from Asif Khan Dehlvi, who spends a lot of his time with Sufi fakirs in the dargah of Qutub Sahib in Mehrauli.
3. Nile Green, *Making Space: Sufis and Settlers in Early Modern India*, New Delhi: Oxford University Press, 2012.
4. I had this conversation with Lubna when I accompanied her to the dargah and she confirmed it by sending me this description email on 19 October 2020.
5. Lubna, Telephonic conversation (confirmed through email description), October 2020.
6. 'The Chains of Pirana', *Frontline*, 10 Sept 2004. Web. July 2022. https://frontline.thehindu.com/the-nation/article30224407.ece
7. Dominique-Sila Khan, *Diversity and Pluralism in Islam*, London and New York: I.B. Tauris and The Institute of Ismaili Studies, London, 2010.
8. 'Aa Mil Yaar | Bulleh Shah', *Sufi Poetry*. Web. July 2022. https://sufipoetry.wordpress.com/2009/11/16/aa-mil-yaar-bulleh-shah/. Translation by Kartar Singh Duggal.

## CHAPTER 15

1. Shafeeq Hudavi, 'A Hindu and His Designer Mosques,' *TwoCircles.net*, 7 August 2015. Web. July 2022. https://twocircles.net/2015aug07/1438935491.html.
2. Susan Bayly, *Saints, Goddesses, and Kings: Muslims and Christians in South Indian Society, 1700–1900*, New York: Cambridge University Press, 1989.
3. Natasha Ramarathan, Email exchange with author, 23 May 2021.
4. This information is from the stone slab installed at his shrine.
5. 'Ameenpeer Dargah – Pedda Dargah', *Kadapa*. Web. July 2022. https://english.kadapa.info/ameenpeer-dargah-pedda-dargah/

6. Bayly, Saints, Goddesses and Kings.
7. Anusha Ravi Sood, 'Quran at temple festival, dargah halt for fair – religious rows can't stop Karnataka rituals', *The Print*, 21 April 2022. Web. July 2022.
8. 'Hindus And Muslims To Celebrate Karaga Festival Together Amid Unrest In Bengaluru', *Sambad English*, 7 April 2022. Web. July 2022. https://sambadenglish.com/hindus-and-muslims-to-celebrate-karaga-festival-together-amid-unrest-in-bengaluru/


## CHAPTER 16


1. G. Hussein Rassool, *Evil Eye, Jinn Possession, and Mental Health Issues: An Islamic Perspective*, London and New York: Routledge, 2019.
2. Bruce Lawrence, *The Qur'an: A Biography*, London: Atlantic Books, 2006.
3. Seyyid Hossein Nasr, *The Study Quran: A New Translation and Commentary*, USA: Harper One, 2015.
4. Sahih Muslim, Book 39, Hadith Number 6757.
5. Lawrence, The Qur'an.
6. Amira el-Zein, *Islam, Arabs, and the Intelligent World of the Jinn*, Syracuse: Syracuse University Publications in Continuing Education, 2009.
7. Ibid.
8. Ibid.
9. Carla Bellamy, *The Powerful Ephemeral: Everyday Healing in an Ambiguously Islamic Plac*e, Berkeley: University of California Press, 2011.
10. F. Islam and R.A. Campbell. '"Satan Has Afflicted Me!": Jinn-Possession and Mental Illness in the Qur'an,' *Journal of Religious Health*, Vol. 53(1): 229–43, 2014.
11. Ibid.
12. Ibid.
13. el-Zein, Islam, Arabs, and the Intelligent World of the Jinn.
14. Ibid.
15. Though I have used the word 'host', some scholars disagree and assert that jinn can only *influence* mankind and cannot literally take up physical space within a human's body – that is, they cannot 'possess' individuals. See: Simon Dein and Abdool Samad Illaiee, 'Jinn and Mental Health: Looking at Jinn Possession in Modern Psychiatric Practice,' *The Psychiatrist*, Vol. 37(9): 290–293, 2013.
16. Bellamy, The Powerful Ephemeral.
17. Ali A. Olomi, Email to author, May 2021.
18. He said that his own personality had been subsumed in his devotion of Allah, and he had no identity left except as a devotee, so his name was irrelevant.
19. *Haal khelna* is used to mean 'to dance with real or pretended ecstasy', but here it is used in a negative sense of thrashing around or dancing with the suppressed energy of the spirit in possession.
20. El-Zein, Islam, Arabs, and the Intelligent World of the Jinn.
21. Nasr, The Study Quran.
22. Christian Troll, *Muslim Shrines in India: Their Character, History and Significance*, Oxford University Press, 2003.

23. Anand Vivek Taneja, *Jinnealogy: Time, Islam, and Ecological Thought in the Medieval Ruins of Delhi*, Stanford: Stanford University Press, 2017.

## CHAPTER 17

1. S.A.H. Abidi, *Memorial Volume: Amir Khusrau*. New Delhi: Publications Division, Ministry of Information and Broadcasting, Government of India, 1975.
2. J.T.P. de Bruijn, *Persian Sufi Poetry: An Introduction to the Mystical Use of Classical Persian Poems*, Great Britain: Curzon Press, 1997.
3. Ibid.
4. Ibid.
5. Arpeeta S. Mizan, 'A Beginner's Take on Sufi Poetry: Does The Sufi Love Transcend Religious Borders to Encapsulate Humanity?' *Journal of the Asiatic Society of Bangladesh* (Hum.), Vol. 61(1): 147–159, 2016.
6. Seyyid Hossein Nasr, 'The Influence of Sufism on Traditional Persian Music', *Studies in Comparative Religion*, Vol. 6(4), 1972. http://www.studiesincomparativereligion.com/public/articles/The_Influence_of_Sufism_on_Traditional_Persian_Music.aspx.
7. Saiyid Naqi Hussain Jafri, *Essays on Literature, History and Society*, Delhi: Primus Books, 2010.
8. Ibid.
9. 'Aṭṭār, Farīd-Al-Dīn,' *Encyclopaedia Iranica*. Web. July 2022. https://iranicaonline.org/articles/attar-farid-al-din-poet.
10. Bruce Lawrence, *'The early Chishti approach to Sama' Islamic society and culture: Essays in Honour of Professor Aziz Ahmad*, eds M. Israel and N.K. Wagle, New Delhi: Manohar, 1983.
11. Dhruv Sangari, one on one meeting and then confirmed on email, 23 March 2019.
12. Regula Burckhardt Qureshi, *Sufi Music of India and Pakistan: Sound, Context and Meaning in Qawwali*, Chicago: University of Chicago Press, 1986.
13. Amira el-Zein, *Islam, Arabs, and the Intelligent World of the Jinn*, Syracuse: Syracuse University Publications in Continuing Education, 2009.
14. Personal communication over email.; Ahmad Sama'ni, *The Repose of the Spirits: A Sufi Commentary on the Divine Names*, Trans. William Chittick, USA: SUNY Press, 2019.
15. Khaliq Ahmed Nizami, *The Life and Times of Shaikh Nizamuddin Auliya*, Delhi: Oxford University Press, 2007.
16. Sunil Sharma and Paul Losenky, *In the Bazaar of Love*, New Delhi: Penguin India, 2011. Known as *tarana bols* (melody), an onomatopoeic string of meaningless syllables interspersed with other bits of poetic lines and sung in any raga.
17. 'Tarana Singing – Ustad Amir Khan.' *Qaul*, 3 May 2008. Web. 30 August 2021. http://qaul.blogspot.com/2008/05/tarana-singing-ustad-amir-khan.html.
18. Ibid.; Dileep Karanth, 'Amir Khusrau's Contributions to Indian Music: A Preliminary Survey', *Sangeet Natak*, Vol. XLII(4): 1–14, 2008.
19. Mikko Viitamäki, 'Poetry in Sufi Practice: Patrons, poets and performers in South Asian Sufism from thirteenth century to the present,' PhD Diss., Department of World Cultures, 2010–2017.

20. Ibid.
21. Farid Ayaz and Abu Mohammad are the descendants of Mian Samat bin Ibrahim, the qawwal *bachha* trained by Hazrat Amir Khusrau. The brothers form an unbroken chain of living tradition of 700 years.
22. This is a literal translation and fails to describe the symbolic meaning of the devotee, who is asking not just for material but gifts of spiritual sustenance and redemption. The *jholi* here refers to the bottom part of the shirt for a man and the scarf of a woman called *daaman,* which is normally lifted in a symbolic gesture of asking.
23. Carl W. Ernst, *Sufism: An Introduction to the Mystical Tradition of Islam*, Colarado: Shambhala, 2016.
24. 'Nami Danam Chi Manzil – Amir Khusrau Poetry', *Qawwal,* 11 March 2010. Web. July 2022. https://qawwal.blogspot.com/2009/02/nami-daanam-chi-manzil.html
25. Sharma and Losenky, In the Bazaar of Love.
26. Sheikh Jamali, *Siyar-ul-Arifin* (*Biographies of Mystics*), Trans Ishrat Hussain Ansari, Hamid Afaq Qureshi and al-Taimi al-Siddiqi, Delhi: Idarah-I Adbiyat-I Delli, 2015.
27. That once Abu Bakr came to her on the day of `Id-ul-Fitr or `Id ul-Adha while the Prophet (□) was with her and there were two girl singers with her, singing songs of the Ansar about the day of Buath. Abu Bakr said twice. 'Musical instrument of Satan!' But the Prophet (□) said, 'Leave them Abu Bakr, for every nation has an `Id (i.e. festival) and this day is our `Id.' – Sahih al-Bukhari 3931, Book 63, Hadith 156, *Sunnah.com*. https://sunnah.com/bukhari:3931.
28. Ibid.
29. Ibid.
30. Jamali, Siyar-ul-Arifin.
31. Personal communication via email, 2019.
32. Saiyid Zaheer Hussain Jafri. 'Adjustments, Accommodation and Adaptations: Chishti Sufis and Indian Linguistic and Ritualistic Traditions.' Paper presented at the Centre for Study of Society and Secularism's International Conference on Sufism and Social Harmony in Mumbai, 22–23 February 2018.
33. Muzaffar Ali, ed. *A Leaf Turns Yellow: The Sufis of Awadh*. New Delhi: Bloomsbury Publishing India Private Limited, 2012.
34. Saiyid Athar Abbas Rizvi, *A History of Sufism in India, Vol. 1*, New Delhi: Munshiram Manoharlal Publishers Pvt Ltd, 1978.
35. Sharma and Losenky, In the Bazaar of Love.
36. Dr Utpola Bora, 'Zikir and Zari: Sufi songs of Assam', *Internet Archive*, May 2006. Web. July 2022. https://web.archive.org/web/20070929060952/http://www.posoowa.org/2006/05/26/305/
37. 'Makkeh Gaya,' *Sufi Poetry*. Web. July 2022. https://sufipoetry.wordpress.com/2009/11/01/makkeh-gaya-bulleh-shah/
38. 'About Wajd', *Wajd*. Web. July 2022. http://www.thewajd.org/index.php
39. Sunil Sharma, Email to author, 13 June 2021.
40. Saiyid Zaheer Hussain Jafri, Communication over telephone, February 2018.
41. Personal communication with the author, February 2018.
42. Khaliq Ahmed Nizami, *State and Culture in Medieval India*, New Delhi: Adam Publishers and Distributors, 1985.

43. Ibid.
44. Ibid.
45. Annemarie Schimmel, *Mystical Dimensions of Islam*, Chapel Hill: University of North Carolina Press, 2011.
46. Nizami, State and Culture in Medieval India.
47. Saiyid Zaheer Hussain Jafri, 'Adjustments, Accommodation and Adaptations: Chishti Sufis and Pre-Existing "Cultural World" of Upper Gangetic Valley'. Paper presented at the Centre for Study of Society and Secularism's International Conference on Sufism and Social Harmony in Mumbai, 22–23 February 2018.
48. Aditya Behl, 'The Soul's Quest in Malik Muhammad Jayasi's Hindavi Romance', In *Islam in South Asia in Practice*, eds. Barbara D. Metcalf, Princeton: Princeton University Press, 2009
49. Rizvi, A History of Sufism in India, Vol. 2.
50. The Niyazi Sufi Order, https://niyazia.wordpress.com/tag/shah-niyaz-ahmed/
51. Nasr, 'The Influence of Sufism on Traditional Persian Music.'
52. Gülru Necipoğlu, *The Topkapi Scroll: Geometry and Ornament in Islamic Architecture*, Santa Monica: Getty Research Institute, 1995.
53. Nader Ardalan and Laleh Bakhtiar, *Sense of Unity: The Sufi Tradition in Persian Architecture*, Chicago: The University of Chicago Press, 1973.
54. Ibid.
55. Hakim Sameer Hamdani, Email to author, January 2022. In response to author's query to him on the concept of sacred geometry.
56. Necipoğlu, The Topkapi Scroll.
57. Making pace.
58. Ardalan and Bakhtiar, Sense of Unity.
59. Ursula Weeks, Email to author, 22 June 2021.
60. The *Bahr al-Hayat* or *Ocean of Life* is an illustrated Persian book written in 1602 by Muhammad Ghaus Gwaliori and is the earliest surviving book which gives an illustrated account of Yoga *asana*s used for meditation.
61. Translation by Prashant Keshavmurthy.

## CHAPTER 18

1. Nile Green, *Making Space: Sufis and Settlers in Early Modern India*, New Delhi: Oxford University Press, 2012.
2. In south India, *urs* celebrations are known as kantūri (derived from the Persian word used for a tablecloth).
3. This is attributed to Hadith collection Mishkaat, BaabuIthbaatil-Qabr. In hadith collection Jami` at-Tirmidhi1071, Vol. 2, Book 5, Hadith 1. It is translated as 'Sleep as a newlywed, whom none awakens but the dearest of his family.'
4. John T. Platts, 'A Dictionary of Urdu, Classical Hindi and English,' *Digital Dictionaries of Southeast Asia*. Web. July 2022. http://dsal.uchicago.edu/cgi-bin/app/platts_query.py?qs=tasawwuf&matchtype=default.
5. Green, Making Space.
6. Ibid.
7. Ibid.

8. Found in the *dibacha*, preface of his book *Golestan.*
9. The words are popularly attributed to Amir Khusrau, but as per Prof. Syeda Bilqis Hussaini (who spoke to me over the telephone), famous Persian scholar Prof. S.A.H. Abidi had said that it was written by the Afghan poet, Muinuddin Haravi.
10. 'Wajd: Chronicling Ecstasy,' *Wajd*. Web. 2022. https://thewajd.org/about.php
11. Saiyid Naqi Hussain Jafri, *Essays on Literature, History and Society*, Delhi: Primus Books, 2010.
12. Saiyid Zaheer Hussain Jafri, 'Adjustments, Accommodation and Adaptations: Chishti Sufis and Pre-Existing "Cultural World" of Upper Gangetic Valley'. Paper presented at the Centre for Study of Society and Secularism's International Conference on Sufism and Social Harmony in Mumbai, 22–23 February 2018.
13. Ibid.
14. Jamshid is the fourth Shah of the mythological Pishdadian dynasty of Iran according to *Shahnameh*, the epic poem written by the Persian poet Ferdowsi.
15. Jafri, 'Chishti Sufis and Pre-Existing "Cultural World" of Upper Gangetic Valley'. A lesser-known poet of Salon, Ishtiyaq Ahmad Mushtaq has composed a poem on the *gagar* procession. This is included in his collection, *Bagh-I Naim*, MS (compiled in AH 1350).
16. This was during the Basant celebration in 2014 in the dargah.
17. Song attributed to Amir Khusrau.
18. Dargah Quli Khan, *Muraqqa-e Dehli: The Mughal Capital in Muhammad Shah's Time*, trans Chander Shekhar and Shama Mitra Chenoy, Delhi: Deputy Publications, 1989.
19. In the aftermath of the Fall of Delhi and the victory of the British in suppressing the Uprising of 1857, the *sair* was stopped for few years. Ghalib refers to that period. They later restarted it.
20. Sunil Sharma and Paul Losenky, *In the Bazaar of Love*, New Delhi: Penguin India, 2011.
21. Ankur Tewari, 'No Janmashtami show at Sarkhej Roza this year.' *The Times of India*, 18 August 2014. https://timesofindia.indiatimes.com/city/ahmedabad/no-janmashtami-show-at-sarkhej-roza-this-year/articleshow/40360290.cms.
22. Prabhakar Machwe, *Kabir*, Sahitya Akademi, 1968. 22–34.

## CHAPTER 19

1. Nizam ad-din Awliya, *Morals of the Heart*, trans. Bruce B. Lawrence, recorded by Amir Hasan Sijzi. Mahwah, New Jersey: Paulist Press, 1992.
2. Sa'diyya Shaikh, *Sufi Narratives of Intimacy: Ibn 'Arabī, Gender, and Sexuality*, Chapel Hill: University of North Carolina Press, 2012.
3. Annemarie Schimmel, *My Soul is a Woman: The Feminine in Islam*, trans. Susan H. Hay, New York: The Continuum Publishing Company, 1997.
4. S.M. Azizuddin Hussain, *Sufis of Punjab: A Biographical Study*, Delhi: Kanishka Publishers, 2021.
5. Amina Wudud, *Qur'an and Woman: Rereading the Sacred Text from a Woman's Perspective*, New York: Oxford University Press, 1999.

6. Ibid.
7. Schimmel, My Soul is a Woman.
8. Ibid.
9. Ali B. Uthman Al-Jullabi Al-Hujwiri, *Kashf al-Mahjub: The Oldest Persian Treatise On Sufiism*, trans. Reynold A. Nicholson, London, Leyden: E. J. Brill, Imprimerie Orientale, 1911.
10. As-Sulami, *Early Sufi Women: A Bilingual Critical Edition of as Sulami'sDikr An-Niswa Al-Muta 'abbitdat As-Sufuyyat*, trans. Rkia Cornell, US: Fons Vitae, 2001.
11. Ibid.
12. Ibid.
13. Alyssa Gabbay, *Gender and Succession in Medieval and Early Modern Islam: Bilateral Descent and the Legacy of Fatima (Early and Medieval Islamic World*), London: I.B. Tauris, 2020.
14. John L. Esposito, *The Oxford Dictionary of Islam*, Oxford University Press, 2003. Esposito describes it as: 'Muhammadan light; also called al-nur al-muhammadi. In the emanation scheme of cosmology characteristic of Sufi and Shii metaphysics, refers to the pre-cosmic soul of Muhammad, which is equivalent to the active intellect of Neoplatonism and associated with the perfect person (al-insan al-kamil) and Muhammadan truth (haqiqa hmuhammadiyyah). Represents the first creation (or emanation) of God, the self-manifestation of divine consciousness. All prophets preceding Muhammad derived their prophetic ability from the Muhammadan light. The doctrine appears in the writings of such early Sufi writers as Sahl al-Tustari and Hakim al-Tirmidhi and was later developed by Ibn al-Arabi and his school. The concept plays an important role in both Sufi and Shii concepts of sainthood (walayah).'
15. Karen G. Ruffle, 'May Fatimah Gather Our Tears: The Mystical and Intercessory Powers of Fatimah al-Zahra in Indo-Persian, Shi'i Devotional Literature and Performance', *Comparative Studies of South Asia, Africa and the Middle East*, Vol. 30(3), 2010: 386–397.
16. Camille Adams Helminski, *Women of Sufism: A Hidden Treasure*, India: Shambhala, 2003.
17. Hassan Abbas, *The Prophet's Heir: The Life of Ali Ibn Abi Talib*, Yale: Yale University Press, 2021.
18. Gabbay, *Gender and Succession in Medieval and Early Modern Islam.*
19. Sahih al-Bukhari 3714, *Sunnah.com*. Web. July 2022. https://sunnah.com/bukhari:3714.
20. Ruffle, 'May Fatimah Gather Our Tears.'
21. Helminski, Women of Sufism.
22. J. Spencer Trimingham, *The Sufi Orders in Islam*, London: Oxford University Press, 1971.
23. Annemarie Schimmel, *Mystical Dimensions of Islam*, Chapel Hill: University of North Carolina Press, 2011.
24. Margaret Smith, *Rabi'a the Mystic and Her Fellow-Saints in Islam*, Cambridge: Cambridge University Press, 2010.

25. Priyanka Chanana, 'Indian Sufism and the women: A Study of the Two Dargahs of the Women Sufis in Delhi.' Unpublished MPhil diss., Delhi University, 2008.
26. Ibid.
27. Ibid.
28. Carl W. Ernst, *Eternal Garden: Mysticism, History, and Politics at a South Asian Sufi Center*, India: Oxford University Press.
29. Chanana, 'Indian Sufism and the Women'.
30. In a conversation with me in January 2019, when I had gone to her house to meet her. She passed away from cancer in 2020.
31. Hussain Siddiqui, *Composite Culture Under The Sultans of Delhi*, New Delhi: Primus Books, 2016.
32. Chanana, 'Indian Sufism and the Women'.
33. Bihar al-Anwar, Vol. 74.
34. Helminski, Women of Sufism.
35. Trimingham, The Sufi Orders in Islam.
36. Ibid.
37. Richard Maxwell Eaton. 'Sufi Folk Literature and the Expansion of Indian Islam.' *History of Religions*, Vol. 14(2): 117–27, 1974.
38. Ibid.
39. Ibid.
40. Ibid. He has created it with His own power –

    (refrain): Say '*La-illah*',
    Dwell in '*il-Allah*.'
    God Himself came out from the hidden treasure
    And showed Himself in the guise of the Prophet.
    (refrain): In the presence of God, the Prophet is the chief
    Allah, Muhammad,
    Are our leaders whom we trust most And obey as slaves.
    (refrain): Our *pir* has taken our hands in his;
    He has given us connections whole-heartedly.
    May he keep this connection forever.
    (refrain): Say '*La-illah*',
    Dwell in '*il-Allah*'.
    41. Ibid.

42. Nizam ad-din Awliya, Morals of the Heart.
43. Helminski, Women of Sufism.
44. Nizam ad-din Awliya, Morals of the Heart.
45. Ibid.
46. Ibid.
47. Ibid.
48. Personal communication via email, April 2020.
49. The most widespread being prostitution according to Schimmel, and one that is well-documented. See Schimmel, My Soul is a Woman.
50. Sunan Al-Nasa'i, vol. 3, 76; and Sahih Muslim, vol. 3, p. 64 chapter

51. 'Sunan Ibn Majah 1570', *Sunnah.com*. Web. July 2022. https://sunnah.com/ibnmajah:1570.
52. al-Islam.org which quotes Sunan al-Nasa'i, vol. 3, 76; and Sahih Muslim and vol. 3, p. 64 chapter of Al Qabr ma yaqaaleinddakhool
53. Christian Troll eds., *Muslim Shrines in India: Their Character, History and Significance*, Oxford University Press, 2003.
54. Email to author, May 2021. In response to author's query about her experiences of visiting dargahs.
55. Raziuddin Aquil, 'Retrograde Custodians,' *Economic and Political Weekly* 50, no. 45 (2015). https://www.epw.in/journal/2015/45/postscript/retrograde-custodians.html

# Other Works Consulted


Abbas, Shemeem Burney. *The Female Voice in Sufi Ritual: Devotional Practices of Pakistan and India*. Austin: University of Texas Press, 2002.

Abbasi, Reema. *Ajmer Sharif: Awakening of Sufism in South Asia*, Niyogi Books, New Delhi, 2017.

Alam, Muzaffar. *The Languages of Political Islam: India, 1200–1800*. Ranikhet: Permanent Black, 2004.

Al-Ghazali. *The Ninety-Nine Beautiful Names of God.* Translated by David B. Burrell and Nazih Daher. United Kingdom: The Islamic Texts Society, 2007.

Aquil, Raziuddin. *Days in the Life of a Sufi: 101 Enchanting Stories of Wisdom.* New Delhi: Pan Macmillan India, New Delhi, 2020.

Armstrong, Karen. *A History of God*. UK: RHUK, 1999.

Ashahti, Aishah Binte, *The Lion Hearted Lady of Karbala*. Translated by Atia Rizvi. Bluerose Publishers, India, 2019.

As-Suyuti, Jalal ad-Din. *History of the Umayyad Caliphs: Tarikh Al-Khulafa*. Translated by Tobias Sahl Anderson. Ta-Ha Publishers Ltd., 2015.

Baldick, Julian. *Mystical Islam: An Introduction to Sufism*. New York: New York University Press, 2000.

Dandekar, Deepa and Torsten Tschacher, eds. *Islam, Sufism and Everyday Politics of Belonging in South Asia.* Milton Park, Abingdon: Routledge, 2016.

Denny, Frederick. *An Introduction to Islam*. London and New York: Routledge, 2016.

Eaton, Richard Maxwell. *Sufis of Bijapur 1300–1700: Social Roles of Sufis in Medieval India*. New Delhi: Munshiram Manoharlal Publishers Pvt. Ltd., 1978.

Ernst, Carl W. *Refractions of Islam in India*. New Delhi: Sage, Yoda Press, 2016.

'Ghazal 98 Verse 11.' *Columbia.edu*. Accessed 30 August 2021. http://www.columbia.edu/itc/mealac/pritchett/00ghalib/098/98_11.html.

Hazleton, Lesley. *The First Muslim: The Story of Muhammad*. UK: Atlantic Books, 2014.

Holland, Christopher Paul. *Rethinking Qawwali: Perspectives of Sufism, Music, and Devotion in North India*, Thesis presented to the Faculty of the Graduate School of the University of Texas at Austin, 2010.

Ibn Arabi, Muhyiddin. *Journey to the Lord of Power: A Sufi Manual on Retreat*. Translated by Rabia Terri Harris. Vermont: Inter Traditions International, 1981, 1989.

Iraqi, Shahabuddin. *Bhakti Movement in Medieval India: Social and Political Perspectives*. New Delhi: Manohar, 2009.

Islam, Md Sirajul. *Sufism and Bhakti: A Comparative Study*. Washington DC: The Council for Research in Values and Philosophy, 2004.

Kugle, Scott Siraj al-Haqq. *Homosexuality in Islam: Critical Reflection on Gay, Lesbian, and Transgender Muslims.* United Kingdom: Oneworld Publications, 2010.

Kugle, Scott Siraj al-Haqq. *Sufi Meditation and Contemplation: Timeless Wisdom from Mughal India*. Omega Publications Inc., 2012.

Kugle, Scott Siraj al-Haqq. 'Strange Bedfellows: Qur'an Interpretation Regarding Same-Sex Female Intercourse.' *Theology & Sexuality* 22, no. 1–2 (2016): 9–24. https://doi.org/10.1080/13558358.2017.1296685.

Laughlin, Vivian A. 'A Brief Overview of *al Jinn* within Islamic Cosmology and Religiosity.' *Journal of Adventist Mission Studies* 11, no. 1 (2015): 67–78.

Lawrence, Bruce B. *Who is Allah*. New Delhi: Dev Publishers and Distributors, 2015.

Mishra, Neeru, eds. *Sufis and Sufism: Some Reflections*. New Delhi: Manohar, 2004.

Myer, Wali Hali, Bilal Hyde, Faisal Muqaddam and Shabda Kahn. *Physicians of the Heart: A Sufi View of the Ninety-Nine Names of Allah*. San Francisco: Sufi Ruhaniat International, 2011.

Shah-Kazemi, Reza. *Justice and Remembrance: Introducing the Spirituality of Imam Ali*. London, New York: I.B. Tauris Publishers in association with The Institute of Ismaili Studies, London, 2006.

Shah-Kazemi, Reza. *Imam Ali: From Concise History to Timeless Mystery*. London: The Matheson Trust, 2019.

Siddiqi, M. Zameer Uddin. 'Shaikh Abdul Quddus of Gangoh and Contemporary Rulers.' *Proceedings of the Indian History Congress* 31 (1969).

Sikand, Yoginder. *Sacred Spaces: Exploring Traditions of Shared Faith in India*. Penguin Books, Gurgaon, Haryana, 2003.

Snehi, Yogesh. *Spatialising Popular Sufi Shrines in Punjab: Dreams, Memories, Territoriality.* Routledge India, 2019.

Starr, Frederick. *Lost Enlightenment: Central Asia's Golden Age from the Arab Conquest to Tamerlane*. USA: Princeton University Press, 2015.

'Sufism, an Inquiry.' *A Journal for People of the Heart* 17, no. 3 (2016). https://issuu.com/iasufism/docs/sufism.vol17no3.

Taylor, John B. 'Ja'Far Al-Sadiq the Spiritual Forbearer of the Sufi's.' *Islamic Culture* 40 (April 1966): 97–113.

Tirmizi, S.A.I. *Ajmer through Inscriptions (1532-1852 A.D.)*. New Delhi: Indian Institute of Islamic Studies, 1968.

Topbaş, Osman Nuri. *A Path Towards the Internalization of Faith (Ihsân)*. Erkam Publications at Smashwords, 2011.